THE
BRONX
NOBODY KNOWS

THE **BRONX** NOBODY KNOWS

AN URBAN WALKING GUIDE

WILLIAM B. HELMREICH

PRINCETON UNIVERSITY PRESS
PRINCETON AND OXFORD

Published by Princeton University Press
41 William Street, Princeton, New Jersey 08540
99 Banbury Road, Oxford OX2 6JX

press.princeton.edu

All Rights Reserved

Library of Congress Cataloging-in-Publication Data

Names: Helmreich, William B., author.
Title: The Bronx nobody knows : an urban walking guide / William B. Helmreich.
Description: Princeton : Princeton University Press, [2023] | Includes bibliographical
    references and index.
Identifiers: LCCN 2022030957 (print) | LCCN 2022030958 (ebook) | ISBN
    9780691166957 (paperback) | ISBN 9780691244013 (ebook)
Subjects: LCSH: Bronx (New York, N.Y.)—Social conditions. | Neighborhoods—
    New York (State)—New York. | Community life—New York (State)—New York.
Classification: LCC HN80.B76 H45 2023 (print) | LCC HN80.B76 (ebook) |
    DDC 306.09747/275—dc23/eng/20221117
LC record available at https://lccn.loc.gov/2022030957
LC ebook record available at https://lccn.loc.gov/2022030958

British Library Cataloging-in-Publication Data is available

Editorial: Meagan Levinson and Erik Beranek
Production Editorial: Mark Bellis
Production: Erin Suydam
Publicity: Julia Haav and Kathryn Stevens
Copyeditor: Molan Goldstein

Cover and frontispiece photographs by Antony Bennett
Interior photographs by Christopher Holewski

This book has been composed in Adobe Caslon Pro, Futura Std
and Public Notice JNL

Printed on acid-free paper. ∞

Printed in China

10 9 8 7 6 5 4 3 2 1

A NOTE TO THE READER

MY HUSBAND, WILLIAM HELMREICH, passed away on March 28, 2020, due to COVID-19. Only two months earlier, he and I had been walking the streets of Staten Island together, neighborhood by neighborhood, for a future book project. He had already completed the manuscript for *The Bronx Nobody Knows*, except for certain sections, like the acknowledgments. Had he lived, he surely would have thanked many more people than those listed.

The Bronx is an amazingly fascinating and complex borough, as you will learn by reading these pages. Walking with him down just about every block, as I did, was a tremendous joy and privilege. Each day was a treasure hunt. Bill had a discerning eye for all that was new and unusual, and a unique capacity to describe his "finds" in beautifully clear and accessible writing. But by far, his greatest gift was his ability to get strangers on the street to open up to him, to share their stories, and to laugh with him at life's foibles.

This book is a tribute to his memory.

Helaine Helmreich

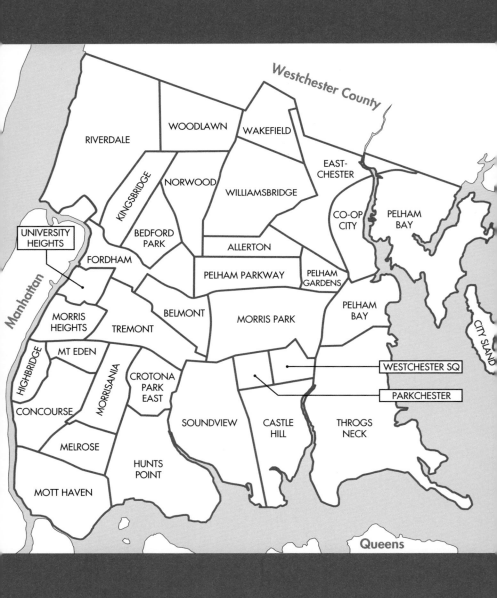

CONTENTS

INTRODUCTION

DESPITE ITS REPUTATION in the popular imagination—Tom Wolfe's best-selling novel *The Bonfire of the Vanities* and films like *Fort Apache*, which portray the borough as a sinister, crime-ridden area—the Bronx I discovered long after these two portraits were drawn does not really resemble them. Since many still view the Bronx through this lens, it's critical that this impression be dispelled. In the course of my walks through this remarkably diverse and truly interesting borough, spanning hundreds of miles and including strolls through public housing projects, I never felt scared. On the contrary, I met hundreds of people who were friendly and helpful to me. In the afternoons and early evenings, they sat outside on the stoops, chatting and joking with each other, answering my hello with a cheerful or at least polite response. On weekends the parks were filled with youths playing ball and older adults relaxing on benches. There were, however, some parks that people avoided, with almost everyone knowing the score. The poverty still gripping some of these areas was also starkly evident. In particular, the New York City Housing Authority (NYCHA) properties, which include project housing and privately built apartment tenements and buildings, continue to be eyesores. Regardless of income, the Bronx is home to thousands of people who live in one-, two-, and three-family homes, all working hard to achieve the proverbial American Dream. The tenements are slowly diminishing in number, and affordable housing, while not luxurious, is newer and far more attractive. A careful look at these residences—the hanging plants visible in apartment windows and the neatly kept homes with well-tended lawns—makes it amply clear that those living in them take considerable pride in what they have. Not everyone, of course; there are dilapidated areas strewn with litter and dog poop, but it's no longer the norm, as was the case from 1970 to 2000. Everything is in the midst of changing. The main commercial streets are filled with shoppers, day and evening, and the subways are crowded, though neither is the case, with some exceptions, after, say, 10:00 p.m. The tour buses that now regularly ply the South and East Bronx, just as they have been doing for years in Harlem, are yet another harbinger of a better future.

The following five traits and realities are what most characterize the Bronx. First, there's a great amount of *hope* among the residents and those who work there. Second, the borough's *history* is truly fascinating. Third, it has great *beauty*. Fourth, it is characterized by a strong *sense of community and friendliness* on the part of its residents. Last, it is full of *surprises* with regard to what there is to see. And now, let's evaluate this subject in greater depth.

It's a bright, chilly, early spring morning in the South Bronx. The skies are partly cloudy, with long, angular shafts of sunshine breaking through the cobalt-blue skies embossed with fluffy white clouds and hitting the gray waters of the East River. I'm standing on Locust Avenue near E. 138th Street, where Silvercup has created four film studios, spanning 115,000 square feet, in what amounts to a savvy expression of *hope* and confidence in the Bronx, an often underappreciated borough in this great city. It is the first of many characteristics that reflect the Bronx and that, taken together, make it a truly special, even wondrous place. This area is known as Port Morris, a subsection of Mott Haven, located at the southernmost tip of the borough.

The swirling murky waters around it bespeak the rich and sometimes dark history of the area. Adjacent to it, not far from the shore, is South Brother Island, designated by the city as "forever wild." Next to it is North Brother Island, which played a role in a disastrous event of epic proportions. On its way to an afternoon excursion on Wednesday, June 15, 1904, the *General Slocum* was steaming toward Locust Grove, Long Island. Suddenly a fire broke out on board as the captain was navigating the treacherous currents by the Hell Gate Bridge. Over one thousand passengers, almost all of them women and children, perished in what was the greatest loss of life for a single occurrence, until it was eclipsed by 9/11.

About 150 passengers were rescued and taken to nearby North Brother Island, where they were treated at Riverside Hospital, which then housed people suffering from typhoid fever, smallpox, tuberculosis, and other contagious diseases. As soon as the survivors could be moved, they were transferred to city treatment centers, among them Bellevue Hospital. Today, there's no trace of what happened here a century ago, except for the remains of what was once Riverside Hospital. Nor is it a forlorn island any longer. It has been turned into a quiet bucolic place where youths from the Bronx are optimistically involved in an effort to restore it as a natural habitat. Both North and South Brother Islands, respectively twenty and six acres in size, are chiefly bird sanctuaries.

Beyond these islands to the east lies Rikers Island, where the thousands of people who are incarcerated there exemplify the inadequacies of our judicial system, many of them languishing for months, even years, before their cases are heard and adjudicated. The Bronx is included in the efforts to "improve matters." Plans call for those currently held at Rikers to be distributed and placed in smaller jails throughout the city. If carried out, they will have serious ramifications for the Bronx, a matter taken up in the discussion of the Melrose community, adjacent to Mott Haven. To the west, you can see Randalls Island, which is conjoined with Wards Island. It's home to all manner of recreational facilities and activities—ballfields, playgrounds, sports events, and music festivals—and can be reached via a pedestrian bridge in Port Morris. And, of course, it offers spectacular views of the Robert F. Kennedy Bridge and Manhattan itself.

Back on shore, Port Morris can boast of many enterprises, which, like Silvercup, provide ample evidence of a firm belief in the Bronx's future. Another case in point is the Bronx Brewery on E. 136th Street, where I speak with Patrick, who expounds about both his business and the Bronx in general: "We're a no-nonsense craft beer, very approachable, not as gimmicky, by which I mean throwing all kinds of fruit in. We like to keep things straightforward, like the people who live in the Bronx. We always let the beer be the hero. Bronx people are very proud of where they live. . . . They're the kind who are gonna tell you how it really is."

And there you have it. An entrepreneur begins to brand the Bronx as a gritty, tough, no-nonsense town, made up of folks with a large dose of pride in who and where they are. And it will work because Patrick's an authentic character with a realistic dream. The brewery produces about 200,000 cases a year, and Patrick does his best to hire workers from the Bronx.

Another alcohol-based undertaking is the Port Morris Distillery on E. 133rd Street. There's good reason for Rafael Barbosa, the owner, to be in the Bronx because he sells Puerto Rican rum, and more Puerto Ricans live in the Bronx than in any other borough. Barbosa elaborates on his company and gives me a little history lesson at the same time: "Our main item is Pitorro Shine. Everywhere where liquor was once illegal, people made moonshine, and this is our special mix. The Hondurans have their moonshine, the people in Tennessee had theirs during Prohibition. Our history began in the seventeenth century in the mountains of Guyama, Puerto Rico. Our moonshine was made from sugar cane since that is a major crop in Puerto Rico, not molasses or corn mash. While Pitorro is technically a rum, it's stronger than 80 or 90 percent proof."

Loyalty to the Puerto Rican community is a factor, but Barbosa still has to risk his money, and that's what hope translates into when it's strongly felt. Not only is the plant here, but an outstanding tavern with great bar food is attached to it, and the decor would match up well with anyplace in Chelsea, Tribeca, or the West Village. Barbosa then throws in a charming tidbit about how the brew is mixed. Pointing overhead he asserts: "The Hell Gate trains go over that bridge. The Acela runs by here all the time, and when it does, our distillery vibrates—and that actually helps the distilling process by agitating it." I assume he's not giving Amtrak a percentage of the profits!

Another business, located on E. 136th Street is New York Sluggers, founded in 2009. It's a sports academy for kids who take lessons here, and it's also the only place in the city that makes wooden baseball bats. The *New York Post* has operated a plant in this neighborhood for almost twenty years, and there's a multitude of other companies here, like Fresh Direct, Fedex, and many smaller operations.

Hope also comes in the form of new people moving in. The Grand Concourse, from 157th to 167th Streets has undergone a renaissance of sorts. The Executive Towers building near 165th Street has improved significantly. Most of the residents there are middle class, and it's more racially mixed. The same is true at number 1075 on the corner of 166th Street, where I speak with one of several new arrivals to the building. The man felt he didn't have enough space in his Murray Hill apartment, and since the Bronx was "gentrifying" he moved here to "beat the rush." His apartment is indeed quite beautiful. Another local resident raves about the new Italian eatery on E. 161st Street, Porto Salvo, opining that "It's a sign that the Bronx will rise again."

And who can deny or minimize the impact of Sonia Sotomayor's selection to the Supreme Court of the United States? She grew up for the most part in the NYCHA Bronxdale Houses and graduated from Princeton University and Yale Law School. The Bronxdale Houses were renamed the Justice Sonia Sotomayor Houses in 2010, and the message is clear: you can succeed in America even if your origins are humble. What stands out here is the incredible heights to which she rose, making her an inspiration to millions.

People are investing in the Bronx in big ways, and one of the largest such projects is the Cary Leeds Tennis Center. A group of New York's leading philanthropists decided to spend $27.5 million—a staggering sum—so that underprivileged youths could learn to play tennis. They built twenty-two outdoor/indoor tennis courts in what was not so long ago one of the city's most dangerous places, Crotona Park. As an avid tennis player for fifty years, I can testify that these courts are world class. Indeed, some of the toniest private schools in Manhattan rent these courts, when available, for their own intramural matches. The director is Liezel Huber, a champion doubles player who was ranked number one in the world for 199 weeks. High-quality courts are also being built elsewhere in the Bronx. The goal is to give the thirty thousand area youngsters a chance to learn how to play tennis and to just have fun. Outstanding performers will receive scholarships to pay for their university education. Hopefully some will turn pro, while others teach future generations.

History is another reason to explore the Bronx.[1] Despite all the destruction of buildings, mostly during the 1970s and '80s, much of the borough is still standing. A great number of buildings from the late nineteenth and early twentieth centuries remain, some in good condition, others not. Of all the boroughs, the Bronx still feels the grittiest and most authentic, precisely because it has hardly been gentrified and thousands of the original buildings remain. Strolling up and down the hundreds of streets feels like a trip into the distant past. As I gaze at the old structures with their original lintels, bow and bay windows, terra-cotta, keystones, turrets, parapets, and quoins adorning the brownstones, row houses, Queen Annes, and Victorians in all their faded but still impressive glory, I'm sometimes tempted to become a tour guide just so I can see the pleasure on people's faces as they look at the architectural treasures that most people are unaware of. The Bronx has thankfully landmarked a number of areas, most notably the Longwood Historic District in the South Bronx, with its terrific collection of former mansions and private homes.

But this is a book about the relatively *unknown* aspects of the Bronx, including historical ones. These fill more than several pages of the book, and I'll simply touch on a few to make clear just how fascinating they are. The important musical and art form of hip-hop began in the Bronx in the 1970s. One location was in the West Bronx at 1520 Sedgwick Avenue, overlooking the Harlem River.

Here, in 1973, DJ Kool unveiled hip-hop at his sister's party. Others trace its origins to a violent street gang called the Black Spades, which controlled the public housing projects of the South and East Bronx, most notably Bronxdale and Bronx River. The genre has had millions of followers. One fascinating way to appreciate this is to circle a block on the Grand Concourse beginning on McClellan Place, walking down to E. 166th Street, making a right to reach Walton Avenue and another right onto McClellan, and walking up the hill back to the Concourse. An amazing wall with hundreds of drawings runs around this square block, and many of the murals are of famous musical artists, with accompanying names and/or comments. When you see it, you'll understand why it's worth checking out.

For a real change of pace, there's a virtually unknown majestic former synagogue, high on a hill on E. 167th Street, between Findlay and Teller Avenues. During the mid-twentieth century some 600,000 Jews, more than half of the Bronx's population, lived in the borough. Today, most are gone, except in Riverdale. With their departure, the hundreds of synagogues in which they worshipped have either become churches or disappeared entirely due to neglect, old age, and fires that consumed them. Yet, here, inside the Daughters of Jacob nursing home, which today serves an entirely non-Jewish population, stands a magnificent high-ceilinged temple in the shape of an amphitheater, with sparkling chandeliers, a balcony, a holy ark, seating for hundreds, intricate moldings, richly painted in soft blue, bright gold, and white. The building is well maintained by an Italian American owner who respects its history. Built in 1917, it's in mint condition, looking as if it had been preserved in formaldehyde. How did this happen? Because it's a building *inside a larger edifice*—the home itself. It was, therefore, immune to the destructive fires, winter cold, wind, and general decline that would tremendously weaken a century-old edifice. The two-story walls surrounding it, the high gates, plus tight security discourage vandals, and obtaining permission to visit it is not easy. It's all described in the section on the Concourse. Perhaps one day, gentrifiers will discover and use it.

I also came across a fascinating piece of Bronx history when reading an obscure unpublished manuscript in the local library in the Highbridge section of the Bronx.[2] It recounts the terrible fate that befell a six-member family of Inuit brought to the United States in 1896 by the famous Arctic explorer Admiral Robert Peary at the request of the world-renowned anthropologist Franz Boas, who wanted to study them in person. They were interviewed and examined by the staff of the American Museum of Natural History, who saw them as human subjects rather than as human beings. The *New York Times* referred to them as "unfortunate little savages" in a piece about the group, which lived for a short time in the Bronx on Macombs Road. Tragically, four of them died very soon thereafter, from either the flu or tuberculosis, having acquired no immunity to these diseases. Another was returned to Greenland.

The last, a youngster named Minik, remained here and was adopted by the superintendent of the museum, who lived on West Tremont Avenue. Minik went to Public School 11, which still exists in Highbridge. He became the city's only known Inuk at the time. Peary was criticized by many for having brought Minik and his family to a place where he was treated as a specimen and where he would surely be exposed to illnesses that could and ultimately did kill most of the family members. Peary was no doubt aware of this, as some twenty to forty million people perished from the flu during this period—more than died in World War I. A popular ditty sung by children skipping rope was:

I had a little bird
Its name was Enza
I opened the window
And in-flu-enza.

When, in later years, Minik attempted to retrieve his father's skeletal remains, the museum denied having them in its possession. An embittered Minik returned to Greenland with a parting salvo:

"You're a race of scientific criminals. I know I'll never get my father's bones out of the museum. . . . I am glad to get away before they get my brains and stuff them in a jar." It wasn't until 1993 that the museum made amends and sent the remains to Greenland, where they received a traditional burial.[3]

This story matters because it demonstrates how the powerless are often neglected and denied justice and how history is often a creation of the powerful. Such incidents, when they do come to light, emerge only by happenstance. The individual history of all immigrants, both before and after they came here, is significant and eminently worth passing on to their children and grandchildren. It also reminds us that all immigrants deserve respect, even if their numbers are tiny. Some examples are Bhutanese (who lived in the Bronx nearby, in University Heights, when they first arrived), Paraguayans, Nepalese, Uruguayans, and the Garifuna who hail from Central America.

Information about a community's history can be gleaned not only from printed materials but from direct observation—a monument, a building, even a street sign, as the following account reveals.

Walking through a subsection of Throgs Neck called Spencer Estates, I happen upon some streets with strange names. These are Ampere, Outlook, Library, Research, Ohm, and Watt Avenues, as well as Radio Place. Perhaps it was once a research center, I thought. But after some research of my own I discovered the answer. Isaac Rice was president of a company founded in the early twentieth century, the Electric Storage Battery Company. He also headed the Electric Boat Company, which built submarines used by the British and United States navies in World War I. His companies were critical to the war effort because submarines used electricity while underwater. After Rice died, his widow Julia donated what was a very large sum in those times, one million dollars, to build Rice Stadium inside Pelham Bay Park. The neighborhood borders the park, and the streets were named in memory of both his generosity and his contributions to this country.

One discovery can sometimes lead to another. Julia Rice founded the Society for the Suppression of Unnecessary Noise. She was annoyed by the whistles and horns that frequently broke the quiet in her residential community on Manhattan's Riverside Drive a century ago. While it sounds like an eccentric project, even "tilting at windmills," since cities are noisy places, it actually led to something of importance that remains with us to this very day. The quiet zones that are the norm today in school and hospital areas have been traced back to the work of her organization, founded in 1907.

A third aspect that characterizes the Bronx is its great *beauty* in many of its neighborhoods. To begin with, it has 26,897 acres of parkland. This encompasses the stunning Pelham Bay Park, which, at 2,765 acres, is the largest in the city. Many parks have attractive topography and are described in this book. Aside from Pelham Bay, they include Van Cortlandt, Bronx, Claremont, Crotona, Ferry Point, and St. Mary's Parks. One of the loveliest sights lies in Tremont, where E. 180th Street and West Farms Road intersect.

I'm standing on a path in front of the Bronx River in River Park where a stunning waterfall, about a third of a block wide, cascades swiftly over the rocks, forming crystal-clear arc-like patterns because of how the waterfall descends from the top at different levels. Ahead, the river and thick woods stretch northward as far as the eye can see. It's the largest waterfall in the city, and if you drown out the urban area behind you it feels like the Adirondacks, or, at the very least, the Catskills. The land here is shared with the New York Botanical Garden and the Bronx Zoo.

Far away in the West Bronx, on a small, obscure street called Andrews Avenue South, I stumble upon a private park belonging to a small development consisting of two apartment buildings. In theory it's open only to the residents, but no one prevents me from entering through the open gate and the residents tell me no one is ever denied entry unless they're unruly. Pillars covered with light-colored mosaic tiles and likenesses of animals, birds, and fish frame the entrance. Inside are comfortable benches encrusted with tiles. On the walls of the buildings facing the park are two murals with brightly painted geometric shapes. There's a fuller description in the section on Morris Heights. It's a gem and must be seen to be appreciated.

Over in the adjoining community of University Heights is the Hall of Fame for Great Americans, situated on the campus of Bronx Community College, which was once the uptown branch of Manhattan's New York University. It features ninety-eight bronze sculptured busts of famous Americans, which stand on each side of a semicircle that resembles a Greek stone colonnade. They're arranged by category—physicians, judges, artists, military leaders, presidents, and so on. Among them are Robert Fulton, Thomas Paine, Booker T. Washington, Charlotte Cushman, and Nathaniel Hawthorne. What makes the display even more beautiful is the way it's laid out, with a walkway made of diamond-shaped tiles with interlocking herringbone tiles. To top it off, there's a breathtaking view of woodlands and of the Harlem River, a gently twisting ribbon of shimmering blue, making its way up to the tip of Manhattan Island.

Off the quad that centers the campus, which was designed by the legendary late-nineteenth-century architect Stanford White, is a magnificent library called the North Hall, created by the vision of another famed contemporary architect, Robert A. M. Stern. Inside, there's a coffered ceiling with white pilasters set against the white walls. The central reading room, boasting well-crafted lamps with shades on the wooden tables, is reminiscent of the New York Public Library's reading room. The furnishings in general are made of rich wood, accompanied by Ionic columns with a Greek key design. Appropriately enough, a series of excellent paintings of street scenes in the borough, by the Bronx artist Daniel Hauben, grace the walls of the library.

This is only a fraction of what the borough has to offer in terms of beauty. There's much more to be seen in the Bronx, especially the many outstanding wall murals. And then there are the private homes in Riverdale, some of them breathtaking, particularly in the Fieldston section, and also the Riverdale Historic District in the 250s, west of the Henry Hudson Parkway. Note, in particular, the fantastic mansions along Sycamore Avenue. The Riverdale section offers many more scenic viewing opportunities, not to mention Wave Hill, a twenty-eight-acre estate with delightful gardens and vistas of the Palisades, and in southern Riverdale, Spuyten Duyvil, with its equally spectacular Palisades views. The Country Club section in the far-off Throgs Neck section also has some very pretty homes with excellent views of Eastchester Bay.

Last, there are the Art Deco buildings for which the Bronx was famed. While many of them have deteriorated over the decades, victim to the blight that overtook the Bronx, there are still some worth seeing. These are described in the book, but if you only have time to look at one such structure, I recommend the exterior of the Park Plaza Apartments at 1005 Jerome Avenue. As you stand in front of the building, with the new Yankee Stadium at your back, what's most striking is a series of polychrome, or glazed ceramic, terra-cotta representations on the building's face done in very bright colors—blue, green, orange, and silver. The designs include the traditional Art Deco motifs: a sunrise, flamingos standing by a fountain, pyramids, and a rendering of the Parthenon. It's the best example of the glory that once was.

A fourth trait that marks the people in the Bronx is *friendliness and a sense of community*. This was validated over and over in hundreds of conversations I had with residents. They spoke of the Bronx as a warm, inviting place where they lived among others who felt similarly. Many believed that the city did not consider their borough to be a priority. Yet, at the end of the day, it was home to them. In a tiny corner in Eastchester, hard up against the Westchester County border, I met a middle-aged white homeowner, whose house overlooked the Hutchinson River. If I hadn't walked every block in the borough, I would not have discovered it because it lay in a five-block-deep area behind a commercial strip with big box stores that blocked the view. A very friendly man, he told me he loved living there because "It's kinda like a hidden community." The sense that only a small number of people lived there made it special for him.

A great example of friendliness came in the form of a cheerful middle-aged Black woman with yellow highlights in her curly hair, whom I met two miles away, outside of Seton Falls Park. As it's not considered very safe, the park isn't heavily used, which in turn makes it even less safe. Still, it has beautiful forests, large trees with gnarled trunks, and interesting large rock outcroppings. As I cased it, I saw some young men that the locals confirmed to be drug dealers or users. I don't have a death wish, but I was intrigued. I asked the woman if the park was safe, and she said she wasn't sure because in the twenty years that she lived three blocks from the park, she had never been inside. Her next comment was surprising.

"I'm ready to walk with you. Why not? You know, I've never done this. It's going to be interesting. You know, this isn't like Central Park." She was genuinely concerned for my welfare and her own, but she wanted to go. This turned into a very interesting experience, but what struck me was her willingness to take this walk into an isolated forest with a total stranger. Race apparently made no difference either. She had been a school crossing guard for many years. What happened? Read the Eastchester section.

One of the elements that makes for cohesive communities is having distinct boundaries. Another is sharing a common culture, and a third is having common needs, interests, and goals. I found more than a few neighborhoods that possessed these traits, among them Harding Park, Silver Beach, Parkchester, and Co-op City. The Bronx has many ethnic and racial groups, and these retain a strong sense of community revolving around identity. Many eat the same foods, have often come from the same countries, and hold the same religious beliefs. There are Italians in Pelham Bay, Morris Park, and Belmont, and Albanians often coexist with them in these communities.

There are West Indians in Kingsbridge and West Africans in the Concourse neighborhood. Bangladeshis have established communities in Castle Hill and parts of Soundview, as well as Westchester Square. African Americans and Hispanics have created subcommunities in parts of Mott Haven, East Tremont, and Morrisania. One clear indication of how friendly people in the Bronx are is that not one person refused to speak with me when I engaged them.

A more fluid, yet definitive, trait of the Bronx is *surprise*. I discovered many things about the Bronx, both large and small, that amazed me. How is it that so few people know about them, I thought? Take, for example, CUNY's Lehman College, in the Bedford Park section of the Bronx. James Lyons, as borough president of the Bronx, invited the United Nations to locate at the college. College administrators were unhappy because they wanted space for overflow students in the postwar era. But City Hall, which had authority over public city colleges, won out and the rest, as they say, was history. When it was first established, the United Nations Security Council was located on the Lehman campus, then a part of Hunter College, for six months. The fledgling organization gained real credibility during this period, when the council successfully pressured the Soviet Union to leave Iran. Few people are aware of this.

Even more amazing and virtually unknown is what occurred during World War II, when the Lehman campus became a major training center for the WAVES (Women Accepted for Volunteer Emergency Service, the women's division of the US Navy), with 91,138 women receiving training there. That was news to me too, but then I learned in a conversation that the program had another secret purpose. Concerned about possible spying from the air, the Navy, and possibly the Army, decided to store secret materials at the college. The WAVE program was the perfect cover, and they found the ideal hiding place: a subterranean network of dimly lit tunnels connecting several campus buildings. I was fortunate to have gained access to it and toured it myself, discovering only on my way out that walking in the area was officially prohibited. The tunnels were a maze of passageways that twisted and turned at sharp angles, with old pipes overhead and rooms off to each side containing machinery and other items whose purposes I was unable to decipher. The full story appears in the Bedford Park section.

There were other unexpected finds, too. A Catholic church in the West Bronx that performed exorcisms every Friday night for years is one example. Another is the Andrew Freedman Home on the Grand Concourse. Freedman, a millionaire, almost lost all his money in the Panic of 1907. Recognizing that it could happen to anyone, he built a retirement home for older adults who had lost their fortunes and became indigent. Here they lived free of charge, enjoying free meals and use of a library, plus other amenities, including being attended to by servants. They were, however, required to be formally attired for dinner. Freedman obviously had a soft spot for such types and felt they would suffer grievously as paupers because they had once had so much. I was aware of the general outlines of the story, but research and a personal visit turned up a treasure trove of additional information. There's more to the story and it's in the Concourse West subsection.

These are only a few of the *surprises,* as I like to call them, and they came about because I re-walked most of the Bronx. As opposed to the first volume on the city, I now had the opportunity to explore everything in greater depth.

Of particular importance for this walking guide is how the Bronx is generally perceived in popular contemporary culture. While it's home to the New York Yankees, the world-famous Bronx Zoo, and the New York Botanical Garden, it is all too often viewed in negative terms by the general public. As noted earlier, its relatively high crime rate, drug dealing, gang violence, and dangerous streets are often portrayed as a way of summing up the borough. These descriptions of what is clearly a problem are nonetheless an exaggeration of the truth. In 2018, while the Bronx still had the second-highest rate of major crimes, it was lower than prevailed in Brooklyn, a borough widely perceived as much safer. On the other hand, in terms of the overall violent-crime rate, the Bronx was first, ahead of Brooklyn. No one can deny that the Bronx has a high rate of crime relative to Manhattan, Staten Island, and Queens, but the most important practical question here is, can you safely walk it? And the answer is yes, under most conditions. The overwhelming majority of crimes are directly related to gang violence and drug dealing, and statistically, innocent bystanders are rarely victims. When crime does happen, there's a major outcry because such incidents are rare. It's also important to emphasize that at least half of the Bronx, in terms of area, is quite safe to walk in, day or night, and the other half is pretty safe to walk in during daytime hours—provided you are alert and careful, as you should be in any major city.

The focus on this topic tends to obscure the reality that crime has dropped to historic lows in the Bronx and everywhere else in the city, part of a long-term trend. In 2018, the number of murders in the city as a whole dropped to below 289. This is a level not seen since the end of World War II, more than seventy years ago. The rate in the city in 2018 was 3 murders per 100,000 people. Compare that to the three other largest metropolitan areas in the nation: the rate in greater Los Angeles was double that of New York at 6 per 100,000, Chicago had 19 per 100,000, and Houston had 15 per 100,000. In short, crime statistics in New York are trending downward, including the number of communities where dangerous situations can and do occur. Twenty years ago, Bushwick, Boerum Hill, Fort Greene, Harlem, and other areas of the city were considered unsafe, and today it's a totally different story.

What of the future? While the book's focus is on exploring the borough, this question is certainly worth a brief discussion. One harbinger of change is gentrification. There's much talk about it happening in the part of Mott Haven that's near the water. Whether it's hype or reality is hard to say. A visit to this area makes it clear that gentrifiers are coming, but not yet, it would appear, in great numbers. On a pleasant Sunday morning, when you might expect to see young families and couples out and about in the streets, the gentrifiers don't appear to be especially visible. But the few people I do encounter are mostly visitors. Another problem is that rent reform laws limiting how much developers can charge if they rehabilitate apartments will also result in fewer high-quality apartments that attract gentrifiers.

A return visit yields the same result: no one in sight, save for a gaggle of Italian tourists snapping photos. There are two antique shops next to a storefront church on Alexander Avenue, neither of them open on a Monday at 11:00 a.m. This feeling of seclusion is, to put it bluntly, a universe away from East Williamsburg, Carroll Gardens, or DUMBO. I speak with some artists who live here, who tell me nothing is happening yet, and that makes them happy because gentrifiers will cause rents to go up. The facts speak for themselves. The main drag here, Bruckner Boulevard, is simply a semi-industrial street with cheap takeout places, auto repair joints, delis, and the like, all rather unattractive. Pulaski Park, on the boulevard, is in bad shape, consisting of a run-down basketball court and a playground. It doesn't even have restrooms, and its major attraction may be a couple of metal figures of cows attached to a fence. There are few restaurants or cafés besides Charlie's Bar and Kitchen on Lincoln Avenue. There's a history here, as the neighborhood seemed poised for takeoff in the early 2000s, but then it fizzled with the 2008 economic meltdown. What will happen now is hard to say at this juncture.

On the one hand, the immediate area is simply not very safe. There's no getting around it, as evident from overall crime statistics supplied by the New York Police Department for the 40th Precinct, which includes the Mott Haven, Port Morris, and Melrose communities. Amenities like taverns, eateries, cafés, boutique shops, supermarkets like Whole Foods, movie theaters, and nightclubs are in an embryonic state. There isn't much available upscale housing yet, though there is some construction going on. Part of the problem is that there are many large NYCHA projects in the immediate vicinity, namely two blocks away. There are similar housing projects next to gentrifying areas in Brooklyn, but they are nowhere near as large, and the area available for gentrification here is much smaller than, say, in Boerum Hill or Fort Greene. Manhattan also has many NYCHA projects, but they are smaller in size or counterbalanced by a large stock of good housing in areas like the Upper West and Upper East Sides. Some observers have even hinted of a conspiracy to prevent the Bronx from gentrifying because if it happens, the poor will be forced out to faraway housing, perhaps in Long Island or New Jersey, leaving those city industries that employ poor people without enough workers. To date, there doesn't seem to be any hard evidence of that, but there may be some merit to the argument.

On the other hand, a strong case can be made by those who believe the Bronx will gentrify just as Brooklyn and Queens have. The reason it matters so much in terms of the Bronx as a whole is that gentrifiers make a community safer, both by their presence and by the fact that they cause the city to pay closer attention to their needs. This, in turn, has a trickle-down effect for everyone—except, of course, those who cannot afford the resulting higher housing prices and may be forced to move elsewhere. As I've discussed extensively in my first book, *The New York Nobody Knows*, which presents a general analysis of the city, it's a complex issue, with some scholars saying it's bad for people in poverty and others arguing it benefits them. A big problem in determining who's right is that there has been no serious research on what happens to those who were forced out, or how many were actually forced to leave. There aren't even any data on where they went and exactly why they left.[4]

In any event, let's look into the arguments that the borough will gentrify. Large lots along the Harlem River totaling four acres were purchased by Somerset Partners and the Chetrit Group in 2014 for about $58 million. There are renderings of twenty-four and twenty-two-story towers—seven in all are slated—plus 20,500 feet of retail space. Part of what made this purchase so significant was that it was for residential purposes. Until then, most of what was bought was for commercial investment. But these groups then sold the site in 2018 to the Brookfield organization for $165 million, a pretty tidy profit. Brookfield announced that the residential focus remained and that 30 percent of the apartments would be for affordable housing. It's still not 100 percent certain whether Brookfield will follow through and build residentially or commercially, or perhaps go for a sports stadium on the site, but if it takes the plunge and builds apartment towers, many others will surely follow. The plan as of 2019 was to build a $950 million residential development with 1,350 apartments. Keep in mind that most neighborhoods in Brooklyn, Manhattan, or Queens that gentrified were once not gentrified. Many observers doubted it would happen, and then it did. There are, in fact, plans to build a soccer stadium in this area to provide a permanent home for the New York City Football Club. Like the Barclays Center in Brooklyn, that would certainly generate more interest and investment in the surrounding neighborhoods.

A key factor for gentrifiers, the majority of whom work in Manhattan, is transportation. The Bronx has no fewer than eight subway lines—the 1, 2, 3, 4, 5, 6, D, and B—and the ride to Manhattan from Mott Haven is very short, depending on where you're going. There's also the beginnings of ferry service, something that's already happening in the more distant East Bronx, like Soundview, Castle Hill, and even Throgs Neck, which would add considerably to the borough's allure. Plus, new train stations are planned for the Metro-North line. People looking for diversity will also find the South Bronx appealing, though many may not be as interested in this option as they claim to be. Perhaps the most critical factor is the real estate market. If the cost of apartments continues to rise in the other boroughs, then many would-be buyers or renters will be priced out there, which will generate lots of interest in the Bronx.

While gentrification isn't occurring yet on a large scale here, more small and middle-range investors are purchasing individual buildings. Their tenants are mostly working-class Black and Hispanic people who are nongentrifiers. In the past, landlords were able to renovate and raise rents by 10 percent or more whenever the lease is up. Rents for these apartments, a big two-bedroom or a "chopped up" smaller three-bedroom are around $1,700 a month. However, new rent reform laws passed in 2019 have made it much harder for landlords to raise rents substantially. It remains to be seen what the long-term effects of these new laws will be on gentrification.

Summing up, there are many push and pull factors that could affect whether or not gentrification comes to the Bronx. A constellation of factors—the economy most of all, but also levels of crime, changing patterns of movement in the city and elsewhere, decisions about what to build and where by the city (a major owner of properties here), and the strength of local groups in fostering a sense of community—can generate momentum, which then becomes a self-fulfilling prophecy. The level of investment interest in the Bronx by more affluent people in recent years seems to have undergone a significant increase. They have already been preceded, to some degree, by artists and musicians, who have typically been the first wave in areas that ultimately gentrify. However, even if it does happen, no one can predict how quickly it will occur.

One hopeful sign is that in 1990 the Bronx had 1.2 million residents, and in 2015 there were 1.4 million, an upward trend that has continued. All of the boroughs have had population increases, but Brooklyn and the Bronx have reported the largest, with each one recording about a 5 percent increase in 2016. In 2018, the city's total population reached a new high of 8,622,698. This number does not include undocumented residents. In 2017, the population in the Bronx reached 1,471,160, a total not seen since 1970, some fifty years ago.

Mott Haven has generated the greatest amount of interest, but this scenario can also be applied to the parts of Concourse, Soundview, and enclaves in the West Bronx because of their proximity to Manhattan. But there's also local opposition by community groups representing people in poverty who fear they will be driven out of their neighborhoods by rising costs and a decline in the availability of inexpensive stores and apartments. A large mural described in the Morris Heights section strongly attacking gentrifiers and builders and vowing resistance is a perfect instance of such hostility. But such opposition, because it is weakened by people willing to accept buyouts, has not succeeded elsewhere in the city to any degree.

And so, will the Bronx gentrify or not? I'd say yes, without specifying when, but stay tuned because no one can control all of the pieces in this complex puzzle, and no one can predict the future.

My love for walking the city can be traced back to a game my father played with me as a child, called "Last Stop." On every available weekend, when I was between the ages of nine and fourteen, my dad and I took a subway from the Upper West Side, where we lived, to its last stop and walked around for a couple of hours. When we ran out of new last stops on the various lines, we did the second to last, then the third, and so on, always traveling to a new place. In this way, I learned to love and appreciate the city, which I like to call "the world's greatest outdoor museum." I also developed a very close bond with my father, who gave me the greatest present a kid can have—the gift of time.

In walking, actually re-walking, the Bronx, my approach was the same as when I did the research for *The New York Nobody Knows: Walking 6,000 Miles in the City*, a comprehensive guide to all five boroughs. I walked and observed what was going on around me, all the while informally interviewing hundreds of people. No one refused to talk to me, once again confirming my past conclusion that New Yorkers are a remarkably open group if approached in a friendly and respectful manner. Sometimes I told them I was writing a book, but much of the time I didn't need to, and simply engaged them in freewheeling, casual conversation. I often taped what they were saying, using my iPhone recording app in front of them. Hardly anyone asked why, and if their attention lingered on the phone for even five seconds, I quickly explained why I was recording. No one seemed to mind. Perhaps that's a statement about what we've become—a society accustomed to cameras and recorders, which accepts that few things are really private anymore. Clearly, this is a great boon for researchers. Greater tolerance for others in general and an abiding belief that the city is safe are also contributors to this state of affairs.

I walked in the daytime, at night, during the week, on weekends, and in all seasons whenever I could, in rain or shine or snow, from April 2018 to January 2019. That's nine months, averaging about ninety miles a month. I attended parades, block parties, and other events and also hung out on the streets, in bars and restaurants, and in parks. Much of the time, my wife, Helaine, who was great company, and our dog, Heidi, a Cavalier/Swiss mountain dog hybrid, and an excellent icebreaker, accompanied me. People, especially women and dog lovers, are both less apt to feel threatened and more inclined to be friendly in such cases. My wife, a keen observer of human life, ended up being my research associate. She saw many things that I missed and was especially helpful in describing the architecture of the borough and in discussing and evaluating my own work. I began in Mott Haven and finished in City Island, traversing every community for a total of 804 miles, as measured by my Omron pedometer and iPhone.

I had, of course, walked almost every block in the borough for the first book, and probably sixteen times before that, albeit more selectively. I wore Rockports, in my view the world's most comfortable and durable shoes. In fact, I was able to do the walk on just two pairs. Walking is, for my money, the best way to explore a city. It slows you down so that you can see and absorb things and literally experience the environment as you talk to those who know it best: the residents. And the more you walk, the greater the chance you'll get really good material. You just can't know whether it'll happen in the first or the fifth hour of your trip on any given day. It's also very healthy. Bicycling is the next best option.

I would recommend exercising caution when walking certain Bronx communities. The reader can decide based on what's been written about them in the book. Walking at night and in the summer, when school is out and gangs are initiating new members, is riskier. Regardless, much of the borough is perfectly safe. In the parts that aren't, the chances of being in a particular spot on a certain day and time are very low. The media inadvertently contribute to a sense of apprehension, because as low as the odds might be, when people read about an assault or murder, they tend to picture it happening to them. Keep in mind, as noted earlier, that about 80 percent of the city's murders are of people who knew their assailants, and that most are drug or gang related.

Clearly you don't have to actually walk the Bronx to learn about it. Simply curl up on a sofa or in an easy chair and read about the communities as you would about a foreign land that you can't or won't visit. Perhaps you grew up in the Bronx and want to vicariously read and reminisce about the old days. For those intrepid travelers who wish to walk everywhere, tips on how to stay safe can be found in appendix A.

The book does have the same theme as the first book, dealing almost exclusively with the unusual and unknown aspects of these communities. Its inclusion of quotes from interviews with residents, its musings on life in general, plus many anecdotes about all manner of things, and its focus on sociological explanations of why things are the way they are, all combine to make it what I believe is a rather unique guidebook.

Hopefully, these walks will whet readers' appetites and entice them into wandering these streets on their own, where they are likely to make new discoveries. In order to make this book easy to carry around, it was necessary to limit the discussion to six or seven pages per community. Had I described everything of interest in these locales, the book would have been twice as long.

There's a street map for each community, and you can walk it in any order you'd like, searching out whatever moves you. The order of communities in the book is strictly geographical. Most of the north-south thoroughfares extend for long stretches and are the best way to traverse the borough; the east-west streets are not nearly as orderly and many of them quickly become dead ends. Starting with Mott Haven, a good way to walk is to generally head north, ending with Riverdale; then south from Woodlawn through Castle Hill; and finally, north from Throgs Neck, ending with City Island.

The majority of Bronxites simply say they live "in the Bronx" when asked, or sometimes the South, East, West, or North Bronx. They might just tell the questioner the name of their street. When you mention their community's name, they will either say yes or no, or give you a puzzled look. More than any other borough, the exact boundaries of each neighborhood are often disputed, sometimes with great vehemence, by both residents and experts. In an interview with me, the venerable official Bronx historian, Lloyd Ultan, explained that the Bronx had already been annexed to the city before the other boroughs were created, and its leaders saw no need to give new names to individual sections. Despite that, it and the other boroughs eventually created communities, which they then duly named.

I've decided to go, in most instances, with the local community boards' designations (the borough is divided into twelve community boards). This has been augmented by consulting the *Encyclopedia of New York City,* whose boundaries often differ from the boards', and by other sources. In some instances, a community's history, population, topography, buildings, natural boundaries (e.g., highways, bridges, industrial parks, etc.) have been considered, as well as using common sense. As there is no universal agreement about many of these borders among city agencies and scholars, I exercised my right to make decisions based on what I saw, learned, and knew. In any case, there aren't any instances of great distances separating people's views about where a community should be. It's more a question of where a community begins or ends within a relatively small geographic space.[5]

One exception worth noting, however, is the South Bronx. Until perhaps the early 1950s, the label referred to the industrial area below 138th Street. Gradually, as blight, poverty, and crime became endemic in a number of Bronx communities, the very words "South Bronx" became synonymous in popular culture with these conditions, and the boundaries shifted northward. Today, the South Bronx is viewed by many as extending northward to Fordham Road. However, this boundary line is disputed by many residents and professionals who regard it as an unfair stereotype, since crime has dropped precipitously in many communities below Fordham Road.

Almost everything in the book is based on new material. I used almost nothing from the first book, as I didn't want it to be seen as a rehash. There were other contributing factors, such as the different structure. The first book about the entire city had chapters focusing on larger themes, such as ethnicity, gentrification, spaces, immigration, social life, and community. These subjects continue to be main topics, but they are now embedded in the narrative that discusses the unique aspects of each community. Because the intended audience here is largely tourists, curious residents of these communities, nostalgia seekers who grew up in or lived in these areas, and New Yorkers looking for interesting local trips, the book discusses in detail every single neighborhood in the Bronx. This means that there must be a few pages on every community, regardless as to how interesting or uninteresting it appears to be. That forced me to work really hard at uncovering new material. What surprised me was that every area *is* interesting. I just had to look deeper and be more creative in some cases.

Another reason why the book is new is because the city is constantly changing. New stores, murals, and buildings go up; parks change; and there are different events every year, like concerts, comedy shows, protests, parades, feasts, and town hall meetings. Everyone with whom I spoke was a new respondent, and the conversations often led in different directions. Some of the places described here may no longer exist when you take your walks. But, no doubt, there will be new places to explore of equal or even greater interest.

Some historical information is included in the sections, but not all that much. This is, after all, a book about the present. The Bronx has a significant number of famous residents, past and present, a few of whom are noted here. If that's your area of interest, I suggest looking them up on Wikipedia and other internet sources, which often provide addresses and other details. And if you're searching for specific topics, like parks, African or Italian restaurants, or gentrification, you should definitely consult the comprehensive index.

There are two critical ways in which this guidebook differs from the typical one. First is *the focus on impromptu conversations* with people from every walk of life. What these folks do is breathe life and energy into the material. By listening to what they had to say, I gained a much deeper understanding of what the Bronx is all about—its complexity, the joys and struggles of its inhabitants, the challenges its residents face, and what helps them get through life. This enhances the reader's or walker's ability to see life as the people who live there do.

The second major distinction between this and most other guidebooks is *its focus on the unknown parts of the city*. Clearly, these areas weren't completely unknown, but they were unknown to most people who live or visit here. I deliberately ignored the sites that appear in most other guides. It's not that those places aren't critical in making the city what it is; they are, but they've already been covered. My aim was to unveil new, hidden aspects of the borough. Hopefully, readers will find the effort to have been worthwhile.

The vignettes, interviews, and descriptions have one overall goal: to capture the heart, pulse, and soul of this endlessly fascinating borough. Whether or not this has been accomplished is for the reader to judge. This is the fourth in a projected "Nobody Knows" series of guidebooks—one for each borough—with Staten Island, the last one, up next.

One last minor, yet practical, point. The Bronx is the only borough prefixed by the word "the." Whether or not that word should be capitalized is a matter of debate. Taking no sides, I'm deferring to common usage and am following the practice of Kenneth Jackson's *The Encyclopedia of New York City*. According to several authoritative sources, a Scandinavian named Jonas Bronck settled in the area in 1639. The tributary that ran near his farm thus became known as "*the* Bronx River." It's the only freshwater river in the entire city, and the borough itself is also the only one that is part of the US mainland. When the borough was named, the "the" stuck. The spelling change from "ck" to "x" happened simply because his name was easier to pronounce that way. And now, welcome to the Bronx!

MOTT HAVEN

MELROSE

CONCOURSE

HUNTS POINT

CROTONA PARK EAST

MORRISANIA

TREMONT

MOUNT EDEN

HIGHBRIDGE

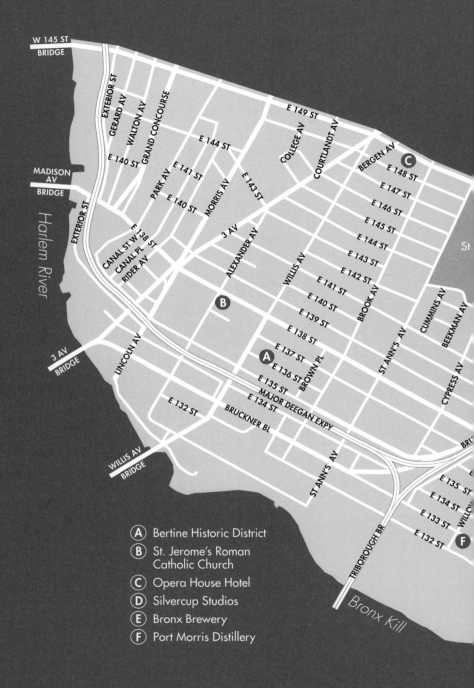

W 145 ST
BRIDGE

EXTERIOR ST
GERARD AV
WALTON AV
GRAND CONCOURSE

E 149 ST

COLLEGE AV

COURTLANDT AV

BERGEN AV

E 148 ST

C

E 144 ST

E 140 ST

E 141 ST

PARK AV

E 140 ST

MORRIS AV

E 143 ST

E 147 ST

E 146 ST

E 145 ST

E 144 ST

MADISON
AV
BRIDGE

EXTERIOR ST

CANAL ST W 138 ST
CANAL PL
RIDER AV

3 AV

ALEXANDER AV

WILLIS AV

E 143 ST

E 142 ST

BROOK AV

ST ANN'S AV

CUMMINS AV

BEEKMAN AV

St

Harlem River

E 141 ST

E 140 ST

E 139 ST

E 138 ST

B

3 AV
BRIDGE

LINCOLN AV

E 137 ST

BROWN PL

A

E 136 ST

E 135 ST

MAJOR DEEGAN EXPY

E 132 ST

E 134 ST

BRUCKNER BL

CYPRESS AV

WILLIS AV
BRIDGE

ST ANN'S AV

BR

E 135 ST

E 134 ST

TRIBOROUGH BR

WILLO

E 133 ST

E 132 ST

F

A Bertine Historic District

B St. Jerome's Roman
Catholic Church

C Opera House Hotel

D Silvercup Studios

E Bronx Brewery

F Port Morris Distillery

Bronx Kill

MOTT HAVEN

MOTT HAVEN'S BOUNDARIES ARE E. 149th Street on the north, E. 149th Street and the East River on the east, the strait known as the Bronx Kill on the south, and the Harlem River on the west. Jonas Bronck, a Swedish sea captain after whom the Bronx was named, established his farm in Mott Haven in 1639. In 1670, the land was bought by the Morris family, one of whose members, Lewis Morris, was a signer of the Declaration of Independence. In 1841, Jordan Lawrence Mott purchased the land for his ironworks factory. In the latter part of the nineteenth century, it became more heavily settled, and a good number of handsome brownstones and row houses were built there. The area became much more densely populated in the twentieth century as tenement houses proliferated throughout the area.

Until the 1950s, Mott Haven was largely German, Irish, and Italian, along with a small Jewish population. It was famous then for a large annual Irish parade sponsored by veterans of the Irish Republican Army, who marched proudly on Willis Avenue on Easter Sunday. Puerto Ricans began moving into Mott Haven in the early 1940s, a pattern that accelerated in the '50s. African Americans also settled here in the early '40s and were drawn to the NYCHA Patterson houses that were built in 1956. Situated on Third Avenue between E. 139th and E. 141st Streets and with almost 1,800 apartments spread through its fifteen buildings, the complex is one of the city's largest housing projects. This community is where the South Bronx's reputation began and where illegal blockbusting tactics resulted in a mass exodus of white people from the area. The 1960s, '70s, and '80s, were marked by arson, abandonment, and crime here and in the neighboring communities of Hunts Point, Morrisania, Melrose, and beyond. These problems and issues, including the lack of opportunity and lack of adequate social programs for those experiencing poverty, have been discussed at length in my first book, *The New York Nobody Knows*.

In recent years, there have been some attempts to gentrify the area, centering on Alexander and Lincoln Avenues, west of the Major Deegan Expressway. It is still in an embryonic state, and whether the trend will grow is uncertain. Mott Haven also has one of the largest concentrations of public housing in the city, with most of it located in the area immediately east of the Major Deegan, a block from the gentrifying area. The major commercial thoroughfares of Mott Haven are E. 149th and E. 138th Streets; Third, Brook, Willis, and St. Ann's Avenues; and Bruckner Boulevard. There's only one decent sized park—St. Mary's—and crime is a significant problem in Mott Haven. While, like the city as a whole, it's safer than, say, fifteen years ago and you can walk through it in the daytime, anyone who is unfamiliar with these streets should exercise caution. This is, of course, true of other South Bronx communities as well.

I begin my trip on the corner of Brown Place and E. 136th Street. There's a charter school—Mott Haven Academy—across the street from the pretty Public School 154, named after Jonas Bronck, as in "the Bronx." The Haven Academy is beautifully painted with a large mural in bright colors: aqua, turquoise, purple, and pink.

Bertine Historic District

Painted on the upper part of the building are leaves and circles in various colors. Below, near the second and third floor is a bird that's very eye-catching because of its plumage and graceful body, notwithstanding that it's impossible to determine what species of bird it is. It's perched on a tree branch of gorgeous shades of blue and yellow. At the bottom of the wall are fanciful designs, some of which look like leaves. What makes this mural so different is its dreamlike quality. The colors are soft, and the bird is the fruit of someone's fertile imagination, especially the upturned beak.

Returning to 136th Street via Brown Place, I make a right and, after passing a brand-new playground built by the city, find myself in front of a group of handsome homes, part of the Bertine Historic

District. Built in the late nineteenth century by Edward Bertine, the homes are structures featuring nice stonework with orange and tan brickwork, mostly in the Queen Anne mode. What stands out is the architectural detail—the gables, arched doorways and windows, fan lights, ziggurat designs—with each home looking different. They are exceptional, but visitors must be cautious, for the block also has a NYCHA-owned and -operated tenement that is an active drug-dealing scene, notwithstanding the drug-free zone sign outside the building. Of course, this may well have changed since I last saw it, but it's symptomatic of a general problem in Mott Haven.

Turning left on Willis Avenue I go one block to E. 135th Street, turn right, and then left onto Lincoln Avenue. As I proceed under the highway I am entering the heart of what's considered to be gentrifying Mott Haven. This area was once a major center for piano manufacturing, and some enterprising real estate people have re-named it the "Piano District."

Many articles have been written about Mott Haven being the epicenter of the newest geographical trend in gentrification. They state that gentrifiers are moving in, mostly on the south side of the Major Deegan Expressway along Lincoln and Alexander Avenues, Bruckner Boulevard and the surrounding streets. Among the eateries touted are Charlie's Steakhouse, which occupies the first floor of the Clock Tower, originally a piano factory and now a residential building on the corner of Lincoln and Bruckner.

Leaving the waterfront area, I turn my attention to the nongentrified areas east of the Major Deegan, walking up Lincoln Avenue and turning right on E. 139th Street. I soon arrive at a small three-block historic district of handsome two-story row houses on Alexander Avenue between 138th and 141st Streets. This street was known variously in earlier times as "Politicians' Row," "Doctors' Row," and "the Irish Fifth Avenue." It also includes the historic St. Jerome's Roman Catholic Church, a large and handsome Italianate Revival and Spanish Colonial building, founded in 1899. But these three blocks are atypical for this area. About 80 percent of

Mott Haven, the part from 149th Street on the north, the Bruckner Expressway on the east, and the Major Deegan on the south and west, is very much a low-income area with little upscale shopping anywhere. The stores on Brook, Third, and Willis Avenues, as well as on 138th and 149th Streets, cater to a low-income population. Therefore, unsurprisingly, investment seems to be, as in Melrose, overwhelmingly in affordable housing. And today, such housing may have amenities like a small fitness center and a rooftop garden.

At 138th Street I turn left and pass block after block of plain and sometimes drab retail outlets that typify the community, with one exception. At number 570, on the corner of St. Ann's Avenue, my attention is drawn to a Chinese takeout joint, with a most unusual name: "Worship Super Heroes—Best Chinese Food in Bronx." This is probably a result of hearing the words "worship superheroes" in a positive context and thinking, why not use it as a name for the store? In any case, it's clearly eye-catching. I swing left onto Cypress Avenue, walking several blocks until it dead-ends at St. Mary's Street.

Here, I enter St. Mary's Park and immediately see a dog run that isn't well maintained. Several pit bulls are gamboling about, with their owners keeping a watchful eye on them. St. Mary's is the largest park in the area, and I stroll down a wide walkway running through the center of the park and flanked on both sides by majestic London plane trees. People are sitting on benches, talking, playing with their smartphones, and taking in the sun on a warm afternoon. Beyond the trees on the right side are sports fields and playgrounds. While one of the playgrounds has been renovated, the others are not in great shape, and the athletic court surfaces are cracked in many places. There are bleachers, but they have no seats. On the left is a maze of pathways winding through hilly and rocky semi-wild terrain interspersed with grassy spaces and trees, offering a commanding scenic view of the neighborhood. I ask a Jamaican couple whether the park is safe at night, and they say it is. But the consensus is that it's definitely safe in the daytime, but not at night. I exit the park at St. Ann's Avenue and walk up to 149th Street, the major shopping thoroughfare and the border between Mott Haven and Melrose. In five minutes, I arrive at number 436, home of the Opera House Hotel.

A long time ago, in the early twentieth century, 149th Street was a center for theater and film. And one of the outstanding venues for live performances was the Bronx Opera House, which opened in 1913 and closed in 1920. It seated more than 1,800 people and was lavishly decorated in various colors, with silk damask curtains, beautiful ornamentation, and a stunning crystal chandelier. It had several reincarnations as a movie theater, Latin dance club, and Pentecostal church. Today, in its latest iteration, it has become a boutique lodging house. In its heyday, the Opera House was considered the best of several such spaces in the area. Today, nothing remains of it except the site itself. Don't expect a luxurious-looking lobby. It looks more like a Best Western hotel, but it provides a chance to connect with the old days. Among those who performed there were Lionel Hampton, Ethel Barrymore, Harry Houdini, and Fats Waller. And tourists may enjoy telling the folks back home, "Guess what? We stayed in the South Bronx."[6]

The rooms at the Opera House are quite nice, especially for about $200 a night or even less, depending on how busy things are. One of its biggest markets seems to be people from out of town going to Yankee games desiring a nice place for half the price of a Manhattan hotel. Cabbies are reluctant to go there because the stereotype of the dangerous South Bronx remains alive in their minds and because they're unlikely to get a return fare to their favorite borough, Manhattan. On the other hand, it's a pretty quick ride by express subway to the 149th Street station and then less than a ten-minute walk. The community hums with activity until late at night, and the walk is quite safe on the populated streets. I cannot imagine that this area is big on nostalgia, but you can never tell. Many people grew up in the Bronx and can remember their shopping expeditions to the Hub (described in the Melrose section). And there are business people who need to be in the Bronx for one reason or another. The bottom floor of the Opera House has several establishments including a Crunch gym, a pharmacy, and a medical care center. Metropolitan College is across the street; it's small, with seventeen classrooms for now, but its goal is to serve the local community, which sees such institutions as an expression of faith in the future of the South Bronx.

On another day I explore the portion of Mott Haven known as Port Morris, which turns into a very interesting experience. Its boundaries aren't really fixed, but it's fair to say that the main part lies generally between Bruckner Boulevard and the East River, from E. 141st to E. 132nd Street. Some have taken to referring to the gentrifying area as Port Morris, which sounds more catchy and upscale. They're free to do so, and the name may even take root, but in my view, it's a reach geographically. People also call this area the Piano District, hoping to attract well-to-do buyers, but that hasn't really caught on either.

My walk begins on 141st Street off Bruckner Boulevard as I head east toward the river. At the end of that brief jaunt I'm on Locust Avenue, which is where Silvercup Studios, whose headquarters are in Queens, has its Bronx location, running from 141st to 138th Streets. Fully operational, with "SILVERCUP" signs everywhere in large letters, it's a 115,000-square-foot facility with four separate studios. Access is restricted, with fences, gates, and guards, just like those you see in Los Angeles studios. It's located on the waterfront and on the other side of Locust as well. Its presence here gives the community some cachet and is a major boost to the local economy in terms of jobs and local businesses.

At 856 E. 136th Street I stop in front of the Bronx Brewery. Smaller breweries like this have become a hit in the city, especially in Brooklyn. This one offers a tasting room and tours. I speak with an owner, Patrick, a man wearing a New York Rangers jersey, with large, almost hypnotic, pale-blue eyes and a neatly trimmed brown beard.

"How would you say your beers differ from others?" I ask.

His answer almost humanizes the product, gives it real personality: "We like to say we're a no-nonsense craft beer, very approachable, not as gimmicky, by which I mean throwing all different kinds of fruit in. We like to keep things straightforward, like the people who live in the Bronx. We always let the beer be the hero; we don't sacrifice it just for a gimmick." As he speaks, I remember having chocolate beer in Bushwick. It really didn't taste at all like beer, so I know what he means.

"How do you define a Bronx personality?"

"People who are very proud of where they live and who they are. People here in the Bronx are the kind who are gonna tell you how it really is."

The brewery produces about 15,000 barrels, or 200,000 cases a year, and tries to hire employees from the Bronx. It offers a number of different flavored beers and sells everywhere in the tristate area, and now in Massachusetts. This is the type of business for which a location like this works. It's not retail, so it's not dependent on people passing by; it's in an area zoned for industry, near the highway; and it's safe.

A block farther, between Willow Avenue and Bruckner Boulevard, I see four brick row houses in the Federal style, dating back to the 1920s. I wonder what it's like to live here, as there are very few private homes in Port Morris. Shopping requires a drive if it's a major trip. For small items, I guess you could walk to a nearby grocery store or under the expressway to St. Ann's or Cypress Avenue, perhaps a fifteen-minute trip. But there doesn't seem to be a real community here. I chat with an older man who has a small business that he runs here.

"Do you live here?"

"No, but I grew up in the Bronx, over on Hoe Avenue."

"What's it like to live here?"

"Well, it's quiet, but prices are going up. One of these homes sold not long ago for about 600K. They've doubled in the last couple of years. People were here for about a month, filming a movie. And they did another one two years ago." Clearly, this area is newsworthy. And, he adds, the neighborhood got better.

"What do you mean by better?"

"More white people moving in." This is stated not in a necessarily racist way, but simply as a descriptive fact. White people have more money and more options. They live in safer and wealthier communities. Thus, if they move in, then the neighborhood must be getting better. He doesn't know my views on the subject. All he sees is that, like him, I'm white.

Across the street from the homes, at number 728, in a large older commercial building, is a baseball school, called New York Sluggers, offering training, lessons, and programs for kids from the surrounding area and beyond. Inside the building is a fully equipped batting range. Some of these students seem to be well-heeled, with their moms pulling up in Mercedes-Benzes and BMWs to drop off their charges. To appeal to this market, the school advertises that it's only seven minutes from the Upper East Side, namely 96th Street. It has five batting cages with pitching tunnels, and the kids can belong to travel teams. This is another example of the interesting enterprises that flourish here. The *New York Post* has long had a plant here, one owned by the Dow Jones Company. In an urban metropolis there are plenty of takers for property near Manhattan for the right price.

On the corners of Willow and 136th Street are two homeless shelters, one for women and one for men. They are not identified as such, and you couldn't guess it just from walking by. People in the area appear to view it as a mixed blessing. A local worker who pointed it out to me said: "Around Christmastime we give them [homeless people] something. They used to hang around in an alleyway by the building, but we closed it off. I've used some of them a couple of times to load up trucks and to clean up the snow. I give them a couple of bucks and they're happy."

This is clearly a symbiotic relationship, with each group finding ways to benefit from the shelters' presence here and with one group controlling behavior it doesn't like. The worker also observes that a number of the occupants have prison records. But even this is mitigated by the relationships that have developed. Another man told me: "My gate got stuck one night. It wouldn't close and I had to leave it open. I came out here later at 10:30 p.m. and my heart was in my mouth. The cops came and checked the cameras. No one had even gone in there, much less taken anything. And they had to know it was open. They surely saw it since it's right next to them."

At 780 E. 133rd Street, I enter a well-configured tavern, with floor-to-ceiling windows and very modern, light-colored wood paneling, which turns out to be attached to the Port Morris Distillery next door. The owner, Rafael Barbosa, introduces himself to me.

"Who's your main market?" I ask.

"New York City and anyone else who will buy what we produce. We do focus on the Puerto Rican market. Our main item is Pitorro Shine. Everywhere where liquor was once illegal, people made moonshine, and this is our special mix. The Hondurans have their moonshine; the people in Tennessee had theirs during Prohibition. Our history began in the seventeenth century in the mountains of Guyama, Puerto Rico. Our moonshine was made from sugar cane since that is a major crop in Puerto Rico, not molasses or corn mash. While Pitorro is technically a rum, it's stronger than the typical 80 or 90 percent proof."

"By the way, just to understand, what's the difference between brewing and distilling?"

"Both require fermentation. When you're brewing you simmer it warm. You're cooking it. Alcohol, which is distilled, is actually vapor that results from a mixing and heating process. Once it hits cold air, it condenses and becomes alcohol."

"Why did you come to Port Morris?

"We had a different business here, which we closed, but we knew we wanted to remain in the area. I actually grew up in Manhattan and was the superintendent for a while of the NYCHA Frederick Douglass Houses."

"What's this bridge overhead, fifty yards away?"

"That's the Hell Gate train. It goes over that bridge. The Acela runs by here all the time, and when it does, our distillery vibrates, and that actually helps the distilling process by 'agitating' it. We've had people that have come here and said, 'I saw your sign from the train.'"

I take a tour of the spanking-clean, gleaming distillery. Rafael describes it: "We have a German-made ultra-modern copper still. And here on the side we have an old moonshine still. It's smaller, but it works in a similar way and was homemade by my partner, a sheet-metal fabricator. We don't use it anymore. It's just a trophy piece. This small silver still is what you would have seen in the mountains in the old days."

It's evident that Rafael takes great pride in what he does. He's producing a distinctive blend, similar to rum, packaging it in beautiful bottles, and introducing the public to it. He's also relating it to his own Puerto Rican culture and that island's rich history. Moonshine is often associated with Appalachia, but Puerto Rico has its own region, history, and ways of producing alcohol. In addition, Rafael has remained close to his New York roots by creating a business here even as he seeks to expand his market elsewhere. Perhaps the most important component is that he really loves what he's doing. It's clear from his voice and from the fact that he uses the finest-quality products, such as his imported copper still. To top it off, the tavern he owns and operates next door is beautifully configured, with excellent food and service. It would fit in perfectly in the best neighborhoods of Manhattan, places like Midtown, Chelsea, or Murray Hill.[7]

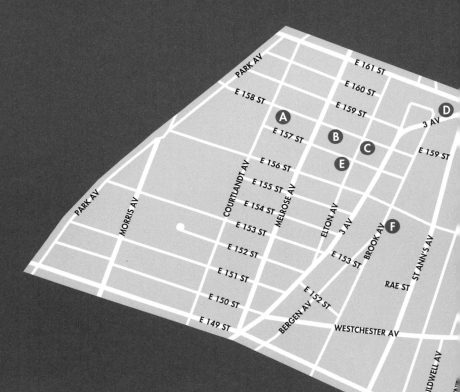

(A) Veterans' Memorial Garden
(B) Fort Apache
(C) La Resurreccion United Methodist Church
(D) Old Bronx Borough Courthouse
(E) "Heart of the Hood" Mural
(F) Via Verde

MELROSE

THE BOUNDARIES OF MELROSE ARE, roughly, E. 163rd Street on the north, Prospect Avenue on the east, E. 149th Street on the south, and Park Avenue on the west. Melrose's modern history begins in the late nineteenth century, when it was home to a substantial German community that was anchored, in part, by the Haffen Brewing Company. In fact, beer gardens were quite popular then throughout the area. Melrose also became more urban during this period because of the construction of the elevated Third Avenue line, which was followed by the subway line in 1904. After World War II, it became predominantly Irish, Italian, Jewish, and, after 1960, Hispanic and Black. Many will see this pattern of ethnic succession as emblematic of how the South Bronx declined, but it's important to remember that for many Blacks and Hispanics, quite a few of them working- or middle-class, coming here was a dream come true, a chance to escape overcrowding in the lower-income neighborhoods of Manhattan. That this didn't happen is due largely to factors that developed or existed here and elsewhere in the city and in other metropolises, a number of which are discussed in the introduction.

The central business thoroughfare is 149th Street, also known as "the Hub." Here, four major streets converge—149th Street and Melrose, Willis, and Third Avenues. It's like a Times Square for shopping and restaurants, accessible to transportation from all points in the Bronx and beyond. Back in the 1930s, it was also an entertainment center, with both theaters and movie houses. The surrounding streets, especially Third Avenue, are also lined with stores. Melrose is undergoing a bit of a renaissance these days, with lots of new affordable housing, including many one- and two-family units. The northern part of Melrose between 161st and 163rd Streets has experienced quite a bit of affordable-housing construction in recent years. This upturn in available housing, in turn, is attracting new business investment. And it's home to a large and still growing number of community gardens. Boricua College, an independent, private liberal arts school, has a beautiful new building with a nice plaza at 890 Washington Avenue near E. 162nd Street in an area called Melrose Commons. In short, Melrose is nothing like its past reputation, and the best way to appreciate that is to walk the community. Nostalgia lovers or just people who want to combine a Yankee game with an evening in the Bronx will find inexpensive lodging here, too. One place that's clean and modern is the Umbrella Hotel, at 681 Elton Avenue, where rooms can be had for about $150 a night.

I begin my first community trip here at the Andrew Jackson Houses, which run along Park Avenue between E. 156th and E. 158th Streets. It's one of five NYCHA projects in Melrose. At 158th, I turn right, heading east. Quite a few of the old-style tenements remain here, mostly five-story walk-ups, but the majority of structures are attractive though not fancy two- and three-story brick homes. They're generally two- to four-family affordable housing, and there are also apartment buildings, many with air-conditioning units for each room. These blocks are a perfect example of the dramatic changes that have occurred in the South Bronx. The buildings date back to the 1980s and more recent decades. Some are, in fact, quite new. Here and there you can also find old private houses that go back a long way. I speak with a young Hispanic woman who lives in a three-apartment brick home, which she owns and rents out to two other families:

"How do you like it here?"

"Very much. It's pretty safe and the mortgage was low, so I can pay it. The only problem is some crime from the Andrew Jackson Houses. And, you know, nothing is ever 100 percent safe. It's New York," she says, with a resigned shrug.

Regardless, I think to myself, this is a great improvement from the lunar landscape of burnt-out hulks of apartment buildings and empty lots that typified this area in the seventies and eighties. And yet, in a reminder that this community isn't crime free, many of the low-story houses still have bars on the windows, most of which were put in during the 1980s.

On 158th, east of Courtlandt Avenue, I see, on my right, opposite a long row of beautiful townhouses, the Veterans' Memorial Garden, also called the Courtlandt Avenue Association. I walk in through the unlocked gate in the back and meet an older Puerto Rican man, a volunteer, who's doing spring-cleaning. He greets me and says: "In the summertime it's gonna be real nice. We're growing green peppers and eggplants. Then we give them away to the people who live around here. Here we have chickens, which lay big beautiful brown eggs. These cost money. My daughter, she pay eight dollars for a dozen in the store. And here we have apple trees and a peach tree."

The place is quite attractive, with colorful little fences, wishing wells, and other decorative items that blend in nicely with the garden. There's also a memorial to Puerto Rican war veterans in the form of two polished wooden benches with backs and a table in the middle. This is, in fact, a point of pride in the Puerto Rican communities. In many ways they are immigrants like Dominicans, El Salvadorans, Mexicans, and other groups, but there's one huge difference: because Puerto Rico is a territory of the United States, they are full citizens and therefore serve in the US armed forces, which they do with great pride. Many of the homes are owned by Puerto Ricans and fly Puerto

Rican, American, and armed forces flags, and it's the same in many of the community gardens in their communities.

"Do you live around here?" I ask the volunteer.

"No, I don't. I live on 151st Street."

"How long does it take you to get here?"

"Ten minutes. I live there thirty-two years."

It's interesting that in his mind, a ten-minute walk is not considered "around here." What it reveals is the relative nature of distances. In a more spread-out area, ten minutes would mean nothing, but the density of the Bronx in terms of population makes each block seem much farther away. The Bronx is, in fact, the third most densely populated county in the country. Two blocks away, and certainly seven, can be another world, given how many people live on each block. This concentration has a way of reducing the feeling of community to that of a block or two.

On the next cross street, Melrose Avenue, I see a nice-looking red-brick apartment building called the Peter Cintron Houses, with air-conditioning units beneath every window and an entrance on E. 158th Street. A replica building is next to it on E. 157th Street. Attractive-looking retail outlets take up the first floor—a nail salon, barbershop, insurance business, and an embroidery store. The setup reminds me of a typical block on gentrified Frederick Douglass Boulevard in Harlem, though the community isn't nearly as safe. Entering the embroidery store I learn about high-priced hats called "distressed hats," meaning they have loose threads to make them look old. "I have hats like that that look old because they *got* old," I joke. "But don't worry; I'm not in this business." The Peter Cintron Houses looks pretty plain inside, no frills, but it's clean and well maintained—not surprising, as it's a NYC Housing Development Corporation building intended for lower-income wage earners looking for affordable rental housing.

Farther down, at 416 E. 158th, I see a pretty private house with an oval wooden sign on which is carved a Native American with feathers. Beneath it are the words "Fort Apache." That was the famous moniker given to a nearby police precinct back in the "wild west" days when chaos ruled in the South Bronx. The Fort Apache precinct was a grim place surrounded by streets where violence was commonplace. But so many years have gone by that it's now simply a reminder that those days are thankfully no more. I see three more community gardens near each other on various blocks and realize that they represent a cottage industry, all of them run and funded by the city with the intention of beautifying the area and giving residents pride in where they live.

On Elton Avenue and E. 156th Street, I stand in front of the La Resurreccion United Methodist Church. The architecture is Gothic, with bright red-painted bricks and white stone, arched stained-glass windows, and a rose window, all very quaint-looking. Established in 1878 to serve the German community that had settled here, it's still in good condition. Amidst all the modern housing it's a bit incongruous, though it can serve to remind people that the Bronx has a long history and that this nineteenth-century house of worship was constructed just after the Bronx first became a part of New York City.

At Third Avenue I turn left and in one block, where it meets E. 159th Street on an angle, I see the 42nd Police Precinct, a typical-looking precinct structure from the old days. This isn't Fort Apache; that was the adjacent precinct, the 41st. Yet it has an important place in another sense, as an older cop explains to me: "We have tour buses, Greyhound buses, coming from all over the world, practically every day, especially from Spain. Over there, when they go to college, they have to see the movie *Fort Apache*. They want to see the South Bronx, and especially Fort Apache. The problem is, when they did the movie about it, they had to film part of it here because their building over on Simpson Street was too small. So the tourists come here, and we let them inside to look around a bit."

The film, starring Paul Newman, appeared in 1981, despite objections by Bronx leaders about how it would damage the borough's reputation. Predictably, not everyone's happy about the tour buses. Sam Goodman, a city planner in the Bronx Borough President's office, tells me that many locals resent these tours because they remind people of how bad things once were. This was also the case with Harlem, but once Harlem became more gentrified, the resentment died down.

"Would you say that this community is safe today?" I ask the officer.

He appears a bit dubious as he responds: "It's a lot better now than back then. You can walk safely in the daytime, and even at night if you're careful and know how to walk the city at night—you know, take precautions."

"Do these nicer buildings make the area safer?"

"Somewhat. People care more about the community when it's nicer, but remember, when you take an apartment, you're living next to somebody with Section 8, unemployed most likely, and that could be a problem."

To the right of the police station, at 513 E. 161st Street is a still magnificent-looking white building created between 1905 and 1914 in the Beaux-Arts style. It's known as the Old Bronx Borough Courthouse. Today, it's been gutted from the inside, and the outside could use a makeover. Still, it's well worth seeing for its external granite stone architecture, which includes an impressive statue of Lady Justice, flanked by two giant Tuscan columns. While the inside may be put to commercial use, with offices or a community facility, the exterior, a national and New York City landmark, will remain in place for the foreseeable future.

From here, I walk south down Brook Avenue as it crosses Third Avenue. After a block, on 159th Street, I see on the left a tall, imposing Gothic-style cathedral, Saints Peter and Paul's Church, founded in 1932. It's an outstanding structure, made of rectangular gray and brown stone in different sizes, with a very ornate entranceway. The statues of Jesus and other holy figures, along with an exquisitely designed rose window, definitely merit a look. All in all, it's reminiscent of the types of Catholic cathedrals you see in Europe. The parochial school building, founded in 1912, with the separate "Boys" and "Girls" entrance signs is still there, but today it's a charter school. I make a left on 159th Street and in one block turn right on to St. Ann's Avenue.

Old Bronx Borough Courthouse

At 156th Street I make a left and go east one block, up a hill. Turning right on Eagle Avenue, I see on the right side of the street an amazing collection of ten old, mostly brick houses, built around 1901. They are painted in a rainbow of bright colors—yellow, blue, red, gold, gray, et cetera. They have arched doorways and windows and are two stories high. One woman, a Honduran lady, has lived here for at least half a century. On each side of her home, atop a brick pillar, is a gorgeously designed stone or granite gnome. Three signs with arrows near the home's entrance point to the house. One says "gone fishing," a second sign reads "gone paddling," and a third claims "gone surfing." I speak with William, a friendly Puerto Rican, who's just entering the house next door.

"Excuse me, but can you tell me about these houses, please? They're so unusual-looking."

"Sure. I bought mine ten years ago and I paid 150K for it. Today, it goes for more than half a million. There are three bedrooms on the first floor and three on the second floor and I rent out the basement."

"What's it like to live here?"

"It's the best. You won't find a nicer block in the Bronx. It's very quiet and very safe. All the people on this block, they look out for each other. We are friends and it's a real community. And the police patrol here regularly too. We know them and they know us."

I wouldn't say that these are the nicest houses in the borough, but what matters is he thinks they are, and the reality is that in this community they are among the prettiest. There is a feeling of peacefulness here because traffic is practically nonexistent and the street is sort of hidden away. At one point, Eagle Avenue has its own little bridge as it crosses high above 158th Street, thus leaving the visitor a bit mystified as to how to access it. I found it on a map, but because I was driving, it took a little while before I figured out how to get there, given the numerous one-way streets here. Gentrifiers would probably find this an ideal home because it's quaint and only a few minutes from the Jackson Avenue subway station. The only problem is that most of the stock available here is affordable housing for low-wage earners. And with so few houses, there isn't much incentive for entrepreneurs to create the stores and shops—restaurants, cafes, boutiques, and the like—that gentrifiers like. Regardless, seeing these homes is worth the trip.

Just as I'm leaving I ask another Puerto Rican homeowner about his Yankees hat: "I see you have a Yankee hat, but it's not the usual navy blue; it's a camouflage color. How come?" "My son got it for me as a present," he replies. "When he told a friend who makes hats that I was a war veteran, the guy decided to make me an army camouflage hat. I love it." This gift combines two loves of many Puerto Ricans, their patriotism for the United States, which has given them special standing among the many groups who have immigrated here, plus their love affair with the Bronx Bombers in the borough with the largest Puerto Rican population in the city. Yet it's more than what they do for the Yankees by supporting them. It what the Yankees do for the Puerto Ricans here by deciding to remain in the Bronx, even as their well-heeled fans must make the trip from Westchester, Manhattan, and towns in New Jersey and Connecticut to see them play. And when the Yankees doubled down by building the new stadium only a few blocks away—in the South Bronx, at that—they sent yet another message: that the Bronx is their true home. These two considerations are strengthened even more when Puerto Ricans get discount tickets to the games because they are veterans.

From here it's back down the hill to St. Ann's, a quick right and a left onto 157th Street. Just beyond Melrose Avenue I see a mural dedicated to the memory of a Hispanic-looking man named Cisco, who died in 2016 at the age of thirty-seven. The colors are mostly red, green, black, and tan. An inscription reads "Heart of the Hood." I also see dice and rolls of hundred-dollar bills. Perhaps he enjoyed shooting craps. On the right in big red letters framed against a white background are the dates of his life—1978–2016. There's also a parchment scroll drawing on which are the words: "Money come & go, but Legends Live Forever." I chat with two Hispanic men who live near the mural. They tell me that Cisco was shot to death one night as he walked home. I think to myself, at least people did something to remember him. In fact, the Bronx has hundreds of such murals.

As it turns out, there's more to the story, but I learned that only because the *New York Times* chose to make a major story out of it as an example of what life can be like here. As it turned out, Francisco Perez, a.k.a. Cisco, was a street-level heroin dealer who did business at Melrose and 157th for many years. He had expensive tastes, as if to make up for an impoverished life as a child, born to a mother who used heroin and died when Cisco was thirteen and a father whose name he did not even know. Then, as he approached middle age, he advised young people not to follow his path and to choose honest work instead. But it was too late for him. He kept dealing and met his end at the hands of rival drug dealers, his body riddled with bullets. There are still plenty of people here whose lives revolve around drugs, but thankfully they are fewer in number. These murals remind us of how bad things once were. I ask the men about the community and receive an instructive response.

"It's better than before. People are living in nicer places. But it's still a lot of the same bad people. Look, a girl was taken to the roof of the Andrew Jackson Houses two blocks away last week and raped. Of course, nothing's ever really safe in New York. And the only project I know that's safe is the Roberto Clemente Houses in Williamsburg where the Jews [read: Hasidim] live. They can keep their baby carriages in the lobby and no one will steal them." Underlying this is the resigned view that in a big city you can't feel completely safe anywhere, even in a safe community.

My trip ends on a somewhat hopeful note as I visit the award-winning Via Verde development at Brook Avenue near 156th Street. It's one of a number of LEED (Leadership in Energy and Environmental Design)-certified apartment buildings in the Bronx. It's a beautiful group of buildings that emphasize healthy living as the rationale for much of its design. Health is a major issue in lower-income communities, where obesity, asthma, and poor diets are common. There are ceiling fans in the hope that people will limit their use of air conditioners, along with rooftop gardens, plus a health education and fitness center. The buildings are configured in a way that allows maximum use of sunlight. At the broader level there's a South Bronx nonprofit organization called Nos Quedamos, or We Stay, dedicated to supporting ideas about healthy and sustainable community growth. Its members consist of business people, homeowners, and residents in general. Groups like this make an emphatic statement that people are determined to improve their neighborhood and infuse it with new life.

I visited Via Verde and was impressed by the way it looked. But appearances don't always tell the whole story. I speak with one

Hispanic resident, a professional with small children, who tells me that there are problems.

"Look, it's a nice place, but that isn't enough. You need professionals to plan activities that bring people together. Without that you don't have a community. You see, I'm an owner and I'm friendly with other people who own their apartments. And then you have renters who live on the other side of the development. We have nothing to do with them, but some of us would like to meet them. But there's no vehicle through which to do it."

"Have you asked management to try to make something happen socially through programs?"

"Yes, but they haven't done it yet. Hopefully they will. But that's not the big problem. What's bothering me and others is that just a few blocks from here, they're building a facility for people with HIV-related illnesses, and we are very concerned about what this will do to the community. And then there's the fact that Rikers Island is being broken up. It's moving into different communities in New York City. And one of the new facilities is going to be ten blocks from here."

She's right, unfortunately. Via Verde, built with the best of intentions, cannot fight city hall, as they say. These decisions will provoke protests, and the projects may be scaled down but probably not enough to have much of an effect on community stability. In a sense, history is repeating itself as city officials, looking for an easy solution, place controversial projects into communities that don't have the clout to resist. Unfortunately, the South Bronx is one of those places. The tragedy is that "solutions" like this dash the hopes of so many people who have made enormous efforts to reinvent the borough into an attractive location for working- and middle-class people. The same goes for gentrifiers, who have begun moving into neighboring Mott Haven. But Melrose is different in this regard. In addition to what has already been said, the city has bought up so much of the land that developers who want to attract market-rate buyers have little to offer them.

CONCOURSE

(A) Thomas Gardens
(B) River Avenue
    Skateboard Park
(C) Macombs Dam Park
(D) Executive Towers
(E) "Fish Building"
(F) Bette's Rose Garden
(G) Daughters of Jacob
    (Geriatric Center)
(H) Andrew Freedman Home
(I) Lorelei Fountain in
    Joyce Kilmer Park

THE BOUNDARIES OF CONCOURSE ARE E. 170th Street on the north, Webster and Park Avenues on the east, E. 149th Street on the south, and the Harlem River on the west. As the map shows, this large area is divided into three subsections, Concourse Village, Concourse East, and Concourse West. The first contains an area that is home to many employees of the court system and people who are employed at Yankee Stadium, along with thousands of other local residents. It is said to be gentrifying, revolving especially around the Grand Concourse, with its nicer apartments and parks, and that may turn out to be the case. It's also important to note that Black and Hispanic gentrifiers are choosing to live here just as much as white gentrifiers. In short, gentrifiers can come from many backgrounds. It also helps that the Grand Concourse, from 153rd Street to 167th, has been designated a historic district.[8] As it happens, the name Concourse Village also applies to a New York State Mitchell-Lama development located in this section. The other two parts of the community have many lower-income residents and tend to resemble the demographics of the South Bronx in general.

The history of this area follows the familiar cycle of succession. First, Native Americans lived here, then the Dutch, followed by the British, and then after the Revolutionary period, the Americans have ruled the roost. For a good part of the nineteenth century, the Morris family owned much of the land. After the development of transportation in the form of rail and subway lines, the population greatly expanded. Irish, Germans, Jews, and Italians were the major ethnic groups who settled here. In the late 1950s and 1960s the community became home to Hispanics and Blacks, and in the early 1970s a period of steep decline began as the poverty caused by lack of opportunity led to crime, drugs, and abandonment of buildings by landlords. Even established complexes like Executive Towers on the Concourse felt the effects, and the prices of apartments there went down accordingly.

Beginning with the twenty-first century, crime began to decline throughout the city, and this community became more attractive to middle-class professionals. Some liked the charm of the older Grand Concourse buildings; others were enticed by new housing developments. Also, the designation of sixty-one older apartment buildings along the Concourse as landmarks gave the community a certain degree of cachet. It was also part of a changing perspective by a newer generation of New Yorkers who welcomed diversity so long as their communities were safe. Many of today's residents come from outside the area—journalists, lawyers, businesspeople, and the like—and they are a multicultural group who wish to take advantage of easy access to Manhattan, lower rents, and the new stores that have been sprouting in response to this change. The area that has shifted the most in this direction is Concourse Village, but there has been some spillover to the edges of the Concourse East and West areas. These two portions, however, are not affluent on the whole, and it remains to be seen what will transpire there.

One anchor of the community is Yankee Stadium, which attracts millions of visitors annually to that immediate area. This keeps the area "in play" as a possible community to live in. Another is the numerous courthouses and administrative buildings associated with them. There's also the Bronx Museum of the Arts, another attraction that enhances the community's reputation. Hostos Community College, part of the CUNY system, serves the local population and beyond and is situated on the Grand Concourse at E. 149th Street. It's named after Eugenio Maria de Hostos, a Puerto Rican educator. Most of its students are Hispanic, and it brings cultural access to the local community through its well-regarded Center for the Arts, which includes an excellent art gallery and which has been offering programs for the students and the community for decades.

The major parks include Joyce Kilmer, Franz Sigel, Macombs Dam, and Mullaly Parks, quite a few for one community, all of them with much to offer and well-maintained. Crime has gone down quite a bit in recent years and it is one of the safer parts of the South Bronx. The major thoroughfares are the Grand Concourse; Jerome, River, Morris, and Webster Avenues; and 170th, 167th, and 161st Streets. Jerome, Inwood, and Cromwell Avenues are industrial streets, with Jerome specializing in automobile-related shops— body work, radiators, alignments, tires, spare parts, et cetera. In fact, people come here from everywhere in the tristate area to have their cars repaired at cut-rate prices.

CONCOURSE VILLAGE

I peek inside the lobby of 750 Grand Concourse near E. 156th Street, an Art Deco structure entered via a steel door with glass bricks on the side that allow light to flow into the lobby. It has a terrazzo floor, with panels in the shape of palm leaves. The lobby is in the round, encircling a large pillar. It's pretty well preserved. There's a seat and desk for a security guard or concierge, but no one's there. Maybe they're literally out to lunch. I've gained entry by following someone else in who apparently doesn't think I'm a mugger. When you're my age you're invisible, a distinct advantage when doing fieldwork.

Next, I stop in at 840 Grand Concourse. A walk-up complex, built in 1923, it was considered one of the first examples of what we consider garden apartments. Also called Thomas Gardens, it's named after Andrew Thomas, the landscape architect who laid out the elaborate gardens. Sam Goodman, an urban planner in the Bronx borough president's office, is with me for part of the time as I explore the Concourse areas. Extremely knowledgeable about many aspects of the borough, he weighs in here.

"This building, like many in this area, is shaped in the form of an H. It has cross-ventilation, meaning windows letting in air on both sides, as opposed to the Lower East Side, which didn't have this sort of layout. The market was working-class families, and it was funded by John D. Rockefeller Jr., one of the few complexes financed by him in the Bronx. A long time ago, there was a brook running through it, with Japanese fish in it and a little bridge going over it."

My next stop is 888 Grand Concourse, an Art Deco gem, on the southeast corner of E. 161st Street. The *New York Times* writer Constance Rosenblum has penned an outstanding book about the Grand Concourse, with its six lanes for cars and promenades for walkers. Her description of this building in her volume, *Boulevard of Dreams*, is as good as any I've seen: "a medley of curves, scallops and concave spaces executed in polished black granite, bronze, stainless steel, marble mosaic, and gold stripes that was unique on the boulevard."[9] Some of the designs aren't so clearly defined after all these years, but there's still enough worth seeing, and there's even talk about restoring parts of it. I would add that mirrors surround the lobby, with its round ceiling-light fixtures, and there's a huge golden bowl in the center of the lobby made from mosaic tiles of the same color.

Crossing 161st Street, I pass, on the northeast corner, what was once the finest hotel in the Bronx, the Concourse Plaza Hotel. Today, it's a housing complex for low-income senior citizens. What was at one time an elegant ballroom is now an open-air space, with some trees and benches for the residents. On the west side of the boulevard I head south past the Bronx Courthouse and enter Franz Sigel Park near E. 158th Street. Named for a co-founder of the German-American Institute and writer for the *New York Times*, it has some sports facilities for basketball and baseball, but mostly it's a park with winding paths over gentle hills that's just fun to walk through on a nice day. The park runs along the Grand Concourse from E. 158th Street to just before E. 152nd Street. I walk the length and width of it, finishing on Walton Avenue and E. 157th Street. I meet almost no one on an early afternoon in July, even though it's a beautiful day, save for a chap nodding off on a rock and a middle-aged tourist from St. Kitts.

Walking down the hill on 157th, I come to the River Avenue Skateboard Park, on the corner of 157th and River. Rails, gaps, banks, and ledges are interspersed throughout in this unsupervised space. Two teenagers, one Hispanic, the other African-American, are whizzing around on their skateboards and they're quite good at this activity.

"Hey guys," I say, "is this a good place for skateboarding?"

The African-American teenager, James, responds: "It's not the biggest, like some of the ones in Queens, but it's pretty nice and many people come here in the late afternoon. This one has good concrete and a variety of obstacles."

"You guys look in great shape. Where do you go to school, James?"

"Harvest Collegiate High School on 14th Street. It's a public high school, near Fifth Avenue."

"But you live in the central Bronx. Aren't there high schools here?"

"Yes, but I don't like the quality of most of the schools here. Harvest has really cool writing and reading courses, and the classes are small. It has a great academic environment. The teachers are great, and most of the students end up in good four-year colleges. I'm into business, public relations, and public speaking, and they're fantastic in these areas. No school around here has programs at their level."

This is an example of a young man who chose options outside his community, in this case Morrisania, where very few students attend quality high schools. There are, in fact, many people who find a way out of the life of gangs, crime, and drugs.

I cross the street and explore Macombs Dam Park. It occupies the footprint of the old Yankee Stadium and is across the street from the new one. It has three championship baseball fields, and you're actually playing where the great Yankee teams of the past could once be seen in action. There's a sign by one of the fields reminding visitors of this in the shape of a giant ticket. On one side it says: "Lou Gehrig at Yankee Stadium." The other side has a date, "July 4th, 1939," followed by the following declaration: "Today I consider myself the luckiest man on the face of the earth." This is the date when Gehrig, known as the "Iron Man," was honored at the stadium as he retired from baseball, already living with ALS disease. Babe Ruth hugged him in an emotional farewell. Gehrig's speech on that day is considered one of the most memorable in sports history.

There's also a 400-meter running track that has the same surface as that used for the Summer Olympics. Another excellent field can be used for soccer or football, and there are handball and basketball courts as well. It's just a first-rate sports park. And in case anyone forgets the long history of the first stadium, the sports shops, featuring everything you ever wanted to have that's related to the Yankees, are still on River Avenue, on the block that comprises the eastern border of where the old stadium used to be, and right next to the new one as well.

From here I walk south on River Avenue away from the park and make a sharp right onto E. 151st Street, and then a left between the shops of the Gateway Center Bronx Terminal Market, followed by a right onto Exterior Street. Off to my left across the street is the Stadium Tennis Center. It seems an unlikely place for such a center, except that there's inexpensive space for it along the river. These are excellent courts and they charge $30 an hour, so I wonder if there's a market for it. It turns there is, as explained to me by a young woman who works there.

"There aren't any other courts around here," she says, "The Crotona Park place is mostly for neighborhood kids and for organized teams. We get a lot of people from northern Bronx and from Manhattan. After all, we're near the Robert F. Kennedy Bridge and the 145th Street Bridge. Jerry Seinfeld's family and Tom Cruise's come here from Manhattan." It does make sense, since in Manhattan courts of this quality will cost more. Behind it is Mill Pond Park, which has picnic areas and a nice walkway along the river.

I also do a quick walk through the Terminal Market, which has a number of big stores like BJ's, Home Depot, Raymour & Flanigan, Bed Bath & Beyond, and Marshalls. It's a seventeen-acre property with about one million square feet of retail space, and it's conveniently located just off the Major Deegan Expressway. Part of it was once the Bronx County Jail, a hideous detention center, one of the worst in the city. There's a parking garage, and the price is right. This center has filled a real need in the Bronx, as did the one in Manhattan on E. 117th Street in East Harlem. It provides a shopping experience for lower-income residents that's more similar to the suburbs than places like the Hub on E. 149th Street, though the Hub may be more convenient.

CONCOURSE EAST

This area is also known as Fleetwood, after a racetrack that was once located here. Walking down Sheridan from 167th Street, I notice an interesting parallel to the Concourse, two blocks west of it. Notwithstanding the occasional gang mural, Sheridan, Sherman, and other avenues seem to be somewhat better in terms of the buildings and stores, and there's a feeling of safety between 167th and 161st Streets, as opposed to the portion from 167th, heading northward through the low 190s. This is probably because the Concourse is a more expensive neighborhood from 161st to 167th as well. Here you have the Bronx Museum of the Arts, the classy Executive Towers apartment building, and the courthouses, and this has a trickle-down effect on the surrounding streets. For example, in the 170s, both the Concourse and the streets parallel to it are much more rundown.

I turn right on E. 165th Street. On Carroll Place I spot an interesting wall mural. It's not a great work of art, actually rather childish-looking, but it's painted on a slant rather than a vertical wall, so that you almost have to stand over it to draw or paint on the surface. I meet the artist, a pleasant woman who is supervising and running a program for children in the schools to counter gun violence. The work is childish because children are the artists. They seem quite excited and happy to be doing it. Lady K Fever is the artist's name she goes by, and this is only one of her numerous art projects. I think to myself that this is art therapy at its best and where it's much needed, given the challenges kids here face every day.

Up the hill, on the Concourse and to my left, is Executive Towers, the last such building constructed with private money, having opened in 1963, when the area was beginning to fall apart. It has those white bricks on the outside that so many buildings on the Upper East Side possess. Its curved shape and the murals and designs on the front entrance as well as the mosaic tile canopy also make me think of the beachfront towers along Miami Beach, maybe even South Beach, especially when I see a gold-painted sculpture of a bare-breasted woman just off the entrance. The lobby has marble tiles, large painted murals, and comfortable couches, like a hotel. In the seventies people began leaving, when graffiti appeared on the building and garbage spread through the streets and sidewalks. But the building came back as the neighborhood improved. Interviews with residents reveal that they are mostly middle class and very racially mixed. The subway is nearby, there's a concierge, and the building is well maintained. It is a notable exception to the older housing on the boulevard. Most of the latter are from the prewar era, but a good many are also well kept.

On the northeast corner of the Concourse at E. 165th Street, number 1040 is the address of the Bronx Museum of the Arts. It is certainly not unknown, but it might as well be on museum row in Manhattan, for all its relevance to the Bronx. Once in a while it has exhibits about the Bronx, but in general its showings are of artists not focused on the borough. This is not to knock the roster of artists whose works I've seen here, which is of high quality. When the museum waived its entrance fee in 2013, it experienced an upsurge in visitors from 25,000 to 50,000 annually, as of 2018. Free admission was made possible by a grant from philanthropists, and a large part of its funding comes from government agencies.

My next stop is at 1150 Grand Concourse, best known as the "Fish Building," near E. 166th Street, and designed by Horace Ginsbern. The exterior of the yellow-brick building with brown trim is highlighted by mosaics on each side of the entrance, with aquatic motifs. They depict marine life with fish and plants, all of them very lifelike. The fish look like angelfish, but instead of being black and white, they display every color of the rainbow and then some. The modest-sized Art Deco lobby is exquisite. There's a painted mural portraying a man playing a cello, with nymphs dancing and animals seemingly listening to the music. There's quite a bit still there from the original design, like the white marble panel above the fake fireplace, inlaid with gold-colored glass disks, which are covered with small glass beads. The elevator doors have Art Deco designs in black, red, and gold metal. To fully restore the lobby would cost $300,000, says the superintendent. She adds that most of the current tenants don't appreciate the value or historical importance of the building. The stained-glass panels with flowers are a new addition which, even if they don't match up with the general décor, look nice. The apartments are pretty intact, and the bathrooms were custom built.

I walk east on 166th Street to check out a tree-lined, landmarked historic block on Clay Avenue running from 166th to 165th Street. *The American Institute of Architects Guide to New York City* has called it "one of the richest rowhouse blocks in New York City."[10] It's a group of mostly two-family homes, in the Renaissance and Romanesque revival styles, with gables, keystones, cornices, and bay

Mosaic at the entrance to the "Fish Building"

windows with stone-gray colors of varying shades. These homes, built in 1902, sit on what was once the Fleetwood Trotting Course, which operated from 1870 to 1899 and whose fans included John D. Rockefeller and Ulysses Grant. Reportedly, several Daitch Milk Company executives owned homes on the block. The company's plant was on Park Avenue near E. 165th Street, a block away. Incidentally, the Sheffield Farms plant was close by as well, at 1051 Webster Avenue, between 165th and 166th Streets. I spy a sign, "Sheffield," which remains on an old building at the site. I speak with one of the homeowners, Randall, a Black man in his early fifties who happens to be a 2004 graduate of the college where I teach, City College of New York.

"I think gentrification is coming here too," Randall says. "There are two Anglo gentrifiers who have houses on this block. [One] just bought the house, a year ago, so I haven't had the chance to interact with him. This block is pretty good, but other blocks could be dangerous. It's about what they could afford. They're priced out of Brooklyn, so they're migrating north. But it's going to take time. The development of the new Bronx is happening in sections." Randall's view about gentrification is shared by many observers, including myself. It will be a slow process, but it will most likely happen. Teaching at City College, by the way, is a rapport-building advantage. On more than one occasion, I have met present or former students from the college while on my walks.

"Why did you choose to live here?"

"Good question. I lived in Florida for a while, but my mother owned this house and I returned to take it over. I also have two sisters, one of whom lives in Brooklyn and is very successful." Running and caring for the home may have been the deciding factor, but I can tell from the conversation that he's very comfortable here, talking with his friends and effusively greeting passersby whom he knows.

Next, I turn west on E. 165th Street and then left on Teller Avenue. A short distance down the block I come across an exquisite garden. It has an intricately designed, eight-foot-high wrought-iron fence, which, luckily, is open. I walk in and see a small space with beautiful roses, most of them white, growing amongst lush bushes with large green leaves. There's a small curved stone bench to sit on and a folding table and also a small vegetable garden. Basically, it's primarily a place to sit in and enjoy the roses, which I do. A sign on the gate reads "Bette's Rose Garden." Bette is none other than Bette Midler, founder of the New York Restoration Project, and the garden was created in honor of the organization's tenth anniversary in 2005. It's across the street from a public school, and the students have used the garden to learn how to grow vegetables and have also created a butterfly garden.

I head north on Teller. The safety of a neighborhood depends, in part, on what time of day and season you're walking it. This is a rough patch in the Bronx and I'm here at a risky time. It's 6:00 p.m. on a ninety-degree day in July, which means that teenagers are hanging out, drug dealers are fully awake and plying their trade, and the heat can shorten people's tempers. Nevertheless, an area must be visited at various times to understand it. In March, the streets would be pretty deserted in the morning, and you wouldn't get the same picture. There would be no music playing in the streets, no basketball games going on, no one sitting on the stoop, and so on. Without people to speak with, learning about the community is almost impossible. Little do I know that I'm about to have a really interesting experience.

On 167th Street, between Teller and Findlay Avenues, I see a red-brick Greco-Roman temple-like edifice, with white Corinthian columns, seemingly rising into the cobalt-blue sky at the top of a steep green hill. The hill on which it stands is the equivalent of perhaps five stories from street level. This is an area with lots of tenements, public housing, and papers and other detritus strewn along the streets, and this magnificent structure is totally at odds with this part of the South Bronx. Yes, it appears to be a building from long ago, but I've seen lots of those in the borough. This one is really unusual and I want to gain entrance to it, but the two-story-high thick stone wall surrounding the perfectly manicured grounds is a real barrier.

However, luck is on my side and I find a way in. Persistence, I've found, almost always pays off, depending on just how persistent you want to be. There's a large metal sign near the gate that says "Daughters of Jacob (Geriatric Center)." I look around and see a tall building on each side, one on Teller Avenue, the other on Findlay Avenue, each with a connecting covered walkway or bridge leading to the central building. A quick Google search reveals the complex to be a nursing facility for older Jews, but that was in the early and mid-twentieth century. Today, it's run by the Triboro Center for Nursing and Rehabilitation, serving primarily Black and Hispanic residents. Opened in 1920, it was designed by the architect Louis Allen Abramson, whose specialties included health facilities, synagogues, and restaurants.

I climb the stone steps to the top. Off to the side there's a large gazebo with benches inside and a doubled-tiered slate roof that has a cupola with a weather vane. I walk into the building just behind the Corinthian columns. A circular building with eight spokes, or wings, it's immaculate, with polished marble floors featuring several circular decorative terrazzos, which generally consist of combinations of glass, quartz, granite, and marble. As I walk the halls I see some medical offices, meeting rooms, a library, and a few residents who are sitting in some easy chairs scattered about. Perhaps they live in the apartments in this structure. No one, including some maintenance workers, questions my presence.

Angling off to another wing, I walk along a hallway filled with white marble plaques that have Jewish-sounding names engraved on them. Other hallways in this section are also filled with plaques, most of which date back to the 1920s. There are at least a thousand of them. These plaques have been here for ages and are meant to recognize donations made to the home. In truth though, who sees them that would recognize the names? It's almost pointless to display them if very few people will pass through here, and most likely none of them will be Jewish since it no longer serves Jews. Most Jews left this part of the Bronx by the mid-seventies at the latest, though the patients in the new wings that were built were still heavily Jewish at the time. So what's the point of having them here? Perhaps that was part of the agreement struck with Daughters of Jacob when a new group took over.

At one point, I see, off to my right, some doors with small windows. Looking through one, I see a very large space. As a door is open a bit, I walk through and find myself in a large amphitheater that looks like a house of worship. The lights are off, yet there's enough light from some windows to see what it looks like and it's stunning. There are rows of curved wooden pews for worshippers and a large balcony with a railing around it in front. Beneath it are a series of delicate raised, sculpted dark-colored designs. These consist of urns with vines and roses curling around them, set against a sky-blue background with white-painted trim. Underneath the blue panels and running the half-circular length of the balcony is a Greek key design, interspersed with small panels of flowers, each containing a dark flower, again with the same blue background. The temple's exterior is crowned with a silver-painted domed cupola, with a large Star of David at its apex, something I know from having seen it when I was outside the complex.

I look around for religious symbols in the front section of the space, but there are none. Above it, the high round ceiling is dominated by a large medallion with embossed blue and white designs that are different from those along the balcony. From it hang several ornate pendant chandeliers. There is what appears to be an ark, with a magnificent gold-coffered arch around and above it, with bands of blue and gold. High above is a small blue Star of David, confirming my suspicion that this is or once was a synagogue, and a beautiful one at that. I ask someone passing by what this is, and he informs me that it's used as a church every week for services. Yet there are no Christian symbols—not even a cross. Another room nearby has a door encrusted with glass designs, and some of it is Tiffany glass. It's the rabbi's former office. Upon entering I see a desk and wooden bookshelves. Behind the desk there's an ornate carving made from blond wood featuring biblical stories. One panel shows Moses breaking the tablets; another has scenes from the book of Ezekiel.

The significance of this discovery for the guidebook is that almost every old synagogue in the core neighborhoods of the Bronx where most Jews once lived is either gone, abandoned, or in terrible shape or has been taken over by a church and significantly altered. You have to look carefully to see any Jewish symbols, and with intervening paint jobs and structural additions, they are often quite different from their original appearance. This synagogue, though, is in pristine condition, giving me an eerie feeling of literally having gone back in time as I stand in the silent center of the amphitheater. It does not seem to have been changed at all. In the soft glow of twilight streaming in from the windows, it looks like it had been preserved in formaldehyde. It's unsurprising that it looks unscarred by the passage of time because it was an interior synagogue, inside a building and thus untouched by the elements or by vandalism. I would venture that this is one of the most perfectly preserved synagogues, certainly in the Bronx, and perhaps in New York. The style and designs are markedly different from those of most synagogues I have seen. It goes without saying that if this were a church it would be an equallly significant find. The trick is gaining entry, possibly by talking to the current owners of the facility or perhaps obtaining informal access through the help of a security guard. It would certainly be worth the effort for anyone interested in the subject.

Fortunately, I was able to speak with Joseph Cicciu, owner of the building, a prominent real estate developer, who answered my questions. Educated in Catholic elementary and high schools, Joe then went to Lehman College, graduated in 1973, and regards himself as a history buff. He's also conscious of his own community's history. Born and raised in the Belmont section, he is a strong supporter of that area to this very day and is the executive director of the Belmont Arthur Avenue Development Corporation.

"Daughters of Jacob ran the facility until 1979," Joe said of the center. "And then it fell into disuse, as the Jews who were there gradually passed away. In 2007, we bought it and put thirty million dollars into . . . bringing it back to life, and receiving help from the government as well. Today, we have 165 studios and one-bedrooms for seniors, most of whom are Black and Hispanic. There's only one Jew living in the building, so Christian groups use the synagogue. We allow them to because they were using it as such before we came. We allowed the Daughters of Jacob to remove holy items like Torah scrolls from the sanctuary. But we recognize the historical importance of the synagogue, and we leave it the way it was, with no Christian symbols there. The Holy Ark is there, and there's a Star of David on top. Plus, all the plaques of the donors are there. After all, the Bronx once had hundreds of thousands of Jews. The churches—one's Hispanic, the other's Black—provide a service for the residents so they can stay, but we've told them it's not a permanent space for them, and we're open to letting others, including Jewish groups, use it as well and also to having plays, music recitals, and other events. I'm very interested in anything that helps the Bronx revitalize, and I do tours for visitors to my own neighborhood, Belmont. The really bad old days are gone, but the media often makes it look scary."

Joe's a very bright and successful real estate developer, the owner of more than seventy properties, most of them affordable housing. He's also a great booster of both Belmont and the Bronx in general. He identifies very strongly with his roots, especially the Italian-American community, noting that he resents people who tend to think of the community only in terms of the Mafia. Of course, he's right since the overwhelming number of Italian-Americans have nothing to do with organized crime. He's far from the only member of his group to take this personally. I have an Italian American cousin who feels the same, as does an Italian-American colleague of mine at CUNY. What's interesting is that his respect for his own culture has clearly generalized into respect for other cultures. He lets the African-American and Hispanic groups worship in his building free of charge, and he respects the history and culture of the large Jewish community that once resided here by preserving the synagogue and its religious symbols.

Across the street on Findlay Avenue is the assisted living facility that was built by the Daughters of Jacob. Another part of the complex is the nursing home on Teller Avenue. Today, there's only one Jewish resident in the place, but as a recent arrival, she knows nothing about the home's history. In the lobby of the Findlay home there's an exhibit of great interest. Chris Pignone is the manager of the building and he enlightens me further: "I was here when they were taking out what was left in the synagogue. And I saw some scrolls in a garbage can. They had left them outside on the street to be taken away by the sanitation truck. I looked at them and I said to myself, 'Hey, wait a minute. These are Torahs, holy Bibles.' So I took them out of the can, cleaned them up, and eventually they became this exhibit you see here. But Joe Cicciu is the one who made the building into what it was. He put in millions to fix it."

The exhibit is quite remarkable. There's a Torah in a velvet coverlet and several other velvet covers without scrolls. On the wall, in a frame with glass inside is a page from a scroll of the book or "Megillah" of Esther, part of the third section of the Hebrew bible. The rest of the book isn't there. According to Rabbi Harold Stern, the last rabbi of the Findlay facility, the Torah scrolls were given to various synagogues around the country. Rabbi Stern came up with an interesting idea: "We knew that in the early 1920s, people from the community donated $25, a significant sum in those days, so that people would say kaddish, the prayer for mourners, for them. So this became a condition for synagogues receiving these Torahs, which are worth many thousands of dollars."

A bronze scale model of the central building with the Greek columns rests on a baby grand piano. The centerpiece of the exhibit is a large, intricately carved tall wooden chair, with two lions adorning the chair posts. Presumably it was a chair in the synagogue, probably where the congregation's president or rabbi sat during services. A small metal plaque is nailed into where a seated person's back would be: It reads, "Chair of Wm. H. TAFT at his reception as a guest of honor at our Fifteenth Annual Grand Ball, January 27, 1912." Next to it is the smaller velvet chair on which Mrs. Taft sat at the event. Taft was president from 1909 to 1913. I'm amazed that the society was able to get him to come to their dinner during his term of office and wonder if I'll ever find out why.

Chris is concerned about the display, asking me, "Is it standing right? Are the letters upside down?" He is a large man, with a booming voice and friendly manner. I also conclude that Chris has a big heart. He's kind and a bit rough in his manner, but he's the sort of person who genuinely wants to be helpful and do the right thing. Without him, none of these pieces of history would have been preserved. Chris was also director of activities at the home for many years. As a young man he was an amateur boxer, and in his office there are photographs of him as a pugilist. He takes me into a social hall on the first floor. I look at large colorful posters advertising the many shows he put on.

"I don't care whether someone's black, green, white, blue, Christian, Jewish or Muslim," Chris says to me. "I accept people as they are. I did all these shows; well-known Italian singers performed here, and we had great times here with the residents. Today, it's all forgotten. And I'm afraid *I'll* be forgotten, and no one will remember how hard I worked for twenty-five years. I spent money outta my own pocket and no one knows about it. They just don't care. We had barbecues; I had famous musicians here, jazz concerts, Christmas parties. Larry Chance—that's a famous group—performed here. And Gene DiNapoli. I built a kitchen over here. Say you was a resident here, you couldn't get enough of these shows. I'm like the forgotten man, not that I wanna be anybody, but. . . ."

Chris's voice trails off, and he chokes up, overcome by emotion as he thinks about what once was. This is a person whose deep feelings reflect what so many human beings want—to be appreciated and remembered for what they gave of themselves to others. His voice conveys great passion, joy in his work, yet also regret for a time that he cannot bring back to life.

CONCOURSE WEST

I begin my walk on the Grand Concourse and E. 168th Street. In two blocks I come to what was once the Andrew Freedman Home, which runs from McClellan Street to E. 166th Street. This place has a unique history. Freedman was a millionaire who came close to losing all his money in the Panic of 1907. Realizing that this could happen to anyone through no fault of their own—after all, how many astute investors lost their wealth during the Depression?—he created a Renaissance-style retirement home at 1125 Grand Concourse, near 166th Street, with a capacity of about 130 people, for older adults of means who had lost their fortunes.

Here they would be able to live in the home free of charge, meals and rooms included, and they even had servants so that they could live out their days in the splendor to which they had once been accustomed, not to mention gardens, oriental rugs, chandeliers, and more. Residents were also required to wear formal dress for dinner, as if to highlight the idea that even if you're no longer rich, you can live like someone who is. When he died in 1915, he bequeathed the money and placed it in a charitable trust. He was worth over $4 million, equal to about $100 million today. Alas, nothing is forever, and the trust ran out of money in the 1960s. Eventually, the home began charging rent, and as the neighborhood deteriorated, people began to leave and the home closed. It reopened in 1984 as a nonprofit home without these prerequisites for acceptance. It was, basically, open to people regardless of income.

I had known about this place for many years and was curious to learn about its current status. My attention is diverted to an artist's creation on the front lawn near the entrance called "Garden of Hallucinatory Delight" by Natalie Collette Wood. It reminds me of an Alice in Wonderland portrait. To me, they look like plants and flowers wrapped against furniture, fanciful creatures, and other items. In her artist statement, Ms. Wood explains that they are meant to look like futuristic representations from another planet, and they are certainly original and interesting. There are also other sculptures on the front lawn.

Today, the building is devoted primarily to displaying art, having performers sing and play music, and activities for children, like Head Start, after-school programs and adult education as well. Walking around inside I see the old ballroom, now available for private parties. The wood paneled library behind a set of glass doors contains many volumes and, with its easy chairs, looks exactly like an old private library that would be at home at the University or Harvard Clubs in Manhattan. This is where the old residents of the building used to go when they wanted to spend some quiet time reading. Some people say, Sam Goodman informs me, that the library is haunted and that at night, ghosts move the ladders from shelf to shelf, remove books, and read them on the building's third floor.

Near the library is an alcove that has a brightly painted baby grand piano, with a woman's face on the piano's lid, and a cityscape of buildings, possibly meant to represent a New York City street. The artist's name, Alice Mizrachi, appears just above the keyboard. It was created for the Sing for Hope organization, a nonprofit that allows artists to give back to communities around the city. I speak with the security guard, Kaldar, to learn more about the home, and he explains: "We have artists-in-residence who actually live here for varying amounts of time. And our art exhibits are constantly changing. There's also a bar down the hall that was used by the former residents in the old days. We give tours of the home to visiting groups. And we have all sorts of kids' programs."

Goodman shows me an interesting building at 1075 Grand Concourse, on the corner of 166th Street, opposite the Andrew Freedman house, that was built in 1927. The ceiling is made of coffered dark wood. The entrance is sheathed in a richly designed, very thick pair of iron doors, with fluted pilaster columns on either side. Once upon a time, it had stained-glass windows but the landlords sold them when they could no longer find any tenants willing to live there. It's also the only residential building on the Concourse that still retains its service elevator.

I speak with a new arrival to this building, whom I'll call Dave to protect his willingness to be candid with me. An advertising executive, he now does consulting on a part-time basis. Dave is a friendly, highly intelligent individual who moved here a few years ago because he didn't have enough space in his Murray Hill place. It's very nicely furnished, with a good collection of books, and the rooms are pretty large, with attractive moldings along the wall and a very pretty kitchen. I ask Dave what it's like to live here.

"It's pretty good, close to the city, there's more space, and I have many friends. My friends are from all backgrounds, and race isn't a factor. What's a dividing line is people who don't care about keeping the area clean, who don't care about their community. They'll throw papers and bottles into the street and I find that very annoying. Another hot-button item for me is neighbors who make a lot of noise. A major issue is that there are no cafés or good restaurants in the immediate vicinity. One reason is that one isn't allowed to open a café on the Grand Concourse between 161st and 167th Streets, part of the historic district. And the fruit markets here charge much more even than those in midtown Manhattan. They've cornered the market. Of course, you can get better food at Yankee Stadium, but the prices—'I'll have the twenty-dollar hot dog!' And there are no good gyms here. I and my friends here do go to one in Manhattan." All these points are valid, but there is a good Italian restaurant about ten blocks east of the Concourse, called Porto Salvo, at 424 E. 161st Street, between Melrose and Elton Avenues.

"What about the Bronx Market shopping center?"

"They have no upscale stores, and none of them carry really good stuff. If I want to get a leather jacket, it will have to be a very low-grade product, what I'd call leatherette, rather than good leather. And if you go up to Fordham Road, you'll get what I call homeboy leather, which looks ridiculous on me."

"What's homeboy leather?"

He seems momentarily at a loss for words and then counters with: "It's not what guys like me wear. It has silver on it and patterns woven into it, and the best restaurant in the Bronx Market is an Applebee's. That says it all! But obviously, this situation is good for the poor. The Target store next to the market is the third most popular one in the whole country."

Clearly, moving here from the Murray Hill section of Manhattan has its challenges. Dave is right to say there are almost no restaurants of any quality, no clothing stores that carry high-end products; people are wont to throw litter into the street and are noisy; and getting good-quality fruits and vegetables is a problem as well. I'm sure this came as no surprise, as he had friends living here already who surely told him what to expect. And in fact, this area has more beds for the homeless than anywhere else in the city. But experiencing it firsthand is always different, and anyway he has a right to complain. At the same time, it's these shortcomings that made buying here a financial bargain for him. But there's something else at work. He can always hope the area gentrifies, and then he can be ahead of the curve. In this sense, his final observation to me is telling.

"It may not look like it, but this area is actually gentrifying. I see it from how many people like me are starting to move into this building. So, it is happening, though slowly and maybe someday, when I don't know. . . ." And his voice trails off. Yet there are statistics to back him up. Already, back in 2012, more people moved into the Bronx than out. Joseph Salvo, head of the population division in the city's planning division observed in 2013: "You've got to go back to the postwar period in the 1940s, when we had a surge of people moving into the Bronx."[11] This trend has only grown since then. In 2017, the Bronx experienced the largest population gain of any county in New York State, up 6.2 percent.

Heading down the hill on E. 166th Street, I'm jolted into the near past when I read the graffiti on a wall that encircles the Freedman property, from the Concourse to 166th to Walton Avenue and to McClellan Street, a full square block. Artists of all kinds have been invited to "do their thing," and I noticed there's quite a bit of homage to hip-hop, a phenomenon that began in the Bronx. Hip-hop encompasses music, art, and culture, and it's the art that's on display here.

First, I see an image of Dr. Soul, a hip-hop artist, whose real name was Foster McElroy. Then there's the Ebony Dukes G.C. (stands for Graffiti Clique), widely believed to have been the first subway "piecing group." Piecing is the term for those who want to turn graffiti into art by using large, intricate and colorful letters for their names, mottos, and slogans. Inspired to some degree by the Black Panthers, they originated in the gang culture of the South Bronx and were also affiliated with hip-hop. I also see a memorial explicitly devoted to hip-hop.

Another panel depicts a Black youth listening to a record on an old phonograph and a TDK cassette. It states: "T-Connection presents the battle fantastic with Cold Crush." T-Connection was a music group from the Bahamas that had a number of hits in the late 1970s and early 1980s, and Cold Crush was another famous hip-hop group. Thus, for those familiar with hip-hop, these drawings speak volumes and commemorate a vibrant part of Black culture in America and elsewhere.

I continue south on Walton Avenue and take note of some nicely renovated red-brick row houses, near E. 165th Street, mixed in with standard apartment houses and more modern townhouses. As always in this part of the Bronx, the architecture is eclectic, often reflecting the different periods in which residences were built. At the corner of 165th, I turn right on Gerard Avenue. At 1068, I see an older but well-maintained apartment building. I slide inside, past a closing door and take a look around. It's mostly affordable housing, and yet it has an indoor parking garage, left over from the old days when this was a fancy place. In the back there's a splendid garden, called "May Peace Prevail on Earth," with at least a hundred potted plants, many of them quite large. It's a beautiful tableau to look at, enhanced by the sight of a woman watering the plants, and one of the nicest such gardens I've seen in these precincts that's attached to an apartment building. Apartments at market rate are around $1,000 a month for a one-bedroom and an estimated $1,500 for a two-bedroom. I ask the superintendent if this area is safer than other parts of the South Bronx. His answer is instructive.

"We have less crime because we have many Africans living here, most of them Muslims. These people don't do drugs, and they go to work in the morning. Of course, there are always jerks in any neighborhood who make trouble, but not the Africans." It's an interesting thought, and most research to date has shown that immigrants do not cause the crime rate to rise. And people who work in the community agencies, not to mention cops, have told me anecdotally that Africans commit relatively few crimes on the whole when compared with other groups living here. I haven't found any serious research on this topic.

Returning to 165th Street, I go right and soon come to Mullaly Park on Jerome Avenue. It's a large place, with ball fields and a very nice swimming pool. There's a playground with some interesting equipment, one of which is two large silver plates set opposite each other. Children stand between them and yell or just talk and the sound comes at them as in an echo chamber. I try it out for size and it's great, the echo of my voice being very clear and resounding. Nearby, I step on a gold square, which emits a musical tone, something the kids enjoy tremendously, from my observations. Two years ago, the park stopped allowing people to cook in it because it was so popular that the park facility was overwhelmed. On a typical weekend there would be mountains of leftover food, paper, and bottles to clean up. Even the grass stopped growing in many places. Today, it's a much more tranquil venue, not nearly as crowded and, yes, the grass is growing once again everywhere.

Turning around, I head uphill back to Walton Avenue and turn right, to the south, soon arriving at Joyce Kilmer Park, on my left, which lies between Walton and the Grand Concourse, across the street from the old Concourse Plaza Hotel. The park is named after Alfred Joyce Kilmer, a writer for the *New York Times*. A poet, he wrote "Trees," which is well known to millions of schoolchildren. It's about the beauty of a tree and concludes with the memorable lines

Poems are made by fools like me,
But only God can make a tree.

There's a statue in the south end of the park honoring an important local figure, Louis Heintz, a Bronx commissioner of streets who played a major role in the creation of the Grand Concourse. Nearby is the Heinrich Heine, or Lorelei, Fountain, honoring the memory of this great German writer and poet. Lorelei, a mythological German maiden, was changed into a siren after throwing herself into the Rhine River. Heine's poem, "Die Lorelei," garnered international recognition for this maiden who hypnotized sailors into their death. Heine's profile face is on the statue.

Why did the white marble statue and fountain end up here? It was supposed to be placed in Düsseldorf, Germany, but the city rejected it in 1893 for political and aesthetic reasons. A group of German Americans stepped in, bought the sculpture, and had it placed in this park. Düsseldorf belatedly and tacitly acknowledged its failure to accept the artwork by sending its deputy mayor here for a ceremony honoring it in 1999, more than a century later. Not all monuments in parks have such an interesting history, but this one does. According to Sam Goodman, there was also an effort by New York City to move the Lorelei Fountain to Riverdale, but

Lorelei Fountain

after fierce local opposition, the city backed off and the statue has remained here.

As I've learned in walking the city, many of the statues and monuments have stories behind them about where, why, and how they were selected and erected. They are often intertwined with egos, politics, and finances, but since they are inanimate objects, you must dig to find out their stories.

PROSPECT AV
HOME ST
E 169 ST
E 167 ST
E 167 ST
E 167 ST
W FARMS RD
LOWELL ST
SHERIDAN BLVD
A
SIMPSON ST
E 165 ST
WHITLOCK AV
LONGFELLOW AV
FAILE ST
HOE AV
BRYANT AV
REV J A POLLITE AV
HALL PL
INTERVALE AV
E 165 ST
WESTCHESTER AV
B
SOUTHERN BL
ALDUS ST
ROGER PL
KELLY ST
TIFFANY ST
FOX ST
SIMPSON ST
BRUCKNER BL
BRUCKNER EXPY
BRUCKNER BL
E 163 ST
E 162 ST
REV R TAÑON AV
E 163 ST
EDGEWATER RD
DAWSON ST
BARETTO ST
IRVINE ST
SENECA AV
Bronx
MACY PL
BECK ST
TIFFANY ST
F
GILBERT PL
LONGWOOD AV
FOX ST
GARRISON AV
C
SOUTHERN BL
BRUCKNER BL
LAFAYETTE AV
LONGFELLOW AV
WHITTIER ST
BRYANT AV
KELLY ST
LEGGETT AV
D
E 156 ST
BARRY ST
HUNTS POINT AV
DRAKE ST
HALLECK ST
BECK ST
ST JOHN AV
LONGWOOD AV
FOX ST
WORTHEN ST
SPOFFORD AV
BARETTO ST
MANIDA ST
COSTER ST
FAILE ST
PROSPECT AV
SOUTHERN BL
E 156 ST
TRUXTON ST
GRINNELL PL
RANDALL AV
TIMPSON PL
LEGGETT AV
CASANOVA ST
E 149 ST
WORTHEN ST
TIFFANY ST
CRAVEN ST
BARRY ST
DUPONT ST
TRUXTON ST
OAK POINT AV
DRAKE PK S
BRUCKNER EXPY
EAST BAY AV
E 149 ST
OAK POINT AV
WHITTIER ST
DRAKE ST
VIELE AV
E
RYAWA AV
East River

HUNTS POINT

THE BOUNDARIES OF HUNTS POINT ARE, roughly, 169th and 167th Streets plus a bit of Westchester Avenue on the north, the Bronx River on the east, the East River on the south, and E. 149th Street and Prospect Avenue on the west. Europeans came to Hunts Point in the 1600s and purchased land from the local Native Americans. The community is named after one of its earliest settlers, Thomas Hunt Jr. In the modern era, it became part of New York City in 1874 and attracted many people to its environs once the IRT subway line was extended in 1904. It was largely a Jewish area but also had smaller representations of Italians, Germans, and Irish. In the 1960s, it suffered the same fate as the rest of the South Bronx, when poverty, arson, drugs, and crime became the norm. During this period, the population became predominantly Hispanic, mostly Puerto Rican, with a smaller Black community.[12] Today the area is still lower-income and not especially safe, though things have nonetheless improved, as is the case in the neighboring communities.

While mainly residential, a good portion of Hunts Point is industrial because of its ready access to rail lines and waterways and the available space in the eastern section of the community. This is also the location of the large and very well known Hunts Point Market, perhaps the largest such enterprise in the country. An important subsection of Hunts Point is Longwood, which is discussed first. The main thoroughfares are Southern Boulevard, as well as Westchester and Hunts Point Avenues. Barretto Point Park is the largest in the community, and there's also Riverside Park by the Bronx River and Joseph Rodman Drake Park, at the intersection of Hunts Point and Oak Point Avenues. This latter small park contains a burial site for members of the Hunt family and for enslaved African Americans.

I begin my trip through Hunts Point in the Longwood neighborhood, which lies between E. 167th Street on the north, the Bronx River and the Bruckner Expressway on the east, E. 149th Street on the south, and Prospect Avenue on the west. I'm heading north on Kelly Street, where former secretary of state Colin Powell lived as a child. After his father hit a lucky number, the family moved to Queens. Though things in Longwood have improved in the past fifteen years, it's still a scruffy neighborhood, with drugs and crime still part of the picture. But in the residential areas there are many blocks with modest two- and three-family homes that seem well maintained.

This was once home to a sizable Jewish population, and I'm reminded of that at 1078 Kelly, which is today a Hispanic Assemblies of God church. Inside there's no trace of it having ever been a synagogue, but outside the words set in stone in Hebrew read: "Congregation Netzach Yisrael B'nai Yaakov." It's not a grand building like some of the temples on the Grand Concourse, but rather a neighborhood synagogue, one of many that once existed here. Colin Powell has often spoken with fondness of his friendships with his Jewish neighbors, recalling how he lit kitchen stoves and turned on electric lights on the Sabbath for those Jews whose beliefs prevented them from doing so. While there was ethnic succession in these neighborhoods, it didn't happen overnight. It usually occurred over several years, and during that period the groups had contact with each other, sometimes superficially and at other times more meaningfully.

At 167th Street I hang a right and then another right onto Simpson Street. I stop at number 1086 in front of what used to be Fort Apache, or the 41st Police Precinct. The building is made of large concrete blocks, in the traditional style of many older police precincts in the city, with arches over the first-floor windows. The nickname was adopted by the officers who worked there because they felt they were in a lawless territory in the Wild West of old when the United States was settling that part of the country. All around them, in the 1970s and 1980s, were abandoned or burnt-out hulks of buildings, tons of garbage in empty lots, and a population of people who committed crimes of various types. Today it looks completely different. The block itself consists mainly of two- and three-story multifamily homes and is quiet. The same is true of the surrounding area, Fox and Tiffany Streets. Nearby, Westchester Avenue has the usual array of shops selling furniture, auto parts and supplies, clothing, grocery items, and so on, interspersed with nail salons, barbershops, and fast-food joints, similar to those seen on thoroughfares in other poor parts of the city. There's no feeling of real danger in this part of Hunts Point, at least during daytime.

Is it worth it to make a special trip here? Not to see Fort Apache perhaps, but there are some outstanding murals here and you can also walk through the Longwood Historic District. Take the IRT 2 or 5 train to the Simpson Street station or drive there. On Simpson, where it intersects with Westchester, there's a special mural of the Bronx. As I approach, I see a small group of tourists from Spain. They're here to see the fabled South Bronx of old. The mural consists of five panels, each with a letter of "BRONX" and, arrayed within it, scenes of the borough.

Inside the B these include the Bronx Zoo, Yankee Stadium, the Bronx Botanical Garden, and a bunch of kids playing stickball in the street. The R contains within it a subway coming down the

I love the Bronx mural on Simpson Street

tracks, the George Washington Bridge, and a group of people seemingly buying property from the Native Americans who once lived here. The *O* has a disc jockey at the bottom, a man selling ices with bottles of different flavors, a drawing of a kid break-dancing in the street, and a bus that rides into the next letter, the *N*. Here children are playing the game of double Dutch, jumping rope. I see sneakers hanging from a wire (possibly a territorial gang marker), and a portion of Yankee Stadium. The letter *X* features the Hell Gate Bridge, some maracas, a domino and a pair of hands beating a drum. There's more, but I'll stop here. It was done by tats.cru in 2012. What makes this mural stand out is its comprehensive portrait of the Bronx plus the quality of the artwork.

On the other side of the street there's a more contemporary mural by the same group, but painted more recently, in 2018. The style is more typical of the murals around the city, such as in Brooklyn's Williamsburg or Bushwick neighborhoods. Basically, it's a jumble of images, but in a more cartoonish style. It also aims to represent the Bronx but is designed in a more avant-garde manner. A young man with a red Mohawk-style haircut, carrying a peace sign, is holding a boom-box and an aerosol spray can, as if he's creating the mural. Above him a bright orange fire hydrant shoots out a stream of water, a common sight in the city during the summer months, and a purple-painted number 2 train is next to it, seemingly running off the tracks. On the left side, there's a gray image of a mermaid floating, as it were, through the air. One can surmise that were it not for the Hernandez repair shop at 1025 Simpson, the mural would have continued expanding.

At 1045½ Westchester Avenue, there's a small bakery called La Nueva Giralda, crammed in between two shops, but it's the bakery window that really draws me in with its decorated cakes. One is a small baby carriage, somewhat hollowed out so that it looks like a pram with a hood on it, very realistic; another has a skyline of the city and a moon in a purple sky; a third has a figure of a woman in a red gown standing in the middle of the cake-top, with roses on each side, and a purple garland around it. There's a cake with a toy drone. Still another has sports figures standing on a field throwing a ball to each other. Finally, I see a cake featuring a Barbie doll, clad in a voluminous skirt, with swirls consisting of icing. The quality of the designs is first rate, and the store is crowded with customers, some having breakfast.

Heading back along Westchester, I turn left on Fox Street, passing empty lots and lots of pit bulls, eventually cutting to the left onto Barretto Street and then right onto Southern Boulevard. On my right I pass an interesting building on the corner of Southern and Tiffany Street. This Italian Renaissance style structure is one of twenty-nine city libraries financed by Andrew Carnegie and opened in 1929. It has large arched windows surrounded by red brick, and the air-conditioned interior is equally classic. The old sign from that era "children's entrance" is etched into the concrete wall on Tiffany Street.

I turn left onto Longwood Avenue and begin my tour of the Longwood Historic District, so designated in 1980. The boundaries are Longwood, Beck Street, Leggett Avenue, and Hewitt Place. It's a marvelous collection of historic semi-attached row houses, most of which were designed between 1897 and 1900.[13] Architecturally, they have neo-Renaissance and Romanesque Revival elements, and they're typically clad in brick and stone. A good example is 759–761 Beck Street. It's in Roman red and beige brick, with stonework on the edges, bow windows on the side, and a large staircase leading up to the entrance. Atop the entrance doors are floral designs with curlicues, and several Ionic columns, plus lions and wreaths.

On the left corner of Beck and 156th Streets is a very special mansion behind a large iron fence set in front of a spacious lawn. This structure, the former home of Denison White, a businessman, and now called Fox Hall, was built in the Greek Revival style of the 1840s and restored in 2009. It's currently used by local residents of the historic district for various purposes. It sits on what was once the seventy-one-acre Longwood Forest. A quite remarkable house of worship stands nearby at 764 Hewitt Place, on the corner of Macy Place. It was originally a synagogue that looked like the ones in Eastern Europe. Inexplicably, it's topped by two onion domes. Today, it's shared by at least two churches, one Mennonite, the other Seventh Day Adventist. In truth, walking any, or better yet, all of these streets will be a rewarding experience. For a detailed guide to the district consult the July 8, 1980, Landmarks Preservation Commission Designation Report.

The next day, having completed my trip through Longwood, I start walking down Hunts Point Avenue to the east from where it crosses underneath the Bruckner Expressway. It's a typical thoroughfare with modest apartment buildings and small shops,

Longwood Historic District

bodegas, nail salons, barbershops, and a charter school. At Lafayette Avenue, I turn left and notice something unusual for this part of the Bronx: malls with grass and pretty trees running down the center of the two-way street. It's amazing how an added touch like this can make a street look so much better. Lafayette soon ends at the entrance to the Hunts Point Riverside Park, part of the South Bronx Greenway. Off to my right is an entrance to the Hunts Point Produce Market.

Immediately to my left, right before the park entrance, is the Point Campus for the Arts and Environment, at 1399 Lafayette, an organization dedicated to helping young people in the community learn about the arts and the environment in which they live. Peering through the fence I see several small boats on the ground near the Bronx River. They belong to a program called Rocking the Boat, which teaches youths to appreciate the Bronx River and its beauty through rowing. Running alongside the property is a combination wall and fence, which contains actual metal grids, cogs, gears, and wheels, as part of the fence and painted in a variety of bright colors. It was created by tats.cru, the same group that made the Bronx mural, discussed above, on Simpson Street. Immediately to the left inside the campus is a small mural that speaks to the temper of the times. The title is "Cop Watch," and a child with a camera is standing beneath it. The sign tells people they have a right to observe and report on what police officers are doing.

I enter Riverside Park. The twenty-three-mile Bronx River empties out two miles south of here into the East River. The area on the river banks was industrial but had so degenerated by the end of the nineteenth century that it was referred to as "an open sewer." Since then, the city has been making many efforts to reclaim it, removing debris, tires, and even cars from its waters. I once had a student at City College who explained his absence from class as due to the fact that his brother had accidentally driven his car into it. Establishing the greenway is part of that program and it has shown some success.

The river at the east shore of the park actually looks very pretty, even pristine. A short distance from the entrance to this small park I spot a display of several white rowboats, with pilings, sculpted barnacles, and seashells, all of which look quite realistic. But everything here is made from concrete or cement. I head down to the shoreline of the Bronx River nearby and talk to a Hispanic fellow who's fishing with his four-year old daughter.

"Hey, catch anything?"

"No."

"Have you ever caught any fish here?"

"Yeah, mostly bluefish, bass—big ones too."

"Do you eat them?"

"Yeah."

"Aren't you afraid they might be poisoned by the water?"

"There's no signs about that. I come here a couple of times a month from where I live, the project up the hill." New York City has about 520 miles of shoreline, according to nycgovparks.org, and fishing is an important activity for thousands of residents. And these are two of them. No doubt his daughter will remember this experience fondly when she grows up.

The entire area around here, to the left along Edgewater Street, to the right along Drake and Halleck Streets, is industrial, filled with factories, plants, and warehouses, not surprising since it's beneficial for many businesses to be near the Hunts Point Produce Market and the Cooperative Market located right next to it. Continuing my walk up Spofford Street, I notice that, like Lafayette, it also has attractive street malls. Crossing Manida Street, I see Puerto Rican and American flags strung across Spofford. Expressing pride, these flags are hung across many other streets in the Bronx, a feature of the landscape, just as they hang across thousands of windows in the borough. I turn left on Tiffany, heading south, and the neighborhood is industrial, with a few old residential buildings here and there, just like the entire section within the general boundaries of

Lafayette on the north, Halleck on the east, the East River on the south, and Bruckner Boulevard on the west.

There isn't much to see here, though it is true that some of the city's Sabrett hot dog stands make this their overnight home at the end of a long day, only to reappear on the streets the following morning. The size of this section, similar to parts of Long Island City in Queens and Bushwick in Brooklyn, gives the explorer the opportunity to understand the city's important role as a place of industry, not just one where people live. There are few flaneurs strolling by, but this industrial role is critical for New York's economy. Without it, businesses would have to pay far more to get their products, and that would affect what people must pay to own them.

Turning left on Oak Point Avenue and then right two blocks later onto Barretto, I walk several blocks to where it dead-ends at Ryawa Avenue. Here, on the water, is Barretto Point Park. It overlooks the East River, and from it you can see a vista that includes North and South Brother Islands, the Manhattan skyline, and Rikers Island. South Brother Island belongs to the Wildlife Preservation Society and will remain, as they say, "forever wild." While it has the standard playground, basketball court, and a volleyball net, the park's real attraction is the grounds themselves, with large open grassy spaces where people can sit and relax, have a picnic, and just be outdoors, enjoying a great view of the surrounding waters, not to mention sit in an amphitheater on inlaid stones. They can also canoe and kayak if they so choose. The adjacent gritty industrial buildings seem far away as I sit on a nearby park bench and gaze into the distance. It's hard to believe that this park was once the location of a gravel plant. One unique attraction is the "Floating Pool," inside a barge that's docked at the park. It has excellent amenities, including locker rooms with showers, lap lanes, swimming instruction, a kid's spray shower, and so on. In this community this is all very special, and most of the people who use it are local, in part because it's a bit out of the way—a twenty-minute walk from the nearest subway.

I head back up Tiffany Street and at East Bay Avenue, enter the Oasis, a restaurant catering to those who work here. It's pretty clean, but definitely low frill, with very reasonable prices. The locals swear by it, praising the friendliness of those who run it. On the next block there's a large water tower on the right, visible only by standing on the west side of Tiffany, that looks like a prehistoric monster with arms and a head because of the way the ducts and pipes are attached to it. It's an unintentional visual highlight of the community. Three blocks up Tiffany crosses Garrison Avenue, and I turn right.

At 940 Garrison I walk into the Point Community Development Corporation, a nonprofit group dedicated to bringing programming, arts, and culture to the residents of Hunts Point, offering classes in music therapy, photography, and art therapy. In general, the Point deals with social and environmental issues that affect the community, and not in an abstract way. Participants have worked on projects like restoring a natural habitat on North Brother Island and learning how to grow their own food in the local community gardens. Students also take classes in technology, résumé writing, public speaking, computer programming, and applying to college, among others.

The Point has partnered with J. P. Morgan and the J. M. Kaplan Fund, and receives funding from the city, including the New York City Department of Small Business Services. The center is clearly sensitive to the particular needs of its community. Thus, National Reading Month works at the local level by featuring a reading of *Sun, Stones, and Shadows: 20 Great Mexican Short Stories*, edited by Jorge F. Hernandez. It is acutely aware of the community's reputation for crime, poverty, and bad schools. One newsletter tells of nineteen-year-old Yesenia Adorno, an activist from outside Hunts Point involved in advocacy techniques, who said, "I once had a very rude person say to me 'If you ever enter Hunts Point, you should enter with a gun.'" There are hundreds of such organizations and programs in poorer sections of the city, and they play a critical role in breathing life, excitement, and enthusiasm into the city's many communities.

Continuing one block on Garrison, I turn right on Manida Street and at the next corner, Lafayette Avenue, I go right again. I'm now in front of a block-long structure at 1231 Lafayette Avenue. It's a landmarked building that once housed the American Bank Note Company. Founded in 1909, the company was best known for printing currencies for various countries throughout the world, including Ecuador, Cuba, Mexico, Brazil, and others. It also printed stock certificates, traveler's checks, food stamps, lottery tickets, and, as its name suggests, bank notes. In its heyday the factory had over two thousand employees. The company also employed a counterfeiter whose job it was to produce copies of the currency. If he succeeded the company then made appropriate changes. Despite tight security, the building was bombed, in 1977, by the FALN (Fuerzas Armadas de Liberacion Nacional), a Puerto Rican revolutionary group, which perceived it as a willing enabler of capitalism. Completed in 1911, the imposing red-brick building featured tall arched windows that allowed for maximum light to enter the plant, unusual for those times. Today it has a much more prosaic identity, with its owners leasing it out to commercial tenants.

I leave the community via Hunts Point Avenue, and it's only fitting that I should see an outstanding mural in resonant colors on the left side of a building near Lafayette Street that exhorts, "You don't have to move out of your neighborhood to live in a better one." Painted green vines encircle two women, one of whom is a Black woman wearing a beautiful bright blue tunic and nice jewelry, who appears to be cupping the rays of the sun in her hands. Birds are flying around her and some buildings. Water cascades down from a water tower on the roof of one building to a Latina-looking woman holding a plant. Other people are looking out the window. Gnarled tree roots jut out on a grassy area. The mural's basic message is that this is, or can be, a beautiful place to live in. A mother is reading a book to her child and small boats are gliding on a river formed by the water pouring down. In short, Hunts Point may not have that much to offer, but it's definitely not short on imagination and hope for the future.

CROTONA PARK EAST

THE BOUNDARIES OF THIS MILE-SQUARE South Bronx community are, roughly, the Cross Bronx Expressway on the north, the Bronx River on the east, E. 167th and E. 169th Streets on the south, and Prospect and Crotona Avenues on the west. Its history closely resembles that of Hunts Point. It was settled by the Dutch in the seventeenth century and eventually became the property of several estates. With the advent of a subway line in 1904, many apartment buildings were built and the population was largely Jewish, along with smaller groups of Irish, Germans, and Italians. In the 1960s, large numbers of poorer Blacks and Hispanics, mostly Puerto Rican, arrived. Arson and crime destroyed the community, and it became a symbol of poverty and failing inner cities because of a visit to the area in 1977 by then president Jimmy Carter.

It was only in the mid-1980s that things began to improve, and today they have stabilized somewhat. The population remains mostly Black and Hispanic and increasingly working and middle class. Much of the community's appearance is rather ordinary, but it possesses some truly interesting, even unique aspects. And there's lots of construction going on here, both residentially and commercially. The major thoroughfares are Southern Boulevard, Boston Road, and to a lesser extent, E. 174th and E. 167th Streets. The largest park is Crotona Park, and quick transportation is available to Manhattan via two major subway lines.

I begin my walk on Southern Boulevard and E. 169th Street. Near Freeman Street, at number 1254, I pass by what was once the Bank of the United States. The bank was built in 1921 by Joseph Marcus, and by 1927 it had more than sixty branches with 400,000 depositors and 18,000 stockholders, huge numbers for those days. Alas, it had dummy corporations and was corrupt. On December 10, 1930, when the Depression swept the world, thousands of account holders tried but failed to withdraw their funds, and mass panic ensued. As the *New York Times* writer Sam Roberts, observed, the great economist Milton Friedman called it "a day of monetary infamy." Today it's a Laundromat. Roberts wryly notes: "Unlike the bank . . . the laundromat has had a working A.T.M. that dispenses cash."[14]

A bit farther north, I come to Help on the Way, located at 1338 Southern Boulevard. With public and private funding, it has many programs and serves young, generally post–high school people with disabilities, from ages eighteen to twenty-one. One of its specialties is helping those with autism. I speak with Eli Bonilla, a supervisor, who further enlightens me and who clearly loves what he's doing. He explains: "We bring them here from their homes in the morning and they take classes, receive therapy, play games, and engage in team sports. In fact, our teams have won several basketball tournaments. We also take them on trips to museums, parks, and shows. People here tend to be higher functioning, more independent. We show them how to manage their money, write resumes for employment, and [practice] the social skills needed to hold down a job. They also do volunteer work, like delivering meals to people are sick.

We have seventy-five people in the day programs. Generally, we're there for them, and if there's something they want to do, we try to make it happen."

I look off to my right and see some folks doing Zumba. Others are participating in a talk about nutrition, and a third group is just returning from a trip to the Museum of Natural History. This program is typical of so many administered by the city government. This is what the city is supposed to do for disadvantaged neighborhoods, and the South Bronx certainly qualifies. And when I walk through these areas and see how many such programs exist—after-school activities and sports for people with physical disabilities, older adults, and the like—I'm reminded of how essential they are, giving people hope and inspiration. A quote from basketball great Michael Jordan beneath the trophies displayed here sums up it up very well: "I failed over and over and over again and that is why I succeeded." The moral is to keep trying; don't give up.

Heading south on Southern Boulevard, I come to Louis Niñé Boulevard and make a right. I pass by several taller, handsome-looking apartment buildings, affordable housing developments where prices vary according to income, with some Section 8 tenants residing in them as well. I pass by the Food Universe Marketplace on the corner of Jennings Street and saunter in to sample the wares. The aisles are spacious, the displays advertising deli items, seafood, and other products are very well done, and the shelves are neatly kept and well stocked. The employees are friendly and eager to help.

I turn right, off Louis Niñé, and make a quick left onto Charlotte Street, the place Jimmy Carter saw when he visited the South Bronx and declared it to be one of the worst places in America. Ronald Reagan also toured the area, with a similar reaction. As a result, new and roomy ranch houses were built in 1985. If you closed your eyes you'd think you were in a quiet suburb of Long Island. Most of the residents here are either African American or Hispanic. I speak with an older Black resident who's outside his home tending his garden.

"I was one of the first people to move in here," he tells me. "I like it. It's a very nice house. The area's safe."

"Does that mean you can walk to the subway at night a few blocks away?"

"Well," he retorts, "I didn't say it was safe at night." He was an ambulance driver at Harlem Hospital and is now retired.

"How'd you get this house?" I ask.

"I got it for 33K and it was dumb luck. They were filling out applications here."

"Would you ever think of moving?"

"Where am I going to go to?"

"Are you friendly with your neighbors?"

"We're friendly with the neighbors but there's no community association here. We tried, but people were thinking: 'Are you gonna get something out of it?' So, we never did it." This is unsurprising. Given the challenges of living in these areas, such as the constant worries about crime, people become cynical about being able to make a difference if they form organizations. Another, younger man named Juan, also tells me he loves it here. He claims it's safe even at night when he walks home from the subway at the Freeman Street stop a few blocks away on Southern Boulevard. A contradiction? I don't think so. It's probably a matter of being thirty years younger. I tell Juan that I'm taping our discussion so I can remember it better. He does not mind at all. In fact, when I meet him again a month later, he tells me that he remembers that I was using a tape recorder and asks where it is. He likes being taped, it would seem, probably because it lends importance to the discussion. It means he is worthy of being recorded for posterity by a person writing a book. Incidentally, it isn't only Charlotte Street that has these ranches. They are also present on adjacent Seabury Place, Minford Place, 172nd Street, and Louis Niñé Boulevard.

Perhaps nothing symbolized the South Bronx's decay in the 1970s more than Tom Wolfe's novel *The Bonfire of the Vanities*. Its locations—Longwood, Hunts Point, Morrisania, Melrose, et cetera—became synonymous with urban decay, landlord abandonment, mass arson, poverty, high crime, drugs, and general hopelessness. And today, nothing more clearly represents the hopes of urban renewal—no, of rebirth—than that same area. The problems were dramatized when then president Jimmy Carter visited Charlotte Street. When he visited the area on October 5, 1977, he was greeted by cries for help: "Give us money." "We want jobs." In response, an $870 million program was unveiled that same year by Mayor Abraham Beame to rehabilitate the area and create new housing, and it was backed by large amounts of federal money as well. But it didn't pass under his successor, Ed Koch, as the City Council voted it down. A scaled-down $375 million proposal met with opposition in Washington. We were now in the Reagan era. The Crotona Park East section, just south of the Cross Bronx Expressway wasn't, strictly speaking, in the South Bronx, but rather in the Central Bronx. But because of its blighted nature, the area north of 167th Street to Fordham Road and all the way west to the Harlem River came to be seen by many as part of the South Bronx.[15]

Charlotte Street encompasses the ebb and flow of many New York City neighborhoods. In the first half of the twentieth century, they were seen as nice communities and attracted upwardly mobile residents of modest means. Then, as the years went by, an area would become rundown, seemingly reaching a point where things seemed hopeless. And then it is reborn in the midst of devastation as a symbol of hope for renewal, and a new group of people comes in to claim it as their own. It's a variation, though, because the area around them remained dangerous for many years, and also because building suburban-style ranch homes in the South Bronx was very unusual. When I asked Lloyd Ultan, the official historian of the Bronx, why ranch homes were chosen, he said: "The idea was to build what people desired at the time. They were moving from the cities to suburbia. Even those living in devastated areas were demanding homeownership, not rentals. They were modular homes, brought in from outside in halves and then attached. Because [these

Junior High School 98

homes were] built, private developers with government subsidies began building attached townhouses and that spread elsewhere."[16]

Walking one block west on Charlotte, I turn right on Boston Road and come to where it intersects with Minford Place and 173rd Street. Here, on my left, I see a truly outstanding Art Deco–style public school, made of both stone and brick with richly decorated Art Deco and some Beaux-Art elements. It's actually Junior High School 98, named after Herman Ridder, a prominent publisher. Standing tall and broad, it is topped by what looks like a large dome. Designed in 1930 and constructed in 1940, it was the first Art Deco–style public school in the city. I see carvings of books and people's faces above the windows. The entrance resembles a skyscraper. It towers majestically over the area and is a must-see, especially for architecture buffs.

Turning left, I go up 173rd and left again onto Crotona Park East. I turn right into Crotona Park on Claremont Parkway and then right onto Crotona Avenue. In a few minutes I come to the stunning $27.5 million Cary Leeds Tennis Center, part of New York Junior Tennis (NYJT), a citywide organization dedicated to promoting tennis for young people. Leeds was a world-ranked player who taught many youngsters how to play the game. Crotona Park sits in the middle of a low-income and not-that-safe area, especially at night. While not very well maintained, its topography is quite appealing, with its lake, rolling hills, and recreational facilities for the public, including a swimming pool, the largest in the borough. But this sports palace is the pièce de résistance. The Bronx center is NYJT's flagship facility, with a magnificent modern complex, a well-designed welcome center, classrooms, a gym, and programs. It has two first-rate exhibition courts and twenty outdoor/indoor courts in all. Its first role is to serve the underprivileged kids, but it also rents out courts to high school students from some of Manhattan's most exclusive private schools. To better understand its significance, I speak with its director, Liezel Huber, a champion doubles tennis player, who was ranked number one in the world for 199 weeks. She is very forthcoming and happy to talk about the program.

"People in the Bronx often think tennis is just for white kids. We have 30,000 kids in this area. Harel Srugo, a former ranked professional player from Israel, has begun an intensive training program for them. We now have scholarships for promising players that will pay for their university education. As a result, they will be able to get the best training and perhaps became professional players, or teachers who will train the next generation of kids. And we're going to get funding for additional first-rate courts in the Bronx. We have 500 kids who come here."

Liesel and Harel are very dedicated to their work. She says: "We are very proud that this place welcomes everyone from the community. Here you can forget momentarily what you don't have, but also see the possibilities that may come your way. It's all about creating opportunities." This is an inspiring mission and a pathway for kids who live in poverty to leapfrog over the incredible obstacles so many of them have.

(A) Uptown Sitting Park
(B) Trinity Episcopal Church
(C) Morris High School
(D) Levin's Crosstown Supply Store

MORRISANIA

MORRISANIA WAS FIRST SETTLED IN ABOUT 1670 by the Morris family, hence its name, and their descendants owned the land there until the mid-1840s. In 1874, it became part of New York City. By 1900, significant numbers of Germans, Irish, Jews, and Italians were living here in tenements, just as they did in other parts of the South Bronx. Earlier in the nineteenth century, the predominant dwellings were small wooden frame houses. Population growth increased dramatically when, in 1904, the IRT subway line was extended to the area. Public housing on a massive scale was created here in the 1950s, designed primarily to provide living space for the impoverished. In the seventies, the area became mired in poverty due to a wave of arson, drug addiction, and crime, which accelerated as white people left and were replaced by poorer Hispanics, the majority of them Puerto Rican, and by African Americans. Schools deteriorated, families fell apart, and community services declined precipitously.[17] In recent years, Morrisania has become home to newer Hispanic groups and to Africans, many of whom are Muslim.

The general boundaries today are the Cross Bronx Expressway on the north,

Crotona and Prospect Avenues on the east, E. 163rd Street on the south, and Webster Avenue on the west. (This community is sometimes called Claremont.) The main commercial thoroughfares are Third and Webster Avenues, and Boston Road. There's also a small historic district, so designated in 1982. Crotona Park is shared by Morrisania with Crotona Park East, the community east of Crotona Avenue, which in turn bisects the park. Affordable housing exists here, but it's nowhere near the amount present in adjacent Melrose.

Crime is still a serious problem in this neighborhood, which has the highest number of incarcerated residents in the city according to DATA2GO, a mapping and data site. The median income level here is $22,343 compared with $53,896 for the city as a whole. There are twenty NYCHA developments in Morrisania, some of them very dangerous. Half of the residents live below the poverty line. A walk through the area and conversations with the police, school officials, shopkeepers, mail deliverers, and residents confirm the feeling that this is perhaps the least safe part of the Bronx, if not the entire city. It isn't even seen as completely safe during the daytime hours. The only positive observation I can make is that things aren't nearly as bad as they were thirty years ago. Then again, that's true everywhere in the city.

I begin my walk on Third Avenue by the Cross Bronx Expressway, which runs east-west above the avenue. Krino's Foods, which specializes in Greek and Mediterranean foods, is located here. At street level, along the sidewalk, this approximately two-square-block company is pretty much surrounded by some truly creative and colorful murals that run for several city blocks in a rectangle—down Third, then turning right along E. 174th Street, then right again on Bathgate Avenue, which is sort of an industrial park, and then right again on E. 175th Street back to Third.

The Third Avenue side features cartoons, species of fish perhaps known only in the artist's imagination, palm trees, a volcano erupting, a planet, a large worm. What predominates is the cartoon faces, with eyes everywhere, in all sizes and shapes, belonging to an array of weird-looking creatures, some with many eyes staring in different directions on one body; others with smiling teeth, some of which are missing. On Bathgate Avenue, there are white geometric designs with various brightly colored lines in the background. The background colors tend to blend with each other, purple into green, orange into gold. The white foreground, with thin lines cutting every which way, looks like a complex stencil. Various items have been drawn inside the shapes: fire hydrants, hearts, cars. Possessing a dreamlike kaleidoscopic quality, it was made by an artist named Victor Matthews in 2016. The E. 175th Street side is characterized by scientific displays: a person's body in anatomical form (human skeletons and muscles in a detailed diagram), a depiction of a chemical reaction, atoms, crystals, and what purports to be DNA. Mischa Most created this exhibit, also in 2016. All three of these murals have different styles, and they are uniformly quite incredible.

I cross E. 175th Street and go east one block to Fulton Avenue and see on my right what must be the city's smallest park. It isn't even on the internet. It goes by the name of Uptown Sitting Park. It's about a quarter of a block long and quite narrow in width, maybe ten yards. Inside, there are a couple of concrete tables, each with the outlines of a checker or chess board. In the back there's a trellis made of leaves and flowers. You could have a small wedding here, I think. The park is across from the much larger Crotona Park, and surely only the locals know it's there.

By the entrance, there's a sign with the usual admonishments to the public—no littering, no drinking, no loud noise, no cooking, and no monopolizing. What does this last prohibition mean, I wonder. No monopolizing of space? Of conversations? No financial monopolies? No Monopoly games? Who knows? As I relax inside on a bench I can see the Cross Bronx Expressway through the bushes. Gazing at the passing cars, trucks, and buses I am struck by the contrast between the busy highway and the stillness of the park, whose shrubbery muffles the sounds of the outside world. To my left I have a clear view of Third Avenue. People are passing by on the sidewalk, unaware of this mini-Shangri La, just as I was until I stumbled across it.

Returning to Third Avenue, I head south and turn west onto E. 172nd Street, turning left in a few minutes onto Washington Avenue. I remember it well, for I was a caseworker long ago, in the summer of 1966, making home visits for the New York City Welfare department in this part of the Bronx. As far as I can tell, the tall NYCHA projects have not changed one iota since then, and the Gouverneur Morris Houses still spell danger for its inhabitants and those who visit there. There's a backlog of 55,000 repairs that need to be made, and rats, roaches, and other vermin are present in large numbers, just as they were more than fifty years ago. The public housing projects have nice trees, leafy and verdant, with grass around them. But space is often a study in contrasts and the looming red-brick buildings easily overshadow Mother Nature.

On the corner of Washington and E. 163rd Street, I detour into a BP gas station convenience store that's run by a tall middle-aged Sikh wearing a turban. He gives me the bathroom key, and I immediately notice that there are two chains around the toilet tank. On my way out of the store, I ask the man: "How come there are chains around the toilet tank? Are you afraid someone will make off with it?"

"Are you kidding? They steal *everything* around here. They will race out of this place and sell it to a scrap dealer. Even the toilet paper. I put zip ties around them. They cut them and [take] off with the paper. And they also steal the soap dispensers." Throughout my journey here, I hear several more tales of woe along these lines, thus anecdotally supporting the crime statistics for Morrisania.

Heading north on Third Avenue, I angle slightly right onto Boston Road, which begins here, just south of E. 164th Street. At the top off the hill, I enter Morrisania's small historic district. Its boundaries are Home Street on the north, Forest Avenue on the east, E. 166th Street on the south, and Boston Road on the west. Trinity Episcopal Church runs along 166th, its architectural glory and majesty still visible through the scaffolding surrounding it, and it is, in fact, the highest elevation in the borough. The oldest building in the district, the cornerstone was laid in 1874. It's a massive red-brick structure designed in Victorian Gothic style and fairly looms over the area from its hilltop location. It has arched windows, a good number of them made of stained glass. Services are still held in the church on a regular basis.

Jackson Avenue probably acquired its name from Washington and Rosetta Jackson, landowners in the area. The brick row houses on the block, built in the early part of the twentieth century, have many features, some of them rather distinctive, and I'll just mention a few: pressed metal cornices; limestone pediments, trim, and banding; raised keystones; conical roofs; triangular and curved gables; and corbels carved in the form of heads. Their overall designs include Renaissance-style Flemish, Italian, and English characteristics. While worth looking at, the homes have become multiple dwellings and are not in good condition. And while they might be attractive to some of the more daring gentrifiers who appreciate good housing stock, such people are unlikely to brave what they see as an area that's perhaps the least safe in the South Bronx. This general perception is confirmed by several residents and by Tony, an employee of a UPS-type company, who delivers packages on a regular basis and is familiar with the buildings.

"This is a really tough area," Tony explains. "I live in the East Bronx, no piece of cake either, but nothing like this. I watch the news, and it's a really bad place. I have a tough area to cover, especially the projects. Even in the daytime you could have a shooting. These row houses are a little better, but look at the location. The dynamics are changing in Harlem, Bed-Stuy, and in other places, but not here. But it's still better than in the old days. In the eighties and nineties, people were dealing in crack and whatnot that turned them very violent. Nowadays the drugs are still here, but they're more mellow, like pills. But there are still stupid people, knuckleheads, who are engaging in petty crime, like stealing old ladies' pocketbooks."

"Have you yourself ever been robbed?"

"No, thank God. So far, so good."

"Why do you think that's the case?"

"Well, I trust no one. No matter who."

"Even an old guy like me?"

"No one. I never put my guard down. But what I do is I try to treat everybody the same, from the oldest to the youngest, with respect. If I see a group of teenagers on the street, when I pass 'em I say, 'What's up fellas? How ya doin? You saw the game last night? Le Bron. I'm goin' for LeBron.' It's from the heart." It surely helps that Tony's Black, but his approach to the teenagers is the same as mine; be friendly without any "attitude," but also be wary of anyone you meet and don't know well. It goes without saying that anyone who works in these parts of the city has to have some street smarts, or they will get into trouble sooner or later.

My next and last stop in the historic district is at Morris High School, around the corner from Jackson on Boston Road and 166th Street, built in 1901. It is a magnificent Collegiate Gothic structure, a designated landmark, and the first large public high school built in the Bronx, in 1901. Many colleges in the United States feature the Gothic style as well, one example of which is City College of New York. The high school's exterior is light-colored brick with limestone and terra-cotta trim. There's a central tower, numerous turrets, with Tudor touches at various points, all making for a marvelous outdoor visual experience.

I'm dying to see the inside of the school, and since I'm in need of a restroom I ask the guard inside if I can use it, showing her my ID, which almost always does the trick. It doesn't work here, however, as she informs me that security in the building is very tight, pointing to the metal detector and saying, "You have to be visiting someone specifically in the school or you can't come in." I've learned never to take no for an answer when doing research and in response to my pleas she half-heartedly calls someone who ends up backing her position. I tell her I desperately need a restroom, though only for a minute. As luck would have it my salvation arrives in the person of Quayson, an African American man and local resident, who happens to be passing by and who is part of the school's security team. He agrees to let me in and escorts me to the facility. Along the way I pepper him with questions about what I see and am surprised to find that he's into the history of the building and has quite a bit of knowledge regarding it.

Quayson is actually very proud of the structure and takes me into the auditorium, which is really quite stupendous. It's also done in the Gothic style and is encircled near the top by some very pretty stained-glass windows. It seats more than five hundred people altogether and the chairs are of polished blond wood, resembling the seats in many school auditoriums. There are gold nameplates behind them, one of them, by a Lawrence Taylor (not the NY Giants star linebacker), reads: "If a C student like me could make it in life, so can you." There's also an organ that was once functional in the rear of the stage. I tell Quayson how impressed I was by his ability to get these tough kids in the hall to quiet down almost instantly.

"Well," he says, "I'm the muscle in the building. We have about 1,200 students, quite a few of them foreigners."

"Let me feel your muscle," I joke. And he does; it's the real deal. I say that I'd love to have him join me on one of my nighttime forays in the Bronx, and he agrees to do it if I wish. I am not trying to butter him up—he's already cooperating. Rather, it's that to do this kind of work, cozying up very quickly to strangers, one needs to have an outgoing personality and I'm just being myself.

Quayson tells me more about the organ: "It broke at some point but they weren't able to get it fixed. Maybe it was a money issue.

Anyway, the acoustics in this room are terrific. Even when the wind starts blowing in here you can hear it. You see these railings? A couple of years ago some guys broke in by kicking in the windows and they stole the railings, figuring the brass had to be worth something. The windows are Tiffany and each one's worth ten grand according to the insurance company. The railings that are here now look like brass but they're just reproductions. One of our famous graduates recently is Fat Joe, a well-known rapper." Perhaps one lesson of this story is that from a simple request to use a bathroom one can end up learning a great deal. Another is that even though this school isn't considered a good school today, academically, at least some people who work in it take pride in its rich and storied history and its appearance.

Walking along Boston Road, I come to a very old-looking place called Levin's Crosstown Supply Store at number 1347. It sells plumbing and heating supplies, with landlords making up a large part of their customer base. I spoke with the owner's son, who is part of the business, which his father still operates.

"We started in 1900 in the Bronx on Westchester Avenue, and we moved here in 1960. I'm fourth generation," he adds with apparent pride in that fact.

"So, you've survived for over a century. There are very few places like this still around in these poor communities. What's the secret?"

"Well it helps that we own the building." He smiles wryly. I've spoken to entrepreneurs in the same situation elsewhere. They cannot get a good price for the property, but there's no mortgage either. So, as long as the customers keep coming they'll stay, at least until they get tired of doing it or simply age out without a buyer or children in the business. There may also be a desire not to break the chain of being in a family business for so long. In this case I didn't feel that this was much of a factor or that there was an emotional connection to the business. He lives way out in Rockland County, and yet he comes in every day. But would he do so if the business was failing, like the piano store owner who told me nobody wanted what he was selling anymore? I doubt it. He has customers, and the business appears to be thriving, with a full inventory in the many square wooden cubbies behind the counter. In short, survive and thrive!

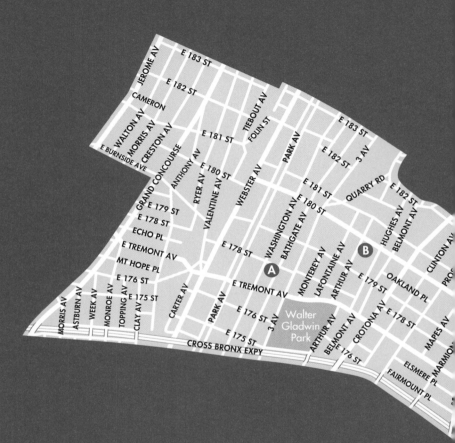

(A) St. Joseph's Church
(B) First Glorious Church
(C) West Farms Soldiers Cemetery
(D) Bronx River waterfall

TREMONT

THIS COMMUNITY, ONCE FARMLAND, became more populated when subway transportation became available and was settled in the late nineteenth and early twentieth centuries mostly by Jews, but also significant numbers of Irish and Italians. In the 1960s it became part of the white exodus from the south-central Bronx, as politics, economics, and immigration resulted in large numbers of poorer minorities, mostly Blacks and Puerto Ricans, moving in. This generally accepted description is an oversimplification, however. As Constance Rosenblum has noted in her book about the Bronx, the first Black people to move into the area were as upwardly mobile as the white people who greeted them. But when the Black Power movement arose, panic set in, especially because those who followed it were often living below the poverty line.[18] Arson, crime, abandonment of buildings, drug dealing, a lack of social programs, and general neglect by the city caused the white population to flee, almost en masse. Another major contributing factor was the construction of the Cross Bronx Expressway, which opened in 1955. It completely bisected the Bronx from west to east and cut through many established communities, including Morrisania and Tremont, thus disrupting and changing forever the patterns of community life.[19] In the 1980s, other groups began moving into Tremont. Most of them were Dominican, but there were also groups from Honduras, Panama, Ecuador, Guyana, and the West Indies, and the community began to improve somewhat.

The boundaries of Tremont, which are not precisely agreed upon, have been established here in a particular way because they fit together ethnically, geographically, and economically, and also in terms of walking them in a productive manner. They are E. 183th and E. 182nd Street, plus Bronx Park South, and E. 180th Street on the north; Boston Road and the Bronx River Parkway on the east, the Cross Bronx Expressway and a small section of E. Burnside Avenue on the south, and the Grand Concourse and Jerome Avenue on the west. The area east of Webster Avenue is also referred to by many as East Tremont. The major thoroughfare is Tremont Avenue which runs east-west for almost the entire width of the Bronx to Throgs Neck. Here, it's a very crowded and busy shopping area. Webster and Third Avenues are also commercial streets, and they run north-south.

Today things are better, yet Tremont, like its southern neighbor, Morrisania, remains a high-crime area. My advice to visitors is to be careful where and when you walk. While the chances of something serious happening are slim, when it does occur, it's often in communities like Tremont and Morrisania.

My walk begins at the intersection of the Grand Concourse and E. Tremont Avenue. I go one short block east on Tremont and make an immediate right onto Monroe Avenue. This is the Mount Hope neighborhood, and it's a rude introduction to the tiny section. The boundaries of Mount Hope are E. Tremont on the north, Webster Avenue on the east, the Cross Bronx Expressway on the south, and the Grand Concourse on the west. It acquired its name because there was a mountain in the area called Mount Hope. Once a Jewish neighborhood, it went the way of the rest of the South Bronx. Unlike other South Bronx neighborhoods, this tiny enclave remains impoverished. There's not even much affordable housing, just decrepit tenements for the most part. The streets are littered with garbage, knots of hard-looking men hang out on the streets and strangers are eyed with even more than the usual degree of suspicion. There is, however, one standout, a stone mansion at 1857 Anthony Avenue and Mount Hope Place, built around the turn of the twentieth century. The gates are rusted, there are bars over the windows, and locals say it's haunted. It certainly has the traditional appearance of a haunted house, with its gables, towers and stone figures seemingly staring at you from every floor no matter which way you turn. This is especially true of two human size figurines standing guard, as it were, on either side of the door. They seem to be wrapped in a shroud, fiercely glowering at passersby. This is, to my knowledge, the only large home of this sort in the urbanized south-central Bronx.

As I leave this enclave and head east on E. Tremont, I come to a homeless shelter just past Anthony Avenue. Next to it is the small hilly Richman Park, whose natural beauty is enhanced by outcroppings of large rocks that give it a wild, untamed appearance. It was formerly called Echo Park because of the sound waves that reportedly bounced off the ancient rocks. Unfortunately, today it is a place filled with people from the shelter who are seated on the few benches here and on the ground—some nodding off, others aggressively panhandling, clearly discouraging others from entering. The only sign of normal activity is a group of teenagers playing basketball on a court that has seen better days. There's a lesson to be learned here, one applicable to many areas. People who are homeless need to live somewhere, but when shelters are constructed, there needs to be enough security so that the few recreational parts of neighborhoods sorely lacking them are safe. This is a graphic example of what happens when the city fails to address such issues.

Several blocks later I turn left onto Bathgate. Near E. 178th Street I pass by St. Joseph's Church, founded in 1873 by German immigrants. Today it's closed, having merged with another church.

What struck me was the gorgeous garden and paths in an outdoor fenced-in area along the northern side of their property. There are hundreds of roses in full bloom along the pathway leading to a shrine of the Virgin Mary. It's worth seeing if you're in the immediate vicinity. Generally, the Bathgate portion of Tremont is low income and residential with small two- and three-family older homes and tenement walk-ups, but nothing stood out as I walked. The boundaries are E. 183rd Street on the north, Third Avenue on the east, the Cross Bronx Expressway on the south, and Webster Avenue on the west. Webster, Park, and Third Avenues are quite ordinary as well, consisting mainly of auto repair shops, hardware suppliers, storefront churches, delis, barbershops, and so on.

Returning via Bathgate, I turn left onto E. Tremont and turn right onto Third Avenue, which is literally a continuation of Manhattan's Third Avenue. Here, on my left, I climb a steep staircase, built in 1899, now in bad condition, and enter Tremont Park. It once led to the nineteenth-century headquarters of Bronx Borough Hall. The grounds are quite nice in what is the largest park in this community. And it's fairly safe in the daytime. Drug dealers are largely absent, according to the locals. There are reportedly people who use opioids hanging around, but they don't bother others, and I see lots of children and seniors in the park. The elevated western edge offers a very nice view of the West Bronx. There's also a baseball field and racquetball courts. There are benches to sit on in a lush green area and an excellent playground as well. I see a large group of schoolchildren on a day trip. They are playing a game of tug-of-war in a small meadow and having a great time. I think of state-of-the-art sports facilities, the computer simulated games that are so popular. Yet the happiness of these children in this simple, time-honored game demonstrates that, for kids, just being in a park on a beautiful spring afternoon is enough to make them laugh, cheer their classmates on, and just enjoy themselves.

A stroll down E. Tremont Avenue reveals it to be a commercial street for people's day-to-day needs. It doesn't have auto repair shops, hardware stores, or lumber yards, but rather it's a series of small shops that go on for miles—Dunkin' Donuts, income tax preparers, cell phone store, small clothing stores, delis, McDonald's, medical offices, barbershops. People are congregating everywhere on the street, giving it a feeling of constantly being busy. It seems to be a place where folks meet and talk. I pass a small furniture store that advertises "FURNITURE: living rooms and dinning rooms." I have become keenly aware of the inattention to correct spelling often in down-and-out communities, which this is to a large extent. Often, it's due to the fact that immigrants open businesses and simply don't know how a word is spelled. And if it's misspelled, does it really matter? After all, doesn't everyone looking for furniture realize that "dinning" is "dining?"

The old Italian portion of Arthur Avenue, with its restaurants and pastry shops, not to mention gourmet delis, begins at E. 183rd Street in the Belmont section. But from E. Tremont Avenue north to E. 182nd it's an entirely different story. One could call it the unknown part of Arthur Avenue. It's a high-crime area, especially near the intersection of Arthur and E. Tremont Avenues. There one can observe drug sales in the open, with young men stationed as lookouts. Nearby, several members of a motorcycle gang engage in easy banter with those on the street. As I walk north on Arthur and cut to the side streets, I pass several gang murals, some with painted graves on them in memory of dead members.

At 2084 Arthur Avenue, I stop in front of the First Glorious Church. This was once a synagogue, Congregation Sons of Israel. Founded in 1909, it served the local Jewish community for decades, most of whose members were quite poor. The people were, however, dedicated to giving their children a Jewish education of some sort, sending them after a day in public school to the synagogue's Hebrew school. During the Depression the cost for the program was $2.00 a week. The classrooms were often unheated in the winter, but the youngsters went anyway, shivering in their coats. A prominent Jewish school, Yeshiva Rabbeinu Chaim Ozer, was also at the location from the mid-fifties to the mid-sixties.

I say hello to two lovely older Black women who are giving out free food and who offer me a dozen eggs. I thank them but decline and ask to enter the church. They say "Sure," and I walk in where I'm immediately welcomed by Bill Francis, a tall, handsome seventy-year old man who turns out to be a church elder.

"I wanted to ask you a question," I say. "I notice you still have the religious symbols of the Jewish temple that was once here. The stained glass rose window outside has a large Star of David and there's another one on top of the building. There's also a menorah that's part of a Torah scroll, made of stone, above the rose window. And I see that inside you have crosses on some of the stained-glass windows and Stars of David from the old days on others. Since it's a different religion why did you do that?"

"Because we keep the church the way it was given to us. By the way, we are a nondenominational church. It's a holiness church. We're not Baptist, we're not Catholic. You get caught up in these labels and it divides people. We have an organ, drums, and a choir on Sunday and the music and words are gospel. We have some Hispanics who come too, generally if they can understand English."

"I see."

"We're also a church of miracles. There was a woman who came here who couldn't walk without braces. People can be healed if they believe, and that's what happened. She started coming and she received the Word. A friend of this church had brought her here. After about six weeks, she suddenly got up and started stumbling around without her braces. And we ran to help her. She said, 'No I don't need help.' I'm telling you the truth. After all, I'm standing in a Blessed House. She was maybe forty years old. She went and marched like a soldier all the way to that door in the back and marched back. She said, 'I do believe.' Our pastor had laid hands on her. She said she spoke to God and He said, 'You can walk.' I saw it. It happened this year."

"This doesn't happen in every church. Why did it happen here?"

"Because of the spirit that's here. Nothing special. We believe that if you avail yourself through the Father to the Son, you will be helped. We've had people with cancer who said it went away after they came here. Let me show you something. Right now, this year, you're a certain age. But next year you'll be a different age. So, what is true, namely your age, will not be true next year. But the word of God is not true. It's *truth*. It doesn't change, past, present, or future."

"Why did you offer me eggs? Isn't it supposed to be for poor people?"

"What does the Lord say? Give. I don't ask you whether or not you can afford it. I offer, you take. It's because God wanted that to happen." I tell Bill I write books about New York and explain my current project. I tell him the history of the synagogue. He listens intently and thanks me for telling him something about the church's history he didn't know.

"You know, we discovered this window with the Star of David when we saw something covered up. We expected to find organ pipes but we didn't. Basically, there's three religions that believe in one God. Judaism and Christianity believe in the same Father. We have a little different opinion about Christ, but we believe in Jehovah. The New Testament tells us we were grafted onto the vine. And the vine was Judaism, and Jesus was a Jew. So how do we represent to the one we call our Savior?"

Bill's life is suffused with religion. He sees holiness and God everywhere, and he believes in God with all his heart. He grew up in Manhattan on 137th Street and Fifth Avenue. He attended City College for a while during the Vietnam War and served in the Air Force. He wound up working for the Transit Authority and became a manager. The conversation is important in that it reveals how religious people see the world. There are hundreds of churches in the Bronx, and they are filled with believers every week who more or less share a common view of the world. And Bill is here on a weekday, volunteering his time to the church. For most of these people, it's not only about God—it's about fellowship, having a community that engages in social activities as well.

Even though I'm a stranger to the community, Bill welcomes me as a friend. There is genuine warmth and sincerity in his voice as he speaks in a personal and compelling manner. I can also sense it in his penetrating eyes as he looks directly at me, never shifting his gaze. Finally, his attitude toward other religions reveals a tolerant mindset of respecting all faiths. It's also revealed in how he rejects the notion of being boxed into one denomination of Christianity. How does he perceive nonbelievers? I don't know, but I suspect he would see them as potential believers if properly approached.

Resuming my walk, I chance upon a parks department employee on the corner of E. 180th Street. "How come they have all these bars in front of the houses?" I ask.

"I don't think it's that dangerous, but there is crime here," he replies. "I guess they just don't want nobody comin' into their houses and yards. The problem is, this area's a little too quiet at night. And the area over on Hughes is pretty rough. After nine or ten p.m. you never know who's walkin' around. And the projects further down has got dangerous people. You never know who comes around and visits their friend and then they wander off and do whatever. These bars were not put up in the seventies but recently, in the last fifteen years. And the danger's because of the city and HUD [Department of Housing and Urban Development]. They bought up properties all over the city. And they put in the homeless." A common complaint is that the city is often too lax in checking on whom they're allowing to move into apartments.

I head east on 180th and come to Southern Boulevard, where I turn left and explore the avenue a bit. Why? Because while it's not the Grand Concourse, it is somewhat grand. Parallel to it on the right is Crotona Parkway and between these two streets is a green mall that runs a few blocks north to about 183rd Street. It's great for a nice walk in this distinctly unglamorous part of the Bronx. On the right you'll see an entrance to the Bronx Zoo, one of the best zoos in the world, but very well known and therefore beyond the scope of this guide. Every guidebook writes about it.

Retracing my steps to 180th Street, I go left and continue eastward to Bryant Avenue, where I try to access the West Farms Soldiers Cemetery. I cannot gain entry as it's locked, but it looks quite interesting even from the outside. When I was last here in 2010, it wasn't locked. Perhaps graves were vandalized since then, but no one's there to confirm that. There are gravestones that are tilted at odd angles, others that lie on the ground, and still others that, while upright, cannot be read. Here are soldiers who died in four wars, the War of 1812, the Civil War, the Spanish-American War, and World War I. That means it spans more than two hundred years. There are forty graves with plenty of room for more, but who's interested? It's neglected and hidden, though there are many small American flags in front of the graves. Still, it's worth looking at, if only for the spookiness of the place.

West Farms Village itself is very old, having been founded in 1663. The neighborhood's boundaries are Bronx Park South and E. 180th Street on the north, the Bronx River on the east, the Cross Bronx Expressway on the south, and Southern Boulevard on the west. It's a subneighborhood of Tremont, but it's quieter than other parts and almost entirely residential, with modest frame homes scattered throughout. However, the bulk of it consists of affordable housing and old tenements. It does have one outstanding sight that is a well-kept secret because it lies deep in the Bronx in a poor neighborhood.

Inside River Park, which can be entered on the corner of West Farms Road and E. 180th, I walk down a hill through the well-maintained park and am soon standing in front of a railing on a path overlooking the Bronx River, which cuts through a swath of lush woods. The near side belongs to the Zoo and the far side to the Botanical Garden, but it looks very wild and scenic. Off to the left I see an incredibly beautiful waterfall, about a third of a block wide. While technically the result of a dam, it's the largest waterfall in

Bronx River waterfall

New York City that's on a natural body of water, namely the Bronx River. Part of what makes it so special is the way the water falls at different levels from the top. It makes arc-like patterns because of the way the rocks line up. The fast-falling crystal-looking waters remind me of rivers in the Adirondacks or the Catskills. You can see nothing but greenery and trees for half a mile beyond it. So peaceful. See my Instagram post (@nynobodyknows) or surf the internet to get a better idea. It's all very picturesque, with nice sitting areas, and worth the trip even if you don't have time to visit the Zoo or Botanical Garden.

You can also see wildlife from the upper floors of buildings on Bronx Park South, frolicking or snoozing in the Bronx Zoo across the street—zebras, antelopes, wolves. You might even get a wake-up call from a lion's roar! It's a perfect example of what people mean when they write about a view as a "space," in the same way that they talk about plazas, hotels, and bridges.[20] In 2018, a three-bedroom apartment here went for about $1,500 a month. Community leaders and public officials say it's getting better, but crime is a factor. In 2017 there was only one murder. In 2018, by contrast, there were five murders only halfway into the year. Which is the anomaly? Check carefully before taking the plunge. At the very least you get a beautiful zoo and botanical gardens, a few minutes' walk away. And there are great subway lines there, the 2 and the 5, which run express throughout Manhattan.[21]

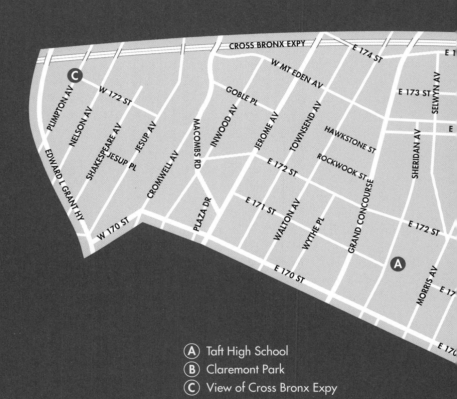

A Taft High School
B Claremont Park
C View of Cross Bronx Expy

MOUNT EDEN

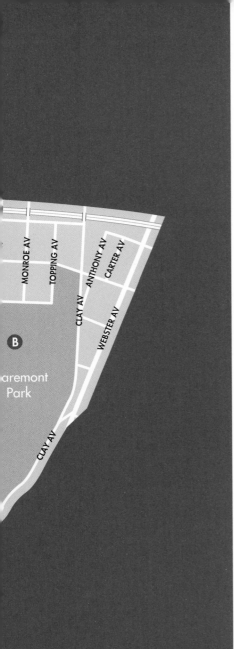

MOUNT EDEN IS A SMALL COMMUNITY IN THE WEST-CENTRAL BRONX. Its boundaries are the Cross Bronx Expressway on the north, Webster Avenue on the east, 170th Street on the south, and Edward L. Grant Highway on the west. In the nineteenth century it was farmland, with the name attributed to Rachel Eden, who owned a farm there. When transportation became available through the extension of the subway lines, apartment buildings were constructed. Most of those who came in large numbers in the 1920s and 1930s were Jewish and tended to be somewhat well off. The community became predominantly Black and Hispanic in the 1970s, as was the case in the surrounding Bronx communities.

The main thoroughfares are 170th Street, Mount Eden and Jerome Avenues, and to a lesser but still substantial extent, Inwood Avenue. It has a lovely park, Claremont Park, which has great natural beauty and nice facilities, including a swimming pool. The terrain is quite hilly, especially the western portion. As to safety, it's not as dangerous as some other communities, but walkers should exercise caution, especially on the streets between the Grand Concourse and Findlay Avenue, as well as in Claremont Park at night. In earlier times, Orthodox Jews went on walks through the park on Sabbath afternoons, where they could meet each other, especially teenagers, and where adults could sit and chat on park benches.

Mount Eden's main shopping area runs along 170th Street, but it's not nearly as extensive as the one farther north on Fordham Road. Still, it does serve those residing in the immediate vicinity. As I descend east down a hill after the Grand Concourse, I see Taft High School, a famous institution founded in the 1940s, situated between Sheridan and Morris Avenues. Its graduates include some famous personalities, like the entertainer Eydie Gorme and movie director Stanley Kubrick, as well as some lesser but well-known figures like Fred "The Furrier" Schwartz, who made a mint and became a household name in the New York metropolitan area. The school, considered one of the worst in the city during the 1990s, has regained a bit of its luster in recent years by rebranding itself. Like other formerly failing schools, it now has mini-schools focusing on specialized career areas: business, medicine, media and communications, and the like. Several parents I spoke with outside the building say it's improved in recent years and that their children were able to get jobs, in part, because they were in these programs—one as a nurse, another as a small business owner.

A few blocks later, I enter Claremont Park, which runs north along Findlay Avenue. Ascending some steps and starting out along a concrete walkway, I'm impressed by its natural beauty. Tall old trees, their leaves gently rustling in the wind, provide a leafy canopy over green meadows and natural rock outcroppings. I stop by a police van parked on the road and ask the officer if the park is dangerous.

"Sure, it is. That's why I'm here."

"Well, I assume that now that you're here, it just became safer."

"I guess you have a point. Actually, it's not really dangerous except at night. And I'm not from around here. Where I work normally, it's really bad. That's the Gun Hill Road section. Don't go there. And don't walk around the Edenwald projects."

I continue on my merry way and soon encounter some park workers on cleanup detail. With a swimming pool, sports facilities, and modern playgrounds, Claremont has great potential. Walking over to one of the workers, a middle-aged African American man, I say: "I just want you to know how much I appreciate the cleanup work you're doing. Without it, the park would be drowning in garbage." He is grateful for the compliment, which is not surprising, since most people probably never praise him, taking his efforts for granted.

"Thank you," he says. "We just had the Ramadan. Over a thousand came and it was pretty messy, but not that bad. You know, we just lost a really old tree the other day."

"How do you feel about that? Do you take it personally?"

"Well, kinda. I mean, you miss it. You miss the shade it provided. There are people, like this lady who always loved to hug the trees, like they were a person. I said to her once, 'What are you doing talking to that tree, like it's a human being?' 'Well,' she said, 'a tree needs love too.' She was Black, in her late forties, I would say. We have all sorts of trees here, many of them London plane trees."

"Is this park safe during the day?"

"Pretty much. But at night I wouldn't trust it," he says, almost chortling at the very thought.

"Did you always do this when you worked?"

"Yes, but for many years I was part of the Park Enforcement Patrol unit. We didn't carry guns, which was good, but we did have Mace."

"Did anything really weird ever happen when you were patrolling?"

"Well there was one really crazy thing that I remember. A call came in when we were on patrol in Central Park, saying: 'We have a report of an exotic animal on the Great Lawn. Please check it out right away.' We went over and, I couldn't believe it. I jumped over a little fence and I saw this huge lion on the lawn, loose it seemed.

They knew, it turned out, but they didn't tell us. Maybe they were afraid we wouldn't go there if we knew it was a lion. And maybe that's true. I had thought it was maybe a bird."

"No! You mean like the big lion you see in the MGM movies picture on the screen?"

"Yeah. It turned out the circus was in town and they were training the lion. It was scary. So, I backed off the hill and started running toward the truck. They could have let us know." Many jobs aren't particularly interesting, but sometimes interesting things happen even in such jobs and this is a good case in point.

The park has a distinct history to it, nonetheless. It was once part of the old Morris family estate, which dates back to 1679. In 1859 a couple, Elliott and Anna Zborowski Montsaulain, built Claremont Mansion and developed the land, with its terraced gardens and scenic grounds, which explains why the park still retains its natural beauty. Apparently there was a curse on the family name, as no male member of the family ever died peacefully in bed. One died in a wheelchair, another was killed by a train, a third was thrown from his horse, yet another drowned in the Bronx River, and a fifth fell from his automobile and was killed.[22] Claremont became one of eight new Bronx parks in 1888 because advocates argued that with so many new arrivals from foreign lands coming in there was a real need for more public green spaces. In 1938, the estate was leveled and a gazebo went up in its place. I visit the gazebo, which has several very pretty chess/checkerboard tables in gold and black hues rather than the dull colors generally found in the outdoor park system.

Exiting the park on the north end, I make my way west along Mount Eden Parkway and turn left on Selwyn Avenue. It's fairly busy, with dominoes players competing against each other at several folding tables, knots of teenagers lounging against the sides of cars or sitting on stoops, not looking especially friendly. By contrast, the next avenue west, Sheridan, has almost no people outside. What it does have is several outdoor stone/concrete staircases leading up to the next street level, which is the Grand Concourse. These staircases,

Claremont Park gazebo

on both sides of the boulevard, exist not only because the streets are hilly, but because the blocks are longer and having stairs between each corner eases access to the other streets. And these stairs have been built on many other blocks in the west Bronx. In short, topography is destiny.

I head up Sheridan, go left onto Mount Eden Avenue, and cross the Concourse on Mount Eden. I then head downhill and past Jerome Avenue, turn left on Inwood Avenue, and see something I've always wondered about, and by this I mean its inner workings. It's a common enough sight in the city, people picking bottles and cans out of garbage cans and on the ground, and putting them into large, plastic, see-through bags, the intent being to redeem them at one of the many such centers in the city. Mostly, they are stand-alone businesses. Here, on this corner, I encounter the manager of one such location, and he turns out to be a most remarkable individual. Charlie's a rail-thin African American man, with a straight mustache. He's wearing a dark, nondescript shirt tucked into a pair of black jeans. There's a constant clatter behind him as the bags are crushed into a mechanical contraption,

"How much can a person get for one of these bags?"

"Twelve bucks," he responds in a matter-of-fact-tone, continuing to check the bags as they come in.

"This is hard work, isn't it?"

"It sure is."

"It's really amazing when I think about it. You have lots of people who don't want to do hard work, and yet these people are willing to do it."

"Yes, and there's millions of these bottles and cans in the city that need to be dealt with. Maybe 100 million. Imagine if they weren't taken away, what the city would look like?"

"How much can someone make doing this on the average in a day? A hundred bucks?

"Oh no, they can earn $300 to $400 a day, cash. You'd be surprised. Some of these people have bought nice houses back in the countries they came from."

"How long have you been doing this?"

"Since the 1990s. I went through my rough period. I had some bad times. I did the drug thing, the alcohol thing, I left a good wife, and now I manage this place."

"How did you get back to a normal life? Any religion involved?"

"Religion was the *only* thing that made me sane again. I became a Baptist. You see, I'm from New Orleans originally, but I was raised in Vicksburg, Mississippi, and also in the city of Greenwood. I came to New York when I was twenty-two in 1964 and I never looked back. But all I had was a high school education, so what was I gonna do? So first I worked for a company that processed shrimp cocktails, called Sau-Sea Foods. I managed the place and had to be there to unlock everything at 5:45 a.m. because they opened at 6:30. Not that I want to tell my whole life story, but I had plenty of ups and downs. I got to the point somehow where I was staying up all night, showing up late, and I started going down, down, down, and there you go. I left my wife and started sleeping in the park. Yet here I am. I'm seventy-seven years old, and I'm fit and working."

"How did you pull yourself together?"

"I pulled myself together through religion because I had been raised a Baptist and so I had something to go back to. You got young people today they never knew about religion in the first place. They will step on you, crush your body and never look back. God says, 'Thou shalt not steal; Thou shalt not rob; Thou shalt not kill.' I used to drink but I only did harm to myself, but not to others because this wasn't me.

"I had a hard life but my mother's was even harder. She was a slave even though she was born after slavery. She lived in a barn on a farm, and the owner impregnated her. His wife used to ask her who was the father. She knew damn well who it was. But my mother never told. She'd say it was some other man passing through. But she was afraid of the owner, and she ran away.

"I worked in Nathan's and was the first Black man to make manager at the Nathan's in Yonkers on Central Avenue. And then I learned this business. I can tell within three or four cans how many there are in a bag of 100 or more. They might tell me they got 110 bottles, and I'll be diplomatic and I'll say, 'I think you might be short four or five.' And they know it. People who bring these cans in, they have to know certain things, like what day they do the recycling in their area, and whatnot. On a hot day like today you can go around the park and maybe pick up five dollars worth of bottles. And you have to wear gloves or you'll get cut up."

"Where do you live?"

"On the Bronxville-Yonkers border. I have six children, and they're all doing well and live near me. My wife passed away."

"Who does most of this work?"

"Many are illegals, like Mexicans. They make cash, and obviously most of them don't pay any taxes. And I believe the city doesn't want to charge them or catch them because the city can't get rid of its garbage anyway, so they certainly won't be able to get the recyclables off the street. So, we'll be in business forever."

Charlie is like a character in Studs Terkel's famous book *Working*. His story is complex, many-sided. He came here from the Deep South and worked at numerous jobs. And then he "fell off the tracks," so to speak. He recovered, and it was because he retained his inner core, one grounded in faith in God. He wasn't educated, but that was due most probably to the fact that it just wasn't what rural Black men did in his day, when the civil rights era was just dawning. He was a manager in a variety of jobs, suggesting that he has smarts and people skills.

His description of the recyclables business explains why it has a place in this city. It performs a valuable service, so much so that law enforcement and city government look the other way, choosing not to regulate it because the workers do what others don't want to do—dirty work. And because others don't want to do it, those who do can make good money, trudging and collecting throwaways in all manner of places. The details of his personal life are both revealing and deeply affecting—the wife he left, the drugs and alcohol he became dependent on.

Why did he open up to me, a total stranger? Because we bonded, had chemistry. Maybe it was being of the same generation despite differences in our backgrounds. I told him I was writing a book on the Bronx and had written one on the whole city. He became excited, wanted to be in it, and wrote down my name so his children could surf the net and tell him more about the books I had written. I'll never forget how every time he mentioned a place in the city I would tell him details about the location, where the road curved, what buildings were on it, even about Yonkers and Bronxville, both of which were familiar to me. And each time, he would exclaim:

"You got it!" or "Right on!" and we would exchange high-fives. I had this experience with many people I met, young and old, rich and poor, one way or another. It's called developing rapport and is essential for ethnographic research. But it isn't only research. You have to enjoy doing this on a personal level and not be at all self-conscious about it.

Somehow or other—many parts to his story remain hidden, no doubt—he made it. He appreciated his mother's struggle, he took pride in the jobs that gave him responsibilities and managed to raise six children, all of whom are gainfully employed. Why did Charlie make it? Because, to put it simply, he never gave up on himself.

I continue down Inwood and turn right on Goble Place, a one-block affair that ends almost immediately at Macombs Road. As I turn onto Macombs, my memory is jolted and I stop dead in my tracks. I'm looking at a building on Macombs, number 1515, and I suddenly realize this is where my first girlfriend lived. Memories flood through my brain as I recall what was my first "date." I was but twelve years old and had taken the D train from where I lived in Manhattan to the 170th Street Station, walking from there to pick her up. My father had tacitly agreed to let me go alone, but it was a sham and we both knew it. He simply followed discreetly behind me at a safe distance—from our apartment, on the train one car back, and up the hill to her house. This game continued, as I picked her up and took the train back to Manhattan.

At the 125th Station, however, we jumped out of the D train just as the doors were closing and grabbed a local AA subway. My father, surprised, couldn't get out in time and the D train (an express), departed for its next stop far away, 59th Street. We got out at 96th Street and caught a movie, *Adam and Eve*—racy in those days but tame by today's standards. An adult bought the tickets for us and we sneaked in. I hadn't thought about this escapade for decades, until the sight of this sturdy surviving apartment building transported me back to a magical time when life was much simpler than today, but so much fun at times. Needless to say, my father and I pretended nothing unusual had happened, but I never forgot it. Nor, I'm sure, did he.

I go south on Macombs Road to 170th Street, hang a right and then another right, striding up a hill on Edward L. Grant Highway, named after Eddie Grant. A 1905 Harvard graduate, Grant was the first major league baseball player to be killed during the fighting in World War I. His last team was the New York Giants, who memorialized him by erecting a plaque in his memory at the Polo Grounds stadium in upper Manhattan, just across the Harlem River. The plaque was stolen, and its final fate is uncertain. There's a replica of the stolen plaque in San Francisco in the Giants' present home, AT&T Park. Why did the Bronx—Yankees territory—commemorate him and not Manhattan, where he played? Because an American Legion post in the Bronx located on the same street, wanted to honor him. According to some chroniclers of his life, Grant declined to say "I got it!" when calling for a fly ball, opting instead for the grammatically correct "I have it!" And why not? He was a Harvard man!

Continuing up Edward Grant, I soon make a right onto Plimpton Avenue. I know it well because I used to visit my uncle and aunt who lived on the block, spending time with their children, my cousins. It's also the place where I take my students in the New York City Ph.D. class to show them what a broad swath the Cross Bronx Expressway cut through the Bronx. It can best be viewed at the intersection of Plimpton and E. 172nd Street. The expressway was the brainchild of Robert Moses. He was a city planning commissioner and chairman of the Triborough Bridge and Tunnel Authority, and he wielded great power over what would be built in the city. Scholars like Marshall Berman and Robert Caro have criticized Moses's lack of sensitivity to local residents and the fact that these were their communities which Moses was controlling by the rule of eminent domain. It's a difficult matter. On the one hand, the expressway did cut through communities and forced people to move. On the other, the city needed a quick way to deliver products to its citizens, and New Yorkers needed to get from one place to the other. Moreover, if highways weren't built, then drivers would be barreling down residential streets to reach their destinations. Finally, new communities were created by the highway separation on each side of the expressway.

I walk down W. 172nd Street and pass by the Shakespeare School, Public School 199. Schools throughout the city play a critical part in bringing the arts to the community, and they use any kind of hook to draw the people in. The Shakespeare School, built in 1929, has presented *The Taming of the Shrew* or another Shakespeare play every year in June for the parents and community because it's the Shakespeare school. In essence, this provides a convenient reason for bringing literature and culture to the school. In communities like Mount Eden, few can afford tickets to Broadway shows, so it is often their only chance to see a real play. Such an experience can provide rich memories for those who went long after they've graduated.

ALEXANDER HAMILTON BRIDGE

CROSS BRONX EXPY

Harlem River

SEDGWICK AVE

UNDERCLIFF AVE

Major Deegan Expy

UNIVERSITY AV

MERRIAM AV

OGDEN AV

PLIMPTON AV

EDWARD L GRANT HY

W 170 ST

W 169 ST

D

NELSON AV

W 168 ST

W 167 ST

SHAKESPEARE AV

SEDGWICK AVE

OGDEN AV

W 167 ST

WOODYCREST AV

ANDERSON AV

W 166 ST

UNIVERSITY AV

W 165 ST

JEROME AV

Harlem River

SUMMIT AV

W 164 ST

W 163 ST

B

W 162 ST

A

W 161 ST

C

JEROME AV

A Noonan Towers

B Park Plaza Apartments

C Highbridge Woodycrest Center

D Highbridge Community Church

HIGHBRIDGE

HIGHBRIDGE IS A COMMUNITY immediately southwest of Mount Eden. It lies on a much higher elevation, with the borders being the Cross Bronx Expressway on the north, Edward L. Grant Highway and Jerome Avenue on the east, Jerome and E. 161st Street on the south and Sedgwick Avenue on the west. The Dutch purchased land here from the Native Americans in 1639. The British controlled the area from the late 1600s until the Revolutionary War. Initially, Highbridge became a resort during the nineteenth century for people hankering for a more pastoral recreational environment. Resorts were built, with most of the people traveling there by steamer across the Harlem River. Highbridge was named for the High Bridge, the oldest existing span in New York City, having been built to transport water from the Croton Reservoir to the city. Construction of the Roman-style bridge, one with large stone arches supporting it, commenced in 1837, and it was completed in 1848. In the late 1920s, these arches were replaced by a large steel span so as to make it easier for ships to pass through.

The High Bridge was closed to pedestrians from 1960 until 2015, though the reasons aren't entirely clear. Some say it was because teenagers were throwing debris and rocks on the Circle Line tour boats as they passed underneath. One person who lives very close to the bridge asserted to me that it was closed "because they got tired of people being thrown off the bridge." That may have happened, but I haven't been able to verify it or that it was a factor. If so, it would more likely have been during the high-crime era of the 1980s, 1990s, and the first few years of the twenty-first century. But the walkway was closed around 1960, twenty years earlier. Today, it's a pretty footpath that features some bricks dating back to the mid-1800s. It's also a boon to the locals who can now walk across the river and enjoy Highbridge Park in Manhattan.

As usual, the community attracted large numbers of newcomers when the subways were extended, first the Jerome Avenue line in 1918 and then the IND line along the Grand Concourse. The primary groups that settled in the area were, first and foremost, the Irish, who made their way to Highbridge in the nineteenth century, and then the Jews, who were leaving the Lower East Side, augmented in the 1930s and 1940s by Jews fleeing Nazi-occupied Europe. Throughout, there were also Germans and Italians who moved in. The most important church was Sacred Heart, founded in 1875 and located today at 1253 Shakespeare Avenue.[23] The Jews established a synagogue that was situated at Nelson Avenue and 167th Street. A unique blending of these two cultures was Sam's Deli on Woodycrest Avenue, which was both a deli and a bar! Today, the area is predominantly Hispanic, with Black people comprising the next most prominent group, especially a growing African population originating in West African countries.

The major thoroughfare running the length of Highbridge is Ogden Avenue, but there are also side streets and corners that feature small stores, especially bodegas, barbershops, and nail salons. In the old days, there were as many candy stores—with stools on which to sit and order egg creams and various flavored sodas, plus candies of every kind, comics or "jokebooks," and daily papers, along with sandwiches—as there are bodegas today. The Bronx entrance to Highbridge Park, reachable by the pedestrian pathway, is at the intersection of Martin Luther King Jr. Boulevard (a.k.a. University Avenue). There is, unfortunately, no park of any size that is, strictly speaking, in Highbridge. Nevertheless, residents can simply cross Jerome Avenue, Highbridge's eastern border, and enter Mullaly Park at E. 164th Street or Macombs Dam Park, at Jerome and E. 162nd Street. Both are, technically, just inside the Concourse neighborhood. Crime is a problem in the area, but no more than in other parts of the West Bronx. Highbridge can be toured, unimpeded in the daytime hours, but caution is advised.

My trip begins on Woodycrest Avenue, a street with old apartment buildings and mansions, many of them rundown. An exception is Noonan Towers, at number 939, which sits at the intersection of Woodycrest and W. 161st Street. Built in 1911, it was once a residence for baseball players from nearby Yankee Stadium. According to some reports, Babe Ruth once lived here. The structure is a mix of Art Deco and other styles, and the lobby has beautiful decorative moldings as well as a richly patterned marble floor. Outside, the entrance is flanked by fluted stone Corinthian columns and elaborately designed iron grillwork that practically blanket the doors. I get a free tour from one of the maintenance workers, who shows me around. On the day of my visit, a hot June afternoon in 2018, there's quite a bit of activity because many apartments are being renovated. I'm shown a one-bedroom, with two bathrooms and a view of Yankee Stadium (the new incarnation) two blocks away. "It's so close, you can hear the radio announcer very clearly," my guide gushes. It's available for rentals at $2,400 a month. There are new gleaming appliances, and the hardwood floors are polished to a high gloss.

Across the street is a historic building, formerly the American Female Guardian Society's Home for the Friendless, established in 1901–1902 to care for children who were abandoned. At the time it served 120 youngsters, who lived in dormitories. Today, this Beaux-Arts style terra-cotta, brick, and limestone mansion, with imposing keystones above Roman-style windows, is home to the Highbridge Woodycrest Center, operated by the BronxCare Health System. It serves as a long-term care facility for older adults and patients with AIDS and disabilities.

Walking north on Woodycrest I see a former mansion near W. 164th Street that typifies these homes. The bottom half is made of stone, with brick on the upper portion, topped by a gray cupola with a solitary nautical window on it. It's well fortified with iron bars. No one is breaking in here without great difficulty. Opposite it is a similar eclectic home, with two angels that are either guarding the home or welcoming you into it. Judging from the two-story high iron fence, I would guess that the angels are performing the former rather than the latter function. Farther up the street I meet John, an Italian-American man in his early forties, by my estimate, who's doing some gardening work outside his detached home.

"Hi," I greet him. "Are you from around here?"

"No, I grew up in Queens, but basically lived in Brooklyn for most of my adult life, around Greenpoint. By the time I was ready to buy a house in Brooklyn I found that I'd been priced out. So, I looked elsewhere and found this place. It's a fairly big house which cost me around $500,000, but would have easily been several million in Greenpoint or North Williamsburg. It's a great house, well built, with all the original moldings. It took a while. I had to do a lot of research and walking through different areas, but I found what I wanted. This may seem weird, but I also like the air up here. We're in a high place and it's a lot cooler here in the summer." John is handsome and fit, with a neatly trimmed beard—a high-tech professional—and I can hear a tinge of regret in his voice as he explains how he ended up here. This was not his dream house, but it was the best deal he could make under the circumstances. He has hopes the high-crime area will improve, but despite seeing a small increase in people like him moving here, he's doubtful about things changing radically in the near future.

"What's it really like to live here?" I ask. "Like, down on the corner, there seem to be some local fellows who maybe deal in drugs. I noticed that they've sort of created a permanent space for themselves. They have an outdoor tent, open on the sides and covered on top with a sheet. They have a table for dominoes, and they also have a grill on the sidewalk where they barbeque chicken. You know, it's across the street from the bodega. Are you friendly with them?"

"I know exactly who you mean. They're kind of old-school guys. I walk by every morning and when I say hello, they say hello. They're not looking for trouble or even attention because they're doing their thing, selling drugs, whatever. When I first moved in here I asked a friendly older African American guy about them, and he said: 'They don't bother nobody and *you* certainly don't have to worry about them because they know if they mess with you, a white guy, the police are going to come flying out of the sky and they're gonna have a big problem.'" John's right. They won't bother him because of who he is, and also because he's local and knows who they are. The conversation is further revealing because it's clear that the African American man regarded him as different because he's white and therefore likely to be treated better by the cops. But he tells this to John, thereby reminding John of the difference between him and the locals in general, despite his having moved here. The African American man simply saw it as a fact of life in a racially stratified world. John also has his own view of where he lives and the challenges it poses.

"Now up in the other direction of the block, on the next corner, there's this younger group that's much more dangerous. They could be horsing around with each other and I come walking by. One of them accidentally/on purpose pushes the other one into me and suddenly I'm in an awkward position. I can't ignore it but to respond angrily could cause a fight, which they might want just because they're bored and I'm not one of them."

"So, what do you do?"

"Well, here's where it pays big-time to be a New Yorker. I don't let myself get into this position. When I see them hanging around I cross the street right away and in that way I'm not in their line of vision. That's why you have to be alert when you walk around here." John is a sophisticated city-dweller, as is clear from this exchange. That's why he can survive in a neighborhood like this. Someone from a small town in the Midwest wouldn't be so aware of the surroundings and would be far more likely to have problems here. John has made a choice. He'd rather have the nice house and convenient subway ride to Manhattan than live in complete safety elsewhere in a small apartment. And this isn't the only disadvantage. John confides: "It's just me and my wife. I would never raise children here.

I mean, what schools would they go to? What play dates could they have? And they could never play alone on the street."

John is an early gentrifier at best. Those who come later, if they ever do, won't have his problems because their group will be much larger. Another reminder of where he resides came in the form of a man who was drunk, standing outside his home late one night and demanding that John sell him some drugs. It turned out that the previous occupant had been selling weed and this person didn't know the man had moved away. These encounters vividly portray what it's really like for outsiders to live here. I thank John for his valuable insights and move on.

I turn right off Woodycrest onto E. 165th Street and take a detour down to Jerome Avenue, where I make another right and soon come to the Park Plaza Apartments at number 1005. This is probably the best-known Art Deco creation in the Bronx. Its most exciting characteristic is a series of polychrome or glazed ceramic terra-cotta representations on the facade, with very bright colors— orange, blue, green, silver—and unique designs that include a sunrise, ostensibly over buildings in the Bronx, flamingos standing by a fountain, and a rendering of the Parthenon. An architect is bending forward, almost in supplication, toward the Parthenon as he cradles a design of one of his buildings. To the side, several animal heads jut out of the wall, seemingly gazing upon those entering the building. The inside is decidedly less remarkable, but it looks better than when I last saw it about five years ago. Because of the exterior, if you only have time to view one Art Deco building in the Bronx, this is the one. And it's right across the street from the new Yankee Stadium!

Returning to Woodycrest Avenue via 165th Street, I make a right onto the avenue and take a quick look at the Nelson Avenue Playground. It's a nifty little place, which has ten humorous-looking representations of green-painted frogs emitting streams of water for the pleasure of frolicking children, who are visibly enjoying this version of a spray shower. And there are some other folks having a good time here. One Jamaican man wearing green Kobe sneakers is dancing with reckless abandon on a concrete table used for chess games, and he's quite good. The music is coming from a large radio on a bench, where two female friends of his are recording it on their iPhones for posterity. Others in the park are cheering him on or, like me, giving him a thumbs-up. This impromptu exhibition demonstrates that people can provide their own entertainment if there's not much happening around them. Incidentally, the park attendant pays no attention to the man dancing on the chessboard.

Continuing up Woodycrest, I pass a low-slung housing development for low-income tenants with an unusual admonition in large letters on a signboard: NO in large letters, with three lines next to it on the right—NO standing, NO loitering, and NO kidding! It's also under twenty-four-hour camera surveillance. Woodycrest merges with Shakespeare just beyond 168th Street. Here I take a look inside the Highbridge Public Library. One of the oldest in the Bronx, it has been renovated since I last visited it in 2011. The librarian, Margaret Fleesak, allows me to spend some time in the inner sanctum, where old photos, books, articles, and unpublished manuscripts about the Bronx are arranged in an uncatalogued collection. It's a treasure trove of memorabilia, and browsing through it I realize how much it does to enrich our understanding of how different the Bronx was in those days, how its people lived, and what mattered to them. I glance at a black-and-white photo of Ogden Avenue and W. 170th Street. What is a busy commercial intersection today was farmland and woods a century ago. It makes one really appreciate whatever has survived until now—apartment buildings, schools, churches, businesses, and so on—though not farms, I'm afraid.

We think of those who settled here and throughout much of the Bronx in succession as the Native Americans, followed by the Dutch, the British, the revolutionaries who became the Americans, the white ethnics—Irish, Germans, Italians, and Jews—and today, the Hispanics, African Americans, West Indians, and Africans. But here, in the library, I read in an unpublished, typescript about an obscure, but fascinating exception. There was a residence called Townsend Poole Cottage, built in 1782 on Macombs Road near Featherbed Lane, in what is today the Mount Eden section, but was most likely Highbridge in those days. During this time the Bronx had fewer people and was not divided into as many neighborhoods as today, when the population is much more densely concentrated. Here, reportedly, for a short time, lived a family of Inuit, who were brought to New York in 1896 by the famous Arctic explorer Rear Admiral Robert E. Peary, to be interviewed and examined by the American Museum of Natural History and who were thus treated more as human subjects than as human beings.

The noted anthropologist Franz Boas reflected the times when he asked Peary to bring back an Inuk for study after one of his Arctic expeditions. Peary outperformed, shall we say, returning with six Inuit. Also mirroring prevailing attitudes, the *New York Times* referred to them as "unfortunate little savages," who, trying to keep cool, "were a source of amusement to several scores of visitors." But their situation was not amusing in the least. They soon succumbed to illness, probably either the flu or tuberculosis, and four of them died, and their remains were acquired by the museum. One of the two remaining Inuit was returned to Greenland. The only one left was a young child named Minik, who was adopted by William Wallace, the former superintendent of the museum's building. He and his wife, Rhetta, doted on Minik. They lived in an apartment on W. Tremont Avenue and sent him to Public School 11 in Highbridge. Peary came in for heavy criticism for bringing Inuit here as "specimens" for research when he must surely have known that their chances of surviving in this environment, with diseases against which the Inuit had no immunity, were very slim. Minik became New York City's only Inuk and called himself Mene Peary Wallace.

According to various sources, Minik attempted to retrieve his father Qisuk's skeleton from the museum's administrators. They denied being in possession of the remains. They were motivated, according to one historian, as was Peary, by a desire to protect the admiral from scandal. This much-honored explorer had received a gold medal from President Theodore Roosevelt. Although he was married, he also had fathered two children with a married Inuit woman. Minik, who had attended Manhattan College in pursuit of a career as a civil engineer, made no headway in his efforts to obtain custody over his father's remains and returned to his native Greenland, declaring that he would never set foot again in the United States. His parting public statement, expressing his anger, was: "You're a race of scientific criminals. I know I'll never get my father's bones out of the American Museum of Natural History. I am glad enough to get away before they grab my brains and stuff them into a jar." Minik did return to this country in 1916, attempting to spark interest in his cause, but no one cared about his predicament, and in 1918 he died a lonely death in New Hampshire, where he had worked as a lumberjack. It was the Spanish flu that killed him, as it did so many others.[24] More people died from the Spanish flu, an estimated twenty to forty million souls, than lost their lives in World War I. A popular rhyme then, to which children skipped rope, was:

I had a little bird,
Its name was Enza.
I opened the window,
And in-flu-enza.[25]

Minik is long dead, but his efforts did eventually bear fruit. In 1993, seventy-seven years later, the museum belatedly sent the Inuit remains to Greenland for a traditional burial. Why is this story so important? First, because these stories teach us about how and why powerless groups are often denied justice. They have no lobby, no financial resources, and people know very little about them. Many people who live in New York belong to small religious or ethnic groups, or hail from very small countries such as Paraguay, Uruguay, and Nepal. They cannot protect their rights. Second, it reminds us that history is written by the powerful. When Black people in

America finally achieved a modicum of power, we began to learn more and more about what it meant to be enslaved in this country. It's only by happenstance and determined digging into history that we learned about these Inuit. By coincidence, the Bronx was also home for a while to refugees from tiny Bhutan, all of whom lived in one apartment building on University Avenue. Because people cared, their plight adjusting to America was publicized. The story of the Inuit left me wondering how many other groups who settled in various New York City communities were ignored. These immigrants count too, even if their numbers are minuscule.

Continuing north on Shakespeare, I make a left at E. 168th Street and take a look at number 139 on the corner of Nelson Avenue. It was once a great Art Deco apartment complex, called Noonan Plaza. Today it's rundown and occupied by poor people, who are friendly enough but are really down and out. Because the building was landmarked, the landlord must make improvements but is not permitted to change anything that would alter the fundamental structure. For example, bricks that fall off must be replaced with nearly identical bricks. In its heyday, the courtyard garden had a waterfall that flowed into a pond filled with goldfish, water lilies, and swans. Dainty Japanese bridges spanned the pond and the apartments were quite opulent. But today, there's no sign that anything of the sort was ever there in the courtyard. This is only worth a visit if you want to see how much things here have deteriorated.

My next stop is the Union Reformed Church at 1272 Ogden Avenue between 168th and 169th Streets. It's a truly impressive house of worship built in 1887–1888 for the Protestant community that resided here. The style is Richardsonian Romanesque, which contains elements of eleventh- and twelfth-century Italian, French, and Spanish styles. It has round arches, short broad columns and cylindrical towers. Union has a bell tower and squat columns, and the materials are rock-faced ashlar, with red trim. The rose window is made of Tiffany stained glass. I stop in and meet Reverend Cora Taitt, the pastor, a lovely African American woman, who was raised

Highbridge Community Church

in Alabama and has some excellent photos of what happened in Selma, Alabama, hanging on her office wall.

"We're called the Highbridge Community Church and belong to the Reformed Church of America. We don't have many Hispanic members because their needs are met by local churches. Most of our congregants are African American or African, quite a few from Nigeria," she informs me. I stand inside the interior and it feels very serene. The pews and timbers are in good condition and the stained-glass windows are very pretty and colorful, covered by a slate roof.

I ask Pastor Taitt about Selma, and she tells me: "I was born [and] raised in Selma, but I wasn't there for what they called Bloody Sunday, when they marched over the Edmund Pettus Bridge and were viciously beaten by Sheriff Bull Connor and his officers. The pictures were given to me by the Bronx Museum of the Arts on the Concourse." We continue exchanging stories about the civil rights movement, and then I ask her, "What's your biggest challenge?"

"I don't know. I guess it's to be seen as the church for this community, to find ways to connect with them. We do outreach programs. Vendors work with us, checking blood pressure and the like. It's a challenge but this is our mission." It is, indeed, difficult to be a Black Protestant minister in a large Catholic Hispanic community. But they only need several hundred people to be a success, and maybe through the efforts of this dedicated woman, that will happen. Across the street is the Highbridge School, or Public School 11, founded in the late nineteenth century and the very school that Minik, the Inuk, attended. The design, Romanesque Revival, is outstanding, with a tower and a mansard roof, to boot, and the building appears to be well maintained. Worth a look for those visiting in this vicinity.

MORRIS HEIGHTS

UNIVERSITY HEIGHTS

BELMONT

FORDHAM

BEDFORD PARK

NORWOOD

KINGSBRIDGE

RIVERDALE

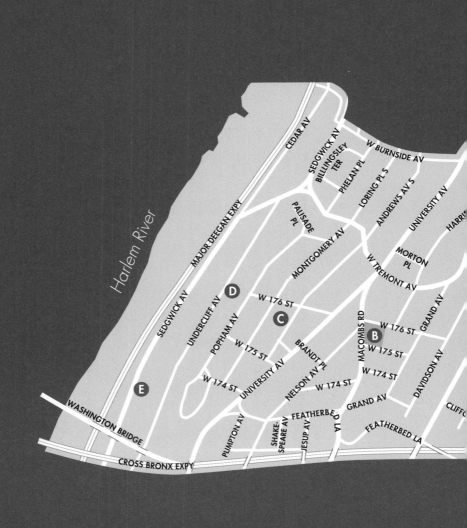

MORRIS HEIGHTS

MORRIS HEIGHTS, WHICH ACQUIRED ITS NAME from the Morris family, whose members raised cattle in this area during the nineteenth century, is by no means a wealthy community. Nor is its neighbor, University Heights, with which it shares a common history. It was home to Fordham Manor, built in 1751 by a Dutch settler who received permission from the British to do so. The British, who called the area Fordham Heights during the Revolutionary War, captured a number of American-built forts there to protect themselves, and it was only renamed University Heights after New York University moved most of its campus there from Greenwich Village in 1894. Public transportation made it possible for developers to build housing, thereby attracting people who wished to escape from overcrowded tenements in Manhattan to both communities. These were mostly Jews, Irish, and also other nationalities of European origin. As these groups then moved out to the suburbs, they were replaced by poorer Blacks and Hispanics, who remain the dominant groups. The ethnic mix today is similar in both communities, but University Heights is notable for having the largest number of Vietnamese and Cambodian immigrants in New York City. At one time, forty families from Bhutan lived on University Avenue in one building when they first arrived in this country, but they have relocated elsewhere in the city as well as to different parts of the United States.

Half of Morris Heights' residents live below the poverty line, as attested to by its numerous NYCHA projects. And yet, grim as parts of the community appear, it also has some very picturesque blocks, augmented by the hilly terrain and winding streets, plus more than a few nice private homes and Art Deco and Art Moderne buildings. The area between the Grand Concourse and Jerome Avenue with E. Burnside Avenue on the north is not clearly defined as belonging to either the Morris Heights or Tremont communities. For various reasons—general fit, walkability, economics, history, and geography—I have chosen to treat it here as part of Morris Heights. In line with this, the boundaries of Morris Heights are Burnside Avenue on the north, the Grand Concourse on the east, the Cross Bronx Expressway on the south, and Sedgwick and Cedar Avenues on the west. The major thoroughfares are the Grand Concourse and Jerome, University (a.k.a. Dr. Martin L. King Jr. Boulevard), Burnside, and Tremont Avenues. The last two have the prefix of East or West, depending on whether they are on the eastern or western side of Jerome Avenue.

I start my walk at the intersection of E. Tremont and Morris Avenues, heading north on Morris. The block between Tremont and E. 179th Street features historic homes that are almost identical. This is most likely an economic decision, since homogeneity is cheaper to construct. The houses are made of reddish and orange brick, but the stone parts are beige in color, a nice combination that exudes warmth. They're bow-shaped to allow for more light and sun and the doors are arched, with quoins on the sides of the stones. On each side of the doors are carved stone faces of men with mustaches and chubby cheeks. The buildings, now landmarked, were erected between 1906 and 1910. The target group, after the 1904 extension of the IRT line, was people looking to escape the lower-income communities in Manhattan. Most settled in apartment houses, but there were also those who could afford to purchase two-family row houses and did so.

I speak with a middle-aged Hispanic man named Raymond, who lives in and owns one of them. He's sitting on the steps in front of the house, enjoying a warm sunny afternoon, with low humidity.

"These homes are really gorgeous, and many of them are well maintained."

"I'm selling. I'm getting rid of it. The whole block," he adds, laughing. "I'm in real estate, and I'm lookin' for people like you."

"Do gentrifiers come here to buy?"

"They're coming because they'll soon run out of room in Brooklyn and Queens. In Manhattan, these would go for five million. Here, $700,000, at least now. Of course, they might be afraid of the neighborhood." Transportation is ideal, with the number 4 train well within walking distance. Part of the problem is that these homes only run for one block, not enough to constitute an up-and-coming community. The rest of this community is mostly apartment buildings, and the private houses are nothing like these in terms of quality. By comparison, the Longwood Historic District in Hunts Point has perhaps ten times as many homes to choose from.

Continuing north on Morris, I turn left onto E. Burnside. At Walton Avenue, I turn left and on the southwest corner find myself staring at a very unusual and intriguing mural on Walton Avenue immediately south of Burnside. It's actually an anti-gentrification cartoon strip, very well done. Interestingly, this is a poor area where gentrification is unlikely to occur anytime soon, if ever. Called "Tales of the Swarm," it features the villainous Dr. Dor, depicted as a "financial exterminator" with giant muscles, bent on killing the local residents, who are represented as a swarm of bees in the mural. In one panel, the bees are fleeing the hive as it's being sprayed.

The next panel presents a giant beehive with the bees underneath, with the cartoonist declaring: "Go my hipster-mites, gentrifying these honeycombs with your appropriation and privilege. Give rise to your condos and coffee shops!" "No," the bees chant in unison, "Not a Whole Foods!" Clearly, the gentrifiers are the hated enemy. And then a rejoinder: "The Royal King Bee will never let the swarm disappear." But underneath, Dr. Dor yells, "Even you can't stop gentrification," as he continues spraying them. The final panel depicts an epic physical battle between the gentrifiers and the people intent on preserving the community.

Why this tremendous hostility in a neighborhood unlikely to gentrify anytime soon? Perhaps because the poorer residents are renters and cannot profit from selling their homes. Instead, they are likely to be forced out. Improving the community isn't worth it for the locals if they cannot afford to remain. And then there's the fear of the unknown, especially of people who are culturally different and far better off economically, people who will want nothing to do with them. Plus, the inexpensive bodegas will be replaced by fancy emporiums and places where coffee is four dollars a cup instead of seventy-five cents. True, the area may become safer, but crime is a reality they've learned to live with. Tremont isn't the only community where resistance is occurring. East New York residents are also very much against gentrification. Both areas are impoverished and have thousands of people living in NYCHA housing. There's an insularity deep in these communities that encourages a kind of perverse solidarity. The author of this visual narrative is identified as www.titonaura.com and can also be reached at 646-894-6811.[26]

On the corner of W. Burnside Avenue at Jerome Avenue, there's a joint advertising two slices of pizza with a can of soda for only $2.75, and a pie for $8.75. Not surprisingly, the line is out the door, and demand ensures that it will be freshly made. Burnside is loaded with inexpensive shops of all kinds, selling clothing, housewares, and grocery items. It's very noisy and crowded, with a vitality that makes you feel the place is jumping with excitement. People are talking loudly, teenagers are laughing in the company of each other. Vendors are hawking their wares with unbridled enthusiasm. Several stores, like the Accra Restaurant one block west on the corner of Burnside and Davidson Avenue, signal the existence of an African community, which has a strong presence throughout the western and central Bronx. An unhappy reminder of the darker side of this area can be discerned from the numerous R.I.P. signs dedicated to the memory of gang members and victims of gang violence—displayed separately, of course—more than a few of whom were cut down in their teens or early twenties.

I turn left on Harrison Avenue and discover a street with very pretty private homes made of brick, along with apartment buildings. Now multifamily dwellings for the most part, they were once home to well-to-do people who have long since departed. This is in contrast to the far more modest housing stock in the South Bronx where the less wealthy tended to gravitate. Also, the arson that gripped the South Bronx didn't happen here to the same degree. On Morton Place between Harrison and University Avenues (the latter now also called Dr. Martin Luther King Jr. Boulevard), the entire block consists of well-kept red-brick attached homes, with a very valuable perk—private parking behind high iron fences. Street parking is at a premium in this crowded community and obviously not as safe, with car break-ins fairly common.

One fact of life here is that the West Bronx is very hilly, with steep, curving streets that weave back and forth to reach the heights that are so common here. Alternatively, many streets have steep flights of stone steps, sometimes the equivalent of six stories, that must be climbed to reach the next block. Art Moderne and Art Deco buildings are very common here, though many plain apartment complexes coexist with them.

I hang a right at W. Tremont and then turn left onto Macombs Road. One block later, at W. 176th Street, I enter Galileo Park. How nice, I think, that this famous explorer-scientist has a playground named after him. I'm even more pleasantly surprised when I see

Galileo Park

what was done to commemorate his achievements. The playground has concrete spheres of all the planets with their names carved into their granite surfaces, and each one is painted a different and often fitting color. Thus Mercury, the hottest planet, is painted yellow and Mars is red. Saturn is much larger than the others, with a silver ring girding it, and Pluto is the farthest away from the rest, as it is in the real universe. It's well known that Galileo was persecuted for asserting that the planets revolved around the sun, not the other way around. Chiseled into the ground at the playground's entrance is this famous man's full name, Galileo Galilei. Galileo was born in 1564. That's also when Michelangelo died and Shakespeare was born, a truly odd coincidence.

From Macombs Road, I veer right onto Nelson Avenue, which begins here. One block south, I walk right onto Brandt Place, cross King Boulevard and proceed a few yards left and then right onto Tenney Place, which, in one minute, dead-ends into Andrews Avenue South. Turning right, I see, across the street, a well-maintained apartment building, number 1665, with the words, engraved into the concrete in block letters above the entrance, "WITH GOD'S LOVE ALL THINGS ARE POSSIBLE." Inside the lobby at number 1665 are some gorgeous wall hangings made from canvas, with designs of people, birds, butterflies, and the building itself. It's affordable housing, with one-bedroom apartments going for about $1,400 a month. Next to it, on the right, is Hayden Lord Park, an amazing private space that belongs to the residents of the two buildings on either side of the park.

According to Nicole, who works with the realty company that owns the building, the park was built, in part, to memorialize a child who became ill and died at an early age. Framing the entrance are several pillars covered with hundreds of light-colored mosaic tiles and likenesses of animals, flying birds, and swimming fish. Off to the left are curving serpentine structures that are actually contoured and comfortable benches completely encrusted with tiles. On the walls of the two buildings, facing the park, are murals of painted geometric shapes. I see gardens with flowers growing within star-shaped beds. And there's a stone wall in the rear with glass bottles of various colors inserted through it.

The thick rubber floor of the playground area is blue with yellow stars everywhere, alongside a rendering of the solar system. There's a gazebo with a ship's wheel inside for kids to turn, with large round boulders off to the side for them to climb. Near the park entrance is a sitting area with brightly painted benches that look like the camouflage that soldiers sometimes wear, only the colors are red, blue, and yellow. It is a stupendous place and I urge everyone to visit it. Describing the individual parts of this Garden of Eden doesn't really do it justice. It's the totality of it, the way all the parts and their placement within the large space harmonize with each other when you look at the benches, gardens, walls, outcroppings. And it's how the setting sun shines through the apertures of the tiled walls, thereby giving it the appearance of pieces from a rainbow. If you're lucky, someone will open it for you. If not, it can still be clearly seen and appreciated from the outside.

Heading north on Andrews Avenue, I turn left on W. 176th Street, where I soon come to Popham Avenue. Looking left and right from the intersection, I see a number of pretty brick private homes, most of them fortified with high iron fences and bars on the first-floor windows. It's yet another reminder that the community isn't safe, which is a paradox because much of the West Bronx, including Morris Heights, appears safer on the surface than Morrisania and other parts of the South Bronx. But that's because the original living spaces here were built for a higher-income population, and also because the South Bronx lost so much more of its housing stock than the West Bronx. Thus, the West Bronx has much nicer buildings and houses that are still standing, though many don't look as nice on the inside.

Popham Avenue is where 176th Street ends. To go farther west one must descend the equivalent of perhaps six stories, which I do, emerging on Undercliff Avenue. I turn around and look up the stairs to Popham and am treated to an incredible view. The back of each step has large X's set against a riotous mix of colors—blue, yellow, green, and orange on each of these hundreds of steps in a wonderful geometric design that's literally dazzling. Readers may want to look at my Instagram entries of Morris Heights to see both the steps and the park with mosaic tiles described above, by entering @nynobodyknows.

Undercliff had an unsavory reputation in the mid-2000s as a street where a gang had taken complete control of it, prompting an outcry by residents and a piece in the *New York Times* on the subject. When this happens, the offending gang simply moves elsewhere. To me, however, judging from those hanging out on Undercliff and conversations with locals, there are still some gang members here. Crossing the avenue, I walk down some more flights, take a roundabout route, and end up on Sedgwick Avenue, which runs parallel to the Major Deegan Expressway.

On Sedgwick I go left and, in a few blocks, pass by some nice old Tudor-style homes, numbers 1620 and 1622, semi-attached and made of brick and stucco. They look out over the Major Deegan Expressway, but also over Upper Manhattan, namely Washington Heights and the Manhattan portion of Highbridge Park. A short distance farther I arrive at my destination, 1520 Sedgwick, where hip-hop originated in 1973. In the mid-eighties and nineties, the place had deteriorated, but today it's been rehabilitated, so to speak. It's a tall red-brick apartment building featuring affordable housing, which happened after a long fight with developers. While there's no discernable physical evidence attesting to its important place in music history, this block of Sedgwick Avenue has been co-named "Hip Hop Boulevard" by the city. DJ Kool Herc unveiled hip hop here at his sister's party in 1973. Members of the Cold Crush Brothers, who formed a group in 1978, and Grandmaster Flash of the same era reportedly were also at the party. Hip-hop has been tremendously influential as a music genre, and I feel like I'm looking at history when I stand here.

I walk up Sedgwick, trot back up the stairs—an aerobic trip, I might say—and go left onto Montgomery Avenue off 176th to W. Tremont Avenue. Then it's left one block to Phelan Place. There are several nice homes, but my attention is drawn to where Phelan Place and Billingsley Terrace intersect, on the right side of Phelan. I look up and see a Roman-style apartment building with some unusual aspects. A large turret sort of hangs from the right side near the top, with a narrow spire crowning it. Squares painted in a gleaming gold hue, are on portions of the building from the ground floor to the top story. These and other doodads, like a large, white-painted curved arch at the entrance, give me the impression that the builders decided to do whatever their heart told them to do and to hell with symmetry or convention. And so ends my visit to this community, one that is definitely among the more unusual ones to visit and savor.

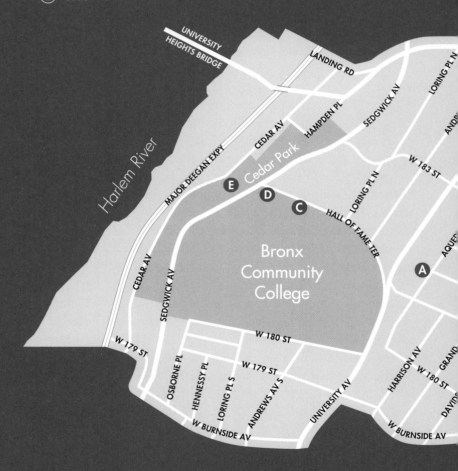

(A) Aqueduct Walk
(B) St. Nicholas of Tolentine Church
(C) Gould Memorial Library
(D) North Hall and Library
(E) Cedar Park

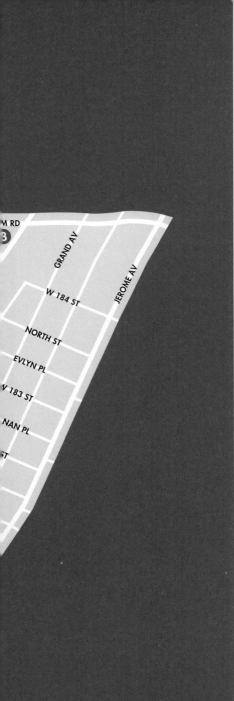

UNIVERSITY HEIGHTS

THE HISTORY OF UNIVERSITY HEIGHTS is the same as that of Morris Heights, as they are really part of the same area. Today, however, they have evolved into distinct communities. The boundaries of University Heights are W. Fordham Road on the north, Jerome Avenue on the east, Burnside Avenue on the south, and Sedgwick Avenue on the west. I begin my jaunt by walking from south to north, starting with Burnside Avenue and ending at W. Fordham Road along Davidson, Grand, and Aqueduct Avenues, located between Jerome and University Avenues (a.k.a. Dr. Martin Luther King Jr. Boulevard—a good decision, but we'll stick with the more common "University" usage). This is the "guts" of the community. It's one old apartment building after another, interspersed at times with frame houses that have definitely experienced far better days. There's really not much to see here, but one does emerge with an understanding of what a plain utilitarian part of this city, which has many of them, looks like. There are also some new, simple buildings, nice but not elaborate, packaged as affordable housing. Jerome Avenue consists of auto repair shops and other small enterprises, fast-food joints, and small stores catering to the population's daily needs. It doesn't feel particularly safe or unsafe, and the most ubiquitous aspect is the bodegas on almost every corner, attended to primarily by Yemenis who have learned how to be friendly to ethnic groups whose members they've never met before coming to this country.

The one exception is Aqueduct Avenue, which has a park running alongside it, sometimes on one side and at other times on both sides. Generally, it consists of a promenade equal to the second side of a normal street, but broad enough to allow people to walk along it, even ten abreast, which some residents actually do. At times the promenade takes center stage, with houses on each side. Several playgrounds are present as well as sitting areas. Even on a weekday at noon, many people are taking advantage of the seating, having lunch, grilling, chatting, or playing ball, just like in a regular park. It extends for about eight long blocks between W. Burnside Avenue and W. Fordham Road. Built in the mid-nineteenth century, the Croton Aqueduct, forty-one miles from the city, carried water to the Big Apple by gravity, traveling about 1.86 miles per hour. Therefore, this street is aptly named, as the water ran along Aqueduct Avenue and then continued under the southern portion of University Avenue.

At Fordham and University Avenues I look up at the tall and stately St. Nicholas of Tolentine Church, built in 1927, and operated under the auspices of the Augustinian Fathers. Gazing up at its stone Gothic twin towers, it's easy to see why it has been dubbed "the Cathedral of the Bronx." Like so many houses of worship in the old Bronx, it faced a choice—adapt to the changing times or simply disappear. St. Nicholas adjusted rather nicely, and services today are held in English, Spanish, and Vietnamese. Architecturally, both inside and outside, it's beautiful and dignified in an old-fashioned sort of way. The stained-glass windows, vaulted ceilings, and marble floors are exquisitely done. The side streets to the west,

Aqueduct Walk

Loring Place North and Andrews Avenue North, have some well-constructed buildings, but nothing outstanding. Continuing south on University, I pass old apartment buildings, some of which sport nicely designed friezes. They look a bit better than those on the side streets, but not by much.

At West 181st Street, I go left to Grand, turning right. Midway down the block I pass a mosque. It's Friday afternoon and Eid al-Fitr, an important Muslim holiday signaling the end of Ramadan, is being celebrated. Worshipers of all races and nationalities pour out of the mosque, as services have just ended. Many are wearing white kufis, the hat of choice for most African Muslims, but also worn by African Christians and Jews. Others are of Bangladeshi, Yemeni, and Pakistani origin. They greet me in friendship and smile in greeting. I cross the street and in two minutes am standing outside a church at number 2112, which has a very unusual approach to Christianity. Located in a semi-attached, three-story brick house, with a metal cross hanging outside, it's called the Ecclesia Catolica. And on the announcements board outside there's an intriguing statement. I've written about this before, but the story merits retelling for anyone walking this area because it's just so interesting. I've also learned more about it since then. I speak with Father Delfin's wife and grandson, and I'm invited inside to see what it looks like. Here's the statement on the signboard:

> On Thursday, September 25, 1997, at 7:11 A.M. the Most Holy Virgin Mary appeared to me and said: "You are St. Delfin the First. Do you know who I am? I am Mary, Mother of Christ. I know that my Son visited you and that he proclaimed you the Second Savior and Messiah for your love of the black, the white, the yellow, the mulato, the American Indian and I am with you now and always. Any blessings will I give for all who believe in Jesus and in you, my second most beloved son."

This is followed by a schedule:

Exorcisms, Friday, at 8:30 P.M.

Sundays, Holy Mass, (one in English and then one in Spanish.)

Everyone is Welcome. The Reverend Father Delfin Rodriguez, Rector

Delfin has been dead for many years. Yet the story of how he became a special holy figure remains on the board, almost as if it were frozen in time. It speaks of a time when this man was vibrant and alive. I talk with a Black woman sitting in a small van outside, a lifelong resident, and ask her what this is all about.

"His wife carries on, but they just have a few people that come sometimes on Sunday," she tells me. "He was a nice guy who helped people a lot. He had a long white beard and was always in white attire."

"Did you believe he was, like, a real saint?"

She pauses, choosing her words carefully, it seems: "I believe there was something special about him. Like, whenever you needed him he was there. And whenever people walked by the house where the church was, they might have remembered him."

The woman passes no judgment on the truth of his claims to be a saint. But in the long run, she seems to feel it doesn't matter. What counts is that he was a good soul who cared about others. Therefore, there's no desire to challenge his assertions. Who can know the truth about such things anyway? A man has a dream. There can only be one version of what happened in it—his own. And we can choose to believe or disbelieve it. As for the story itself, it's highly unusual. There aren't many exorcists in New York City's communities. What isn't unusual, however, is the ubiquitous presence of community characters in general. In a sense, this is a historic landmark, albeit one not formally recognized.

I speak with the imam across the street. He also recalls Delfin and says, "He was a holy man, very kind and wise. I wish all Christians were like him, and if they were, the world would be a more tolerant place."

I return the next day and chat with Delfin's wife, a small, dainty Hispanic woman who lets me into the church. It's in good condition, with small wooden pews and a place in front for worshipers to approach the saints that overlook it. Tears well up in her eyes as she reflects on him and what he meant to her, but she speaks very little English. Her grandson is with her and I ask him if he remembers Delfin.

"Yes, I do. He was a great man, I know, but I was a little scared of him as a seven-year-old. When he did those exorcisms. I was afraid to go into the church. But I loved him, and I know he loved me." Perhaps this isn't as strange as it sounds. Exorcisms are rare within the Catholic Church and widely frowned upon, to say the least. However, the *New York Times* reported on a two-day conference held in Baltimore on how to deal with it. The reason? There are many people out there who believe they have been possessed by the devil and see this as a way to relieve their suffering.[27]

As for me, I find myself wishing that I could have met and had a conversation with him. It's a not unusual feeling for me because cities are dynamic in so many ways, forever changing. What remains are stationary reminders that outlived those who created these places, be they buildings, restaurants that ceased to exist, or whatever. Of course, in this instance at least, the sign is still there, intact. By contrast, many murals last a few years and are then replaced by buildings or simply erased by new owners of the space. I also think about how much less I would have learned about Delfin had this Black woman not been there or had I decided not to interact with her.

Retracing my steps, I return to 181st and University, cross the street and continue up Hall of Fame Terrace to the entrance for Bronx Community College (BCC), where I explore the campus. Formerly the home of New York University's uptown campus, which sold it to BCC in 1973, it feels like an endowed private institution. It was designed in 1892 by Stanford White, who was the architect for some of the city's most famous buildings, such as Madison Square Garden and the Washington Square Arch. The quad is broad and surrounded by impressive buildings, the central and most memorable of which is the old Gould Memorial Library, meant to recall the Pantheon in Rome. It possesses a rotunda with sixteen green marble columns, and a reading room under a grand, coffered dome. But this has been here since 1900. Less known is the new library, called the North Hall and Library, and created by the famed architect Robert A.M. Stern. This latest addition to the campus is well worth describing and seeing.

In a way, this building is a continuation of White's project, since he designed the quad and the buildings and Stern's new edifice is meant to harmoniously blend in, which it accomplishes almost seamlessly. The yellow- and cream-colored bricks used in the old days could not be obtained, but other Roman bricks similar in hue, in alternating shades of orange, beige, and gray were substituted. The cast-stone trim matches that which adorned the earlier structures. Inside are a coffered ceiling with white pilasters set against the white walls, and herringbone-patterned floor tiles. Very modern, comfortable, and brightly lit classrooms are scattered throughout the building.

The library is on the second floor of the building, where I enter into the breathtaking reading room. The bookshelves are on the level above the central reading room and the lampshades on the wooden tables remind me of how the New York Public Library looks. The tables, chairs, and Ionic columns with a Greek key design are made of rich wood, with large windows that sit within bronze-colored frames. They are configured to allow in light, while at the same time maintaining some degree of shade. Couches, comfortable loveseats, and easy chairs allow library users to relax if they so desire. The reading room and main stair landings feature numerous paintings by the Bronx artist Daniel Hauben. Most are about the Bronx: street scenes, including one of Morris Avenue; the Highbridge section; renderings of the old and new Yankee Stadiums; a subway traveling through the Bronx; panoramas of the borough. It's a great display from a truly talented artist. Incidentally, the building adheres to the city and state requirements for sustainability and reduction of gas emissions. The technology is digital and state-of-the-art wireless.

I walk around the right side of Gould Library where I take a short trip through the Hall of Fame for Great Americans. The first "hall of fame" in the country, it dates back to 1900. Its emphasis is not on celebrities but on people whose accomplishments have withstood the test of time. In fact, the most recent entry is former president Franklin Delano Roosevelt. Arranged in a semicircle and resembling a Greek stone colonnade, it consists of ninety-eight bronze sculptured busts. Although their names appear beneath their likenesses, anyone who knows what these people looked like will have no problem whatsoever identifying them simply by studying their faces. They're arranged by category—physicians, politicians, judges, artists, military people, and great teachers. Each section has a diamond-shaped floor tile denoting the group that is memorialized, surrounded invariably by interlocking herringbone tiles. Some famous examples are Robert Fulton, Alexander Hamilton, Nathaniel Hawthorne, Thomas Edison, Booker T. Washington, and Thomas Paine. There are also individuals who are less well known, such as the clergyman William Ellery Channing, the actress Charlotte Cushman, and the inventor Elias Howe, plus many more. It's worth spending some time here if only to discover why these merited inclusion in this august pantheon. Finally, the setting is really scenic because you get a breathtaking view of the lush woodlands below this high point and of the Harlem River.

My meanderings end in an unlikely setting, a park of sorts called Cedar Park, but also known as University Woods. It's located just below the college between Sedgwick and Cedar Avenues at the western end of Hall of Fame Terrace. Having achieved the dubious distinction of being deemed "New York City's worst park" in terms of safety and upkeep by New Yorkers 4 Parks, an advocacy group that aims to improve parks, I wanted to personally learn why. As I'm about to walk in, I meet an older white man with crystal-blue piercing eyes, walking two pit bulls. With flowing white hair, and of slightly above average height, he has a small paunch. Despite that, he still looks fit and trim. He's stylishly dressed, like someone who either has or once had some money, in a nice button-down light blue oxford shirt, belted light-khaki shorts—Bermudas, neatly pressed—and black sneakers with no socks. Let's call him Sean, since he says, with a quick laugh, that his name wouldn't mean anything since no one's ever heard of him. He's a longtime resident of the immediate area.

"Hey, I want to walk around this park. Is there anything worth seeing here?" I ask.

He looks at me in surprise and asks, rhetorically: "Are you kidding? It's a major meeting place and hangout for prostitution and drugs. Are you a New Yorker? I mean, do you know that a walk like this might well be unsafe, depending on who you meet?"

"Sure," I say in a macho way. "I grew up in the 'hood, 105th Street and Columbus Avenue. I've walked everywhere in tough areas, even at 1:00 a.m. in East New York on a Saturday night."

"Well, I don't mean only that. It's a shortcut from Sedgwick to Cedar. But it's dirty, neglected, and very unappetizing. Why would you want to see it? And why would you want anything to do with these disgusting people who sell drugs to kids and their bodies to anyone who wants them? You know, it's a shame. This park was once beautiful. It was put together in the 1930s by Ukrainian workers. There used to be an old fort here from the Revolutionary War."

"Well, I'd like to see it because I'm writing a book about the unknown places in the Bronx, and without going in, it remains unknown to me too. I mean, the Web says they received a $500,000 grant from the city in 2008 to refurbish it."

"Well, that's not enough to fix a park of this size. That was courtesy of Bloomberg." He's right about that. If Di Blasio gave more money, I can only say that the park is in terrible condition in 2018. Sean and I begin strolling on an asphalt walkway, which is pockmarked and cracked. The woods are full of poison ivy and weeds, and the grass is long, with tangled branches everywhere. It's noontime, and I spy two teenage girls from a local public school who are just hanging out, talking, and eating sandwiches. They certainly aren't dangerous, but I do appreciate Sean's point several hundred yards farther in. I spot another teenager. His clothes are seedy, his hair is unkempt, and he sizes me and my friend up, retreating to a boulder just off the path and a vantage point from which to attack or escape into the thick woods. I approach and say hello.

"You guys ain't cops, are you?" he asks, eyeing me suspiciously.

"No," I respond, laughing heartily. "We're the farthest thing from that. If we're cops then they need a new department!" Deciding I'm telling the truth he reaches behind his back, grabs a small pipe that he must have hid when he saw us coming and starts smoking some weed, an odor I easily recognize. I say, "Have a blast toking up," and we continue on our way.

Before he retired, Sean was a career employee for New York State. He grew up and lived on the Upper East Side, moving to University Heights twenty years ago because one could get more living space for one's money.

"I hated what the shopping was turning into," he says. "It had all these small stores where I used to shop and where I knew everybody. And then they began to disappear in a big way. They were building chain places everywhere, impersonal, and so the whole feeling of community went away. I like neighborhoods. I also like cheap. There are two drug dealers in my building a few blocks from here, and I know both of them."

"Do you ever walk around here at night?"

"Not if I can help it. It's not safe. I'm the only white guy on the block."

"Do you ever get lonely for people you have things in common with?"

"What, other white guys?" He retorts, laughing. "Look, I have friends who live in Westchester and Riverdale and in Midtown. If I want to get together with them, it's ten, twenty minutes away. Of course, I never come home at night."

Sean doesn't fall easily into any category. He's really one of a kind, eccentric but not weird, out of place yet someone who has a place in which he has made a life for twenty years. He's not a community character, but he's a character in the community who minds his own business—not your Jane Jacobs eyes and ears on the street and by no means a community activist. His tastes have an aesthetic attraction. Though he tells me the park might be filled with unsavory characters, it's clear that more than being criminals they turn him off because they're physically unappealing. To say they're not his type would be quite an understatement.

Sean's a graduate of an excellent private college, and he dresses well with a certain flair, especially considering this is a down-at-the-heels part of town and it's a weekday. His adopted pit bulls are not necessarily vicious, and I see them more as a Yorkie or French bulldog type. When he says "I like cheap," I think to myself that aside from preferring the shops he grew up with, he might not be able to afford large living quarters, with only some savings, a part-time job, and a state pension. Thus, finding a bigger place might be worth it if that's what's important to him. Obviously, while he has friends in the area, he doesn't at all miss not having them in the immediate vicinity.

Summing up, when you put it all together, it doesn't fit—and that's precisely the point, because New York City is a haven for thousands of oddball types who don't fit the mold and who thrive in a big cosmopolitan city like this, which prides itself on not giving a damn about such things. That's a group that few, if any, sociologists have studied. One might call them deviants who fall somewhat short of being defined that way, and yet are somewhere on the continuum of deviance.

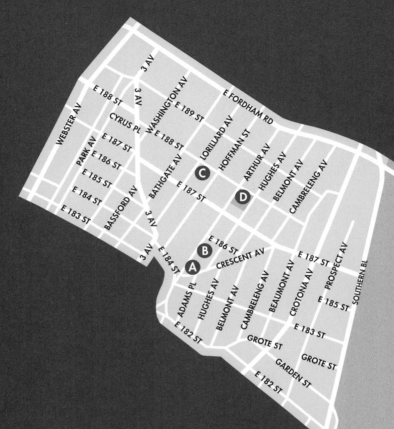

3 AV

E 188 ST

3 AV

WASHINGTON AV

E 189 ST

E FORDHAM RD

WEBSTER AV

CYRUS PL

E 188 ST

LORILLARD AV

HOFFMAN ST

PARK AV

E 187 ST

ARTHUR AV

HUGHES AV

BELMONT AV

CAMBRELENG AV

E 186 ST

BATHGATE AV

E 187 ST

Ⓒ

Ⓓ

E 185 ST

E 184 ST

BASSFORD AV

3 AV

Ⓑ

E 186 ST

E 183 ST

Ⓐ

CRESCENT AV

E 187 ST

PROSPECT AV

3 AV

E 184 ST

ADAMS PL

HUGHES AV

BELMONT AV

CAMBRELENG AV

BEAUMONT AV

CROTONA AV

E 185 ST

SOUTHERN BL

E 182 ST

E 183 ST

GROTE ST

GROTE ST

GARDEN ST

E 182 ST

Bronx

BRONX PARK S

Ⓐ Kosova Deli

Ⓑ Arthur Ave. Retail Market

Ⓒ Lorillard House and Ann Devenney House

Ⓓ Ciccarone Park

DHAM RD

ark

BRONX RIVER PKWY

E 180 ST

BELMONT

THE BELMONT SECTION OF THE BRONX is well known to millions of people. And yet it is totally unknown to millions of other people, and they include many New Yorkers and millions of tourists who visit here. Since it's a living community with demarcated streets, it seems reasonable that it should be included in this book, though not in great detail. Those who are unfamiliar with it but are interested in exploring the Bronx should give it top priority as it is quite unique. The boundaries are E. Fordham Road on the north, Southern Boulevard on the east, E. 182nd and 183rd Streets on the south, and Webster Avenue on the west.

Until the 1880s, the area consisted of estates and farms. Subsequent to that, streets were built by the city and the Third Avenue elevated was extended to Fordham Road. Italians came to the area at the turn of the twentieth century to help construct the buildings for the zoo and botanical gardens. They were also employed to develop the landscaping for these attractions. They settled in the nearby Belmont section in numbers so large that it came to be called the Little Italy of the Bronx. In the 1980s, many Albanians came to this area.

While the neighborhood around it has a high crime rate, Belmont is to this day a very safe place except for the sections around Southern Boulevard on the edge of the community and in the west, between Bathgate and Webster Avenues.

What makes this area even more important today in the larger sense is that the Little Italy in Manhattan has shrunk to about one block. So this is now the largest such center. People, especially Italian Americans, flock to the restaurants here, especially Dominick's, Roberto's (a standout with a 27 Zagat rating), Emilio's, Ann & Tony's, and others that might not be as well known but are still pretty good. These can be found, for the most part, on Arthur Avenue between E. 184th and E. 188th Streets, and from Lorillard Place to Hughes Avenue along E. 187th Street. Incidentally, the street was named after former president Chester Arthur at the request of Catherine Lorillard Wolfe, a philanthropist who owned property in the area and was a great admirer of the man.[28]

On Arthur Avenue I stop in front of the Kosova Deli at number 2326, specializing in items from Kosovo and Albania. It's really the same foods and culture, since Kosovo was once part of Albania. Hanging in the window is the red Albanian flag and next to it are two çiftelis, a two-stringed instrument popular in Albania and Kosovo. Today, Kosovo is considered an independent state by most countries and has large Albanian and Serbian populations. Inside, the store is stocked with delicacies from the region, especially cheeses and meats. It's neat and clean and very enticing. Once almost exclusively Italian, Belmont now has a large Albanian population and is sometimes referred to as "Italy-Albania." There are, in fact, Albanian eateries, pastry shops, and social clubs. The Albanians are also heavily involved in New York's pizza shops in all the boroughs. In the not-so-distant future, they will be the dominant group, if they aren't already.

There's even a Jewish representation, Teitel's, at 2372 Arthur Avenue, which has been here for over a century, since 1915. Sepia-toned photographs outside the store featuring the owners and their families convey what life was like in those days. Modern color photos of the families portray what their descendants look like. The entrance has a small outdoor floor made up of the old-fashioned, small hexagonal tiles. They're white, but in the center lies a star of David, made of red hexagons. Teitel's has gone big now and sells its products on the internet all over the United States. They've adapted, like everyone else who wants to stay in business.

A few doors down at number 2344, I enter the Arthur Avenue Retail Market. Outside, there's a wooden Native American statue with an ad in front reading: "Cigar Rollers for All your Events: Weddings, Baptisms, Corporate, etc." The cigar rollers themselves, Dominican men, are seated in front behind a counter, rolling cigars and smiling shyly at the customers or simply gawkers. It's a very large market with a skylight running the length of the emporium and long thin fluorescent lights beneath it. One area serves pastries, while another has wooden tables to eat on. Exotic Italian cheeses and meats like veal tongues, duck legs, and pig's feet are displayed at several counters, in windows and hanging from beams overhead as well, seemingly competing for space. There are olives in barrels, and fruits and pastas of all kinds. It's like an indoor mall and must be seen to be fully appreciated.

The streets in the neighborhood around the commercial thoroughfares have many well-tended one- and two-family homes. Many date back to the days when this was a thriving Italian residential community.[29] Today, the population is increasingly Albanian, and even some of the Italian restaurants and cafés are now Albanian-owned. In short, this area survived the deterioration of the Bronx. It attracts many tourists, though probably more come from places like Long Island, Brooklyn, and Queens than from far away, largely because it's a place insiders know about and may even have come from. There are gentrifiers living here, as well as longtime older Italian residents, many of whom are looking to sell their homes and the modest-sized apartment buildings they have owned for decades.

Arthur Avenue Retail Market

There aren't only restaurants here. There are professionals with offices too, like Justin Ippolito, a dentist, whose shingle hangs outside his office. Clearly, they serve the residents. It is both a community, as attested to by the bocci court in the local park, and a tourist destination. The area is decorated with Italian and American flags, and there are banners proclaiming it to be "Little Italy in the Bronx. The Good Taste of Tradition." The buildings are well maintained and preserved. Like in Manhattan's Little Italy, with its San Gennaro Festival, the saints are also brought into play here. There's the Feast of Saint Anthony at Our Lady of Mount Carmel Church, held in June, with an annual procession, also featuring games, rides, raffles, amusements, and, of course, the trump card, "the best food anywhere." In addition, there are musical performances by such favorites as the Bronx Wanderers.

Yet for some, even this isn't enough to justify a long trip to the Bronx. A woman visiting from Brooklyn approaches me and asks, "You from around here?" "No." "What's there to see around here? It's just restaurants and stuff. This is my first and last time here. I could go to Mulberry Street in Manhattan; it's much closer." She has a 2:30 reservation at the well-known Mario's. Her reaction is not so bad for business here as it might seem, because tourist areas count many one-time visitors among their clientele. If enough come, it's still okay.

There is also a sizable contingent of Fordham University students who have settled here, in the Arthur Avenue area, at least while they're in school. The university lies only a few blocks away, on the other side of Fordham Road. Since the area around the district is lower income, with a significant crime rate, just as it is around Columbia, there are shuttle-bus stops to be found at strategic central locations, usually outside residences with student apartments. One such place, Lorillard House on Lorillard Place and E. 188th Street, is a very old two-story brick building with a porch and white columns, or pillars. Attached to it, on the left, is the Ann Devenney House, number 2428. Devenney was a community organizer who devoted her life to preserving and beautifying her neighborhood. Outside are stone pineapples, the traditional welcome symbol that proliferates throughout the city. There's a booth in front for a security officer next to a sign announcing that the shuttle bus stops there.

Finally, there's Ciccarone Park, located on E. 188th Street between Arthur and Hughes Avenues. It's a pretty oasis in this crowded neighborhood. Its bocce court was opened in 1934. Teams from the United States Bocce Federation compete there in an annual tournament held in the fall. Surrounded as it is by so many Italian restaurants, it's said to be the only place in the country where you can play bocce between courses, or at least after dessert.

Belmont is obviously an exception to the prevailing state of affairs in the south-central Bronx, with its impoverished communities still struggling to emerge from decades of destruction and neglect. Why is this so? The Italians who came here built a strong community and refused to run when things hit the fan, so to speak. Put simply, they fought physically to keep what they had built up. Those who entered the community with bad intentions knew that robbers and muggers would themselves be attacked. By contrast, the Jews who inhabited this same part of the Bronx, and who through education became upwardly mobile, were less apt to make a last stand. They had options to move to safer areas in the Bronx or to the suburbs. Many Italians did leave, but there was another group of tough, determined immigrants who moved in during the 1980s—the Albanians. They also fought to keep their turf, even as they did battle with the Italians to wrest control of the area from them too. Today, the two groups coexist, having learned to get along with each other. Given the aging out of the Italians, the Albanians will probably become more dominant as time passes. There's much more to be said about this and on the topic of gentrification, which is also touched on below, but not in what is essentially a walking guide.

Can this community gentrify? There are forces against it, most notably transportation. The Bronx has excellent subway lines, but none of them are really near this area. In addition, the Italians and

Albanians are very family-oriented, and they tend to pass on property to their own kind. They are willing to sell, but only at a high price. Unlike Bensonhurst in Brooklyn, an Italian enclave that is succumbing to a very large influx of Chinese and, to a lesser degree, Russian immigrants, those populations are absent here. The rental apartments are most often snapped up by the many Fordham students, whose university is only a few blocks away. Perhaps it will happen someday, but not until there's so little available housing in Brooklyn and Queens that gentrifiers have no choice but to look elsewhere. As is the case with Mott Haven, entrepreneurs are purchasing properties here, betting that it will increase in value someday if the gentrifiers come. On the other hand, until that happens, they can make enough of a profit from other renters.

Harlem River

BROADWAY BRIDGE BROADWAY

BAILEY AV

W KINGSBRIDGE RD

HEATH AV

W 193 ST

MAJOR DEEGAN EXPY

HEATH AV

BAILEY AV

SEDGWICK AV

Kingsbridge Heights

WEBB AV

UNIVERSITY AV

WEBB AV

DEVOE TER

AQUEDUCT AV

W 192 ST

DAVIDSON AV

E 193 ST

E KINGSBRIDGE RD

FR ZEISER PL

W 188

GRAND AV

W 190 ST

JEROME AV

St. James Park

E 192 ST

C

BRIGGS AV

POE PL

D

BAINBRIDGE AV

LANDING RD

W FORDHAM RD

E 191 ST

E 190 ST

E FORDHAM RD

WALTON AV

MORRIS AV

CRESTON AV

GRAND CONCOURSE

A

RYER AV

E 188 ST

TIEBOUT AV

ELM PL

MARION AV

WEBSTER

VALENTINE AV

E 187 ST

B

E 184 ST

(A) World Changers Church

(B) Memory of Wilson mural

(C) Poe Cottage

(D) Bronx Blockbusters

(E) Gothic University Church

(F) Fordham Museum of Greek, Etruscan, and Roman Art

FORDHAM

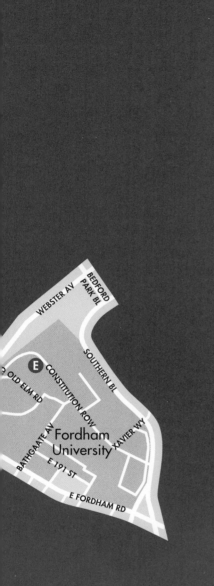

FORDHAM'S ORIGINS DATE BACK TO 1671, when a Dutch settler, John Archer, purchased 3,900 acres of land here from the British who controlled the general area until after the Revolutionary War. The name, actually Fordham Manor, may have come from a Bronx River crossing that people had to "ford" to cross from one side to the other. Much of the land was part of what is today the Rose Hill Campus of Fordham University. The boundaries of Fordham are W. 225th Street, Kingsbridge Road, and E. 194th Street on the north, Webster Avenue and Fordham University on the east, 184th and 183rd Streets and W. Fordham Road on the south, and Bailey Avenue on the west. The area west of University Avenue (a.k.a. Dr. Martin Luther King Jr. Boulevard) to Bailey is also known as Kingsbridge Heights. This neighborhood also extends into a small portion of the Bedford Park community.

Fordham expanded with the arrival of rail service in the nineteenth century, and much more so with the Third Avenue Elevated (i.e., the Third Avenue El) and similar rail lines along the Grand Concourse and Jerome Avenue. From the early twentieth century until the late 1960s, the predominant groups residing here were Irish, Jewish, and Italian. These groups departed after the community became more heavily African American, West Indian, Puerto Rican, and Dominican. Since the dawn of the twenty-first century, Mexicans and Africans have moved here in greater numbers.

I begin my sojourn through Fordham along the Grand Concourse. Here, on the west side of the street, halfway between 184th Street and E. Fordham Road, is what was once the home of Loew's Paradise Theatre. It was one of the five "wonder theatres" created in the 1920s by the architect John Eberson. Among the many stars who once performed here were Bob Hope, Al Jolson, and George Burns. Set in the facade of a very ornate building made of beige stone is a huge sign—Loew's Paradise—against a blue background with rays of the sun radiating outward. Around it are balustrades, a large impressive clock with Roman numerals, shields, crests, garlands, urns, and large Corinthian pilasters.

Today it's the headquarters of the World Changers Church, based in Fulton County, Georgia, with services held both in English and Spanish. The lobby has three ceiling domes with large painted murals on them. Because of its landmark status, the church has not changed them substantially. The interior, with its almost four thousand seats and grand stage, still retains an aura of grandeur from the days when it was a theater. The best way to see and appreciate this magnificent edifice is to visit, as I did, during services on a Sunday after 10:00 a.m. Be prepared to hear some sermons and lots of gospel music. For those who can't make it on that day, there are services on Saturday night as well.

To live in a bad community is to live in a world whose concerns probably seem surreal to outsiders, but they are real nonetheless to its residents, as the following exchange with a Bronx man reveals:

"Why does that house down the block have all the iron bars around it, top to bottom?" I ask.

"It belongs to an Indian guy from I don't know where, Guyana or Pakistan."

"Why does he live on the block, imprisoned like that? That's not a life."

"Because he owns three quarters of the friggin' block. He's protecting his investment."

"Does he also have to come to an agreement with the gangs here?"

"Everybody does. It's a matter of unspoken respect and understanding. He has to come around and have papers signed and shake hands. And the gangs know that." And so, in the end, you do what you have to do to survive.

This is by no means the only reason for bars on windows or doors. It's interesting that on the same block one house will have bars covering its windows from the first floor to the top floor, giving it the appearance of an impenetrable fortress, while another home directly across the street has no iron bars protecting it whatsoever. Do the unprotected just refuse to worry about being burglarized? Do they simply find it too distasteful to live behind bars, almost as if they were in a prison of their own making? Are they unable to afford to purchase protective bars? Are they powerful people whom others will not mess with? Do they have differing perceptions of crime? Are those with the "fortress look" drug dealers protecting their stash, or people making it hard for enemies to attack them, or both? Any one or more of these is possible. In addition, these days the bars on homes could even be an ode to earlier days when the community was much more dangerous, although a good number of people have been removing them as the city has become safer.

There are still parts of the city that have stubbornly resisted all efforts to make them safe. There's a police crackdown—the cherry-picker truck with the NYPD logo is a telltale sign—crime ebbs, the police leave, and a month or two later crime goes up. One such pocket is in the Fordham section. At E. 184th Street, I cross the

Concourse and head east and am soon at Tiebout Avenue where there's an old Verizon building. Here, on Tiebout itself, I gaze upon a large, intricately drawn, and fascinating gang mural that adorns the brick wall. Such portraits are ubiquitous throughout the city's more dangerous parts, but this one's special because of its complexity and the quality of the artwork, and because it ends up not being exactly what it appears to be. Since the corner is quite dangerous, I strongly recommend that it be viewed from the inside of an automobile and even avoided if one doesn't feel comfortable being here altogether. For those individuals, and for folks who want to experience the Bronx from the vantage point of an armchair, the description will be of interest to them. It reads as follows:

To my beloved husband Wilson.
Your love I miss every day of my life.
For all I have now is those precious memories that will always
be in my heart forever.
For I know we lived together in happiness and will rest to-
gether in peace.
Your Wife, Mitzi

It has not been defaced at all and is co-signed by many people, who are identified as family members. There are no fewer than thirty-five names up there—Emily, Joshua, Robbie, Sergio, Olga, Yvonne, Papo. These are all given names, and I initially think of this as an exception to the gang member murals, with their usual R.I.P.s. How nice it is, I reflect, that a woman, her children, and her extended family chose this way to memorialize her life partner.

But then I see a list of people on the right under the words "The Shirt Boys CC Mob," who have also signed on to this. The mural contains entries for "The 184th Street Posse," "The 156th Street Beck Boys" (probably Beck Street), and the "L.A. Boys, West Coast." So, I realize it is almost certainly a gang mural, and there's apparently a national support group as well. Altogether, the names of gang members and affiliates on the mural number about twenty-five people. These are likely gang names, so it's certainly not a simple personal family presentation. The gang and the family are combined into one large grouping. I soon discover that this assessment is on the money.

According to Verizon employees, the company has a tacit understanding with the local gang: the mural stays and the gang leaves the workers alone. That's the price of doing business in the city, and they are far from the only ones to cooperate in such a manner. Businesses of all types throughout the city have similar arrangements, though employees are understandably reluctant to acknowledge them. Reportedly, management will sometimes even give bonuses to people—one referred to it as "urban pay"—to entice them to work in highly unsafe communities.

In an interesting twist to the story, I learn from some local residents that Wilson was apparently a gang leader who reformed in "mid-career," so to speak. He became a businessman who ran a T-shirt company and helped local kids stay out of trouble, and he died in an automobile accident, not in a hail of gunfire or a stabbing. This reveals that one shouldn't jump to conclusions purely based on what it says on a mural, because sometimes there's more to the story.

Heading north on Tiebout, I come to E. Fordham Road, the community's main commercial street. The epicenter is two blocks to my left, where E. Fordham and the Grand Concourse intersect, home to a P.C. Richard, a Marshalls, and other shopping emporiums. This hub has been so for many decades. When I was a kid, the main department store on the corner was Alexander's. Heading east from there, down a hill, one passes many chain stores—Rainbow, Falla's, Dr. J., Foot Action, Zales—just like 149th Street in the Bronx, Jamaica Avenue in Queens, and Pitkin Avenue in Brooklyn. There are pawnshops, convenience stores, and fast-food offerings of many kinds. There's even a tiny triangular oasis with benches, called Bryan Park, near E. Kingsbridge Road, that provides a respite for tired shoppers.

Just beyond the park, I turn left onto Bainbridge Avenue and then left again onto Coles Place. To my right, a very short distance ahead, is Poe Place, a somewhat long dead-end block. It's one of the many byways that reveals the "guts" of the city. All of the houses—two really old apartment buildings, one supported by an ancient-looking stone wall, and a group of modest houses, mostly multifamily—have their "backs" to the street, if you will. On the right, it's Bainbridge, and on the left, Briggs Avenue. Unless one wanted to enter a structure via the back way, there'd be no reason to even walk here. As I explore it, I see garbage strewn about: bottles, empty corrugated boxes, papers, pieces of wood, with nails protruding from them, and so on. The walls of the houses are in fair condition at best, and the porches and balconies all have items on them, brooms, broken tricycles, and flimsy stools and chairs that seem to have been put there because they fall into a gray area—not really worth keeping, but not yet ready to be thrown away. In short, they're inanimate commentaries on how life progresses, often indecisively, with fits and starts rather than the orderliness that better describes the fronts of homes, how people wish to present themselves to the outside world. It's the hidden side of the city that we don't often see unless we happen to come by. This would probably not have been Edgar Allan Poe's first choice of a street named after him.

Why Poe to begin with? Because this is near where he lived for a brief, yet important creative period in his life. Returning on Bainbridge to Fordham, I make a right and then another quick right, walking up one block on E. Kingsbridge. Here, on my left, is Poe Park, which runs along the Grand Concourse on its western border. It's not a big park, but within it lies what has been named Poe Cottage. The writer moved here in 1846, along with his wife, Virginia, and her mother. This is where he penned three of his most famous poems, "Ulalume," "Annabelle Lee," and "The Bells," which many believe refers to the church bell at Fordham University. He lived here until his death in 1849, while on a visit to Baltimore.

Poe Cottage

The cottage has a certain charm about it, and Poe was reportedly very happy to be there. Today, you can visit this restored dwelling, courtesy of the Bronx County Historical Society and take a tour of its rooms. There's a visitor's center, which has perhaps the cleanest restrooms of any park in the Bronx.

From here, I turn right onto E. 194th Street and walk downhill to Bainbridge. This quiet-looking corner is anything but quiet after 6:00 p.m., because it's a notorious hangout for drug dealers. Possibly the city has cleaned it up since my last visit. What this usually means is that the dealers move elsewhere, only to return, in quite a few cases, when the heat dies down. But this reality doesn't tell the entire story, for in densely populated urban spaces, other often-salutary activities or places—Poe Cottage being but one example—coexist in the same locale, albeit a five- or ten-minute walk away. One short block south of the corner on Bainbridge there's a very attractive community garden. It's being tended on this day by a garden member, an older Jamaican woman, who loves what she does and is eager to share.

"Let me show you around this Garden of Eden. Its real name is Bronx Blockbusters. Here's a little garden in memory of a child who passed away at birth. The family lives in the neighborhood. Look at what we're planting and growing here. We have perennials and, look, here's a plastic flamingo who has done his time. He's been here quite a while. We grow tomatoes, peppers, collard greens, callaloo [spinach-like leaves], mints, strawberries, figs, grapes."

"Why do people like to do this?"

"First of all, it's food. Second, these gardens remind us of the countries we came from and where we lived in small towns and villages in the Caribbean lands. We also have an Easter egg roll every year and birthday parties, and little concerts." Her description demonstrates the many ways in which the gardens serve the community, besides providing flowers and food products, that one wouldn't be aware of from just passing by—Easter egg rolls, concerts, memorials, parties. But there are challenges too. First, making it all happen requires organization and hard work. Second, there's vandalism. The woman tells me about how teenagers from a bordering apartment building once lowered a ladder into the garden and damaged it.

There's also a television film being shot here, titled, *The Other Two,* and the signs announcing its presence are everywhere. This is definitely not good for the drug dealers who obviously prefer living under the radar. Another film was made here several years ago using a local home as a haunted house. As I've learned from personal experience, the outer boroughs are of great interest to location scouts searching for authentic old buildings, whether tenements or brick row houses.

About three hundred yards down the block, at 2569 Bainbridge, I come to a private home with several large Mickey Mouse dolls and blow-ups. It reminds me of a friend who has made it clear that she collects anything and everything with a Mickey Mouse in it. Sometimes, when my wife and I travel, we see an item and bring it back for her. At first glance it appears that she has a like-minded soul here, but I soon learn, the reason for it is entirely different. A man clad in blue shorts and a T-shirt is sitting on the porch, fiddling with a small kids' truck. It turns out he's a licensed daycare provider and this is one of his three centers, all of them called Carmen Torres Group Daycare. This center is on the first floor of his four-bedroom home. The house is over a hundred years old and is painted in vivid colors, with several small Corinthian columns supporting the porch overhang.

Rene Torres, a good-looking, jovial man in his early sixties with a gift of gab was raised on the Upper East Side of Manhattan in the Carnegie Hill section and formerly lived on the Upper West Side. Of Puerto Rican origin, he was born in New York.

"Why did you move here?" I ask him.

"More space for less money," he responds.

"What kind of work did you do before this?"

"I was a doorman for a hospital before retiring. I liked it, but I wanted to do something else."

"By the way, why did you choose Mickey Mouse and not Donald Duck?"

"It's all about marketing. Mickey sells best." He gives me a business card and a postcard-sized glossy announcement about the Jose Caraballo Art Gallery, which also happens to be in his house. Caraballo's works have been exhibited in a major Manhattan hospital, at El Museo del Barrio, and the Museum of the City of New York. Rene also owns property. He is clearly a very enterprising individual who combines business with doing what he loves and believes in.

I return to Fordham Road, and turning left, make my way to Fordham University, which begins just east of Webster Avenue. I've placed it in the Fordham section because it has a history in this community, dating back to its founding in 1841, although it borders other communities too, like Belmont. It's a gorgeous campus with traditional Gothic buildings and more modern structures. One of them, the beautiful Gothic University Church, has stained-glass windows, a gift from King Louis Philippe I of France. The altar that was in Old St. Patrick's Cathedral is there too. This church, built in 1809/1815, is located at 260–264 Mulberry Street in lower Manhattan. It was the seat of the Roman Catholic Archdiocese of New York until the present Saint Patrick's Cathedral opened its doors in 1879. The sloping grassy areas and the campus quad are magnificent and have the feel of a university that's far removed from the city. It was, in fact, featured in several films, including *Love Story* and *A Beautiful Mind.* Since it's out of the way, deep in the Bronx, it's not nearly as well known as Columbia, and for those who've never been here, it's eminently worth a leisurely stroll.

I'm here primarily to see the Fordham Museum of Greek, Etruscan, and Roman Art, housed inside the Walsh Family Library.

It's filled with artifacts, 280 of them in all, from these classical cultures—busts, urns, vases, cups, mosaics, statues, even a toddler's sarcophagus. The collection spans eight hundred years, beginning with the fourth century BC. I was especially taken by a tall, colorful Greek water vase from the early Hellenic Period, circa 333 BC, decorated with a female head set within an elaborate floral field, all very complex in its design. It's inside the third glass-enclosed exhibit on the left when you enter. This terrific collection is open to the public at no charge.

Leaving here after a quick nap in the shade of a spreading tree, I walk up Fordham to the other side of the Concourse, hanging a right at Creston Avenue and proceeding to St. James Park, a nice place, certainly more than adequate, with decent tennis courts and playgrounds. Noteworthy is a fitness center with cycling equipment, and films and concerts open to the public.

I walk up Jerome Avenue to W. 192nd Street and turn left. It turns out to be a small pocket of detached, pretty well-maintained brick homes, a good number of them one-family dwellings with tile roofs. The same is true of Davidson Avenue, going up to W. Kingsbridge Road. Grand Avenue is also attractive, though not on the level of 192nd Street or Davidson. I do see some very unusual, differentiated, and lively stone representations of lions in different poses in front of a large multifamily, white-painted home on Davidson. The section beyond University Avenue toward Bailey is very hilly, and some of the buildings there—especially on Sedgwick, Heath, and Bailey Avenues—boast excellent views of the Harlem River. This is also where the large Veterans Administration Medical Center, bounded in part by W. Kingsbridge Road and Webb Avenue, is located.

Heading back to W. 190th and Jerome Avenue, I find myself facing the entrance of Monroe College, a one-block-long no-frills, private, for-profit school. While certainly not as well known as Fordham University and without a penny's worth of endowment funds, it is nevertheless a very special and important institution. With approximately seven thousand students, it has campuses in the Bronx and New Rochelle and in the Caribbean Island of St. Lucia. The Bronx campus offers the full range of undergraduate courses leading to the BA, and the college has graduate programs in business, criminal justice, public health, and other areas. The students hail mostly from the Bronx and other boroughs. Many come from the poorer neighborhoods of the city. Despite their difficult circumstances, they are, by and large, incredibly motivated. For them, this is their Harvard, and that's why it's so important a place. In the lobby of the building, I meet and speak with Jacqueline Ruegger, the director of public affairs, who tells me more about Monroe.

"We probably graduate more Black and Hispanic students than any other college in New York State. We also partner with more than a hundred high schools in the city, mostly in the Bronx, offering an array of wonderful mentoring programs. I hope you can meet our new president, Mark Jerome. We follow an accelerated three-semester program and our students, in effect, get a BA in three years."

When I was last here, I met a student in a nearby vest-pocket park. I noticed a Hispanic youth wearing a gray T-shirt, sitting on a park bench. He's got a shopping cart, inside of which is a large, green plastic garbage bag. "Hey. Ice cold water, one dollar, come get it!" he calls out in a singsong fashion every minute or so. I watch him and see that no one is buying. Out of pity, I stroll over and purchase a bottle from him for a dollar, even though I'm not at all thirsty. He is enormously gratified with making the sale and thanks me profusely. "How do you keep these bottles cold out here?" I ask. "Well, first I freeze them at home. That way they stay cold a long time." "Where are you in school?" "I just graduated high school." "What are you gonna do next?" "I'm going to Monroe College." "For what?" "I'm going to be a rich businessman. It's a great college."

It begins humbly enough with bottles of water, this entrepreneurial spirit. Who knows where the journey will end? And there you have it. This is his horizon. He does not think about an Ivy League university, or even CUNY's Baruch College. This is it, but for him, it's more than enough.

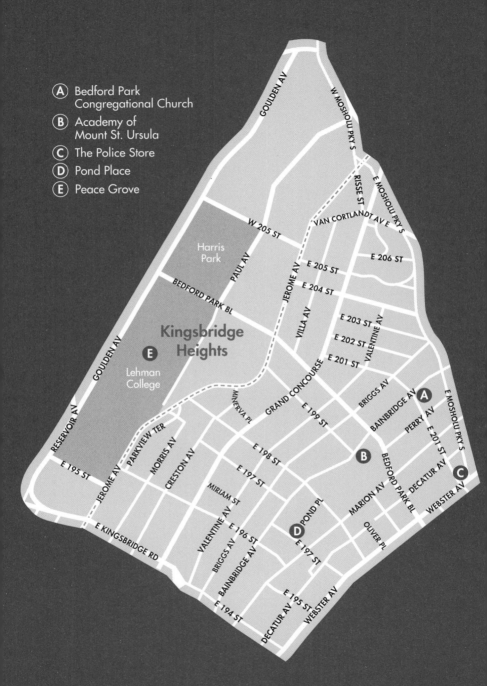

A Bedford Park
  Congregational Church
B Academy of
  Mount St. Ursula
C The Police Store
D Pond Place
E Peace Grove

Kingsbridge
Heights

Harris
Park

Lehman
College

GOULDEN AV
W MOSHOLU PKY S
RISSE ST
E MOSHOLU PKY S
W 205 ST
VAN CORTLANDT AV E
E 206 ST
PAUL AV
E 205 ST
JEROME AV
E 204 ST
BEDFORD PARK BL
VILLA AV
E 203 ST
VALENTINE AV
E 202 ST
E 201 ST
GRAND CONCOURSE
MINERVA PL
BRIGGS AV
BAINBRIDGE AV
E 199 ST
PERRY AV
E 201 ST
E MOSHOLU PKY S
RESERVOIR AV
GOULDEN AV
PARKVIEW TER
MORRIS AV
CRESTON AV
E 198 ST
BEDFORD PARK BL
DECATUR AV
WEBSTER AV
JEROME AV
E 197 ST
MARION AV
E 195 ST
MIRIAM ST
VALENTINE AV
E 196 ST
POND PL
OLIVER PL
E 197 ST
E KINGSBRIDGE RD
BRIGGS AV
BAINBRIDGE AV
E 194 ST
DECATUR AV
E 195 ST
WEBSTER AV

BEDFORD PARK

THE FIRST MAJOR DEVELOPMENT IN THIS AREA was the construction of the Jerome Park Racetrack, which became the first home of the Belmont Stakes. The racetrack was sold in 1890 and the site eventually became the Jerome Park Reservoir. This was where the water from the New Croton Aqueduct was stored. Bedford Park was a planned community whose origins date back to the 1880s. Its name is derived from the town of Bedford, England, and it's one of the reasons why a good number of the houses here have a Queen Anne architectural style and others are Victorian. Its boundaries are West and East Mosholu Parkway on the northeast, Webster Avenue on the east, E. 194th Street and East and West Kingsbridge Road on the south, and Bailey and Goulden Avenues on the west. There's also a small area that's part of Bedford Park, known as Kingsbridge Heights. Its boundaries are W. Mosholu Parkway on the northeastern side, Jerome Avenue on the east, W. Kingsbridge Road on the south, and Reservoir and Goulden Avenues on the west. Incidentally, Mosholu is an Algonquin word, meaning small or smooth stones, which were common in a small creek nearby.

When the subway lines were built in the early 1900s, the area became more developed, attracting thousands of new residents. The predominant groups were Irish, Italians, and Jews. This changed in the early 1970s, as Blacks and Hispanics became the dominant groups. Today, it is home to a diverse population including Guyanese, Bangladeshis, Pakistanis, Koreans, Vietnamese, Africans, West Indians, Mexicans, and Dominicans.

The main commercial thoroughfares of this community are Kingsbridge Road/E. 194th Street, Jerome and Webster Avenues, and Bedford Park Boulevard. Overall, the area east of the Concourse is more upscale than that on the western side. There are quite a few important educational institutions in Bedford Park, namely the

Bronx High School of Science, the Academy of Mount St. Ursula High School, Walton High School, DeWitt Clinton High School, and Lehman College. It's a relatively safe community. The two major parks are Harris Park, which consists mostly of ballfields, and DeVoe Park, smaller in area and used mostly for strolling through a green area.

One of the oldest churches in Bedford Park, the Bedford Park Congregational Church, dates back to 1882. It's on the corner of Bainbridge Avenue and E. 201st Street. It has changed quite a bit since then, in that it is home today to a variety of denominations and groups. There's the Presbyterian Church of Ghana, Iglesia Vida, and the Bedford Park Seventh Day Adventist Church. The very presence of these groups speaks volumes about how the demographics here have shifted. The earlier groups are gone, and the new population must be served. Sometimes, the transition is not as dramatic. The RC Church of St. Philip Neri, on the Grand Concourse and E. 202nd Street, founded in 1900, was always, and remains to this day, a Catholic church. The clientele has changed, however, with Hispanics replacing the earlier group of Irish and Italian worshipers. And they draw a nice crowd on Sundays, as I observed. A stone edifice with Gothic windows, it's in excellent condition, with a beautiful bell tower on top graced by three large bells. Inside, a Procession of the Holy Cross is going on, with the priests and altar boys walking down the aisle, wearing their white vestments. The organ is playing Beethoven's "Ode to Joy" and people are joining in the words. The church has magnificent high vaulted ceilings, with brown wooden beams, gold and red trim around them, and painted floral designs on the surface; exquisite stained-glass windows, and hanging chandeliers. The burnished brown pews shine brightly. In the front section of the church, behind the altar, the walls are a reddish brown, with gold fleurs-de-lis embossed on them. Summing up, this is a classic example of a traditional-style church.

A passerby would likely be unaware of something else about this church: it was once the spiritual home of the family of Joseph Vitolo Jr., born October 29, 1945. When he was nine, Joseph, who lived with his family at nearby 3194 Villa Avenue, a three-block long enclave of Italian-Americans one block west of the Concourse, had a vision. Playing with friends on a rocky hill behind his house that overlooked the Concourse, three passing girls told him they saw something above the hill. He saw nothing, but when they told him to pray, he did; and when he said a Hail Mary, a woman who resembled the Virgin Mary, in a blue dress that turned pink, hovered over the spot and called out to him. When he reported this to his father, he was slapped for lying, but Joey insisted that he saw what he saw. Years later he said: "I was petrified, but her voice calmed me down."

For sixteen nights he came to the spot and recited the rosary, praying as she told him to, for peace on earth. As news spread by word of mouth and through the press, more and more people came to sing hymns, as requested by the vision, and to pray for cures, with some swearing that they had been healed. Even Cardinal Spellman visited, as did Frank Sinatra. More than 25,000 people came, quite a few from far away, on the final night of prayer, November 13, with some claiming to have seen visions in the sky. For young Joey, the attention was overwhelming. He recalled: "People were charging at me, looking for help, looking for cures. I was young and confused."

Vitolo was permanently affected by what happened. Some revered him, but others, especially neighborhood kids, ridiculed him at times, sardonically referring to him as "St. Joseph." He dropped out of high school and studied briefly for the priesthood, but this did not bring the solace he sought. These efforts were followed by a series of menial jobs, the last of which was at Jacobi Hospital, where he rarely spoke about his past. He married, had children, and remained in the house where he was raised, frequently visiting and praying at the shrine. Throughout, he remained faithful to what he saw. As he put it: "I never had any doubts. . . . I know what I saw." In the decades after, thousands of people have prayed at the shrine. The house next door to it, on the Concourse, was purchased by Salvatore Mazzela, who had prayed at the shrine and wanted to protect what he saw as a holy site. He took care of it, planted flowers, and added statues on the walkway, plus a stone with the Ten Commandments engraved on it.[30]

The shrine was never vandalized during the seventies and eighties, when havoc and destruction swept through the Bronx. And when I went there several years ago, that was still the case. Mazzela's house is still there, but it is falling apart, with a number of windows boarded up and a fading wooden "beware of the dog" sign. It appears to be uninhabited. I climb the rickety steps to the home and follow a walkway on the right to what is now called "Queen of the Universe Shrine." No one questions me as I pass the house on the property. There are plastic flowers and also some bouquets with real flowers. A sign reads "This place for praying only." A brief statement recounts the events described above. Anyone interested in visiting this place can do so with relative ease.

Vitolo is not the first one to claim having seen Christ or Mary. In fact, in the University Heights section, there is a discussion of one pastor, Delfin Rodriguez, who reported that Mary came to him in a dream and told him he was her second son. One difference, nonetheless, is that others claimed to have had various visions when they visited Vitolo's shrine. Possibly they were strongly influenced by Vitolo's vision. Perhaps the best-known case of all is that of Bernadette Soubirous, the young shepherd girl of Lourdes who asserted in 1858 that she had seen the Virgin Mary. Eventually she was declared a saint, and the story became known to millions through the Academy Award-winning film *Song of Bernadette*. Not all claimants are so fortunate, certainly not Vitolo himself, but there were other outcomes that had an impact. Though not nearly as well known as Arthur Avenue, Villa Avenue was a strong Italian community, and this put them on the map. They rallied in support of Vitolo, and took great pride that one of their own had brought nationwide recognition to their community. It also served as a symbol of the truth of their faith and its tenets. The Church of St. Philip Neri also derived deferred status since the family belonged to it. Ultimately it isn't only a question of whether it really happened. What counts as well is that people believed it happened, and this changed how they viewed life and how they were seen by others. As for Vitolo, he died on December 17, 2014, a week before Christmas.

Turning around, I head north and soon come to the end of the Grand Concourse. The last building on the east side of the Concourse at number 3224, lies between Van Cortlandt Avenue East and Mosholu Parkway. An imposing red-brick Tudor-style structure, it can only be accessed through a large wrought-iron gate that is locked. It leads into a pretty inner courtyard that features a lush garden and a slate-roof gazebo with steps leading up to it. There are separate entrances to what is a complex of buildings and all of it is landmarked. Across the street, at number 3235, is another charming building, the last on the Concourse's west side. A lavishly decorated light brick structure, which, like 3224, takes up the entire block, its style is eclectic, but predominantly Italianate. There are arches and a band with a floral pattern encircles it. The most stunning elements, tiles, circles, and terra-cotta, are reserved for the top floor, just beneath the roof. The lobby is painted white and the outstanding coffered ceiling is done in colors of blue, green, and red. The pillars have fleurs-de-lis, leaves, and other decorative aspects. Some very well known people grew up there, including Penny Marshall, who played Laverne in the TV show *Laverne and Shirley*, and her brother Garry, creator of the hit show *Happy Days*. The well-known editor of the *New York Times* foreign desk, Bernard Gwertzman, also resided here. These two structures, both dating back to the 1920s, make for a fitting ending to what was once a fabulous boulevard.

From here, I head south along Valentine Avenue, from E. 204th Street down to E. 196th Street. This area on the eastern side of the Concourse is a very pleasant-looking neighborhood, quiet, with well-maintained homes that stand in sharp contrast to the Fordham area south of 194th, which is rougher. The blocks between the 194th

Street border and 196th Street serve as a gradual physical transition between the two communities. On E. 194th, I see a sign on an awning beneath a grocery store that tells the walker something about the ethnic groups residing here. It reads: "African-Bangladeshi-Pakistanis-Middle Eastern-West Indian." These groups come from countries separated by thousands of miles, but what unites them, this being a halal establishment, is Islam.

I walk north on Bainbridge Avenue and pass the grounds of the old St. Ursula Convent on the right, at E. 199th Street, between Bainbridge and Bedford Park Boulevard. The Ursulines were the first nuns to arrive in the New World, in 1639. There are no nuns living at St. Ursula today, reflecting the decreasing numbers of nuns in this country, down from about 180,000 in the mid-1960s to about 42,000 in 2018. But the Academy of Mount St. Ursula high school, founded in 1855, is still open, with about 350 students. It's the oldest continuously functioning Catholic girls' high school in the state.

Yet it has become difficult for them financially to maintain their campus. In a nod to that reality, they have rented out part of their facility to the Protestant New Day United Methodist Church, which I visited on a Sunday afternoon. A service with music and singing was in progress, and I was warmly welcomed. The church's credo is openness, especially to LGBTQ people and members of every ethnic and racial background. I ask them how they get along with the folks from St. Ursula. A man serving as an usher and greeter tells me:

"We get along just fine with them. They might not share our beliefs, philosophy, and practices, but they respect us and are very warm and welcoming. If you just come with your wife for one service, you won't regret it." It's not surprising. In today's times, people are much more tolerant. Forty years ago, renting to such a group might have resulted in a big fuss, but not today, at least in New York City, and not here in Bedford Park, with its population predominantly made up of people of color.

On the north side of Bedford Park Boulevard is the Bedford Park Presbyterian Church, whose worshipers are almost all Koreans.

They have services in English and Korean. The organ is playing and a young woman eagerly welcomes me. There are only eight people in attendance, all of whom appear Korean, singing and then listening to the Korean pastor speak. It's a relatively small space. I ask the woman, "Is this the normal number of people who come regularly?"

"We usually have about twenty-five worshipers. But now it's July and people are on vacation." The church is about one hundred years old, and the Korean group has been here for about fifty years. Their small membership is probably due to large numbers of upwardly mobile Koreans having moved away from here because of the much larger populations in Queens and the suburbs. Today, the Bronx has the lowest number of Koreans, fewer than two thousand, of any borough.

I continue north on Bainbridge Avenue to E. Mosholu Parkway. It's a large six-lane street, with grassy malls and gently sloping parkland between the center and service roads. Walking south on E. Mosholu South, I see, roughly between Marion and Webster Avenues, a sunken meadow with several large trees that is entirely encircled by a wall consisting of round stones, topped by stone pillars. Shielded as it is from passing vehicular and pedestrian traffic, it's a great place to relax in. Driving along the road, one wouldn't even know it exists. On Webster and Mosholu I am startled to see the soccer stadium, called Frisch Field, where, as a small child, I used to watch my cousin Ernie, an all-American college soccer star, play. His parents had lived on Mosholu, and we visited them fairly often.

I head south on Webster Avenue and stop in at the Police Store, on the corner of E. 201st Street, a block from the local police station. Its stock consists almost wholly of the type of items law enforcement officers would purchase. Some, like weapons, are restricted; but others, like police caps, ties, sweatshirts, can be bought by anyone. There aren't many of these places in the city, and usually they're near law enforcement locations. This one sells to police departments both in the city and in nearby Westchester County.

The blocks between Mosholu and Bedford Park Boulevard, from Webster to the Concourse, are some of the nicest ones I've seen in Bedford Park. The apartment buildings are nicely designed and well maintained, as are some private homes. An orange-painted stucco home at 2960 Decatur Avenue is a standout. I speak with a white woman in her early forties, playing with her small daughter and get her take on the neighborhood.

"It's nice but nothing like it used to be. The park on Mosholu is dirtier, and there are people smoking pot in there, and the police don't care. They would rather give out tickets. Look, there are cops in my family. I know. There are many more Hispanics here, but it's still a good area." This is a very typical conversation in the city, demonstrating how people's concerns are mostly local. And what are they? Safety and the police, park maintenance, and ethnic change. Yet, none of these are enough to give the neighborhood a bad rating, as she insists it's still a nice place to live in.

I head down Marion to E. 198th Street, make a right on it, and then a quick left onto a two-block-long attractive street called Pond Place. There are some well-preserved old, brick row houses here. At number 2785, a brick home from long ago has multiple keystones above the windows, and some very pretty cornices near the roof. Another house has an unusual twist, a pair of gold-painted, stone lionesses, not the far more typical males, standing guard in front of a home.

Returning to Bedford Park Boulevard, I head west to the portion of Bedford Park located west of the Concourse. Just after Paul Avenue I turn left through Lehman College's Gate 8 and make a right at the Music Building. It's a very pretty campus, designed with a combination of the old and the new, with classic Collegiate-Gothic buildings, with sandstone colors and mixed in with other modern structures. In front of the music building is a beautiful space below the ground surface of the campus, shaped in a square. There's grass, walkways, and stately trees, and it's called the "Peace Grove," commemorating the fact that the United Nations was on this campus from March to August 1946, with meetings of the Security Council held here. How fitting, since this is a CUNY campus with students from many lands. During this period, the Security Council decided to pressure the Soviet Union to leave Iran, which it did. This gave legitimacy to the fledgling organization of nations.

On the lawn next to the Peace Grove, is the only "official" replica in the United States of the Olmecs, a gift from Mexico to honor Lehman's creation of the CUNY Institute of Mexican Studies. It's a giant version of an Olmec's head and his glowering expression looks a little intimidating, to say the least. Historians believe the statues were representations of their actual rulers. The Olmecs were a pre-Columbian civilization, the forerunners of the Maya and the Aztecs. The original statue that was discovered dates back approximately to 1200–900 B.C. Its place in a university setting is very appropriate since the Olmecs were believed to have made tremendous advances in mathematics and the arts.

Perhaps what's most interesting in a "nobody knows" sense is the college's historical connection to the military. Lehman actually took over the campus in 1968, when it was first established. But before that, from 1931 until 1968, it was a branch of Manhattan's Hunter College, known colloquially as "Hunter College in the Bronx." Until the mid-1940s, only women were enrolled here as students.

During World War II, the college was vacated and the Navy took over the campus, using it primarily as a training facility for its WAVES (Women Accepted for Volunteer Emergency Service) and SPARS (United States Coast Guard Women's Reserve). Altogether about 91,138 women were trained in these programs between 1943 and 1945.[31] But there may be a more clandestine side to this period. Some believe, including employees at the campus with whom I spoke, that the Navy used the WAVES' and SPARS' presence as a cover to place military equipment in tunnels underneath the campus. According to one informant, the tunnels were actually employed to transport cannons and other military equipment from one part of the campus to another, and for storing them where they wouldn't be seen from the air by anyone spying against the United States. In this way, when people would ask why the military was on the campus, military personnel could simply respond, "Oh, the WAVES are training here," and that would end the discussion. I'm not talking only about the standard tunnels at Lehman that students often use to get from one building to another, such as from Shuster, to Carmen, to Davis Halls. Before continuing, it's worth noting that these tunnels are of great benefit to this day for the students and others because people can go through them when it's snowing or when it's very hot. In fact, there are three videos about them.

I went through these subbasements used by students, faculty, and staff but found nothing of interest. But when I reached Carmen Hall, I took the stairs down one more level, to a subbasement directly beneath the above-mentioned one. It was constructed before the more modern one above it and students used it regularly. In fact, given that water from the Croton Reservoir probably went through these pipes, this subbasement was probably in place before the college was even built. For me it was a very surreal, even spooky, experience because of the way it looks. There's a sign outside a heavy door that reads "Authorized Personnel Only." As it happened, a person who works behind the doors let me in and showed me where to walk.

I proceed to ramble through a maze of dimly lit tunnels for a distance of about two miles. Along the way, I pass only one person wheeling a cart, who does not question my presence. I see pipes, many of them corroded, running every which way, along the sides of the walkway and just below the ceilings. Some of the pipes are hissing very loudly, making me wonder if it's really safe to continue my trip, but curiosity gets the better of me. I have the feeling that if I were ever locked in here I would have trouble attracting attention. There are unused light fixtures, and there's a sign on a door reading "Center for Employment Opportunities." It doesn't open and looks very old, judging from the rotting wood on it. Someone seems to have found a great place to put or hide a bike. There are discarded old cabinets and old boilers that look as if they're from the early twentieth century. For those who have nightmares about being lost or chased, this would be the ideal setting. One hallway I walk down is one of the longest straight halls I've ever seen, perhaps four city blocks in all. There are signs pointing to a cafeteria and a mail receiving center, but I don't know how far away they are, on what floor, or even if they refer to places that only existed long ago. There are pieces of old machinery that I can't even describe or explain. Throughout there are small rectangular neon clocks hanging from the ceiling at intervals, giving the correct time.

I leave this area by going up a staircase that leads out, yet bars entry if one is on the other side. So was this the place where weapons or other materials were hidden, rather than the level above? Perhaps both levels were used or possibly neither. Two things are clear. The Navy was in sole possession of the college during the war and could do what it wanted. Second, given the large underground network and useful cover story, it would have been a perfectly positioned location in which to deploy weapons, hold secret meetings, or anything else. Finally, I spoke with Rene Rotolo, assistant vice president for campus planning and facilities, a longtime administrator at Lehman. To the best of her knowledge, the armed forces did store certain materials in the subterranean basements over the years with respect to civil defense in particular, though she doesn't know what all of them were. She does remember the Navy decommissioning a generator in the subbasement beneath Davis Hall as recently as the 1990s.

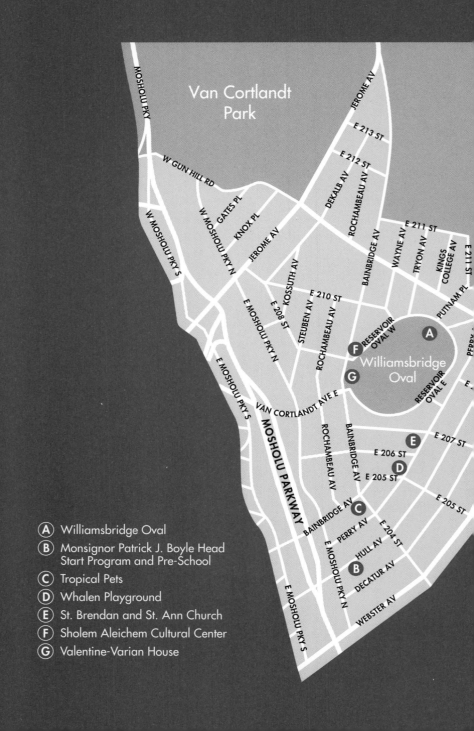

Van Cortlandt
Park

Williamsbridge
Oval

- (A) Williamsbridge Oval
- (B) Monsignor Patrick J. Boyle Head Start Program and Pre-School
- (C) Tropical Pets
- (D) Whalen Playground
- (E) St. Brendan and St. Ann Church
- (F) Sholem Aleichem Cultural Center
- (G) Valentine-Varian House

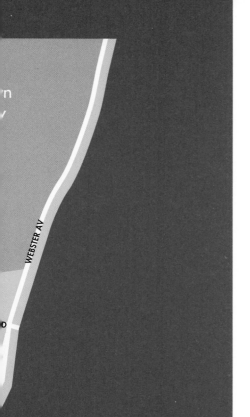

WEBSTER AV

NORWOOD

AN ODD-SHAPED SMALL COMMUNITY, Norwood is bounded, roughly, by W. Gun Hill Road, Jerome and Bainbridge Avenues, and E. 211 Street on the north; Webster Avenue on the east; and Mosholu Parkway on the southwest. The area was first settled by Native Americans, then the British, followed by the American Revolutionaries. Until about 1905, it was farmland owned by the Varian, Bussing, and Valentine families. After public transportation was extended to this part of the Bronx in the early twentieth century, developers constructed homes and apartment buildings. Most of the people attracted to the area were of Irish, Italian, and Jewish descent. Puerto Ricans also began arriving here around World War II and afterward.

From the mid-1970s on, Norwood became home to a number of groups, including Dominicans, West Indians, Mexicans, Ecuadorians, Guyanese, Cambodians, Koreans, and others, but it is predominantly Hispanic. While most of the Jews and Italians had left earlier, there were Irish immigrants, many of them from Northern Ireland, who came here from the 1970s to the 1990s and breathed new life into the dwindling Irish community that was aging out.

In this way the Irish pubs, grocery stores, and restaurants that had served the earlier generations could stay on. The area is perfectly safe during the day and more or less so at night. The major park, Williamsbridge Oval, is a gem. The main commercial streets are Jerome, Bainbridge, and Webster Avenues, and Gun Hill Road.

Williamsbridge Oval is a first-rate park and serves as an important gathering place for the community. Shaped like an oval, it's encircled by a street called Reservoir Oval. It's in the center of the community and fairly small for a city park, about nineteen acres. But the space is organized very efficiently, and there's a lot in it. The centerpiece is a large soccer field, with a running track around it. There are three state-of-the-art, gaily colored playgrounds, and nearby eight tennis courts are open to the public. Basketball courts are on the other side of the soccer field. A skateboard park was also under construction when I visited several years ago. Don't expect much from the dog run, however; it's very small. Kids in a day camp are having a ball, running around and playing under the watchful eyes of counselors. Several teenagers are competing in a hurdle event, with the hurdles set up on the running track. The park is a model of harmony as people of varied backgrounds play and relax together. Older folks are sitting on what appears to be fairly new benches, chatting or reading. There's no debris, and the homeless people who often populate city parks are absent here. It stands in sharp contrast to some of the parks in the South Bronx, which are not well maintained. Whatever space isn't being used for activities is landscaped with trees and shrubs. Inside a stone building there's a recreation center with spin cycling and fitness rooms.

A block away, I walk down the main commercial drag, called Bainbridge Avenue, and then E. 204th Street. There are chain-store outlets like McDonald's, T-Mobile, and Domino's, but also local establishments such as Leroy's Pharmacy and Jerry's Hardware, with some dating back more than forty years. I also see a boarded-up Irish pub, Dwyer's, on E. 204th and Hull Avenue, a reminder that

Ten Commandments above the entrance to the Monsignor Patrick J. Boyle
Head Start Program and Pre-School

this was once a heavily Irish community. Turning right onto Hull
Avenue, I see small homes, but far fewer with bars on them than in,
say, Fordham, Tremont, or Morrisania.

At number 3044, I stop in front of the now gone Mosholu Jewish Center. The sandstone-colored exterior is very well preserved.
It is now the Monsignor Patrick J. Boyle Head Start Program and
Pre-School, run by the Bronx Archdiocese, as well as the Cardinal
McCloskey Community Service Center. The Jewish past is certainly
evident here, with the Ten Commandments and a Star of David,
surrounded by intricately carved pilasters and diamond- and square-
shaped designs on the facade.

There's a plaque to the right of the entrance which reads: "Presented by members of the 52nd Precinct Police Department to the
Mosholu Jewish Center in 1955 at the Community Tercentenary,"
which means three hundred years. In other words, there was a community of some sort, probably Dutch, here in 1655. The synagogue
itself was founded in 1928, and at one time it had thousands of members. Rabbi Herschel Schacter, who was the rabbi here from 1947
to 1999, has a special place in history. He was one of the country's
most influential rabbis, meeting with US presidents from John F.
Kennedy on and chairing national Jewish organizations. Serving as

a chaplain in World War II, Schacter was the first rabbi to enter and help liberate the concentration camps. He walked into the notorious Buchenwald Camp an hour after it fell to the US Army. Not only that, he stayed there for months, helping the survivors find a way back from near extermination and acting as their spiritual leader.

I walk along East Mosholu Parkway North and pass by old five- and six-story brick apartment buildings that, despite the passage of time, still retain vestiges of their former glory. This was once a fancy address, offering large apartments with great views of Mosholu Park. Even today, some of the buildings are well managed, with lovely flower boxes in the gardens outside them. Many of the homes in this area were once brick row houses. Today, they are covered with aluminum siding, and all that's left from the old days are porches and bay windows. Sometimes it's because the brick deteriorated, and other times because they were damaged by water or fire. Thus, when you do see a brick structure, you can get an idea of what this area looked like when most of the homes were brick and had keystones and other designs.

At 3199 Bainbridge Avenue, I walk into Kolb Radiology. Headed by Dr. Thomas Kolb, it's a spanking-clean office that would be perfectly at home on Manhattan's Upper East Side. In fact, Dr. Kolb has an office on Madison Avenue too. He's a radiologist affiliated with Memorial Sloan-Kettering Hospital. The office here is efficient and welcoming. I speak with Sabrina, who's at the desk: "Is there anything about this office that's special in any way?"

"Actually, yes. I've worked in other medical offices so I have perspective. This is the only one I know of where you not only get excellent care, but where, when you have an exam, the referring physician has the results for the patients the same day. Very few places do that." Many people say that if you want to get the best care, you should go to Manhattan. This may be true in certain cases, especially when it's a complicated problem. But if it isn't, then this office, and others I've seen in the Bronx, Brooklyn, and Queens, demonstrates that people outside Manhattan often have access to doctors with excellent reputations.

A block down Bainbridge, at the corner of E. 205th Street, I pass Tropical Pets, a pet shop with a sign that attracts attention: "We buy cockatiels, macaws, and African grays." Curious as to who would be buying these somewhat unusual birds in this out-of-the-way community, I enter and speak with the owner, a gravelly voiced, sharp-tongued New Yorker.

"How do people who don't walk by know you're interested in these birds?"

"Put it this way. I have contacts around the country—Texas, California, and elsewhere. So I'm a known quantity. How do I get 'em? I've been in business for many years. So obviously I know what I'm doing. The African Grays are unusual. They only breed once a year."

"These aquariums are gorgeous. How do you attract customers to your place?"

"Put it this way. Look at my birds and compare 'em with another pet shop. Aren't they just beautiful? You go to Petco. They have three birds, it's a lot."

"Are there other pet shops in this immediate location?"

"You walk around here and answer your own question." And then his voice rising and the volume increasing, he says, in a perhaps belligerent tone: "Hey, lemme ask you a question. If I came in here, a perfect stranger, and started asking you all these crazy questions, how would you respond? Would you be so nice? Honestly?"

I try to respond but don't get very far, so I say, "Well, here's my college photo ID, where I teach, just so you know I'm really who I say I am."

He interrupts: "That's not the point. If I were you and you were me, would you be as kind as I am to you? Answer the question."

"Yes."

"Okay. There you go. There you go. You answered my question."

"Look, my books have many readers, and I've been on TV."

"Awesome, awesome. You look familiar." I'm not sure I believe him, but it doesn't matter. It's a friendly gesture. Perhaps he realizes he might get publicity via the book, which he obviously will. He continues: "My name is Benjamin. Look at how clean this place is. Look at how I keep these animals. Then you know how much I care about what I do, year after year."

"I love you, Benjamin. You're a real New Yorker," I reply, and we slap each other five. This interview adds some color to what many people in these communities are really like. They have personality, pizzazz; they work very hard in these retail businesses. They often have a bit of an edge, attitude—that is, if they're into people and enjoy what they're doing, like Benjamin. When he challenges me as to whether I would act like him, it's impossible to predict how he will respond to whatever answer I give him. He's not really angry, but he's letting me know that I must perform, I must engage, and I must not waste his time. And most of all, I have to be truthfully real. When I say "Yes," his "Awesome" response means I've passed the test. I'm like him, a good person who will help others.

This is a man who clearly loves his work and loves talking to people. Methodologically, the interview is an example of how you must be fast on the draw, look at him directly, smile, gesture, engage in banter, know when to praise, when not to. But much of the interaction is through eye contact, eye-rolling, and gestures that cannot be easily described. Moreover, the conversations are spontaneous; questions cannot be asked in a formal way or a particular order, because they depend on what the respondent says. But for the experienced ethnographer, it's all part of a day's work, a day made all the more enjoyable because the exchange has gone well.

Turning left onto Hull Avenue, I stop at number 3142, a well-kept home with an exquisitely decorated shrine to the Virgin Mary, surrounded by a very well tended garden. There are sculpted animals, including a squirrel and a bulldog, of all things. Perhaps there's a real one inside, and this is his or her shrine. A sign in front of the house says: "I'm Catholic and I vote, with a box checked off." No telling how they will vote, but it's a veiled warning that their views and needs must be taken into account.

I turn left at E. 205th Street, and on the next block I hit Perry Avenue. Here is the Whalen Playground that's right next to a subway station. It's the 205th Street Station on the D line, and the staircase leading to the street is by the playground entrance. The playground is brand new and, having opened only two weeks ago, hasn't even been dedicated yet, and it's also next to a library. Everything is new: the benches, the equipment, and the murals. There's also a stately tree protected by an iron fence. The children's play area has a trapezoid-shaped metal covering that provides shade for those playing there. The sides of this structure consist of panels with brightly colored designs. One has spheres with bubbles, all floating in the sky. Yet another resembles a meat loaf, only it's yellow and black instead of brown and a spaceship is flying by. It's all very fanciful and intriguing.

On E. 206th Street near Perry Avenue, I see the side of a perhaps six-story dark brick building. There are no windows, so I can only estimate. What's most striking about it is that the entire brick wall is covered with "clinker bricks." Called clinker because of the metallic sound they make when banged together, they are blackened bricks in irregular shapes, which don't fit in with the standard bricks. Yet many people think they're charming, and architects will use them as design features. I've seen them occasionally on buildings throughout the city, but never so many. As I look up, I see the top has a large, white, upwardly curved protrusion that makes it appear as if it's soaring into the sky.

Walking around onto Perry I see a large cross on the building and realize it's a church. This side is also covered with clinker bricks. The church entrance is where Perry intersects with E. 207th Street and its name is St. Brendan and St. Ann. Brendan the Navigator, as he was known, was reported to have celebrated Mass aboard a ship while fish gathered to listen. In Irish culture, he is considered the monastic patron saint of mariners, sailors, boatmen, older adventurers, travelers, and whales, and of two dioceses: Clonfert and Kerry. He was born in County Kerry and established a monastery in County Clonfert. Irish tradition has it that, as a sailor extraordinaire, he may have been the first European to land in North America. After learning this, I realize that the upwardly curved part of the building was most likely created to resemble the large prow of a ship. Why is it also called St. Ann? Was she also a nautical person? Not really. It was the name of a church that merged with St. Brendan's. In any case, the design of the church is by no means accidental, and the church website confirms that it was designed this way to honor St. Brendan and what he stood for.

The church looks pretty new, but it was built in 1967. I enter it and see that it has a very modern and austere design, looking nothing like the traditional Gothic structures that prevail in the Bronx. In its simplicity and open spaces, with its many pews, it's quite awe-inspiring, especially the carved modern stone rendering of the Tabernacle in the front. I say to a worker outside. "This is a wonderful-looking church."

He gives me his perspective on my comment: "I know. We're installing cameras for the church. But nothing is wonderful when you gotta work on it." I now realize the truth of the platitude: "Beauty is in the eyes of the beholder." I inform the man that Brendan was the patron saint of travelers, sailors, even whales. "Really. I had no idea that whales were Catholics," is his slightly irreverent quip. A white man who lives on Long Island, he readily admits that he's not Catholic.

My next stop is at the Sholem Aleichem Cultural Center, near the Oval. I get there by walking around the park's perimeter to Bainbridge Avenue. It's at number 3301, a small building that it shares with several offices belonging to Montefiore Hospital. I go downstairs to the social hall, where the members have their activities. It has a wonderful library of old Yiddish and English books on Jewish life in Eastern Europe, not to mention large photographs of famous Jewish writers and leaders from Y. L. Peretz to Theodore Herzl and other luminaries. What's interesting is that Yiddish is enjoying something of a revival today, even though most native Yiddish speakers are no longer alive. Every week, a group of Yiddish enthusiasts meet here to discuss Yiddish culture and history. The center has been here since the 1930s, when it was a place where children learned Yiddish because their parents, immigrants from the old country, wanted to keep that world alive.

This isn't merely a Norwood club though. It was part of a Bronx that once had over a half-million Jews, most of them from Eastern Europe where Yiddish was widely spoken among them. Seeing this small place is misleading because interest in Yiddish culture is enjoying increasing popularity, and one of the main reasons is the National Yiddish Theatre Folksbiene. Dedicated to promoting and preserving Yiddish culture, it was founded in 1915, a time when there were fifteen such theater groups in the city. Today, it's the only one left. Its goal is to make this world accessible, and it does a terrific job—presenting more than 120 events annually, seen by more than 100,000 people. For example, in 2018 it brought the classic play *Fiddler on the Roof* to New York, where, under the direction of the Oscar and Tony Award winner Joel Grey, it ran for several months and was seen by thousands of people. The underlying reason for this great interest among Jews of all ages is best summed up by Jeffrey Wiesenfeld, chairman of the theatre: "More than anything it's the excitement they feel about seeing and hearing Yiddish, as spoken by their ancestors, come to life again."

A block away, across the street at 3266 Bainbridge, I see a very old home from Revolutionary times. It's the Valentine-Varian House, a Georgian-style fieldstone residence with a gable roof. Built in 1758, it's the second-oldest house in the borough, but well preserved (the oldest is the Van Cortlandt House). For those who enjoy museums, the Museum of Bronx History is there, but only open at selected times. One of the owner's descendants was Isaac Varian, New York's sixty-third mayor, from 1839 to 1841. Off to the side of the building, surrounded by grass and bushes, I see a statue of a Civil War soldier with a rifle, titled *Bronx River Soldier*, that has no connection to the home. It actually tumbled into the Bronx River from a granite pier, where it had been on display. Restored by the Bronx County Historical Society, it was brought here and fits in well, although I imagine a casual visitor might think the soldier fought in the Revolutionary War. If so, at least it's the same army, just a different era!

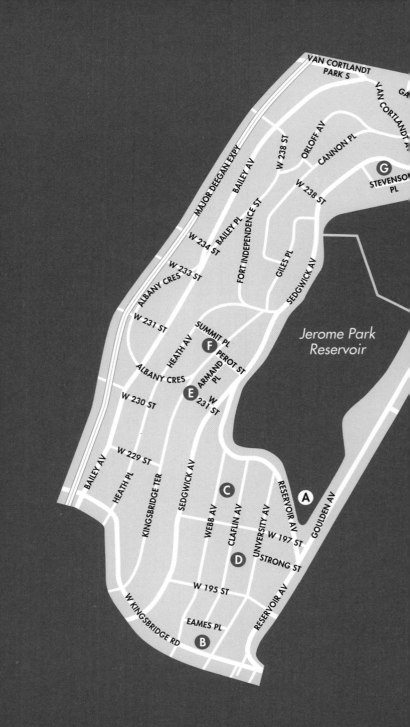

KINGSBRIDGE

THE NAME "KINGSBRIDGE" STEMS FROM THE KING'S BRIDGE, built in 1693 when the British ruled the area. The bridge no longer exists but was located along 230th Street, and parts of it might still lie buried there. The community became part of New York City in 1874 and was developed in the late nineteenth and early twentieth centuries once public transportation, such as subway lines, made it more accessible. The boundaries of Kingsbridge are not agreed upon, but for the purposes of this book, based on the criteria discussed in the introduction, they are Van Cortlandt Park South on the north, Mosholu Parkway and Goulden and Reservoir Avenues on the east, W. Kingsbridge Road on the south, and the Major Deegan Expressway on the west. All of the numbered streets in this area are "W," and for this reason they won't be identified as such each time they're mentioned. Much of the area is hilly, especially from Sedgwick Avenue down to Bailey Avenue.

Ethnically, in modern times, the population was predominantly Irish, most of whom were gone by the 1970s. The community gradually became predominantly Hispanic, with Dominicans as the dominant group. Before the 1970s, Puerto Ricans and some Cubans comprised the majority of the Hispanic community. This changed in the seventies as Dominican immigration increased, with many coming from the nearby Washington Heights and Inwood areas of first settlement. Smaller representations include Blacks, especially west of Kingsbridge Terrace, with some Greeks, Albanians, Asians, and Jews.

The major park is Van Cortlandt Park, one of the jewels of the park system. Since most of it borders Riverdale, it will be discussed in that section, keeping in mind that, like every other public park, anyone from anywhere in the country can walk in it and use the general facilities. The commercial avenues are W. Kingsbridge Road, Bailey Avenue, and 238th Street. It's worth mentioning that Kingsbridge has many older homes, some dating back more than a century. It's a fairly safe area, though not completely so at night.

My trip originates on Reservoir Avenue at 197th Street. I walk the perimeter of the Jerome Park Reservoir, at least the side that runs along Kingsbridge (the rest of it is in Bedford Park). It became part of the New York water supply network when it was completed in 1906. In a strange coincidence, the land on which it lay was also home to a circular structure, the Jerome Park Racetrack, built in 1866 and the host, in 1867, of the first Belmont Stakes race, which is today the last leg of the Triple Crown races.[32] One cannot walk along the reservoir by the shore, but the view just above it is outstanding. Were it not for several tall buildings alongside it, one could easily imagine it as a lake inside a forest, surrounded as it is by wooded areas.

On the other side of the street are several playgrounds and basketball courts interspersed with grassy knolls and ancient rock formations, with boulders scattered throughout. One higher rock has a plaque with the following historical inscription: "This was the location of Fort 4 of the exterior defenses of Fort Washington in

Kingsbridge. Constructed by the American Army in 1776." The memorial was erected here in 1914 by the Daughters of the American Revolution. This site is just before University Avenue, a major thoroughfare that runs from south to north through the West Bronx and dead-ends at Reservoir Avenue.

I climb some stone steps into a small square with a park bench that overlooks the reservoir, noting at the same time that the old apartment buildings that ring the reservoir offer beautiful panoramic views of the water from on high. Because of the way the trees in front are positioned, none of the larger buildings surrounding the reservoir on the far side are visible, as I look out from the bench. I might as well be in the Catskills. While it's a warm day, with temperatures in the eighties, a cool breeze crossing the reservoir creates a ripple effect on the water, similar to small waves.

At Sedgwick Avenue, I turn left and soon pass Our Lady of the Angels, a Hispanic church that was once a parish for the predominantly Irish population here. On the right, 229th Street is actually a steep and long stone staircase leading down to Kingsbridge Terrace, the street below. Turning left, I pass old brick apartment buildings flanking both sides of this thoroughfare, and I soon arrive at one of the major commercial streets of the community, W. Kingsbridge Road, where I turn left.

Here, shortly before University Avenue, I discover a classic Greek diner, at number 101, called Perista Coffee Shop and Restaurant. The menu says: "Selected Best Coffee in the Bronx by the *Bronx Times*. Thanks to our loyal customers." The owners can't resist adding "We think it's the best in the world." It's a very efficiently run place, a hybrid between a coffee shop and a diner serving what reviews describe as delicious food. This is a largely Hispanic section and most of the customers appear to be Hispanic. And while there are some Spanish offerings, the menu is predominantly Greek dishes and generic American food. There's a "Bronx Omelette," consisting of ham, sausage, bacon, and cheese. I don't believe that's unique to the Bronx, but who cares? Perista also claims to have been among the first establishments in the Bronx to offer paninis. While most of the workers are Hispanic, it's a tribute to management that they have stayed true to what they probably do best in terms of food ever since opening in 1978. And lest you forget what this place represents, there are photos everywhere, including on the menu, of Perista, which is the Greek village that the people who started the place, Aris Patilis and George Sicolas, came from.

Farther up Kingsbridge, I turn left on Reservoir and pass the Eighth Regiment or Kingsbridge Armory, reportedly the largest armory in the entire world. On a five-acre site, it's a nine-story red-brick edifice with a metal roof that, with its turrets, arches, corbels, iron gates, and other designs, looks like a castle. Formerly used by the military and also for events like boxing matches, it was taken over by the city and has remained vacant because no one can quite agree on what to use it for. One plan under consideration is to turn it into the world's largest ice-skating rink.

In a quarter of a mile, I turn left off Reservoir onto Webb Avenue and at number 2854, I see a small private home. It's three stories high, but it's a very narrow structure, wedged in between two apartment buildings. I've always wondered about buildings like this. Why are the owners holding on? Is it because they're attached to their home, to the neighborhood, or both? Perhaps such a small piece of land has no practical use. In this case no one's home, and no one I encounter on the street knows anything about the people residing there. I have seen hundreds of such situations. Haven't we all, if we live in a city? Hopefully one day someone will do a study of the subject. The house looks quite neglected. There's life, but not much. It has a mix of siding and stucco and is very old. I peer through the first-floor window and see a tableau of human life—two basketball trophies, a sign about the subway series between the Yankees and Mets, a lone votive candle in front of a Budweiser sign. The windows are dusty and the wood around them is splintered and in need of a paint job. Behind them are some bamboo window shades, with

2854 Webb Avenue

spaces between them. An American flag hangs outside, alongside a colorfully designed flag with seemingly no affiliation. The steps leading up to it are in good shape, but they could use a paint job. It all seems to be saying: "Don't overlook me, even though I'm squashed between two buildings. Here I am, a house, hanging in there, and sometimes I don't know why."

The rest of Webb Avenue is pretty standard, with many red-brick homes that are well maintained, solid but not glamorous in any way. They're large enough to be multifamily, and some of the mailboxes outside indicate that this is the case. I turn right on W. Kingsbridge and go right again on Claflin Avenue. And then, something makes me stop short. I see a pretty brick home, at number 2784, with barred windows on the first floor and with many names on the wall. They run down the center of the house. It seems to be a memorial to many people, and I recognize at least one of the names, Yusuf or Yusef Hawkins, murdered by someone who was part of a group of thirty mostly Italian American youths who attacked him. They suspected him of trying to date a local girl, but it turns out he was in no way involved and had just gone to Bensonhurst to look at a car that was for sale. Another is Amadou Diallo, an African immigrant from Guinea who was killed by four police officers who mistook him for a serial rapist. Of forty-one shots fired, nineteen hit him. An uproar over police brutality ensued, but in the end all of the officers were acquitted.

Most of the names are of people killed by the police. On top of the long list is a banner with a heart superimposed over it which reads: "IN MEMORY OF." On the side of the house but clearly visible are large portraits of two Hispanic young men, Anthony Rosario and Hilton Vega. They are the son and nephew, respectively, of Marjorie, the woman who owns this home. Below Anthony's name are the words "EXECUTED" in red letters, and "No Justice, No Peace, Why are you doing this? We're not resisting. POR QUE?" The words beneath Vega's portrait are: "demands justice from heaven while we demand justice on earth."

The anger in these words and everything else about the mural is palpable and very strong. It is that of the anguished mother of Anthony Rosario, who has done something I've never seen before, plastered her own private home with this story and attached it to a plea that justice be achieved for many others. Every time she leaves or enters her home, she probably looks at it and remembers what happened. Does it result in anything concrete? It must, certainly in terms of consciousness raising. It's in this book and, I'm told, it's been written about elsewhere. A small gravestone in front of the home is etched with the words: "In our grieving hearts we acknowledge police brutality and racial injustice. Thou shall not kill, said the Lord." A Puerto Rican flag is displayed in front of a first-floor window. A next-door neighbor describes what happened to Marjorie's son and nephew as "an unfortunate misunderstanding, a tragic miscommunication." Another person who lives in the house says: "It's very complicated, what happened." They defer to Marjorie, saying, "She can tell you about it in detail." Alas, she's not home, but I leave a message in case she wants to talk.

At 197th Street, I turn left, then hang a right onto Sedgwick Avenue, a left onto 229th Street, and then another left onto Kingsbridge Terrace. In a few minutes I come to a gray house at number 2744, which is made of heavy stone and resembles a castle. The bottom third is a stone retaining wall, and it's only above the equivalent of three floors up that the first story of this multilevel house begins. The outside stair walls leading from the sidewalk to the house stairs are made of gray concrete with carved cutouts of four-leaf clovers along them. Large concrete urns and statues adorn the property, and it has a tourelle with a pointed cupola. There are balconies on the second and third floors of the house, with crenellations running along the top balcony, as well as stained-glass windows. In terms of design and size, it's quite unusual-looking.

My friend, Matt Green, New York City explorer par excellence, has also weighed in about this house on his blog (every once in a while, we unwittingly come across the same items of interest) with a historical take on the "battles" that might well have been fought in these parts, opining, in his usual droll fashion: "This castle redoubt guarded the realm against invading Riverdaleans and the despised Norwooders. Boiling chicken fat was poured through the quadrified buttresses against any invaders who dared to mount a frontal assault." The castle was erected in 1915 [or 1912]. Norwood and Riverdale are communities nearby though there are no records indicating any such battles! The American Institute of Architecture's *Guide to New York City* also presents its view of this edifice: "Here is this tiny monument, a stucco castle with a weather vane, a TV antenna, and a tunnel reputedly leading from the 'dungeon' to the street." And Zillow describes it as a "Kingsbridge castle; feel like royalty as you live in this home, with stunning river views from your private balcony." In fairness, this isn't a block that exudes confidence in the community's safety. Tough-looking characters abound, and there are signs of drug activity as I overhear some conversations of people yelling into their cell phones.

One block north it's a different story. Here Kingsbridge is quiet, almost bucolic. No one's hanging out, and the homes are better taken care of. A bit farther up on the right, at 231st Street, there's a long set of stairs leading up to Sedgwick Avenue. On each side there's a mural of a large tree, meant to be the same tree, but in different seasons, which makes for a creative and startling contrast. On the left side it's nighttime in the winter, and on the right it's daytime in the spring. Thus, on the left the sky is dark, snowflakes are floating down, winter birds like cardinals are perched on the tree's snow-covered bare branches, and there's even a snowman nearby. On the right it's a sunny day, with birds of spring and leaves growing on the branches. It's a large mural extending upward along five flights of stairs on a forty-five-degree angle from the ground. It really must be seen to be appreciated. The mural's creators or artists are Sadie, Jessica, Joy, John, Dillon, Andy, and many more kids, all part of the Kingsbridge Heights Community Center.

Another block north, at the intersection of Kingsbridge Terrace with Summit Place, I spy the Kingsbridge Heights Community Center at number 3101. A long time ago it was home to the 50th Police Precinct. The building is a Beaux Arts Renaissance classic that's very eclectic-looking, dating all the way back to 1902. It's an orange-beige–colored brick building, with the 50th Precinct sign carved into it, large and visible. It's festooned with carvings of scrolls, shields, flowers, and medallions as well as Doric columns on either side of several windows. The corner is curved, and on the Summit side is a crude but effectively rendered painting of several subway cars, next to which is a sign reading: "Building a better Bronx, one family at a time." Another proclamation screams out "BRONX PRIDE." The first subway car is the number 1 train, which runs through this community. Looking out from a window is former president John F. Kennedy. The next one, the number 4 train, features Supreme Court Justice Sonia Sotomayor. Others depicted are Jennifer Lopez, Al Pacino, and the actress and singer Mary J. Blige. Pacino lived in the Bronx, near the Bronx Zoo from the age of two, when his parents were divorced. Jennifer Lopez resided in the Castle Hill section, not far from Sotomayor. Blige actually grew up in the public housing projects of nearby Yonkers, which borders the Bronx on the north.

Perhaps the nicest part of Kingsbridge, aesthetically, is a small section, just west of Sedgwick. The street names are Giles Place, Cannon Place, Fort Independence Street, and Orloff Avenue. They wind around each other in a circular pattern, where they cross each other at intervals. The homes are both single- and two-family, typically brick and fieldstone, in a Tudor style. They're not large, but they are immaculate with manicured lawns and shrubbery, and the reservoir is but a five- or ten-minute walk away. Another beautiful area is marked by elegant prewar apartment buildings, some with charming inner gardens for the residents. They can be found between Sedgwick and Van Cortlandt Park South. One real beauty is at 74 Van Cortlandt Park South, overlooking Van Cortlandt Park, which borders Kingsbridge.

Most of the Jews in Kingsbridge were originally from Eastern Europe and belonged to left-wing political groups that emphasized secular Yiddish life and culture. A good number of them lived in the Sholem, or Shalom, Aleichem Houses on Sedgwick Avenue and W. 238th Street, a cooperative housing complex developed by an organization devoted to keeping alive secular Yiddish culture. Another prominent location, also a co-op, was the Amalgamated Houses headquartered at 98 Van Cortland Park South.

Today, these Jews are largely gone, but there's still a small Jewish presence here. At number 3880 I come to the Van Cortlandt Jewish Center. As a synagogue it's dying and can barely muster a quorum on the Sabbath, but as a central gathering place it has reinvented itself. There's a senior center, and 50 percent of the participants aren't Jewish, with about fifty people who come on a regular basis. In short, it's open to all. Here they eat lunch, chat, play cards and find a second home to escape the loneliness that is often the lot of older adults. Programs include yoga, Zumba, and tai chi. They also assist with bill payments and housing and naturalization applications and are funded by the city and UJA Federation. On the day that I visit, I see an ad for a "Middle Eastern Dance Show," headlined by Nabila Nazem, a well-known belly dancer who graduated from New York University's Tisch School of the Arts. I speak with a volunteer worker about it.

"This seems like a really fun idea, pretty innovative. Is she really going to do a belly dance?"

"Oh yes."

"I mean, maybe some of the guys will lose control."

"I know," she says with a quick laugh. "I told her to dress more conservatively than usual. But of course, she's going to have to remove some of her clothes, and obviously they'll have to see her belly. How can you have a belly dancer without a belly? But that doesn't mean she has to be 90 percent naked, which is her usual outfit, if you wanna call it that."

"Sounds like fun."

And that's how my journey through Kingsbridge ends.

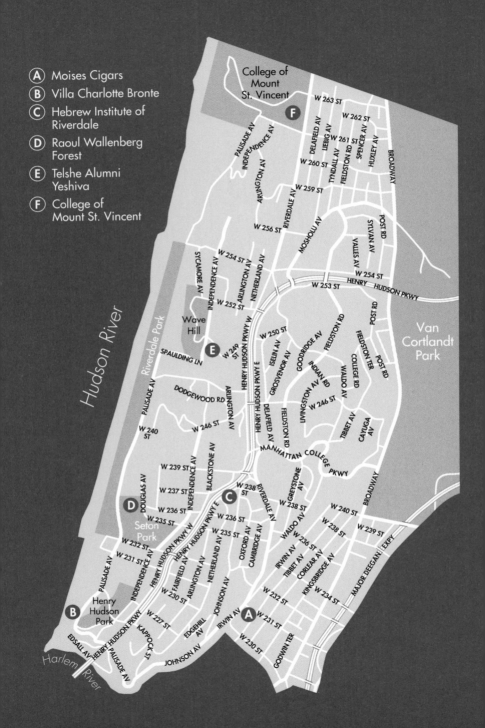

A Moises Cigars
B Villa Charlotte Bronte
C Hebrew Institute of Riverdale
D Raoul Wallenberg Forest
E Telshe Alumni Yeshiva
F College of Mount St. Vincent

RIVERDALE

RIVERDALE WAS ORIGINALLY HOME to various Native American groups, followed by the Dutch and British, respectively. It has been an affluent community ever since the nineteenth century, when many wealthy Manhattan residents created summer estates in the area, traveling back and forth by rail. Typical of this pattern was Fieldston, a designated historic district north of what is today Manhattan College. In the early twentieth century it became a private community, a time when more convenient bus, subway, and automobile transportation made it an attractive place to live in on a permanent basis.

The precise boundaries of Riverdale and its subsections have been disputed by many. Roughly speaking, it's bounded by W. 263rd Street and Westchester County on the north, Broadway and the Major Deegan Expressway on the east, W. 230th Street and the Harlem River on the south, and Palisade Avenue on the west. It has quite a few subareas within it, including South Riverdale/Spuyten Duyvil, from the Harlem River to 239th Street; Central Riverdale, from 239th Street to 254th Street; North Riverdale, from 254th Street to 263rd Street; and Fieldston, whose approximate boundaries are 250th Street on the north, Tibbett Avenue on the east, Manhattan College Parkway on the south, and the Henry Hudson Parkway on the west. The major commercial arteries are Broadway and Riverdale Avenue. There are many two- to three-block-long shopping areas, some of which are 230th, 231st, 235th, and 238th Streets, plus Mosholu and Johnson Avenues. Also, there's a spillover along Broadway of one- to two-block shopping streets between 230th and 238th Streets, both east and west. In particular, Broadway, from about 230th to 239th Streets in Riverdale is a major shopping area and is referred to by some as "Downtown Riverdale."

Riverdale is home to numerous churches and synagogues. Historically and architecturally, the most important are the Riverdale

Presbyterian Church, at 4765 Henry Hudson Parkway West, which dates back to 1863; and Christ Church (Episcopalian), at 5030 Henry Hudson Parkway East, established in 1866. A Gothic revival structure, Riverdale Presbyterian was designed by James Renwick Jr., who also designed St. Patrick's Cathedral. Christ Church is a small exquisite brick and stone structure, whose most prominent members were Lou Gehrig and Fiorello LaGuardia. Both churches are designated city landmarks.

No other community in the Bronx has as many beautiful homes and mansions, and just describing them could easily take up twenty pages. My suggestion is to meander through Historic Riverdale and Historic Fieldston, using the American Institute of Architecture volume as a guide, as well as surfing the internet for other individual homes. The Wikipedia entry for Fieldston also has a useful list of notable homes there. Suffice it to say that Riverdale has many apartment buildings, some of them quite luxurious. All in all, however, the streets of Riverdale have a decidedly suburban feel.

Riverdale did not share the city's history of white people leaving and people of color replacing them. It has always been overwhelmingly white, due to the expensiveness of its high-quality homes and apartments. As of late, though, more racially diverse groups, many of them middle class, have been moving in. Ethnically, most residents are Jewish and Irish, along with small groups of Chinese and Koreans, along with West Indians and Hispanics from various nations. There are more Jews, by far, residing in Riverdale, than in any other Bronx community. Today, it remains a safe, liberal-minded, and highly desirable community.

Educationally, Riverdale, besides having excellent public schools, has some of the best private schools in the city: Riverdale Country School, Fieldston School, and Horace Mann. A high number of the graduates of these schools go on to attend the top universities in the nation. Manhattan College is also in Riverdale and is ranked fifteenth among regional universities of the north.

Riverdale has quite a few parks, including Henry Hudson, Bell Tower, Spuyten Duyvil Shorefront, Brust, Seton, Ewen, and Gaelic Parks. Gaelic Park is owned by Manhattan College, whose sports teams make good use of it. In addition, Gaelic football games and hurling competitions are held there. For information about the activities at the other parks, consult the New York City Department of Parks website. Wave Hill is another park owned by the city, and its gardens and charming paths are open to the public. There are open spaces with benches where one can enjoy unparalleled views of the Hudson River and the New Jersey Palisades. But the most impressive in this area is Van Cortlandt Park. While it borders on several Bronx communities, the Riverdale border on the east is the largest of them. Because of that, and since the size of the park, at 1,146 acres, makes it the third-largest in the city, it merits discussion in the section itself. By comparison, Central Park, at 843 acres, is the fifth-largest in the city.

I begin my walk on Irwin Avenue near 230th Street. The homes are quite nice, not as fancy as Fieldston and other wealthy parts of Riverdale but no different from Rego Park, Middle Village, or Fresh Meadows in Queens, or Marine Park, Sheepshead Bay, or Bay Ridge in Brooklyn. In short, they're solidly middle class.

Welcome to the other part of the Bronx, as much a part of this complex borough as those who unfortunately live here in poverty, plus the ones who are working or lower middle class. It's a mix of attached, semi-attached, and detached homes. Tall apartment buildings, some of them in the luxury category, are also present in this community, towering over the homes, along with smaller pre-war brick apartment buildings. The general area here is sometimes known as South Riverdale.

This is the first Bronx community where I pass, even on a hot summer day at noon, serious walkers, joggers, and runners. It reminds me that such activity is most often the province of those able to do so because their income gives them the time for it. Plus, exercise is very much a part of their lifestyle. Of course, I see plenty of people playing basketball in poorer communities, but they are almost all young. The middle-aged and older adults just aren't into exercise of this sort. Since health is a much bigger problem for the poor, for reasons such as lack of access to health care and limited availability of organic, minimally processed food, residents may not be well enough to exercise vigorously.

Straddling the intersection on 238th Street and Irwin Avenue is a low-slung yellow-and-tan brick building with Roman-style windows that looks both old and shuttered, with no sign of what it is. The windows can't be seen through and the lone door on 238th is boarded up with plywood. A Roman aqueduct design runs the length of one side of the building. But there's help around the corner of the next block, Tibbett Avenue. Here, on the left I see a sign outside on a wooden board: "Robert A. Mahan Manhattan College Physical Plant Complex, 305 W. 238th Street." So, we know it belongs to the college. I speak with the superintendent of construction, Roland Thurman.

"It's going to be a large locker room for the sports facility the college is building for men and women's soccer and lacrosse and for women's softball," he informs me. "It was originally a Con Ed building. I tell you, I played football for Texas A&M for four years, and we didn't have a locker room as nice as they're getting. I also was signed up by the Houston Oilers, played on the practice squad and even got into a game in 1976, but I had injuries."

"No kidding. What position did you play for the Oilers?"

"Linebacker. I played for Bum Phillips [a famous coach]. I live in Texas but I came up here because this is where the construction company sent me. I supervise about forty people, most of them locals. I've worked here on a whole bunch of projects over the years."

"You know, I don't meet a professional football player in the street every day of the week. I'm kind of curious as to how you got to this point."

"I actually blew a knee out and had to stop playing after a year. I was on special teams. And so, after that I went into law enforcement."

"That must have been very disappointing for you."

"Yeah, it was hard for a long time. It's funny, I get mad now because a signing contract back in '87 was $60,000 and now, just to be on the practice team, they get paid $460,000."

"Even so, to get a taste of the big time, even if only for a little while is great. You know how many thousands of college football players never see that?"

"Yep. I grew up in a small town in Texas, Jacksboro, where I was a stud player at Texas A&M and started for four years."

"Well, at least you're the boss here."

"Well, that depends on whether you like getting your butt chewed out at every turn. I travel all the time. I've been to New York four times over the last few years, and each time I lived here for about four or five months. So, I know the city and the people here. In October I'll be in Baltimore. My wife travels all the time on her job too, working for a pharmaceutical company. My company will fly me home to Fort Worth every few weeks. We're married thirty-four years; I have three kids and seven grandchildren. Next month I'll have a great-grand-kid. It's hard and I'm sixty-one, but I'm in good shape. I enjoy traveling because I like meeting people. That was one of the things I liked about being a police officer. I met a lot of people. It was actually a lot more interesting than a football career was."

"In what way?"

"It seems like I was a magnet for action. The reason I'm not in law enforcement now is I got injured. I got shot in a drug raid in Fort Worth. I had gone undercover and we were making this raid against a motorcycle gang, the Bandidos. They have branches throughout the world and their motto is 'We are the people our parents warned us about.' These two guys drove up, one of them shot me in the stomach and the knees. I shot back and killed one of them. I don't complain much, though. I've had sixteen surgeries. I can walk but

I'm not able to run. I don't like to take drugs. This opioid crisis is really bad in New York and New Jersey. Hell, I went up here to this restaurant Havana. Some drunken guy started up with me and I left him layin' there."

Roland is an example of a temporary New Yorker, who nevertheless is integral to the city. He is part of an army of people who go back and forth to the city on various projects and if we multiply that by all the other people who are here temporarily—entertainers, seasonal workers, and people who intended to stay but quit their jobs or were fired, it's a category of its own. Like Roland, they interact with others in the city, supervise and train people, usually New Yorkers, have an occasional fight with them, sleep in hotels, and so on. Their impact will most likely be felt in the views of life they share with New Yorkers. In this case, New Yorkers aren't often exposed to how Texans view matters—their voting preferences, religious outlook, opinions about the economy, values about family, thoughts regarding immigration, and lots of other things. Roland's take on life may not be shared by all Texans, but there are group tendencies based on region, ethnicity, and experiences that people "up north" don't necessarily align with. What's important to realize is that whoever comes here and stays even for a short time can make a difference in ways both large and small.

Also noteworthy is the stability of Roland's life—married many years, with children and a permanent home to return to. He fell into this type of employment because of his injury as a police officer, and became an officer because his professional football career was cut short by injuries. But this brush with fame marks him in a certain way. He reveals this fact almost immediately and enjoys my reaction to it. It makes him special in a way, even if he wasn't a star. In that way he's like a New Yorker, because residents of this town always enjoy telling me about their contacts with the rich and famous, however fleeting they may be.

I walk south on Tibbett Avenue, which has nice homes similar to those on Irwin. At 231st Street, I cross the street, attracted by a cigar store Native American statue with the colorful headdress of a chieftain and stroll into Moises Cigars, which has been at this location for four years. Moise, a handsome Dominican entrepreneur, tells me that the statue was a gift from patrons of his store. It's a well-appointed place, with comfortable leather club chairs with nail-head studs and Windsor armchairs that contribute to a warm welcoming feeling. The lighting is soft, walls are wood-paneled, and the floors are made of dark wood. Attractive straw hats are available for purchase.

"Are there other cigar lounges in this area?" I ask Moise.

"There's a small one over in Bedford Park and another in Yonkers, in Westchester County, and maybe two or three more in the South Bronx. People actually come here from Brooklyn and Queens because they like the atmosphere."

"Do you inhale?"

"Oh no. It's not healthy, but I like the feeling of smoking. It's very relaxing."

"What's the price range of your cigars?"

"The cheapest is eight dollars. You cannot charge less. And the most expensive is $75.00, a Nicaraguan cigar."

The people in the place appear very relaxed, sitting around and chatting with each other, while others watch TV. Chess sets are scattered throughout the establishment, and Moise says he loves the game. I set up a riddle for him, and he immediately becomes engrossed in solving it. Since I must leave, I give him the answer and suggest that he set it up and offer prizes to the first one to solve it. He also has tables for dominoes and stays open until 4:00 a.m. on the weekends. His wife works with him and attends to the humidor, a temperature controlled, glass-enclosed area, where the cigars are kept in boxes. I wish Moise good luck and continue on my way.

Cigar lounges, or bars, became popular after laws against smoking in public became far more stringent. Turning them into physically attractive spaces also appealed to this clientele because it made them feel respected, not derided or pitied. Since most cigar lounges don't permit cigarette smoking, it's actually a compromise between what was and what is. Given these realities, this business will always have a niche, and in a city of this size, one can make a living from it, especially if like Moise, an accountant, one has a fallback option.

From here I head east on 231st, make a left on Kingsbridge Avenue and in a few minutes arrive at the Riverdale Diner at number 3657. It's a large traditional-looking establishment with the usual menu. I ask the manager: "Does this place have a special history?"

"Yeah. One Greek owner had been here for fifty-two years."

"And," I add with a smile, "you can get anything you want here. You got pierogies for the Polish, matzoh ball soup for the Jews, chicken marsala for the Italians, an Irish breakfast, a Greek omelette, and Bacalao Con Huevos [codfish and eggs served with mangu (mashed plantains)], for the Dominicans, and lots more. "

"The way I put it," he retorts, "a diner is a place where you can get everything from an egg to a lobster." He's absolutely right.

It's another day, and I begin my walk heading south on Cambridge Avenue and 235th Street. At number 3212, I see an interesting home. It's made of brick and quite large. The lions on each side of the entrance are dignified and different from each other. The landscaping is first-rate, with pretty patios; there are balconies and stone decorations, including an important-looking shield, and archways over the doorways. The back of the house looks out over the West Bronx. The homes on the rest of the block are also quite nice, and the same can be said for the surrounding avenues. There's a shopping area along 235th Street, with a Key Foods supermarket. Black-and-white photographs of New York's various skylines, displayed on panels along the outside, liven up the streetscape here.

In the old days, local shopping strips in communities generally had barber and beauty shops, delis, grocery stores, dry cleaners. Today, they are increasingly joined by urgent care centers, only this one, at 3509 Johnson Avenue, just north of 235th, is dental instead of the more common medical office. I also see some young children playing the old hand-clapping game in front of some shops. The current version includes the stanza: "Your mother smells like pizza!"

Continuing north on Johnson I turn left at Henry Hudson Parkway and soon come to the Hebrew Institute of Riverdale (HIR), a Modern Orthodox Synagogue founded in 1971. Rabbi Dan Margulies, the assistant rabbi and a graduate of its allied rabbinic school, Yeshivat Chovevei Torah, happens to be in and I chat with him.

"What's unique about the school?"

"It's a very intimate and supportive learning style. The head of the school, Rabbi Dov Linzer, has an incredible teaching style, and he's a very sensitive humanist. He also cares about how Torah [the Bible] affects people's lives. There's also a parallel women's school, Maharat, run by Rabbi Jeff Fox, where women are trained to be female Jewish religious leaders and receive ordination after studying intensively for four years. The founder of these three institutions, Rabbi Avi Weiss, had a vision that the school and synagogue should be in one building so as to unite the concepts of study and prayer, an integrated system."

Rabbi Weiss is one of the leading rabbis in America. He is perhaps best known for his charismatic leadership in the struggles to allow Soviet Jews to leave the USSR and be able to live free and to express themselves religiously. He led hundreds of demonstrations beginning in the 1960s, met with world leaders and advocated for Soviet Jews, resulting in millions of Jews around the world demonstrating on their behalf. He believes in what he has termed "open Orthodoxy," and has been criticized, even condemned, as too liberal by other Orthodox leaders. Yet he has remained firm in his beliefs that Orthodoxy should be open to new ideas and deal with issues like welcoming LGBTQ people into the fold, strongly supporting the State of Israel, and promoting women's rights, but within the boundaries of Orthodox Jewish law. In 1989, he led a group of people who dressed in concentration camp garb and climbed the walls of a Carmelite convent that had been established within the site of Auschwitz to draw worldwide attention to its presence there. In 1993, Pope John Paul II ordered the nuns to vacate the site.

Rabbi Weiss retired as leader of HIR in 2015, and is now Resident Rabbi, with Rabbi Steven Exler serving as the new spiritual leader. The synagogue has an ark where the Torahs are kept. It's in the shape of a large open Torah scroll with two rollers, all of it constructed from thick beige-colored wood, with the ark itself in the center. Uniquely, the Torahs inside the ark are on rollers so that even people in wheelchairs can reach and hold the Torah. The chairs are arranged in such a way that everyone has an equal view and access to where the services are conducted. HIR has 850 families, a large number for an Orthodox synagogue. The rabbi has always sat with the congregation and floats around, sitting in different seats to promote the idea of warmth and approachability that is a hallmark of this house of worship. The new rabbi doesn't "float" that much, but generally sits in the back of the middle section. It's a measure of the progressive elements residing in Riverdale that an innovative synagogue of this type flourishes here.

From here I proceed to Kappock Street and make a right and one block later a left onto Independence Avenue. Walking east on Independence, I make a left onto Palisade Avenue where it descends toward the Hudson River. In two minutes I make a right and in about twenty yards continue left onto Edsall Avenue, where I pass some lovely old homes, including one made from stone. Rounding a curve in the road I pass the Spuyten Duyvil station of the Metro-North Railroad. Spuyten Duyvil, the Dutch words for "spouting devil," refers to the strong tidal currents at this location and is the name of this area.[33]

I'm just in time to see a train stop. The station is literally by the water and affords a tremendous view of New Jersey's Palisades. When I look toward Manhattan, the Henry Hudson Bridge appears to be entering a forest, a forest otherwise known as Inwood Hill Park. Standing underneath the steel arch of the Henry Hudson Bridge nearby feels as if one is inside a giant erector set, a

Villa Charlotte Bronte

remarkable view of the bridge's infrastructure. I continue along Edsall until Palisade Avenue and turn left onto Palisade, from whence I came. The trails along the wooded side of the street are part of Spuyten Duyvil Shorefront Park, which is tranquil, scenic and worth exploring, especially due to the many species of birds that make it their home.

In a few minutes, I see several stunning attached houses that face the Hudson pretty close to river level, just overlooking it. I'm at number 2501, built in 1926 to look like an Italian Villa that would be at home along, say, the Amalfi Coast, called the Villa Charlotte Bronte. Residents have magnificent views of the river, and it's a five-minute walk to the Spuyten Duyvil Metro-North train station.

Thus, they can be in Grand Central Terminal in about twenty minutes. The roofs are tiled and thick, and charming ivy blankets a good part of the beige stucco walls, which have numerous French casement windows and terraces on different levels.

I pass Henry Hudson Park, small with nice walking areas and an imposing bronze statue of the explorer, Henry Hudson. Resting atop a hundred-foot-high Doric column, it gives the impression that Hudson is peering out from the deck of a ship.[34] I've decided to walk the length of Palisade Avenue, which runs north, though it does take a few detours to do that. There are many beautiful homes—colonial, Tudor, brick, and so forth—on both sides of the road and they add to the allure of this route. Just beyond 232nd Street I also pass Seton Park, which has playgrounds and two baseball fields.

The relatively unknown Raoul Wallenberg Forest begins just north of Seton Park and is really worth seeing. Wallenberg was a Swedish diplomat whose courage and ingenuity saved an estimated 100,000 Jews from extermination by the Nazis through the power of his office. He grew up in a wealthy family and was posted to Budapest, where Hitler and Adolf Eichmann were making strenuous efforts to murder almost the entire Jewish population in Hungary. Arriving in 1944 as head of the Swedish legation, Wallenberg created counterfeit Swedish passports. He also acquired homes, villas, and buildings, and decorated them with Swedish flags and sheltered Jews in them. He fed them with food from warehouses that he owned. Following the war, he was imprisoned by the Russians. Despite many efforts to learn what happened to him, his fate remains unknown.

There's room to park on the east side of the road. From there I enter the forest, one with many tall thick trees. I see a European beech tree fifty-two inches in diameter and an equally large white oak specimen. Different kinds of berries and grapes abound here in the lush underbrush, and many species of birds hop, fly, and perch on the tree branches—red-tailed hawks, white-throated sparrows, screech owls, Baltimore orioles, and other varieties. At the entrance there's a huge painted boulder. The path, while paved at times, appears quite neglected and narrows at various points to where you must walk single-file. When I think of the fact that many of those whose lives he saved attempted to hide in forests just like this, I realize how appropriately named this four-acre site is. Despite being just off Palisade Avenue, you need walk only five minutes to feel as if you are deep in the woods. Notwithstanding that, in ten minutes, I come to a staircase in poor but still navigable condition and climb it to Douglas Avenue and 236th Street, which provides another access point to the park, though it's quite easy to miss the small sign identifying its presence. Here I encounter by chance an older woman with a thick European accent walking her pint-size dog.

"Hi. Do you know this place?" I ask.

"Yes. Wallenberg was a wonderful man. He rescued many people."

"Are you from Hungary?"

"No, I'm from an even worse place, Russia." She assumes that this requires no elaboration, and I don't press her on it, as I want to return to Palisade.

The Wallenberg forest is actually part of Riverdale Park, which runs for many blocks along Palisade Avenue, mostly on the left, along the shoreline. The park can be entered through a break in the chain link fence at 232nd Street, and you can enjoy a true wildlife walk with numerous trails breaking through untamed vegetation, in a wild area along the river, exiting at 254th Street. On the other hand, you can continue along Palisade and make a right, for example, on 247th Street, where delightful homes await you on 247th and on wooded lanes that branch off from the street. One of them, Independence Avenue, is a main artery elsewhere, but here it's merely a lane. If you want to live in nature and forget you're in the city, this is an excellent choice. You can also forget about finding a corner grocery store or any other commercial establishment, but it's available perhaps a mile away or less—a five-minute car ride, depending on where you are. This enchanting walk ends at the service road of the Henry Hudson Parkway. On the corner is one of those bright-red old fire alarm boxes that one rarely sees these days, a carved cylinder with a hexagonal box on top. I meander back to Palisade along 247th Street and turn right. In ten minutes it ends and veers sharply right where its name changes temporarily to Spaulding Lane.

I pass several lovely, large mansions and soon arrive at Independence Avenue, where, at number 4904, I see a yeshiva, or advanced rabbinical academy, known as Telshe Alumni Yeshiva, a substantial part of which is situated inside a large stone mansion. A transplant from Eastern Europe, headquartered in Cleveland, Ohio, and known as one of the top yeshivas in the United States, it established a high school branch in Riverdale in the early 1980s that is still there. Jewish schools like the academically outstanding Salanter Akiva Riverdale Academy (SAR), also in Riverdale on 254th Street, are better known to the outside world, whereas this institution avoids contact with outsiders. Its adherents believe that for men, study of the Talmud, day and night, is the highest level that a Jew can aspire to. For those running the Telshe Yeshiva, the personalities who are perfect role models for their acolytes exist in a universe of their own making—outstanding personalities and intellects in Torah scholarship such as Rabbi Aharon Kotler, founder of the yeshiva in Lakewood, New Jersey; and Rabbi Mordechai Gifter, who established and headed the Telshe Yeshiva. They take great pride in the fact that their world and their academies have existed for thousands of years.

The campus doesn't seem to be in very good condition these days, but its history is quite rich. Completed in 1929, it resembles a Tuscan villa, has twenty-eight rooms, and won a gold medal from the Architectural League of New York for its landscape design. It was built by Anthony Campagna, a developer of large apartment buildings on Fifth Avenue and elsewhere and a member of the New York City Board of Education, and is now a landmarked building. It's located across the street from Wave Hill, Riverdale's oldest mansion, built in 1843, whose past residents include Theodore Roosevelt, Mark Twain, and Arturo Toscanini. Wave Hill is well known by many New Yorkers as a first-rate venue for all sorts of events, especially the perfect wedding. It has public gardens, boasts terrific views of the Hudson River, and also holds many concerts. Telshe Yeshiva and Wave Hill directly across the street from each other? It's a juxtaposition which proves that in New York, anything is possible.

At 249th Street I make a left off of Independence onto Sycamore Avenue. Between 252nd and 254th Streets, Sycamore is part of the Riverdale Historic District. Here I see ivy-covered stone walls, expansive manicured gardens, orchards, it seems, and stupendous homes like the ones at 5260 and 5288. At 254th Street I turn left and pass SAR, a Jewish day school and high school (the latter is located on 259th Street), and come to a yacht club reachable by a footbridge, to the right of which is another Metro-North train station. Turning right I head north onto Palisade Avenue, which picks up again here. Soon I pass the Hebrew Home for the Aged, at 5901 Palisade, a massive and impressive-looking facility that's considered one of the best nursing homes in the country. Inside lies the Derfner Judaica Museum, along with several nearby hallways that form an art gallery lined with original signed prints by some of America's most accomplished modern artists. Outdoors at the southern end is a grassy slope filled with colorful modern sculpture, mostly abstract, overlooking the wide Hudson River and the New Jersey Palisades beyond.

At 261st Street, I turn right. This is close to the northern border of the Bronx. I turn left on Riverdale Avenue and come to the College of Mount St. Vincent on 263rd Street, the northernmost street both in the Bronx and in New York City. On the other side of the border is Yonkers, a city in Westchester County. The location is magnificent. The Gothic-style buildings of this co-ed Catholic institution are beautiful and the landscaped campus is memorable, especially as it slopes down to the Hudson River. It was founded in 1847 by the Sisters of Charity and has about two thousand students. It's not a well-known school like Manhattan, Fordham, or St. John's, all Catholic universities in New York City, and that's why it's discussed here.

Serving undergraduates and graduate students, it specializes in business, education, and nursing. Its best-known building is the Fonthill Castle, constructed in 1852, which overlooks the river. While the building is no longer in use, its exterior is really special. Modeled after the novelist William Beckford's Fonthill Abbey in England, it's listed on the National Register of Historic Places. Among the college's most famous students are the playwright Eugene O'Neill and the actor Lionel Barrymore. Academically, it's a good college, typical academically of the colleges attended by the vast majority of students in this country. It's also one of the prettiest campuses I've seen in the city.[35]

I'm now in what's called North Riverdale, which runs north-south from 263rd Street to about 254th and east-west from Broadway to Riverdale Avenue. The homes are not as elaborate as those in Riverdale proper west of the parkway or in Fieldston. They're nice, nonetheless—an assortment of Tudors, colonials, and capes with a middle-class population. Judging from the mezuzahs, wreaths, and flags on display, it seems largely Irish and Jewish. It's both quiet and safe with lots of trees on the streets and modest-sized gardens. One unusual structure, with a cupola and a shingle dome on top, as well as a large Irish flag, is at 418 W. 260th Street. The lower half is a stone wall, with red brick above it, and with balustrades on the second floor. I walk south on Fieldston Road, which traverses the center of the neighborhood. Crossing Mosholu Avenue, I see on my left a very distinguished-looking apartment building with red brick, some of it herringbone-patterned, fieldstone, Tudor elements, clinker bricks, and other elaborate designs, along with a gorgeous garden in front of it. Its name, appropriately, is Fieldston Manor, located at number 5400 and built in 1939.

Continuing on Fieldston Road for several blocks, I enter the Fieldston enclave, a very well known neighborhood. As indicated before, I'll not dwell much on the beautiful homes except to mention a few of these dwellings: numbers 4731, 4629, 4621, and 4503, all on Fieldston Road. The Fieldston School has a very charming campus as well. There's also 4428 Waldo Avenue, with the replica of a cannon in front and a tourelle, or turret, attached to the house. Leaving Fieldston, I turn left onto 246th Street and head east on it until it dead-ends at Post Road. Here I go right and make the first left, which dead-ends at Broadway in just a few yards. I turn south onto Broadway and make a left onto 238th Street. In a few minutes I walk into S&S Cheesecake.

One of my friends told me about the high quality of its cheese-cake, which is basically what it sells, some with strawberry and other toppings and others straight, meaning with no topping for those who like their cheesecake pure. They're not defensive at all about this emphasis, as can be seen from their motto: "Doing one thing well." I ask Yair Benzaquen, the owner, a middle-aged man with a great smile and salt and pepper hair, who hails from Israel, what makes his cake so popular and special.

"Well, I can't say everything about how we make it, but I can tell you a few things. First, it's made with love and with the purest ingredients we can get. We also bake it twice. The first time when it's almost frozen, we bake it and create a skin on the outside to capture and hold the flavor. We seal it so that it remains moist. And then we bake it again. We have a crust too, but it's really a shell whose primary function is to make it look good. People eat with the eyes first. And, of course, we put fat in it because that gives it flavor. We got a great write-up from Mimi Sheraton, of the *New York Times*. Some people think cheese has to be very fresh, but it's not really true. It has to age somewhat, like a steak. You want it to settle a little. Also, I make it myself whenever possible."

Yair is a charming fellow and says he looks like he's sixteen but feels like a hundred, following that up with a quick laugh that expects you to disagree with his self-evaluation. He's opening an upscale steakhouse soon next door and that's his next dream. Yair explained to me that deliveries around the country, once a lucra-tive part of his enterprise, had been diminishing in importance as transportation costs soared. The steakhouse has clearly captured his imagination. He described to me in detail how steaks have to be prepared, telling me about the strongest competitors in the city, places like Peter Luger and Sparks, and how he would make customers feel like a million dollars. He expressed hope that people would eat at the steakhouse and then go next door for the cheesecake. This didn't strike me as very practical, having two separate locations. He had a problem: The cheesecake place was kosher and the steakhouse wouldn't be, making it unlikely that they could be combined. Perhaps he doesn't want to give up the old until it becomes clear that the new business will succeed, a not uncommon dilemma for many business people.

Africans are an increasingly major presence in the Bronx as they are in Brooklyn. A store called Masidi's Urban African Store, at 5616 Broadway, near 231st Street, has a remarkable collection of Africana. It's crammed into a relatively small space that nevertheless manages to present a tremendous number of items. Let's begin with the window displays. I see two black mannequins, clad in dashikis, with huge, graduated orange-colored beads hanging down below the waist, the largest being about four inches. The female figure has a beaded choker with a large disc hanging from it. The male figure is wearing a tie in orange, green, blue, and black. Next to it are two chess sets with African faces on the pieces, one set made from stone, the other wood. There are very ornate drums, painted in many colors; tables made of glass with silver tiles on them, and sculptures of men in pensive poses sitting with gourds, reminiscent of Rodin's famous *Thinker*. There's a table with carvings of three monkeys in "Hear no evil, see no evil, speak no evil" poses. Other bronze animal carvings are also present, as are sculptures that are probably fertility goddesses.

I walk inside and see a woman braiding a customer's hair. "Just looking around," I say, and she goes back to her work. The inside is just chock-full of literally hundreds of items large, small, and in-between. It feels as if I've entered a museum, though the lighting could be better. I see an array of statues, musical instruments, paintings, games, an eagle, and a xylophone, the latter two made of wood. Improbably, in the middle of everything there's a carving of an American Indian with a headdress, which really belongs in front of an Optimo cigar shop. Next to it is a tiny statue of an African Red Cross doctor, with a stethoscope around his neck. On the wall is a photo of a black woman, her hands seemingly raised in supplication to the sky lamenting the departure of her male companion, perhaps husband. Next to it is the following explanatory poem.

A Woman's Work

I may cook and I may clean.
I may even be a former beauty queen.
The bills, they are all past due.
And I still can't get over you.
Oh, our baby, he's fine.
But we both know he's all mine.
Help me with my bag?
That's okay, I'm fine.
If you tell it that all these problems are mine,
Let you tell it all, these problems are mine.
So, as I pull and I slave on the hottest day
I lost sight of myself somewhere along the way.
So, I dropped my bag and began to pray.
This is a woman's work.

This poem may sound like it's the same as "A woman's work is never done," an idiom, and the title of several different poems. But its words bear no resemblance to the usual exemplars. The latter are paeans of praise to the millions of women who are often unappreciated for the household chores they do, while this one's main focus is on abandonment by men of their families. I speak with Aisha, who braids hair in the back and is an employee of the shop.

"This is near an area where large numbers of Africans live, isn't it?"

"Yes, and I'm from Guinea, but the store has things from many African countries."

"Are you on the internet?"

"No, because the minute you put things on the internet, other people are going to copy you." For that she's willing to forgo advertising her wares. Is it worth it? Apparently yes, in her view.

"What are you asking for the chess sets in the windows?"

"The wooden one is forty dollars, and seventy dollars for the stone."

"I'll give you thirty for the wooden one."

"It's not mine. Price is price. And rents are very high in Riverdale. And they have to ship them from Africa."

"But everything is negotiable in New York. And in Africa too." She laughs good-naturedly but doesn't budge. I decide to drop it since it's not a priority for me.

"Are there other stores like this?"

"In Brooklyn and Manhattan, but not in the Bronx." It appears she's correct, as far as I can tell from researching it, which is why I recommend it as a place to visit when exploring the Bronx. The reviews are mixed as to price and service, but this is for the buyer to decide.

When I was doing Inwood, the Manhattan neighbor to the south from Riverdale, I lamented how the old Irish bars, which I had gone to in the past, both to imbibe and listen to Irish music, had become extinct. And now I discover they weren't so much gone as relocated to nearby Riverdale, where a substantial Irish community remains to this very day, while Inwood has become primarily Dominican. It's with this mindset that I enter Mr. McGoo's. Outside, there's a memorial roster of former patrons from the community who had passed on to another world. There's also a list of bands to come, including one with the intriguing name of "The Slippery Chickens." Alas, I'm told inside, none of them are Irish. Nor are they likely to sing the ballads of Tommy Makem and the Clancy Brothers. Those are not the favorites of the younger generation, most of whom have probably never heard of these Emerald Isle legends. I also take note that the borough has a slightly altered moniker on a sign outside, "County Bronx," as in Counties Mayo, Cork, Kilkenny, Wexford, and Sligo. As I peer into the dim light at noon on a quiet weekday, the barista beckons me inside with a wide smile.

"C'mon in; the water's fine."

"Thank you and nice to meet you." It turns out that Mary Coughlan lives in Inwood, where she raised a couple of kids. She also knows about the caveman who lives in Inwood Hill Park and about whom I've written in *The Manhattan Nobody Knows*. She tells me that coyotes have made their way there and into nearby Van Cortlandt Park. Mary invites me to have a look at the outdoor space in the back and I accept. I tell her that, from the photos lining the walls, it's definitely a Yankees joint. She demurs, asserting that Mets fans will be treated "with respect" too.

It's a nice space for a relaxing time, but what catches my eye are the drawings of various personages who have in common their historical connection to the area. One is a former Bronxite, Al Pacino, discussed earlier in the section on Kingsbridge. Another is Ace Frehley, a Kiss band member, who lived in the Bedford Park section on Marion Avenue near E. 201st Street. A third is Lou Gehrig, who lived in Riverdale at 5204 Delafield Avenue for the last two years of his life. Jennifer Lopez, also depicted here, lived at 2210 Blackrock Avenue, in the Castle Hill section of the Bronx, plus Ann Bancroft, whose name originally was Anna Maria Louisa Italiano and who was raised in the immigrant Italian community of Belmont. I go back inside and suggest to Mary that the back be named "From the Bronx and Proud of It." Mary offers me a drink on the house and together we each down a shot, a vodka for her and a Maker's Mark for me. Thus fortified, I thank her and, bidding her a lovely day, head for nearby Van Cortlandt Park.

I enter the park at the intersection of Van Cortlandt Park South and Gale Place. As I begin walking, I notice six birdfeeders hanging from trees. Presumably, they belong to local residents, one indication of how people adapt parks to suit their own interests. About a ten-minute walk past the classic playground, the path briefly becomes a trail veering off to the left and then opens up to a wider concrete walkway with streetlamps on either side. To my right I can see Mosholu Parkway through the trees, and on my left is the border of the eighteen-hole Van Cortlandt Golf Course, built in 1895, the first public course in the country. A bit farther I see Van Cortlandt Lake. I gaze upon it and look across the water to the tree-lined shore off in the distance, where some kids are fishing. If I didn't know otherwise, I'd think I was in the forests of upstate New York. A passing shower chases the birds closer to where I'm standing. There are two magnificent swans, some Canada geese, and a family of mallard ducks. Other wildlife found here includes rabbits, raccoons, opossums, even coyotes, along with cranes, red-winged blackbirds, and herons.

Off to my right is the golf course café. Marino Rosado, a friendly fellow who lives close by, works behind the counter and tells me: "This place is a hidden secret. On a regular weekday it's pretty empty, and on the weekends it's pretty packed, but those who come are just the regulars. We do catering for weddings, bar mitzvahs, you name it. We also have a big tent in case it rains, and the food is delicious and inexpensive. It's also very clean and attractively presented." The lunch and breakfast menus are pretty standard: grilled cheese, tuna wraps, eggs of any kind, hot dogs, and the like. You can eat indoors where there's a fireplace, but what's special is the tables outside, where you can eat while looking out upon the largest freshwater body in the Bronx. I skirt the lake heading west and soon come to the Van Cortlandt House, the oldest surviving structure in the Bronx, made of stone and built in 1748. It's a museum, with furniture-filled rooms offering a look at how people lived in colonial times.

In closing, this is an amazing park with many attractions, including horseback riding, tennis courts; cricket, soccer, and baseball fields; a beautiful swimming pool; plus an incredible network of trails and cross-country running terrain, most of it very well maintained. It's incredible that a park of this size isn't better known.

WOODLAWN

WAKEFIELD

EASTCHESTER & BAYCHESTER

WILLIAMSBRIDGE

ALLERTON

PELHAM PARKWAY & PELHAM GARDENS

MORRIS PARK

PARKCHESTER

SOUNDVIEW

CASTLE HILL

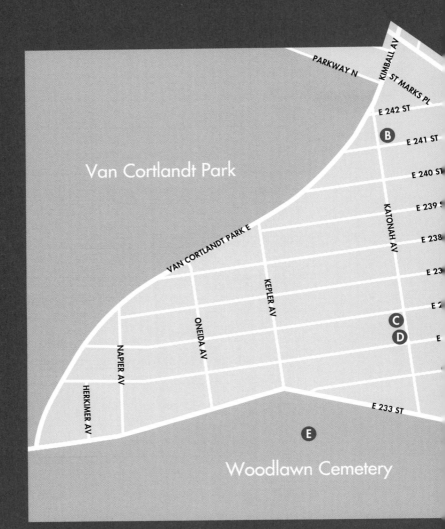

PARKWAY N

KIMBALL AV

ST MARKS PL

Van Cortlandt Park

E 242 ST

B E 241 ST

E 240 ST

KATONAH AV

E 239 S

E 238

VAN CORTLANDT PARK E

E 23

KEPLER AV

E 2

C

D

ONEIDA AV

NAPIER AV

E 233 ST

HERKIMER AV

E

Woodlawn Cemetery

A The Saratogian
B Trinity Community Church
C Emerald Isle Immigration Center
D "The only bench in town"
E Woodlawn Cemetery

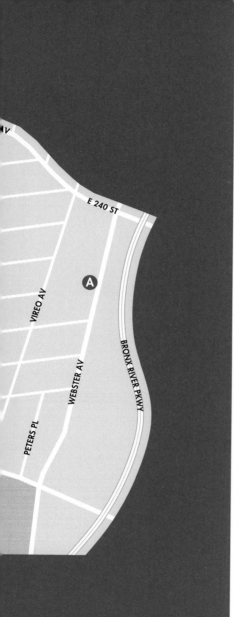

WOODLAWN

THE BOUNDARIES OF WOODLAWN ARE McLean Avenue on the north, Bronx River Parkway on the east, Woodlawn Cemetery on the south, and Van Cortlandt Park East on the west. It has the typical Bronx community history of succession. First, the Dutch arrived and took possession of Native American lands, either by force or subterfuge or both. In 1664 the British assumed control of the area and subsequently lost possession after the Revolutionary War. For the next century, the land was owned by wealthy Americans, then Catholics came in the early twentieth century and established a community in St. Barnabas Church, which began in 1910. The St. Luke United Methodist Church was established in 1875 and moved into its new building on Katonah Avenue in 1913. Germans predominated in the early years, but eventually the Irish became the majority here.[36] The area was called Woodlawn Heights but is generally known simply as Woodlawn.

Today, it's still heavily Irish, with a fairly sizable Italian and Hispanic presence too. The main streets are Katonah and McLean Avenues and E. 233rd Street. McLean is actually in Yonkers just over the city line, but Woodlawn residents consider it part of their community, doing much of their shopping and frequenting the taverns and eateries there. The major park is Van Cortlandt, and there are several playgrounds in the area as well. It is home to both Catholic and Protestant churches; and Public School 19, or the Judith K. Weiss School, is a community anchor with classes from kindergarten through eighth grade. The community is very safe and compact, with clearly defined boundaries.

My trip begins on Webster Avenue near East 233rd Street, the southern tip of Woodlawn. Heading north, I pass older apartment buildings, generally five to seven stories high and well maintained. I take note of the Saratogian, at number 4315, built in 1957, which is actually the name of the daily newspaper in Saratoga Springs. I ask an older West Indian woman why it's called that. Her response: "I have no idea."

"How long have you lived here?" She looks at me with a sheepish expression and says:

"Can you believe, twenty years? I just never thought to ask. I'll call the rental office tomorrow and ask them."

"No need to do that," I say, wanting to avoid an intermediary. "Give me the number and I'll call them myself," which she does, as I thank her for her help. A woman answers the phone and gives me the story: "My family owned property there in the 1940s, and then we bought some buildings here and we needed a name, so Saratogian seemed appropriate." People often have pretty simple reasons for doing things and this definitely falls into that category.

On my right is a steeply sloping grassy area, and just beyond it are the tracks of the Metro-North Railroad, which has a station in Woodlawn, thus making for a quick commute to Grand Central Terminal. At McLean Avenue, the main shopping area for this community, I go left. Heavily used by Woodlawn residents, it's actually only a block or two into Yonkers, Westchester County, but there are no border police, and the physical appearance of the area and ethnic makeup is the same.

Many of the shops clearly cater to the Irish community, either in terms of what they sell or by their names, especially the taverns. I speak with Reverend David Rider of St. Barnabas Church, located at Martha Avenue and E. 241st Street, who corroborates the presence of such a community.

"I think you could say it's an Irish community, judging from the people I see at mass. The majority are Irish immigrants, and there are also Italians. We have nine masses and they're all full. One is in Italian and the rest are in English." There are Italian food shops here too, and there's the US Corleone Club at 1022 McLean, which is up for sale. Its origins may be found in the Palermo area of southern Italy, where it was the name of a municipality. These clubs have a long history in this country, are very tight-knit, and do not really welcome outsiders even if they are Italians. They have declined greatly in number as the older generation passes on. Some have been associated with the Mafia, but the majority are simply places for people to socialize in.

This one does have a connection to the Mafia, and not simply the fictional Don Corleone of the *Godfather* films. Corleone means "heart of the lion," and it was the birthplace of two notorious Sicilian mafia chieftains, Salvatore Riina and Bernardo Provenzano, who ran Sicily's Cosa Nostra in the 1980s. More than a thousand people were killed as battles raged for control of the area. In 2016, the municipality was shut down, with the Italians blaming it on Mafia control of the area. This is a general problem in Italy, with 212 city governments having been dissolved between 1991 and 2016. In addition, there was a strong Mafia presence in Yonkers during the 1970s and 1980s, most notably through the carting industry. Given the waning influence of the Mafia today, these can only be viewed as an unfortunate, albeit colorful, part of Italian American history. Clearly, as has been established over and over again nationwide, the vast majority of this community's residents had nothing to do with the Mafia.

More representative of the community here is Avitabile Deli at number 1016, which has won many chamber of commerce awards for its products. Once again, in a sign of the changing times, almost no one waiting in the long line at the deli counter seems to be Italian. Virtually all of those buying lunch here are either Black or Hispanic. I spot a store here at number 994 with the moniker of How Sweet It Is, referring to Jackie Gleason's quote from *The Honeymooners*. It's a sweetshop, with a photo of Gleason inside, and sells cake toppers, decorative mugs, ice creams, and endless jars of penny candy like jelly beans, jelly apples, and a party room. There's also an old-style bakery, called Anna Artuso's Pastry Shop. A photo of Anna, with coiffed white hair, looks out with a friendly expression. It's been there for fifty-two years. Born in 1922, Anna was an Italian immigrant who hailed from Reggio-Calabria. She opened the shop during the Vietnam War and sent hundreds of packages to soldiers overseas. This mix of ethnic pride and patriotism typifies the city's immigrant communities, who honor and memorialize members of the armed forces. Anna was known as "Grandma," remembered for the free cookies she gave to kids who entered the bakery.

Irish bars abound here. One architectural standout, both outside and inside, is Moriarty's Bar and Restaurant at number 986. The outside is a brightly painted red, including the bricks. A large arched window graces the front. The moldings around the windows are bright white against the red background. Beautiful red corbels can be found here as well. Inside there's a long, polished counter, and all the furnishings are in tip-top shape. The bartender tells me a bit about the community: "The Irish are still here, but not as much as before. We have Irish music from time to time. It hasn't changed ethnically. Not yet. It's still holding up. Now, it's going toward Europe. And another problem is Europeans can't get into the States so easily. There are restrictions."

One might wonder why a community whose Irish population is not as large as in the past bothers to retain the Irish look and ambiance. The answer is clear, however. First, there are still many Irish left. Second, there's nostalgia and possible tourism. Finally, these trappings make the Irish immigrants who still land here when they arrive feel more at home. During the summers, the bars and eateries are packed with revelers on weekends. Another architectural gem is Ned Devine's Saloon, a bar on the corner of Alexander and McLean Avenues, at number 940. It's three storefronts wide and has a fake slate roof, also painted bright red, with black and gold signs. The inside is equally well appointed, with a mural of the movie *Waking Ned Devine*, which was set in Ireland.

I turn left onto Katonah Avenue, which becomes another Irish commercial drag after a few blocks, but not before I linger at a grassy triangle behind which buses stop and pick up passengers. The triangle memorializes sandhogs, or operating engineers, those who work in underground tunnels and those who gave their lives while doing so. This was for the sixty-mile long Tunnel No. 3, scheduled to be completed in 2026, which will bring water from three watersheds—Croton, Catskill, and Delaware. Started in 1970, and boring through miles and miles of undisturbed bedrock hundreds of feet below ground, it's the largest capital construction project ever undertaken by the city, costing some $6 billion. It will deliver 1.5 billion gallons of water to the city every day through gravity alone, without pumping. There's a gleaming flagpole several stories high, with a large flag flying. The names of those who died are engraved into twenty-four separate discs that resemble manhole covers.

Van Cortlandt Park East is a road that angles off to the right here. I walk along it and soon enter a roadway that travels through this part of Van Cortlandt Park. It's peaceful and goes through a wooded area that's being revitalized. There's also a really nice baseball field on the left, followed a bit farther by other fields. And on the right a barrier blocks vehicular traffic from entering. A guard stationed there informs me that I can't go into the area. He creates an air of mystery when I ask him what's inside the one-level stone structure behind him.

"I can't discuss it," he says.

"Who's in charge of it?"

"The EPA [Environmental Protection Agency]. I've been here ten years and I don't know what the place is about. They won't tell

Trinity Community Church at 4390 Katonah Avenue

me." But conversations with others suggest that it's part of the water supply and is completely unguarded at night. As far as I can tell, there's nothing really secret about it, but they do want to prevent vandalism. After all, one cannot get near the Jerome Park Reservoir in nearby Kingsbridge, either. Regardless, there are plenty of tranquil trails to explore here.

At 4390 Katonah Avenue, I come to a church that looks really old. At present, it's in the hands of a Filipino church that's refurbishing the ancient structure. A church official invites me to join them for services and I tell him I'll try. It was known as the St. Luke United Methodist Church back in 1913. With its fieldstone exterior and crenellations on top that give it a castle-like appearance, it would have been very much at home in a small English village. The chipped historic bell outside dates back to 1892. I stop an older local denizen outside and ask him about the church, but that's not what's on his mind. His concern as a Catholic is the growing and seemingly endless scandal of sexual abuse in the church. As I discover in conversations with others, this is a widely shared feeling in this heavily Catholic Irish community.

"I wouldn't know. I don't go to church anymore after the abuses. I'm completely disillusioned, fed up is how I feel. You know, when you put your faith into someone. It's almost like having a wife. You trust each other, and then when they betray you. . . ." His voice trails off and a look of incredible sadness crosses his face. "I was married once, too," he continues. "I had nothing but agony. On the other hand, I'm not perfect either. I have my faults too. And today, it's a new world. What is it coming to? You see, these Protestants, they let the priests marry. They all have urges, but even if you did, why would you want to [go] after a mere kid? When they became priests they didn't know they would get the urge. It's all horrible. Well, maybe I could turn Filipino and join this church. But I'm thinking of Armageddon. I'm a-gettin' outta here." This is typical of what I hear. It seems to be on everyone's mind. Some just make a comment, or shake their heads, while others declare they'll never go to church again.

At 239th Street and Katonah, I come to the Woodlawn Heights Library, which has a collection of Irish books, occupying two shelves, most of them guidebooks. They do have an excellent local history about Woodlawn, which I carefully peruse.[37] Of even greater interest in the contemporary sense is a volume containing memoirs of Irish immigrants to the States, most of whom arrived in the 1950s and early to mid-1960s, with a few going as far back as the 1920s. These provide a fascinating look at their lives, hopes, disappointments and relationships with others. The majority of them lived in either Woodlawn or Yonkers, but quite a few resided in other Irish parts of the Bronx, like Riverdale, Norwood, and Bedford Park.[38]

The library is a really charming refuge from the hubbub of Katonah Avenue. The interior is spotless. On the right in the reading room, a beautiful tapestry created by the Bronx County Historical Society hangs, featuring drawings of important places in the borough, such as Bartow-Pell Mansion, with a rendering of its magnificent garden; Yankee Stadium; the Hall of Fame for Great Americans on the Bronx Community College campus; Bronx Botanical Gardens; Poe Cottage; the Bronx Zoo, with an obviously fanciful image of an elephant entering its portals; and Orchard Beach. Along the library walls are a series of portraits, mostly depicting local scenes in Woodlawn, created by Ann O'Grady, a talented local artist. Depicted are people standing in the street conversing with each other, a barbershop, a beauty parlor, a home with a man gazing out from his porch, and more. The oil paintings have an Edward Hopper-like, old-time, nostalgic quality to them, especially the colors, which seem almost deliberately faded, and they are excellently done. The books are well presented too. Two contrasting works, their spines open, face outward. One is a memoir, *The Lost Landscape: A Writer's Coming of Age,* by Joyce Carol Oates, the other is a book called *The Mayor of Mogadishu: A Story of Chaos and Redemption,* by Andrew Harding. A delicately pink scalloped sign above one section reads: "Young Adults." All in all, it's a perfect example of how enchanting a small library with limited space can look.

Leaving the library, I explore the streets from Webster Avenue to Van Cortlandt Park East and from 234th to 242nd Street. Scattered throughout are brick apartment buildings five to six stories high, with well-tended gardens and attractive wooden doors, topped by pretty archways. The homes are generally nice Georgians, colonials, Victorians, and Queen Annes, which somehow give the community a dreamy quality, almost as if you had stepped into the 1930s or1940s via a time machine. You can walk through these lanes and choose favorites among the homes. For me there were two on E. 239th Street. The first, at number 257, is a colonial, with a closed front porch that has four double-hung windows with small glass panes. The parents or grandparents have put up artworks that have been drawn on regular white notepaper. The garage doors are painted in bright red, with black brackets where the hinges are. Atop each of the garage doors are stained-glass windows, in navy blue, green, and yellow. The second, at number 227, is a Queen Anne, with a wraparound porch that has a ceiling of gleaming boards that are either made of pine or oak. It's supported by several Doric columns along the porch. On the top floor, I see a turret with a torch-like object above it.

Just inside Van Cortlandt Park, along Van Cortlandt Park East where it crosses Oneida Avenue, I see a bronze plaque, mounted on a boulder, commemorating a battle during the American Revolution between the Stockbridge Indian Nation, who were on the side of the Americans, and the Hessian and Tory troops, comprising Americans fighting for the British. The plaque focuses on Chief Nimham of the Wappinger Peoples, who led the Stockbridge militia and was killed along with many of his men when his militia was ambushed. The Tory colonel John Simcoe was wounded.

I return to Katonah Avenue via 237th Street and go right a few blocks. Down the road, I see the Emerald Isle Immigration Center at 4275 Katonah. The organization has helped thousands of people immigrate from Ireland, giving them information and applications, and helping them adapt once they arrive, with medical insurance, employment, permanent visas, and education. It has also advocated for legislation favorable to the immigrants. Today, it remains very active in these areas. I see an ad for a fundraiser, announcements for citizenship classes, guest speakers, films, counseling programs, and so on. This is a highly organized and knowledgeable community that draws upon a long history of immigration dating back to the potato famine of the 1840s, a challenge made easier by the fact that its people are native English speakers, albeit with a brogue when they first come here.

I arrive at Sean's Quality Deli at number 4273, which advertises Irish food, including "roast *lion* of pork." I go in and tell the person behind the counter that it's a great attention getter that causes people to check it out. As it turns out, I'm wrong. He knows nothing about it. The owner, Sarah, informs me that it was just an offering on a chalkboard that changes every day and the spelling was a careless mistake. Clearly, it's always best to check, rather than assume. Accidental misspellings abound in this city's stores, many of them run by immigrants. In this case the deli is run by Hispanics despite its Irish offerings. What's most interesting is a sitting bench outside the place, with a short poetic history that reads, in part:

> It's a long wooden bench of faded brown timber
> Five people sit there on a regular basis.
> The bench is always occupied,
> but by different people at different times
> The bench has been here a long time.
> The bench knows how people are feeling
> The bench knows who's who.
> If one is sad or happy
> It holds the information of the neighborhood
> And feels sad when no one sits on it.
> The bench is the iPhone of Woodlawn.
> The bench has served Woodlawn well.
> It's the only bench in town.

The author, Bridey McMahon, penned this poem in July of 2014. She is a resident of Ireland (not the Sinn Féin activist with the same name) who regularly visits her grandchildren who live in the area. It's an important piece of data about the community, for these are the little things that enhance solidarity among its members by giving expression to it. Observing the bench, I see the regulars and the visitors, who are treated politely but not as warmly as the locals who know each other and gather there almost daily.

Last, but certainly not least, there's Woodlawn Cemetery, just south of E. 233rd Street. It borders Woodlawn but is considered part of it. The roster of famous people buried here is endless—Rosa Parks, Aretha Franklin, Duke Ellington, Herman Melville, Ben Gazzara, Fiorello LaGuardia, Damon Runyon, Frank W. Woolworth, Robert Moses, and Irving Berlin are just a few of the greats. Walking or driving through the cemetery is an architecturally enriching experience, as well. Many of the memorials are quite astounding. One drawback is that these people are scattered among four hundred acres with 310,000 graves. My advice is to take a guided tour by surfing the internet for graves suited to one's interests. The cemetery will give visitors the names of its luminaries, but they are very difficult to find because the map isn't that clear. One of the unusual aspects of the cemetery is the elaborate colorful lifelike carvings of various animals. There's a large representation of an eagle off Central Avenue, not too far from the Webster Avenue entrance, plus an owl and a squirrel.

Ⓐ *Blowing in the Wind* sculpture
Ⓑ Botanica Mama Kengue
Ⓒ Bissel Gardens

WAKEFIELD

WAKEFIELD IS A PREDOMINANTLY working- and lower-middle-class community in the extreme northern Bronx. Its general boundaries are 242nd and 243rd Streets on the north, Baychester Avenue on the east, 233rd Street on the south, and Bronx Boulevard on the west. In the time of the Native Americans it was a wooded area. Once the Dutch arrived in the 1600s, it became farmland, a pattern that continued when the British became the dominant group here. When public transportation was extended here in the early twentieth century, white people moved in, a majority of whom were Italian and Irish.

When immigration laws were liberalized in 1965, thousands of West Indians, most of them from Jamaica, moved here and made the area their home. Other groups from the Caribbean also came, including Guyanese. Hispanics live here too, including Puerto Ricans and Dominicans. While Wakefield was considered a dangerous area during the late twentieth century, things have gotten much better recently. Today it is much safer, though not entirely so. Unfortunately, there are no outdoor recreation areas such as parks, but there are quite a few playgrounds interspersed

EDSON AV

GRACE AV

BAYCHESTER AV

STRANG AV

E 233 ST

throughout the community. The major thoroughfares are White Plains Road, E. 233rd Street, and a portion of Nereid Avenue. The IRT number 2 train runs here; and so does the 5, but only during the rush hours.

I start out on Bronx Boulevard on the western border of Wakefield. The street is mostly commercial and industrial, with many auto and auto-related shops, self-storage buildings, and other enterprises. It's not especially eye-catching until I see a small brick building at number 4380 with a sign, "Anna's Place." What could it be, I wonder, as I notice several rough-around-the-edges types sitting on a bench and a city officer standing nearby. It turns out to be a homeless shelter. In a sense, the innocuous, in fact, pleasant exterior is a way of sheltering the public from the place, perhaps because communities are often opposed to having them. There's a very nice metal sculpture made of graceful intertwining ribbons that could be a design in front of any pretty apartment building. It's called *Blowing in the Wind*, by Linda Cunningham. I ask the officer, a John Jay College graduate who's with the city homeless department, about the name on the building.

"It's named after Anna Charles, a Hispanic woman who ran the shelter."

"Is she still here?"

"Nope. She was murdered a while back by a resident who was really crazy and stalked her, and so the shelter is dedicated to her memory. She was a really nice person." This is an example of how behind a simple name there's sometimes a story. I wonder how those who use the shelter feel about the naming. Do they simply feel it's the right and proper thing to do? Are they a bit uneasy because it reminds people that someone in a similar situation to them committed this crime?

I continue on my way and notice that after Nereid Avenue, Bronx Boulevard changes rather dramatically, becoming a one-way street flanked on both sides by small attached, semi-attached, and detached generally modest homes. The block on Bronx Boulevard after E. 239th Street has a long row of attached, multiple-dwelling two- and three-story homes. Many have plants hanging from their terraces, with their windows nicely decorated. Some of the homes here are clearly very old while others look pretty new. Beyond 240th Street, the homes are even nicer, though not elaborate in any way. At number 4643, I come to a really old brick three-story structure, built 120 years ago in 1901, made of brick and stucco, with narrow double-hung windows. On the side of the building, which overlooks a small lot filled with overgrown grass, the building is sheathed in asphalt shingles in a rarely seen old-style red-and-brown hexagonal design, which unfortunately, shows significant signs of deterioration.

At the corner, on E. 241 Street, I hang a left and then a right to see what Bullard Street, which runs for a short two-block distance parallel to the Metro-North Railroad tracks, looks like. It's rather attractive, largely because the mostly private homes, with huge back-yards, face out onto a heavily wooded area with tall trees that obscure the tracks from view. Someone has actually planted corn here, and, as the song in the musical *Oklahoma* goes, "the corn is as high as an elephant's eye"; only these cornstalks seem to be even higher! Bullard is certainly one of New York's most unknown streets. One backyard contains a decrepit-looking nonfunctioning old Cadillac from the fifties. I imagine it as having once been someone's pride and joy. Despite Bullard's isolation, nothing seems to escape the eagle eyes of the city traffic violations bureau, as I see a recent ticket tucked under a vehicle's windshield wiper.

Rounding the corner on E. 242nd Street, I take note of a 1969 Chevelle in seemingly mint condition, parked outside an auto detail shop, painted a gloriously outrageous bright orange. This is the northern border of the Bronx in this area, abutting Mount Vernon. I turn south onto Carpenter Avenue. It's quiet and peaceful here, with the only reminder of the bad times being a few barred windows and porches. They haven't been removed. Perhaps it's because they still provide protection. Or possibly some of the working-class folks here simply cannot afford alarm systems. Stone walls running along the raised foundations of the homes here indicate that these homes are quite old, and many of them look it. The housing is similar on other avenues and streets in this western portion of Wakefield. Flags outside quite a few of the houses provide evidence of a Guyanese presence. One old three-story apartment building on the right has beautifully carved concrete seashells over the second-floor windows where keystones are usually placed. The area is somewhat hilly and one can sometimes catch great views off in the distance to the west where isolated homes are visible in wooded sections, giving it a distinctly country-like ambience.

Turning left on E. 239th Street, I walk east to White Plains Road and turn south. It's commercial, but not for local shopping, at least not in this upper portion. Overhead, the number 2 and 5 trains rumble by, rather frequently I must say, on their way to the last stop on the line—E. 241st Street, less than a minute away. The shops are mostly auto businesses and a potpourri of other places, a tile shop, a window and door establishment, a fast-food joint, and a Chinese takeout place. At number 4436, I see Botanica Mama Kengue, which sells religious products, many of them potions, and does spiritual readings. These stores are popular among Hispanics, and their religion is Santería. Many of those who come here are also Catholic.

Briefly, Santería is a faith that grew among the West Africans captured by the Spaniards and carried off to the New World as slaves. It means, literally, "worship of saints." The customs, traditions, and practices spread in Africa and among the indigenous populations in the Caribbean. While the precise number of believers is hard to know, there are thousands of people in New York City who go to botanicas and avail themselves of the services of Santeros, as their priests are called. Hence, if one is studying New York, knowledge of this community is important.

In the window, I see a group of figures painted on a piece of metal. On the extreme left I see a dark-skinned woman. She's called a witch doctor or *palera*, and she's originally from the Congo in Africa. In the center is a Cuban Virgin Mary in the sky, dressed in blue and white. She is considered the saint of love, charity, and fertility. Beneath her is a small boat with two white men on each end and a Black man with his hands tied, in the middle, which is meant to convey that he is enslaved. The *palera* in the painting is from Aruba, first settled by the Arawak, a group of indigenous peoples, and the beliefs are a combination of native and African cultures. On her right there's a tarot card, commonly used in Aruba, featuring a naked man on horseback. It has a sun above it, and anything with a sun means good luck. Another African man on the right is a witch doctor, referred to in the Aruban language as a *tata,* which means grandfather.

Santería developed in the New World as a response to oppression. The slaves disguised what was seen as their pagan practices by adopting various Catholic saints and it developed into a synthesis of the two faiths. Many, if not most of those who practice Santería, are Catholics and have been brought up in the church. Protestants are unlikely to be members.

Damian Velado, the co-owner of this botanica, is a good-looking man of Puerto Rican descent, perhaps in his thirties. He is wearing a dark sweatshirt, with yellow, red, green, and blue beads surrounding his throat, all of them related to Santería beliefs. His arms and neck are decorated with tattoos, an infinity sign among others, many of them unfamiliar symbols. Even his face has teardrop tattoos at the edge of his eyes, and there's a ring in his nose. There are tattoos on his hands and LOVE positioned above the knuckles with one letter per finger, plus PAIN, LIFE, and HURT elsewhere on his body. I begin my conversation by asking him about what he has in the store, a well-maintained place where the shelves are full of oils, candles, soaps, and statues, all related to the religion. Damian tells me about it.

"Energy, both good and bad is central to Santería. If you want to be a santero it's where you begin, by learning how to control energy. You see these turtles here?" He says, pointing to one rather large turtle and to two smaller ones, comfortably resting in water. "They remove bad energy from the air, and that's why they're here. When you go up to the higher ranks of priesthood, then you know how to make people feel better, and if someone asks you, you also know how to do something to someone who's done bad things to you. Sometimes you need bad to fight bad, and sometimes you need good to fight bad, depending on the situation. The methods we use are secret. The plants here, magnolias, suck out bad energy too."

"And what are these statues?"

"They're *orichas*, our saints. This one is St. Michael—our St. Michael, not the Catholic one. Here's St. Expeditas. He makes things happen quickly. This one with the axes in his hands fights for you. We cement the secrets and energy into the bottom of the statue to give it power. The beads I wear round my neck and hands are also part of the religion. I got one from a *babalawo*, which is a high-level priest. The red and white is Chango, a royal African ancestor. Any time you want to pray to any of these energy statues, you have to feed them. If you don't feed them, then they can close all the doors. You can give them mints, coconuts, guava paste, pastries. We put them in front of them."

"But they don't really eat them. I mean, do they actually disappear?"

"Not too much, but you can see the nutrients fade away. Like I said, it's more what you believe in and how you look at things. We have all these oils, one for money, one for blessings and curses, and we have herbs. We have potions too, with secret recipes that we make."

"This all sounds extremely complicated. How long does it take to learn all this stuff?" Damian gives me a look as if to emphasize what he's about to say.

"*Years*, man, *years*. You learn from people telling you things. Like growing up with your family. I'm third generation. My grandmother and mother did this. It's deep within my psyche. The weird part of it is that when you do it every day, more things just come to you. The dead are walking with us, letting us know what to do and not do. We have the religious practices that come from the Congo, called *Palo Mayombe,* and it's very serious stuff, both good and bad. Then we have candles for different purposes—to get clients to come to court, to fall in love, to get rid of somebody, whatever."

"Do you feel the energy if a person comes in with, say, bad energy?"

"Yes, but even if they have bad energy, we have to help them. Let's say they want to get back at somebody who hurt them. It's not our place to decide, because we get all types who come in here."

"What do you charge for these services?

"It's all according to what the spirits tell us to charge. They could even tell us not to charge, and then we have to follow what they say."

"So, there must be some very surprised people?" We both have a good laugh about that.

"How about the Catholic Church? Do they agree with what you're doing?"

"Not necessarily, but we have things from Catholicism, like God, Jesus, holy water, anointing. Of course, we don't have confession, because the dead don't have to confess. And we don't believe Jesus was a god. We believe he was a regular person, but one with special gifts who was very spiritual. He knew how to use his energy to heal and do other good deeds. And people like Jehovah's Witnesses, they think this is the devil's work."

I compliment Damian on his tattoos, and he tells me: "I have many more on my body. And I have lots of Japanese stuff. I love their culture, the way they carry themselves."

Damian is difficult to categorize. On the one hand, he's someone who uses potions and energy to cast spells, to heal people, and believes in wearing beads that can accomplish things. But, on the other hand, his comments about energy reveal that he sees it as a representation of what a person is really like. At the same time, he maintains that you have to believe sincerely if you want to achieve your goals. In this sense Santería is no different than a conventional faith, for all religions assert that belief is essential, whether it's to have good health or to achieve salvation of the soul. Also, his beads are the same as the crosses or stars that Christians or Jews wear for good luck and protection from evil, as well as other elements typical of most religious groups—a clear system of beliefs, specific rules about how to carry out acts of faith, priests, gatherings, values, and texts from which members can learn. There's also a, shall we say, "heroic" history. The religion was born from oppression, and its practitioners had the foresight to adapt and to fool the masters into thinking they were good Christians, even as they kept their beliefs and customs alive. And now when they adopt Catholic beliefs, it's on their own terms, as they pick and choose what they wish to preserve and what they have decided to discard.

I walk down the street to where White Plains Road becomes a real shopping area below Nereid Avenue, continuing all the way down to E. 233rd Street. There's a Rainbow shop, West Indian and Guyanese eateries, an armed forces recruiting station, and other stores common in working-class areas of the Bronx. Detouring a bit, I go right onto E. 237th Street. Here I gaze upon one of the nicest homes I've seen in this part of Wakefield. It's at number 654 on the corner of Matilda Avenue. The occupants are Guyanese, as evidenced by the multicolored flags in the front yard. There are polished marble balustrades, accompanied by an intricate floral design on the square marble pillars in front of the house. I also see red and yellow Indian paintbrush flowers.

Turning around, I head east on 237th Street and hang a right onto Furman Avenue. It's a mix of modest homes and old brick apartment buildings, with more of the same on Byron Avenue. I make a left on E. 233rd Street, which is another shopping area, and then another left on Barnes Avenue. Eventually, I spot a large five-bedroom house on the corner of Digney Avenue. It's a good-sized triangular property. On the Digney side, I notice a high stone and concrete wall, with cobblestones inside of it. Curiously enough, there's also a large cornerstone into which is carved the words: "Villa Norma." This turns out to be a relic from the past, when the community was largely Italian. On top of the wall there's a brick and stone planter in the shape of a boat. The owner is Lucille, a very pleasant older Jamaican woman.

"I do all the gardening here, which isn't easy," she tells me. "I bought the place in 1995 from an old Italian family. It's a pretty safe area and I love it. I bought it when things were rough around here. Today, it's almost like a paradise. The community is quite safe."

Continuing my walk, I pop into a grocery owned by a youngish Yemeni man with bushy eyebrows and a beautiful smile. I ask him what it's like to work here.

"Well, here everybody knows me and I know them, so I don't have to worry much about robberies from them. Sometimes shady people come here from other areas like Mount Vernon, but so far nothing has happened. I've been here maybe ten years."

"A Yemeni storekeeper in Brooklyn told me that the Yemenis got into this business when a man, not a Yemeni, lent them money and held on to their green cards until they paid off the loans."

"Yes, I believe that man was Neil Kramer, a lawyer. He's very famous in our community and helped us start in America, for which we were very grateful because no bank would lend new immigrants from a poor country money." This is a welcome corroboration from what I had previously heard. Often new immigrants obtain funds from those from their native land who are already here, but regardless, someone has to start, and that is what happened in this instance.

"You went into this business, which was your father's. Is this what you hope your children will do?"

"Absolutely not," he says. "My father died when I was very young, so I had no choice. I had to be in the store, and also, I couldn't go to college. But for my children, whatever profession they want. Not this, where you must work fourteen hours a day, six and a half days a week."

The New York City subway yards for the number 2 train lie at the end of Barnes Avenue, about a hundred yards beyond E. 239th. It's a large property stretching on for several blocks, almost to the Mount Vernon border. Off to the right is Bissel Avenue, which cannot be traversed by automobile, for it's little more than a dirt road made softer by wood chips on top of it, which runs east at a slight angle. The Bissels were French Huguenots, and some historians claim that one Israel Bissel galloped down this very street to spread the news in 1775 that "from Concord and Lexington" the American Revolutionary War had begun.[39]

I don't know it, but I'm about to discover what is probably the longest community garden in the Bronx and perhaps in the city, a distance of about three city blocks. Called Bissel Gardens, it has loads of individual garden spaces where vegetables and fruits grow, tended by local residents. The fence has quite a few gates where members of the garden can enter with a key. The garden runs along a two-story stone wall that borders the transit yards. The popularity of these gardens stems, in part, from the fact that many immigrants to this country are from rural origins. It's also a very fun thing to do for those who like it. At the intersection of Bissel and Grace Avenues, there's a two-story mural painted onto the aforementioned stone wall. It's a bright blue and white, with flowers and big butterflies adorning it and the words "Bissel Gardens" on it in large letters. Here, Bissel turns sharply leftward and soon ends at Baychester Avenue.

I turn right onto Baychester Avenue and head south. Most of this street is lined with attached and semi-attached two- and three-story red-brick homes. I go right along the streets and see more of the same along the thoroughfares such as Nereid, Pitman, Bussing, and Edenwald Avenues, which cross over streets like Grace, Boyd, Ely, Wickham, and Gunther Avenues. What they have in common is that they're modest yet comfortable homes of varying architectural types. And from the way they are maintained, it's quite apparent that the residents take considerable pride in them. Then it's back to E. 233rd Street, where I begin walking west.

Bissel Gardens

It's a primarily commercial street, with supermarkets. I see a sign near the intersection of Edenwald Avenue over a small storefront church, Open Heavens Prophetic Ministry. In general, I have found that the smaller the church, the more grandiose the name, almost as if this alone will make up for its modest size. By way of contrast, across the street one finds the Philadelphia Seventh Day Adventist Church. The name says it all, with no hyperbole needed. There are, in fact, quite a few churches on this street. My trip ends at my starting point, Bronx Boulevard and E. 233rd Street. When all is said and done, this is a fairly typical lower-middle-class community in a section of the Bronx where there are other pretty similar areas. Yet, as always, they will have some distinctive aspects. In this case it's Anna's Place, the homeless shelter; it's the Yemeni store owner and his take on children and life in general.

E 242 ST

PENFIELD ST

CRANFORD AV

SETON AV

E 241 ST

MURDOCK AV

HILL AV

NEREID AV

WILDER AV

DE REIMER AV

BAYCHESTER AV

PITMAN AV

MONTICELLO AV

BUSSING AV

EDENWALD AV

HILL AV

DURYEA AV

AMUNDSON AV

SETON AV

BELL AV

PRATT AV

HARPER AV

SECOR AV

MERRITT AV

PROVOST AV

WILDER AV

STRANG AV

Eastchester

McOWEN AV

ROPES AV

HUGUENOT AV

EASTCHEST

Seton
Falls
Park

LIGHT ST

HARPER AV

DYRE AV

ROMBOUTS AV

HEATHCOTE AV

PEARTREE AV

NOELL AV

CONNER ST

BAYCHESTER AV

CRAWFORD AV

MAROLLA AV

BOLLER AV

PALMER AV

DE REIMER AV

STEENWICK AV

BIVONA ST

HOLLERS AV

NEW ENGLAND THRUWAY

Hutchinson River

HUT

BOSTON RD

BOLLER AV

HUNTER AV

EDSON AV

GRACE AV

ELY AV

TILLOTSON AV

E 222 ST

GIVAN AV

BOSTON RD

TILLOTSON AV

TIEMANN AV

MICKLE AV

EASTCHESTER RD

WICKHAM AV

GIVAN AV

BURKE AV

FENTON AV

SEYMOUR AV

FISH AV

WILSON AV

BOUCK AV

BURKE AV

Baychester

HAMMERSLEY AV

WICKHAM AV

GUNTHER AV

TIEMANN AV

KINGSLAND AV

MICKLE AV

BRUNER AV

EDSON AV

GRACE AV

ELY AV

E GUN HILL RD

ARNOW AV

BARTOW AV

NEW ENGLAND THRUWAY

EASTCHESTER & BAYCHESTER

THESE TWO ADJOINING COMMUNITIES border each other and share a common history and are today very similar to each other demographically and residentially. They are therefore treated here as sections of one large area. The specific borders are enumerated here for those interested in knowing what parts of the community they are in. Keep in mind as well that there is no universal agreement on the precise borders. Reflecting this uncertainty, many if not most of the residents here simply say they live in either the Bronx, the northeast Bronx, east of White Plains Road, near Dyre Avenue, near E. 222nd or E. 233rd Streets, and so on. I have, in this case, largely followed the borders set by Community Board 12. The boundaries of Eastchester are the city line on the north, the New England Thruway on the east, the New England Thruway and Baychester Avenue on the south, and Baychester Avenue on the southwest. Baychester's boundaries are E. 222nd Street on the north, the New England Thruway on the southeast, E. Gun Hill Road on the south, and Boston Road on the west.

Co-op City is also considered part of Baychester, but given its self-contained nature as a community, it's discussed separately.

The area was first settled by various Native Americans, including the Siwanoy and the Weckguasgeek. They were followed by the Dutch, the British, and the Revolutionary settlers. The area remained farmland until the early twentieth century, when improved mass transportation attracted Italians, Jews, and to a lesser extent, Irish. Some members of these and other European groups still reside here, but the majority are Black, especially West Indians, and there are also Hispanics. The most important parks are Seton Falls and Haffen. The number 5 train is the main transportation option, and many commuters must use buses to get to their homes. Another choice is the Metro-North Railroad. The main commercial thoroughfares are E. Gun Hill Road, Baychester Avenue, E. 233rd Street, Boston Road, Conner Street, and to a lesser extent, Dyre Avenue and Eastchester Road. These communities are fairly safe, but caution should, nevertheless, be exercised.

My meanderings through Eastchester begin on Seton Avenue, on a block that borders Seton Falls Park on the east. The homes have a lovely view of the park. One home worth seeing, number 3860, is a detached stucco Greek revival-style structure, painted a bright yellow with white trim, and Doric columns in the front. There's a fairly large backyard too. I turn around and cross E. 233rd Street and opt to head north on Amundson Avenue, one block east of Seton. The homes here are more upscale than in southern Wakefield, and this is true also for the streets just east of Amundson, from Durea to Mulvey. There are detached all-brick houses as well as large Victorians. Most of the residents are Black and West Indian, or Guyanese. They take great pride in their homes, seeing them and their lives as the embodiment of the American dream as they recall with pleasure how much better their communities are when compared with twenty or thirty years ago.

Rounding the corner onto Strang Avenue I make the next left onto Seton and see, at number 4065, a creatively designed garden with giant sunflowers and crimson-topped cockscomb flowers. Off to the side are bushes pruned into interesting shapes. The next home has a beautiful fence resting on a concrete wall. Mysteriously, a large gold-trim headboard on the home's side near the sidewalk seems to be available for the taking. People do put all sorts of things on their property. It can be an expression of independence, as if to say, "It's my property and I can put whatever I want on it."

I see an especially beautiful home at 4064 Monticello Avenue, the next street to the west of Seton. It's constructed of brick in varying colors. The porch is open and has three arches, one of which is over the entrance. Also, the banisters have pretty balustrades on both sides. Two plaster dogs, Jack Russells, are sipping water from a dish. Across the street, number 4039, is a blue-painted clapboard house with a blue slate roof. Gold ironwork has been placed inside the glass of the windows facing the front of the house. Monticello is one of the nicest blocks in the community, which is about two blocks from Mount Vernon in Westchester County.

Turning left off Monticello at Pitman Avenue, I soon make a right onto Murdoch Avenue and pass by Mount St. Michael Academy, a Catholic prep school for boys, serving grades 6–12. Demographically, its students reflect the area they're in, with Blacks and Hispanics making up about 70 percent of the student body; non-Hispanic whites comprise another 17 percent, Asians 3 percent, and mixed-origin students the rest. Situated on twenty-two acres, the school, colloquially known as "the Mount," features a handsome main building in a Collegiate Gothic style with castle-like turrets on top. It was founded in 1926 and is run by the Marist Brothers. While it has lost some of its luster when compared to the past, it's still a good school, boasting a high graduation rate, with some 70 percent of the students going on to college. Tuition is inexpensive for a private high school, about $8,000 a year.

Continuing up Murdock to the corner of E. 241st Street, I notice on my right at number 942 a stunning, large brick home. What's most noteworthy about it is a giant second-floor porch containing flower-filled planters, which wraps around the house. Arrayed along it are filigreed wrought-iron columns, and the roof seems to be covered with solar panels.

From here I turn around and head south on Murdock to E. 233rd Street, turn right for a few blocks, and make a left onto Baychester Avenue. After several blocks I go left onto Needham Avenue, another portion of Eastchester, and one that is decidedly plainer than the area I've just finished exploring. Walking up and down the cross streets, De Reimer, Palmer, and Boller Avenues, I'm struck by the overwhelming predominance of three-story multifamily brick homes. Make no mistake—in the South Bronx they would look nice, but they don't compare to the detached homes in Wakefield and other parts of Eastchester. I stroll north a short distance on Boller and enter the park on Crawford Avenue, near where it intersects with Boller.

Seton Falls Park is a lovely, somewhat hilly park, heavily forested, with terrific trails and concrete walkways along rocky outcroppings, tall gnarled trees, boulders, and streams. It's a wetlands and bird sanctuary, along with the constructed waterfalls created by the Seton family. The most famous person in the family, of course, is Elizabeth Seton, a convert to Catholicism who was the first native-born American to be named a saint, in 1975. In 2009, almost $1 million was spent on improving the trails, signage, and other aspects of the park. Today, however, there is scant evidence that the park is in good shape. People throw their garbage all around the edges of the park. Even though I saw workers cleaning it up along the edge on E. 233rd, their efforts seemed half-hearted as they picked up perhaps 10 percent of the total. Inside the park there's garbage too. The paths and trails are not well-maintained, homeless people hang out, and people openly smoke and sell weed. One hardly sees any park employees around. In fact, I saw none during my park excursion.

So why bother to mention it here, given the current state of affairs? Simply because it's so naturally beautiful. The trees are tall, many of the boulders are huge and naturally landscaped. This has to be the most literal reality of the signs in New York proclaiming "Forever Wild." The trails wind along circuitous routes and one has the feeling of being hundreds of miles away from the city. And although the waterfalls are only miniature falls, flowing over several large rocks, the views are, nonetheless, breathtaking. For those wishing to see large waterfalls that dwarf these, I suggest the falls at E. 180th Street, between the Botanical Gardens and the Bronx Zoo. Occasionally, crimes are committed in the park, but it's quite unusual. Still, the fear of walking inside the parks is palpable.

I meet a middle-aged Black woman, with yellow highlights in her curly hair. Christine befriends me and offers to walk with me in the park. Aha, an experienced park walker, I think. It turns out she's never been inside, only in the playground along Crawford Avenue. Here, people are playing with or watching their children.

"I'm ready to walk with you," says Christine. "Why not? You know, I've never done this. It's going to be interesting. You know, this isn't like Central Park."

"That's true. You've never been inside, but you live only three blocks away. How long have you lived here?"

"Twenty years," she says, looking a bit sheepish. "I guess I was kinda afraid." We're on a wide walkway, with trails stretching out, right, left, uphill, and downhill in maze-like fashion. I tell Christine I'm going down one that has stairs on it as well.

"Are you sure you wanna do that? You're pretty brave. I can't see anything beyond a little ways. Where that goes I don't know. You're an adventurous guy," she says, laughing. As I begin my descent, intent upon seeing what's there, she adds: "I'll just watch you, but don't go out of my sight." She is genuinely concerned about my welfare and doesn't want anything to happen to me. I hear it in her voice and see it in her eyes. It also dawns upon me that just as I thought her presence would make things safer, she was thinking *my* presence would do so. Thus, my separating from her causes some anxiety. I promise to return but she keeps calling my name after she loses sight of me and I promise to come back soon, which I do. This happens in several different places.

When we leave, finally, having satisfied my curiosity, she proclaims: "Wow, this has really been something else. What an adventure! I can't believe I did this. Wait till my daughter hears about it, and my son." She calls them and describes what it was like. I don't regard her behavior as atypical in any way. Although the city is much safer today, many people remain unconvinced of that. As an aside, there's much talk of racial polarization, and it's true. But what about the fact that a Black woman does not hesitate to walk with a white man in an overwhelmingly Black community into a park that she's a bit apprehensive about?

Christine is a very nice person who grew up in the South Bronx and graduated from Morris High School, a pretty tough place. She has three children, one of whom attends Brooklyn College, the other Westchester College. A third child is a Con Ed employee. Her husband passed away several years ago. She received her degree from Monroe College in the Bronx, a hallowed institution for lower-income people in the Bronx. She worked as a crossing guard, but has a degree in public health. Last week she interviewed for a mid-level medical administrative position at Columbia Presbyterian Hospital. I really hope she gets it.

Leaving the park, I head back down Boller Avenue, cross Boston Road, and wander the streets adjacent to Boller: Palmer, Hunter, Wright, Tillotson. The homes are pretty much identical to what I saw earlier in the section along Needham Avenue—multifamily dwellings of the cookie-cutter variety and small detached or semi-attached homes. As they're near the highway, it's somewhat noisy. There are also NYCHA projects here, which the residents say are "not too bad." They're located along Reeds Mill Lane and Bivona Street. On Boston Road, I pass many auto places and fast-food restaurants. I turn left on Conner Street. There are some old, rather basic private homes here, but it's mostly commercial. There's also a huge sex shop here called Romantic Depot, offering lingerie, dildos of all sorts, and other similar items. I leave after a brief visual encounter with a four-foot-high rubberized penis! These places have to be somewhere, and this commercial drag is an ideal location for one. Returning to Boston Road, I continue up the street heading toward the Westchester County line. Along the way, I take a quick walk through the streets running off Boston Road, like Noell, Peartree, and Heathcote Avenues. All of them are industrial—auto repair and collision outfits and junkyards.

Continuing along Boston Road, I expect to find more of the same and am pleasantly surprised to find it's not true. Just beyond the Hutchinson River (Boston Road briefly becomes an overpass that traverses it) on the right is a hidden neighborhood that is a true oasis. Make a right on any of the following three streets—Huguenot, McCowen, or Ropes—and you'll find it. The homes are almost all detached, well taken care of, though outside of two or three exceptions, hardly opulent. It's a mostly white neighborhood. In the Bronx, white can just as often mean of Hispanic origin, as Puerto Ricans settled early in this borough and many of their children and grandchildren have done well and live in places like this or in the suburbs ringing the city. I speak with a middle-aged resident standing in front of his home on Eastchester Place. He refers to his neighborhood as "the Bronx" even though he knows it's Eastchester. This is true in much of the borough.

"Your house overlooks this river. Really nice."

"Yes, it's called the Hutchinson River. It's kinda like a hidden neighborhood. We're on the edge of Westchester. Used to be woods and a beach here in the fifties. It's a little polluted but used to be worse. It's not completely safe to swim in." Next to his home is an interesting house at number 3480. It's fairly large and has very charming fieldstone blocks embedded in the brick exterior. As a decorative device, the door is also framed in fieldstone.

I make a left and go up Huguenot Avenue back toward Boston Road and see more pretty homes. It's really quiet. Nothing seems

Hidden neighborhood in Eastchester

to be happening here, one might say. One cannot tell there's a residential community here because on the corner of Boston Road and the next street, McOwen Avenue, there's a Wendy's, though one giveaway is a small sign that says "Passenger cars only." Across Boston Road on the left is a shopping center with a Lane Bryant and other shops. The next block going east is Ropes Avenue, and it's the last block in the city. I turn right onto it and then left on Flint Avenue. Here I meet a Hispanic man walking with his grandson and his small dog. I ask him how long he's lived here.

"About nineteen years. It's very safe and quiet."

"How did you even find it?"

"You know, I lived in the Bronx my whole life, but I used to love going to the IHOP, here. I love that restaurant, and it was nearby, so I discovered the neighborhood." So we see that a simple eating choice can lead to a residential choice.

"Do you live on this block?"

"Yeah, second house from the corner. My house cost about $450K. My brother's house, that monster place, I don't even wanna think about what it cost." Indeed, it's a giant house with shiny balustrades, and it must be worth $1–$1.5 million. I wonder what it's like to live next to your brother whose home is so much larger, but decide to play it safe and not go there.

"Can you get to Manhattan from here?"

"Yes, but I need to take a bus to the 5 train, and I don't like doing that route. The 5 train isn't very nice," he says, with a short laugh. I've taken the 5 and it's a long ride, but okay if you have something to read or listen to. Walking to the end of the block, I hit Pelham Bay Place West. Indeed, the extreme western end of Pelham Bay Park is here, as a sign proclaims. It's a large field that's used for soccer but also has room for walking. It's separated from the rest of this giant park by the New England Thruway. I end my trip here, satisfied that I've found yet another hidden corner of the Bronx, unknown to most people who live in the city. I have a feeling it would be a popular choice for many in terms of price, peacefulness, and easy access to shopping.

Baychester is a much smaller, quiet area with decent-looking private homes for the most part, ranging from multifamily to small detached homes, and some apartment buildings scattered throughout the area. The main shopping thoroughfares are E. Gun Hill Road and Boston Road. Of interest is Haffen Park, which can be easily accessed from Hammersley Avenue. It's a compact and well-landscaped three-block-long recreational space. It has a half bandshell and a stage for local performances. There are tennis and basketball courts, a soccer field, even a boxball court, all in good condition. The playgrounds here have been modernized with the latest equipment for children. Plus, there's a pretty good outdoor pool. In short, no space is wasted here, including a pleasantly situated sitting area with benches throughout. Haffen Park is named after the first borough president, Louis Haffen, the son of a German dairy farmer and beer brewer. An engineer by profession, his résumé included a stint working in Colorado mines. Most important, he's also credited with planning various boulevards and parks of the Bronx.

I walk east on Wickham Avenue to Arnow Avenue, where, on the corner at number 1768 Arnow, I stop and gaze upon a charming home whose outside on three sides consists of hundreds of cobblestones on the first floor and on the chimney, with very old pillars partially supporting it. It's a robust survivor from the old days in a sea of nondescript houses. Coming to Eastchester Road, a wide boulevard with tall trees and a small shopping area, I turn right and proceed northwest to Boston Road. Here I turn left and climb a bit of an incline to Corsa Avenue, where I have a chance to look west all the way to the faint outlines of the George Washington Bridge and the area before it. It's a great view of the sweep that makes up the Bronx from east to west.

On E. Gun Hill Road, I make a left and soon come to a bowling alley, also on my left, with the long exterior that has the name Gun Post Lanes in large letters on it. There aren't many bowling alleys left in this city, so I'm curious to see how this one is doing on a weekday afternoon at 3:30 p.m. A heavy-set older white man with reddish-gray hair is sitting on a barstool. He admits to working here and greets me with a wan smile and a barely audible hello, suggesting he's just going through the motions of running a business. Indeed, there's no one bowling except for a couple of Black twenty-somethings using two lanes. The other forty-six lanes are utterly devoid of humanity. The gutters between the lanes are painted in royal blue, and facing the bowler above the pins is a painting of a city skyline. Inside a small luncheonette in the back, I see green, old-style round globes with the word "Budweiser" in script letters as light fixtures. They're thirty years old at least.

"Hi. I used to bowl all the time. Does anybody still bowl these days? Does the place fill up on the weekend?"

"Are you kidding? Bowling's dying. Pretty soon there ain't gonna be no bowling no more."

"I'm very sad to hear that. When I was in my twenties, I used to bowl every week in Queens as a member of the New York Daily News League. What I love most about the game is that when you bowl a perfect 300 game, it's a perfect game anywhere, unlike a sport like basketball where your points scored are always a matter of what level competition you played against. So, who comes here?"

"Not much, just people here and there. We have a school program for five weeks. Friends of the owner take care of his bills, running the place for now. There are maybe ten or fifteen left in the five boroughs. What do you do?"

"I teach at City College of New York. I'm writing a book about the Bronx, and I'm trying to understand what's going on around here."

"Oh yeah? Forget it. You don't understand. You don't live here. It's not like it used to be in the sixties, seventies. It's much more dangerous today. There's a killing every day; four or five every day in the five boroughs, maybe ten or fifteen. They keep it a secret. Everybody's dyin'."

"But the murder rate's way down compared to the old days."

"C'mon. There's gotta be about 5,000 killings a year on the average in the city. I been here since 1970. What do you do with the book? Sell it? They'll kill you if they find out you was talking about them. In the fifties there were a lotta whites here. Then the Puerto Ricans came in the 1970s, and they were fighting with the whites. Then the Blacks came in the eighties, and then in the late nineties the West Indians, and all these years everybody was killing the group that was there before them." I thank him for his time and depart.

This man has a very dour and pessimistic view, no doubt partially influenced by the decline of his business. His statistics about the number of people murdered annually is wildly incorrect, 5,000 vs. the reality of 300. As I've discovered, one's view of this has to do with one's immediate neighborhood and social isolation from newer ethnic/racial groups that have replaced one's own. Keep in mind that Baychester, while not very safe, isn't particularly dangerous, either. Added to that is the frustration that nobody's interested in what he has to offer, and that in itself has got to be depressing to people who have given their all to something and now all that's left are the memories.

(A) Primrose Cricket Club Inc.
(B) E. 221st St. King Bee mural
(C) Zambo Aroma
(D) First Presbyterian Church of Williamsbridge

WILLIAMS-BRIDGE

WILLIAMSBRIDGE'S BORDERS ARE E. 233rd Street on the north, Baychester Avenue and Boston Road on the east, Adee Avenue on the south, and the Bronx River Parkway on the west. What was once a distinct community called Olinville, south of E. Gun Hill Road to Adee Avenue, is now considered part of Williamsbridge as well, and in terms of who lives there and the housing that predominates, is not different from the rest of Williamsbridge. The name refers to John Williams, who had a farm in the eighteenth century along the Bronx River. A small community was established during the nineteenth century, and then came the usual pattern in the Bronx as public transportation attracted people from Manhattan to the area, most of them Italians and Jews, and a smattering of Blacks, who arrived in the 1920s.

In general, Williamsbridge appears to be a bit more upscale than its neighbor, Baychester. It is a viable, fairly safe, thriving place, with community organizations, many churches, and a lively commercial district. Most of the population is West Indian, along with smaller groups of African Americans, and Hispanics. The West Indians, along with some Guyanese and Dominicans, became a presence in the 1980s. The demographic shift from whites to Blacks took place in the early seventies as poorer residents, predominantly African Americans, in search of safety and decent housing, began moving in. Most of the housing is private and multifamily homes owned by those who live in them, and small three- and four-story apartment dwellings scattered throughout the community.

I start out with a walk past, and through, Edenwald Houses, widely regarded as one of the worst crime-ridden NYCHA housing projects in the city. Walking along Shieffelin Place, E. 229th Street, and Laconia Avenue around noon I hardly see anyone around. However, at 4:00 p.m. when I return, there are plenty of high school–age people hanging out, but not paying attention to me. Laconia Avenue has a small shopping area for several blocks, but the rest of Laconia is mostly residential all the way down opposite the public housing projects and south of them, with attached and semi-attached homes made of brick for the most part.

I turn right, or west, on several streets in the 220s from east to west to get a closer look at the community. Of these E. 223rd Street is quite typical of the rest. The houses are in various styles and generally well tended. Most blocks also have a few three- or four-story old apartment buildings. Butler Memorial United Methodist Church is located at 3920 Paulding Avenue where it intersects with E. 223rd. It was established over a century ago, in 1912. The belfry has a silver cross above it, beautifully framed against a brilliant blue autumn sky. East 223rd Street between Paulding and Bronxwood Avenues consists almost entirely of older, solid-looking semi-attached red-brick homes, many of them with a diamond-shaped pattern of bricks at various points. One house here has two small statues of Ganesh the elephant god, where normally lions would be showcased. Not surprisingly, as the prayer flags in the garden indicate, it's owned by a

Guyanese family. The elephants' trunks are curled upward as if poised to take off in flight, and a surefire indicator of ethnic change in the community. At number 929 I see an unusual home with a wall made of small boulders attached to each other in haphazard fashion. A bit farther on I view a multicolored home in bright red, yellow, and blue, which might be seen by some as a "statement home" of sorts.

At White Plains Road, the main shopping district of this community, I turn left and go south toward E. 222nd Street. Here are large pharmacies, Domino's Pizza, Dollar Tree, supermarkets, nail salons, barbershops, realty and attorney offices and the like, numerous eateries advertising curried goat and jerk chicken, and shops offering Caribbean staples. My attention is drawn to a sign over a store called Mercy and Blessing, claiming to offer brand-name clothing. I cross over and enter it and am overwhelmed by the number of items piled sky high helter-skelter, in seeming danger of tumbling down to the ground—small appliances, bedding, and clothing of every description. I ask the Ghanaian storeowner, a woman wearing traditional African garb: "I was wondering why you call this place Mercy and Blessing?"

"We are religious Christians, and we believe all that is good comes from God. Other people have also asked us, and they think we're claiming to be a religious organization so we won't have to pay taxes, but we don't do that. We are believers, but we are not a church." In fact, this community has many storefront churches and for some, say locals, it is a tax dodge. On E. 221st Street, I spy a 9/11 memorial—a grassy area surrounded by a small metal fence, with a plaque memorializing those who lost their lives on 9/11, stating "You will never be forgotten," dedicated by a Frank Pinto. I've seen many memorials like this in the city, but this is somewhat special in that it's not on a wall but right on the street itself. It's a beautiful marble symbolic gravestone embossed in gold. There are also roses on each side accompanied by several gold cherubs. In front is what looks like a miniature lighthouse and a flagpole.

Continuing west on 221st I pass a private home on a triple lot, unusual in these parts. At number 631, there's a home with a large wrought-iron fence and jagged stone pillars. The porch is home to a cat with six of her babies snuggled up against each other.

Returning via E. 220th Street to White Plains Road, I take note of the Jamaican equivalent to the old Italian social clubs. Only instead of a place possibly named a "gun and rod club," it is identified as the Primrose Cricket Club Inc., at number 3836, reflecting the popularity of the game among West Indians. It's old, having been established first in the West Indies in 1913. Next door is a barbershop, called the Ambiance Beauty Salon, that appears to cater to men. It's run by Errol Thomas, an older Jamaican gentleman whom I engage in an impromptu conversation.

"Is this place next door a Jamaican club?"

"Not necessarily. There are people from different countries. Yes, Jamaica, but also Barbados, Trinidad, and other lands."

"If I told you I had a favorite singer from Jamaica, who would you think I mean?"

"Probably Bob Marley."

"No. It's Beres Hammond."

His face actually lights up upon hearing this because Beres Hammond is not well known to white folks like Marley, or, say, Harry Belafonte. He's a contemporary crooner who draws thousands of Black people to his concerts, one of which I attended at Lehman College where I was the only white person in the audience. I just wanted to see the look on his face and I was rewarded. He actually said, "Wow, I never thought you, a white guy, would know him."

"I'm writing a book about the Bronx and want to include your place, but, of course, I won't mention the scantily-clad pinup model you have."

"Why not?" he says. "She's beautiful. People should come in and appreciate the photo."

"Spoken like a true barber," I respond, laughing.

"How long have you been a barber?"

"For fifty-two years. I've lived here since 1987." Barbers usually lay out their private lives via photos. I see pictures of his children—one, a psychologist; another, a postal worker—and a photo of his brother who has passed away.

"Do you visit Jamaica?"

"Yes. I love it there, and if I had the money I would go back home for good. Life is better there. I have free movement there and everything, a beach, fresh food."

"But how about your children? Didn't they have opportunities here?"

"In what way?"

"Well, one became a psychologist."

"There are opportunities there too, and the people are nicer there. Look, they arrested this man for bombing a synagogue. He was white, so they took him alive. Had he been Black, they would have shot him dead."

At 3828, I see a Laundromat named "Fun-o-Mat," which strikes me as a funny name for a business. Whoever heard of seeing a launderette as a fun place? After all it's just a locale where people sit and wait, hoping it won't take too long. Except that they came up with the name as an attention grabber. Across the street at 3809, is another interesting name, this one for a Chinese takeout joint—Dream Station.

Just off of White Plains Road, on the northeast corner of E. 221st Street, is an intricately designed, captivating, and quite colorful mural. Starting from the left side is a drawing of two couples dancing what appears to be the tango, at least from the positioning of the dancers on an outdoor deck. The woman, clad in a bright red dress is quite curvaceous. Another woman, wearing a pink sleeveless dress, with matching high-heeled pink shoes, is seated at a table doing something on a laptop and facing the dancers. She's also holding a pink cup. Bright floodlights above illuminate the deck, which is surrounded by a black railing, beyond which is a green grassy area. Next to a fence post, a man wearing a hat and a yellow suit is perusing a newspaper. Off to the side, a train is entering a station, perhaps the Metro-North Railroad. Nearby is a bridge resembling the Throgs Neck Bridge, but that can't be because there is no train that passes near the Throgs Neck at ground level. Next to it is a group of tall buildings, in orange, purple, and other colors, that appears to be a city skyline, but not one in New York City. Near a fence, I spot a blue fire hydrant. Above is a magenta-colored sky, with black birds flying under it. The creator of this tableau is the well-known artist King Bee (www.kingbeeuw.com). It's really worth seeing, especially because this one is not on his website.

Zambo Aroma is also situated on this corner, at 3818 White Plains Road. The mural runs the length of the place. Aromatherapy involves the use of substances extracted from plants to maintain and nurture the health of the body and mind. I walk into the store and meet Tree, the co-owner, a young Black man, who hails from Chicago.

"First, tell me how you ended up with the name of Tree?"

"Well, I chose it because it stands for ability to withstand all seasons, being deeply rooted."

"That's a great name. How did this business begin?"

"We started with different types of soaps, and then we grew to loofas and other skin care items like bath salts, essential oils, and soon we'll have an oxygen bar."

"Your place is so beautifully designed and very spacious. Are there other places like this in the Bronx?"

"Stores with this kind of ambience and which offer these services are very rare in the Bronx. I began doing this seventeen years ago in Chicago, where I grew up and learned how to do this. I graduated from college in Chicago and then moved here. We opened three months ago."

"What made you choose this area? An enterprise like this would be more common in communities like Greenwich Village, or Brooklyn Heights. I mean, it's a luxury rather than an absolute necessity, and this is predominantly a working-class community."

Zambo Aroma

"Well, first my partner and I bought a house here, and we have six kids—seventeen, six, four, two three-year-olds, and last, a newborn. All except the last one are adopted. The newborn was carried to term by a female friend."

"Was your house the only reason for locating the store here?"

"My parents were heavily into the civil rights movement and believed strongly in supporting the Black community. So since I bought the house here, I want to invest in my community. And it's a necessity to work nearby because I have so many kids. Of course, it's a strange place to build a business like this. A lot of people stand outside for a few minutes trying to figure out what exactly this is. But we get the word out online, and we're attracting customers. Tomorrow we're having a Halloween party for local kids."

Before leaving the store, it's worth describing what this open space looks like. On the right there's a long black wall, almost like a blackboard, with writings in colored chalk and people have signed their names on it. There's also an orange wall, decorated with hanging fabrics, baskets, and other art objects. On the left is another long wall with attached wooden shelves on which rest many small bottles of oils, and also wax candles, identified as pumpkin, seabreeze, vanilla-bean, and other aromas. There are many different types of soaps, body rubs, bath salts, lotions, and hair tonics. I also see stones and crystals. In the back, there's an attractive curtain with painted fruits and leaves and background paints in white, black, gray, and orange.

I'm not sure that this effort will succeed, but the determination and outgoing, warm personalities and incredibly hard work of these people make me feel that either it will or they'll adapt their business to the community's needs if necessary. Having children and a nearby home will likely be a great motivator for them.

Heading north on White Plains Road, I make a right onto E. 225th Street and soon come to the First Presbyterian Church of Williamsbridge at number 730, built in 1903. It has red wooden shingles, surrounded by yellow trim, and seems very old. It has large stained-glass windows and a square belfry tower with a pagoda-shaped roof. At number 806, I notice, on my right, a plain four-story brick apartment building, called the Towers. Yet there's absolutely nothing remotely resembling a tower design, and four floors does not a tower make. But the most interesting aspect of it is a metal sign, admonishing "No loitering, No bicycles, carriages, ball-playing, skating, de-facing, loud music," and then "No mutilating"! Who is being mutilated? What types of mutilations are being performed? Who knows? It's rather humorous in a bizarre way.

Returning to Williamsbridge the following day, I begin my trip heading west from where E. Gun Hill Road crosses Boston Road. I can't help but notice that Williamsbridge has many churches, most likely because many of its residents are West Indians and devout churchgoers. On one short block on Gun Hill, I pass four storefront churches, and that's not atypical.

At number 974, my attention is drawn to what I consider an unusual establishment, a music school run by an Italian man, the Palomba Academy. While it's clearly a leftover from the old days when this area was an Italian redoubt, inside it's flourishing, with people waiting their turn. It's a serious school with an enrollment of 500 students and a large selection of programs. The school's motto is "We don't just teach students, we build musicians." Its prices are very reasonable, thirty dollars for a half-hour private lesson. Right now, it's focused on enrolling students to play in ensemble groups. I speak with Michael Palomba, the proprietor, a man with blue eyes and gray hair, with a stocky build.

"October 22nd was our sixty-second anniversary," he tells me.

"That says a lot. It's a really long time."

"Yes, it does. It's a family business and I'm sixty-one. I'm born in this building. It's nice to see all these people from the more recent cultures that moved here come in and express interest in music. Yes, you can say Black, but that's like saying white. The Blacks are African, West Indian, Haitian. Some are French and others are English. Unfortunately, many of our politicians are seeking to divide us. We also don't need to have homeless people brought into neighborhoods where people have paid $500,000 of hard-earned money to live in peace and quiet. It just doesn't work and it's not right. This neighborhood was a mix at one time—Irish, Italian, Jewish, Black, and Puerto Rican. We lived and played together on the same blocks, and we were proud of who we were. We weren't the same, but our ethnicity or race defined us. We had an identity, a past."

"Now that the community has changed, doesn't the music that's 'in' change too?"

"Yes, but it's not clear-cut, because it depends on who influences the young people. If it's the parents, then they'll go for R&B; if it's the kids in school, then it could be rock or hip-hop; if it's the minister, then maybe gospel. It's a compliment to the community that the people here are loyal to us. These people are hardworking and they pay $1,500 a year to learn music, and we are dedicated to giving them the opportunities. And when they come to apply, we interview them about their lives and goals. We're a caring place, and I love what I do."

Michael is a man who clearly cares deeply about his work. The school is his life. How has he survived? He might have good business skills and organizational abilities, but it's his drive, passion, and pride in having been here for so long that keeps him going. Businesses fail all the time in this city, but it's the people that have these traits who succeed.

I pass by the Wisdom Nail and Hair Salon. Could this be another gimmick to attract passersby? Is there a religious theme at work here? Nothing of the sort it turns out. The woman bought the salon from a friend whose last name was Wisdom, and so she kept it but will change it soon to her name, Tracy's. I turn right onto White Plains Road. Turning right on E. 215th Street I head toward Barnes Avenue, and on my right there's a curious oddity, a one-story brick apartment building with a flat roof, located at number 768, dating back to 1901. It has nice corbels and there are six apartments, all on one level. I wonder why they never built it any higher. The buildings in this portion of Williamsbridge are older than other sections and have more character as a result. They reflect a bygone era that has been somewhat preserved.

My trip ends in what was once called Olinville, the area from E. Gun Hill Road to Adee Avenue. There's not much to say here. It's a quiet, less commercial section with homes that are a bit nicer than in the rest of Williamsbridge, especially between Duncan Street and Burke Avenue. Some of the older four-story apartment buildings can also be found here. I leave here with the realization that there are peaceful, entirely livable communities in the northeast Bronx waiting for people who feel they're good enough, or who think of them as a way station to greater success.

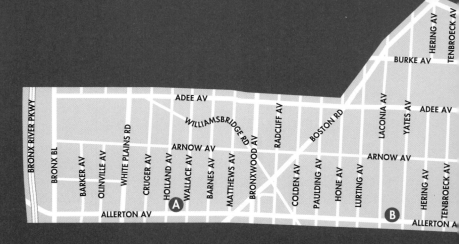

Ⓐ Bruce Lee Mural
Ⓑ Sal & Dom's Pastry Shop

ALLERTON

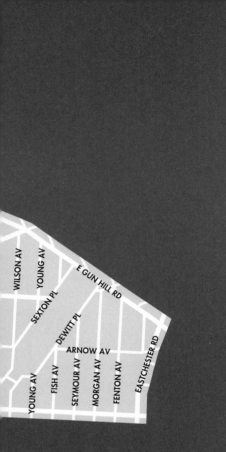

THE BOUNDARIES OF ALLERTON ARE Adee Avenue and E. Gun Hill Road on the north, Eastchester Avenue on the east, Allerton Avenue on the south, and the Bronx River Parkway on the west. Like Williamsbridge, its name is derived from a farmer, Daniel Allerton, who tilled the soil in this area. In the early twentieth century, with the extension of the IRT subway line, it became a destination for working-class white people seeking to escape from Manhattan's poorer communities. Generally speaking, the Jews were concentrated west of Bronxwood Avenue and the Italians to the east. There was also a small concentration of Irish who resided here.

In the 1980s, the community became home to many Blacks, primarily West Indians, who, like their white predecessors, were also working class. Other groups who settled here were Dominicans and Guyanese. Today only a small number of white people, namely Italians augmented by Albanians, remain, and their numbers are shrinking. The western part of Allerton Avenue is the main commercial drag here, plus small portions of Boston and Williamsbridge Roads, both of which cut through the community at an angle. Overall, this is a fairly safe community. The main park is Bronx River Park, which runs between Bronx Park East and the Bronx River Parkway.

I begin my voyage through Allerton from Bronx Park East with an eastward walk along Adee Avenue. It's a quiet street, and most of the homes are semi-attached and attached two-story brick homes, and a few apartment buildings. They are well kept and modest, as befits this working-class community. There's also a NYCHA housing project, Eastchester Houses. One especially nice Tudor-type brick apartment house is at 808 Adee between Barnes and Matthews Avenues. Built in 1927, it has multicolored bricks—brown, red, orange, and beige in alternating colors—with the Tudor part of the building consisting of white stucco. The impressive front entrance has a large A-shaped design made of wood that is positioned above a Gothic arch. Surrounding the entrance are large blocks of very attractive beige and gray stone, topped by a mock roof-front with slate stone above it.

Intermittently, I go right on the streets I'm passing—Cruger, Bronxwood, Radcliffe, Paulding, Lurtig, and so on—and explore the housing there. There isn't much worth commenting about, other than to say the homes are well maintained and mostly attached, with single-family homes as well.

Eventually Adee temporarily dead-ends into Sexton Place before reappearing on the other side of it, the same being true of Arnow, which runs parallel to Adee south of it. As my way is blocked, I go left on Sexton for a block, turn right on E. Gun Hill Road, and then make a right very soon onto Eastchester Avenue, taking it down to Allerton and making another right, thus heading west. From Eastchester to about Hone Avenue, Allerton is mainly residential and, therefore, a quiet stretch. In a few blocks, just past Yates Avenue, I come to an Italian bakery at number 1108, Sal & Dom's Pastry Shop. One of the few stores in this section, it's been in business for sixty-two years. The young woman working there informs me that it's been a family-run business for three generations. Today, Dom

Sal & Dom's Pastry Shop

still comes in every day, even though he has a hard time getting around at age eighty-seven. I guess he can't let go of something he spent his whole life doing. A youngish man emerges from the back and introduces himself as Carlo.

"I'm third generation. How can I help you?"

"I'm writing a book about the Bronx, and I have a couple of questions about the bakery."

"Well, I'm really busy now. I'd love to help you but I got some things in the oven. If you wanna come back I could spend some time, but it's the holiday season and I'm really busy."

I decide not to do that because there might not be another time and just ask him: "Who are your customers?"

"Well, the area has changed. In the old days, the people were mostly Italian. Today, it's everybody—Jamaicans, Dominicans, Asians, you name it."

"Do you try to make items that they would like?"

"We have a Hispanic type of cake, but that's pretty much it. Everything else, cakes, pies, cookies, bread, is traditional Italian or American."

"Are you the last of a kind here?"

Carlo pauses briefly before answering, as if it's a vexing question: "I don't think my kids are gonna want to work here. They're fourteen- and twelve-year-old girls."

"Then why did you, in the third generation, decide to go into it? Couldn't you also have said no?"

"That's a good question. I don't know. I just don't know." I look at the words emblazoned against the wall in large letters: "Family, Inspire, Memories" and wonder if he ever felt inspired? Did he do it out of guilt? Italians are, of course, very family-centered as a group, and often well into adulthood. He will have memories no doubt of the time he put in here, but apparently, his children most likely won't.

The family clearly takes pride in what they do, emphasizing their approach as a craft, an art, not simply a business. Their website, in essence, says so: "You can still find quality, fresh baked products made from the original recipes. We don't buy products baked or even part baked. We still make our own cannoli, something our competitors can only dream of. Everything from our famous rainbow cookies to beautifully decorated wedding cakes, are all done the same way since 1956."

Tradition and a belief that the old way is the best way is their stock-in-trade. One has to be impressed by people who make their own cannoli. They must believe it's better that way, I think. It would be easier to buy it wholesale. And then there's the implication that if they've been around since 1956, they must have something special to offer. But there's trouble ahead. Carlo is obviously pessimistic that the pastry shop can outlast him. I have seen this time and time again. A business becomes irrelevant, and the owners have no real desire to adapt to a changing clientele. And so, nothing is left behind for others to remember. Perhaps he could have moved to a suburb with an Italian community, but who would have paid him enough for his business so that he could start over again? In the end, places like this—restaurants, bakeries, barbershops, and the like—are really representations of life itself. They're born, or rather created, they have a prime period when demand for what they have to sell is high. And then, they decline and eventually they die.

Thus, the stores mirror the life and times of those who toiled in them for years, even decades. Their past exists only in the minds of their owners and those who purchased their products. And then they are replaced by a new generation of customers who literally buy into something else that appeals to them, a Dominican bakery, a roti shop for a Jamaican clientele, a hair salon. And eventually, they may well suffer the same fate.

As I leave, I bump into an older couple on their way into the store and ask, "What do you think of this place?"

"It's great, just great. And I come from all the way over on East Tremont and Leland Avenue." That's not really far, perhaps a five-minute drive. But everything's relative and for a man who looks to be in his early eighties, it's far.

"My husband's a cake man," his wife chimes in. "He really likes his cake. He gets these cheese buns and their Napoleons are delicious. So, every week we make the trip. There's only one other place that's nearby which is similar, but they're not as good. They're just passable." His wife recalls having delicious pepper sticks, made from semolina, pepper, and olive oil. People have their own favorites. As long as Carlo has enough customers like these, he can make a go of it. There is, in fact, still an Italian presence here, but the locals tell me it's declining quite a bit. I see a man standing in front of his home who appears to be Italian. He has straight black hair, tied in a small bun and he's wearing a black muscle shirt. He reminds me of some of the people who populated *The Sopranos*.

I detour north onto Yates Avenue, which has quite a few charming homes, some of them new. At number 2712, there's a square home, made of large, gray-colored stone blocks, with a two-car garage, an unusual sight in this modest area. There's a balustrade-lined staircase leading up from the garage level to the first floor. The entrance to the house, an arched doorway with a wood-paneled door, features a metal design that gives it a medieval appearance. Some of the side streets here have rows of semi-attached, well-constructed red-brick colonials, many with nice gardens. In fact, almost an entire block of Pearsall Avenue, between Allerton and Arnow has these homes. Walking up and down Tenbroeck, Throop, Wilson Avenues and others in the area, I have the impression of a quiet neighborhood tucked away in the northeast Bronx. But as I head west, the area becomes more crowded and somewhat noisier.

Signs that at least some Italians still live here can also be discerned from a number of businesses here. I come to Dominick's Pizzeria at number 1015 Allerton. And Dominick turns out to be here, an older bald man who greets me with a friendly hello.

"I love that photo you have on the wall of that pizza shop with the old neon sign, 'Pizza, 15¢ a slice.' I remember that from when I was a kid. Of course, the subway was only fifteen cents too."

"That's the early sixties. You don't look old enough to know about that." I accept the compliment even as I realize from the twinkle in his eye that he's just trying to make me feel good. Next to his place is the Italia 90 Club. It claims to be a restaurant, but the sign says: "Members Only." These clubs were once fixtures in every Italian community.

A bit farther down, at 925 Allerton, you'll find Bruxelle's Lounge. It seems to be closed. Peering through the window I see a silver suit of armor, complete with helmet. There's a bar and red and white banquettes in the seating area. A large interesting looking clock with Roman numerals hangs behind the bar. There's something strange about this place, I think. The banquettes are from the fifties; the knight in a suit of armor doesn't really fit in there. Why is it padlocked? I wonder. I step into the florist next door. An older Korean couple is sitting down, cutting flowers. The woman has an excellent sense of humor.

"Hello. Do you speak English?"

"No I don't," she says cheerfully. "But I can speak Korean." She laughs, only the laugh's on me and I join in, thinking it quite funny.

"What's the story with your neighbor, Bruxelle's?" Much to my surprise there's quite a story behind it and she's not shy about telling it either.

"Oh, very bad. They're closed. The owner said he's had enough. There was a shooting, a man got killed; another guy got stabbed. They were having trouble getting a liquor license, so they made it into a party place and people rented it and brought their own liquor. But then there was this shooting. People rented it for a party and there was a big fight. So now, nothing."

I check out the story. Not only is it true, it's even worse than what she told me. According to a story posted on August 25, 2018 in the *Bronx Times:*

> Multiple people were shot and stabbed over the weekend in Allerton. . . . Three men and a woman sustained injuries after an argument inside the Bruxelles Lounge turned violent . . . on August 18th at 4:30 am. Four people were shot and two were stabbed. The shooter allegedly fired into a crowd from a passing vehicle. A 24-year-old woman was shot in the head and a 25-year-old man was stabbed in the head.[40]

The victims were listed in critical condition and the woman died shortly thereafter.

You can walk on a street, and there's nothing to indicate what happened there. In that sense, walking through a community is a snapshot in time. If I had been here that night, I could have been caught in the crossfire. Local residents asserted it was a quiet community, and there was no history of fights at Bruxelles. Bad news sells, and it's unfair to taint an entire area because of what happened. It could have happened anywhere, but once people know this is where it occurred, their view of the community can change in a hurry. Local sources say that it's not as safe above Allerton as below it, but they don't feel that the area is especially dangerous; nor is it known to be a war zone. In short, it is New York, it is the Bronx, and there are no guarantees, especially at night. Moreover, chance often plays an unheralded role in research. Had I not popped into the florist, I wouldn't have known the backstory of Bruxelles.

Halfway between Wallace and Holland Avenues, on Allerton, there's a narrow alleyway and along a wall I see a beautifully done wall mural of a young Bruce Lee. If you were driving by or even walking fast, you wouldn't notice it. Sporting a chiseled body, he's in a martial arts pose, and his face and chest have been cut. On either side of him are elaborate gray dragons, looking equally fierce. It's definitely worth a look. The mural was placed here, according to the owner of the store next door, because this was where room was available. The "alley" turns into a dirt road, almost but not quite wide enough for a car. As I walk between the backs of houses on either side, with the grass underneath my feet, and the trees on the side, I can almost feel I'm walking down a rural country road.

West of White Plains Road, Allerton is more of a honky-tonk thoroughfare, with pawn shops, takeout joints like Kennedy Fried Chicken, a US Armed Forces recruiting station. It's somewhat like that east of White Plains Road too, though not as much. I make a right where it dead-ends into Bronx Park East. The first building is a block long, ending at Britton Street. A brick structure, it has Tudor elements and an interior garden in a diamond shape. The next building has thousands of clinker bricks. But instead of being hap-hazardly placed, these bricks are arranged in a very orderly pattern. I also see a flyer offering a $2,500 reward for information on the murder of a Black man, Don Ross Granville, in October of 2018, in front of 2824 Bronx Park East—the very building being described here. It has a very pretty interior courtyard with evergreens, rose of

Sharon, and other flora. The complex is in the Romanesque style. Like the rest of this book, what's written in the present context has historical antecedents, ones where other dreamers of a better life carved out communities. Here's one example of what it was like eighty-nine to ninety years ago in these buildings on Bronx Park East, near Allerton Avenue:

"The co-ops were apartment buildings for working class people of all ethnicities, a grand experiment in cooperative living, built by the Union. It was *the* gathering place—I'd go from working all day to dance, to Jewish chorus with my papa, and later participated in my children's Yiddish education there. There was even a restaurant with a section especially for young people. It was where I met my husband."[41]

Across the street is Bronx Park, situated on a block-wide strip between Bronx Park East and the Bronx River Parkway. It runs north-south from E. Gun Hill Road to shortly before Morris Park Avenue. It's very nicely landscaped, with thick, wooded areas, trails, concrete paths, ballfields, and playgrounds running the length of it. Worthy of mention too is a skateboard park across from where Arnow Avenue ends. Parallel to Bronx Park on the other side of the Bronx River Parkway are the Botanical Gardens and the Bronx Zoo, which are also the largest parts of Bronx Park. In a large city, every parcel of land tends to be used, and Bronx Park, occupying a narrow strip of greenery along a very busy parkway, is a good example of that.

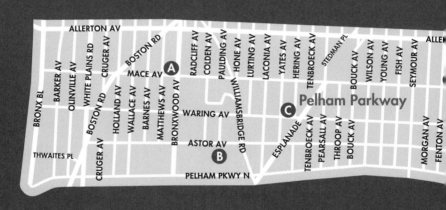

- (A) The grotto at St. Lucy's Church
- (B) New York Institute for Special Education
- (C) Waring Ave. Italianate houses
- (D) Battaglia's Market
- (E) Christmas House

PELHAM PARKWAY & PELHAM GARDENS

THESE TWO COMMUNITIES border each other along Eastchester Road. They share a generally similar history and are discussed together here. They are also similar residentially and socioeconomically. The boundaries of Pelham Parkway (sometimes called Bronxdale) are Allerton Avenue on the north, Eastchester Road on the east, Pelham Parkway on the south, and the Bronx River Parkway on the west. Pelham Gardens' borders are E. Gun Hill Road on the north and east, Stillwell Avenue and Pelham Parkway North on the south, and Eastchester Road on the west.

Originally, this was part of the land belonging to the Siwanoy, then followed by the Dutch, British, and the Revolutionary forces. The area was settled in the nineteenth century and remained a small community until subway lines were extended in 1917. The number 2 train services Pelham Parkway, running along White Plains Road. Farther east, on Esplanade Avenue the number 5 train is available. Substantial numbers of

Jews moved to Pelham Parkway during the early twentieth century, but today many have moved away, replaced by Albanians, Hispanics, African Americans, West Indians, and various other nationalities.

Pelham Gardens is still an Italian stronghold, although other groups have moved here too in recent decades, namely Albanians and Hispanics. The major commercial thoroughfares for both communities are Boston, White Plains, Williamsbridge, E. Gun Hill, and Eastchester Roads. As for parks, there's Bronx River Park on the west and, throughout, Pelham Parkway, a giant thoroughfare that boasts park-like areas for recreation in the center sections of the roadways. Both areas are considered quite safe on the whole.

In general, these communities are more upscale than Allerton, as evidenced by the quality of the real estate and how well it's maintained. As I stroll along Wilson, Seymour, Woodhull, Mickle Avenues, and others like them I'm struck by how quiet, and safe this area is, almost like a suburb on Long Island. And what does one do when there's nothing of import to write about? One sublimates. I think about my work, my family, and what a great workout it is to walk for miles.

I begin my trek through Pelham Parkway heading south on Bronx Park East. On the right side is Bronx Park, which runs the length of the Pelham Parkway community. It's a really attractive recreational space with wooded trails, and a wide concrete walkway for walkers, joggers, and bike riders. The landscape is just hilly enough to make traversing it interesting. Playgrounds are here too, as well as several ball fields, and it feels safe. This area extends to the west to the Bronx River Parkway. Here, just where Bronx Park East crosses Mace Avenue, one can walk over a bridge spanning the highway and gain entry to the Botanical Gardens—for a fee, of course.

On the corner of Mace Avenue, number 600, and Bronx Park East is a large house that was a single-family two-story home at one time but has now been converted into several apartments. The style has Tudor elements, and the material is white stucco and red brick, some of it in a herringbone pattern and in the shape of a diamond. There's a dramatic entrance because of a tower reaching the height of the structure, featuring a small Juliet balcony in front of a small window. A stone wall encircles the home. On the Bronx Park East side, someone apparently painted the trim a royal blue, as opposed to the red and white pattern that predominates on Mace. I wonder if there was a discussion among the neighbors about the added blue colors.

In about fifty yards, I spot a modern building in the spare style of structures commonly seen in North Williamsburg—minimal design, plain windows, with glass panels, and red and white colors. On the right side, on the fifth floor, there seems to be a rooftop deck. Because so many of the traditional older apartment buildings have been preserved, the contrast is quite startling. Next to it, number 2320 is perhaps ninety years older and yet it's much more beautiful, and I don't think many people would disagree with that assessment. The style is Mediterranean, a tiled roof over three arches, the center of which is the entranceway, with iron designs over the doors, giving it the feeling of a hacienda. The walls have alternating bricks, some of which are inverted to increase its visual appeal, not to mention the delicate fluted columns. Moreover, the next building, number 2300, is a repeat of the first one. These are followed by an Art Moderne building, with its corner windows, horizontal lines, and rounded-off nautical-style fire escapes.

Strolling up Olinville Avenue, at 2260, I glance at an older building with multicolored bricks, some in checkerboard patterns underneath some of the windows. Triangular-shaped pediments also enhance the building's old-world charm. Near Waring Avenue, I pass a classic Art Deco apartment building on the right. The exterior has the chevrons, vertical lines, columns, and other designs, and inside there's a gold-and-black terrazzo floor. The Grand Concourse and the surrounding area boast the greatest number of such buildings, but it's important to remember that Art Deco structures exist in many other Bronx communities.

On the left side, there's a long wall supporting a large parking lot. Beneath it is Mother Nature's own example of a wall, a long outcropping of ancient boulders which have been painted a bright green. The wall is dominated by children's renderings of flowers, trees, insects, and birds as well as tall and medium-sized buildings. The latter display has hundreds of small, not-so-neatly drawn round and square yellow-painted windows. Drawing them must have taken a great deal of time and patience. Its appeal lies in the fact that it's not done by professionals, but by local kids. The green boulders have the same type of artwork created by children. At one point, there's a serviceable drawing of a white youngster, featured on the upper-level wall, helping a Hispanic girl climb up from a real boulder underneath the wall, thus combining the two projects of natural rock and wall. Alas, Barker Avenue, which runs parallel to Olinville, is not especially interesting.

Turning left onto Thwaites Place from Barker, I head east a short distance to Boston Road, then left, and a quick jog to Astor Avenue, where I turn right and continue east. On the left are some of the Pelham Parkway Houses, a NYCHA project. At Bronxwood Avenue, I walk north a couple of blocks and at Mace Avenue arrive at a large and famous American grotto, the "American Lourdes," that of St. Lucy's Church, also called "The Lourdes of the Bronx." The city tap water flowing from the rock, blessed annually by a priest, is believed to have healing powers. In addition to the grotto, the grounds contain various other shrines. The grotto was created in 1939, meant to be a replica of the world-renowned grotto at Lourdes, where St. Bernadette had a vision of the Blessed Mother appearing to her. Here also, it is claimed, curative water flows from a spring. At St. Lucy's, a white statue of the Virgin Mary stands atop the rocks. Statues of various saints and trumpet-blowing angels abound elsewhere on the grounds.

The grotto at St. Lucy's Church

As I observe the scene on a cold and windy mid-week November afternoon, several Hispanic women approach and wash themselves with ice-cold water, pouring it from a bottle onto their bodies and then walking backward from the grotto as they cross themselves. One of them is explaining what it all means to a small girl, perhaps her daughter. There are written testimonials affixed to the walls describing how many people were cured of cancer, gained eyesight, and were otherwise helped. In the end, what matters is that many fervently believe in it. I recall the famous dictum coined in 1928 by the sociologist W. I. Thomas: "If men define situations as real, they are real in their consequences."[42] The thousands who have traveled here, as well as locals—Italians, Hispanics, and more recently, Albanians—provide eloquent testimony to what Thomas wrote. Such is the strength of this belief that people sometimes fill up buckets of this water and wash their cars and clean their homes with it.

Returning to Astor Avenue and continuing eastward, I pass the grounds of the former Institute for Special Education (the front entrance is at 999 Pelham Parkway, a block south of Astor), founded way back in 1831. The property is fenced in, three blocks long, with numerous low-rise red-brick buildings, set amid spacious grounds. Today, it's the New York Institute for Special Education, serving the needs of those with emotional and learning challenges as well as physical disabilities, especially blindness.

While many are plain, attached two-family structures, there are also some very nice homes along Astor, like numbers 1350 and 1352. A beautiful arched door, with a delicate wrought-iron design and arched window, graces the front of 1363. I also pass by the Blessed Mary Convent, which doesn't look like the traditional austere setting. Rather, it resembles a very large brick, quoin-embossed colonial, complete with a chandelier, visible through a large top-floor window. Outside are two large very brightly painted statues of Jesus and Mary. Jesus is dressed in a red robe and Mary is wearing turquoise robes and a headdress. The window seems to have gold filigree within it. Opposite is the Engine 97 firehouse with a painted image of a muscle-bound fireman, sporting a huge grin, holding a blue fire hydrant against a background of flames. Ironically, he's chomping on a cigar, which I hope hasn't caused the fire.

I turn right onto Eastchester Road, a small commercial section providing for the community's daily needs. Making another right in a few blocks, I find myself on one of the most impressive boulevards in the city, Pelham Parkway (officially called Bronx and Pelham Parkway), created in 1911 as a one-lane road. Today it has two three-lane main roadways plus service roads on each side. Lawns, boulders, and many trees, some of them quite large, which provide ample shade can be found in spacious areas on both sides of the central roads. There's also a bikeway on the north side.

The housing stock along the parkway is a mix, ranging from elaborate homes to more modest ones, as well as apartment complexes, plus a few medical centers and churches. West of Williamsbridge Road is the front of the New York Institute for Special Education campus. Standing proudly is a huge colonial-style building, with large ionic pillars, and a golden dome above it. But it's the greenery along the parkway that's really impressive, even elegant, as a place that people can stroll through or relax in. I head north on White Plains Road, which has a shopping area with a supermarket, gas station, Dunkin' Donuts, pretty basic in all with nothing standing out. The same is true of Boston Road, which crosses White Plains here.

At Waring Avenue, I make a right and walk it to Eastchester. It's residential, quiet and unremarkable. An exception to this is six homes on the north side of Waring, beginning with number 1125. They are Italianate, with arched grid-paned windows and fan lights. Keystones and cement squares alternate with multicolored bricks in a pretty pattern. All have the exact same design, and the effect is more noticeable because it's six nice homes in a row. Turning left on Eastchester, I go left again at the next corner onto Mace Avenue, this time heading west. Eventually, I come to a narrow home at number 1283, covered with white siding. The house is a strange shape with two distinct sections. One of them is in an oblong form, which is connected to the square-shaped front part of the building. Both have crenellations or crenels, battlements on the parapets of medieval castles. These are spaced at two- to three-foot intervals here, but look somewhat out of place because this isn't a home that looks like a castle. In front, around the garden, is a small wall, about three feet high, made of cobblestones. The door is set on the diagonal. It's definitely unusual-looking.

Just as I'm almost done with the area, I have an interesting encounter. I'm standing outside the Serie A Café at 1480 Mace Avenue, near Eastchester Road. Walking in I see that it serves no food, just expresso, lattes, cappuccino, and regular coffee. Liquor is also available, and there are large framed photos of Marilyn Monroe, Audrey Hepburn, and Carmen Basilio, a well-known boxer from the old days. As an aside, there's a small contraption off to the side that resembles a slot machine, but it isn't. I say hello to the manager, Carolin, a young Dominican woman with a friendly smile, and ask her who the clientele is.

"Mostly, we have old people, Italians and Albanians, who like to come in and have a coffee, talk, and watch TV. And sometimes they hang out so long, I think I should put a mattress in here."

"Do they drink?"

"No, they're not interested in drinking. I never saw anyone get drunk here. It's just there because we have a license for it."

"What about the back room? I see you have tables for card games, and you also have slots around the tables to hold gambling chips."

"Yes, but there's nothing going on with these guys. They never play for money. They just play for fun, games like rummy and pinochle." In truth, the café was at one time, in 2011, a social club where some people affiliated with the Genovese family took bets and hung out, but now there are different owners and it seems to be a pretty placid place. Unfortunately, the Mafia is intertwined with the Italian community in general, but only a fraction of the people residing in it have anything to do with the mob. In the Bronx, the same would be true of the much larger Belmont and Throgs Neck communities.[43]

"How did you get into this type of work?" I ask Carolin.

"I came to the US ten years ago from the Dominican Republic. For a while I worked in nail salons, and then I thought I'd try this and I'm enjoying it, especially," she's says, laughing, "because my Albanian boss goes on vacation to Europe and brings me back delicious chocolates."

"How do you feel about the fact that people in the US come from so many different lands, while in the Dominican Republic, that's not the case?

"I like it. I meet many people from different cultures. But it depends. I certainly don't feel positively about Haitians."

"Have you met any Haitians in New York?"

"No. If I did, I didn't know they were Haitians. But I'm not looking to meet them. Their country is right on our border and throughout our history they have killed many Dominicans after starting a couple of wars, and so that's it for me."

One of the things I've noticed in my research over the years is that groups who disliked each other in the old country get along here for the most part. Some examples would be Indians and Pakistanis, Arabs and Jews, and Puerto Ricans and Dominicans. Among the reasons for the easing of tension is that people here have an opportunity to meet on neutral ground and realize that they may have unfairly stereotyped or even demonized members of other groups. Also, in the United States, the sources of hostility, such as disputes over territory, simply don't apply. That said, increased tolerance doesn't always happen. Some people harbor such deep hostility that they reject any contact with groups they don't like, despite people's best efforts at outreach. When that happens, it's important to accept it. Of course, Carolin is just one Dominican, and others might feel differently.

I begin exploring Pelham Gardens, walking along Eastchester Road, its western border. My route takes me through a main shopping artery. I notice a liquor store, two large pharmacies, a supermarket, several pizza shops, legal and medical offices, and other businesses. Jumping into the Good Fellas Barbershop, I ask the barber if there's anyone in this community who doesn't know what Goodfellas refers to. He declares that he would be extremely surprised to meet such a fellow.

Next, I hit Fratelli's at number 2507. It's a family-oriented place, serving generous helpings of classic Italian foods and drawing from several Italian regions. It's lunch hour, and there's a large church group enjoying the food. I realize how important these daytime groups are to the restaurant business. If it were open only in the evening, it would starve in areas like this, which don't have the nightlife of Manhattan. The manager shows me a menu that has a very young version of the Fratelli brothers, wearing knickers, superimposed over the menu, looking as they did when they arrived from the old country. One of the brothers is the head chef here, giving it an aura of authenticity.

A few doors down, at 2503, is Battaglia's Market, screaming out, "old school," just by the name. It was established over thirty years ago, and the newest owners have kept it as it was, with a butcher shop that carries Italian-style meats and a deli featuring Italian delicacies. There are no fewer than twenty-six specialty sandwiches on the menu. While what's in a sandwich may bear no relationship to its name, it suggests a fertile imagination at work. Some examples:

> Italian Stallion—Ham, cappy, mortadella, prosciutto, sopressata, mozzarella, roasted peppers, lettuce, tomato, oil, and vinegar
> Blazin Buffalo—Fried franks, red hot cutlet, melted pepper jack cheese, lettuce, w/blue cheese dressing
> The Big Bambino—Pepper turkey, sweet sopressata, Muenster cheese, roasted peppers, mayo, Balsamic vinaigrette

And, in a nod to the relatively small Jewish population residing here:

The Katz—grilled pastrami, melted Swiss cheese, your choice
   of sauerkraut or coleslaw
The King David—Imported prosciutto, sharp provolone, and
   olive oil

This last offering is followed, perhaps in an attempt to be ecumenical, by

The Virgin Mary—House made fresh mozzarella, tomato,
   basil, olive oil

As noted, in general, the combinations don't appear to have anything to do with the name, but it's a great gimmick, since it draws people's attention to what's available. By the way, all these treats cost less than ten dollars each.

The best-known attraction in Pelham Gardens is the Christmas House, or Garabedian family house, at 1605 Pelham Parkway North, on the corner of Westervelt Avenue. The Garabedian family owns the house, and they have a fabric trimming business, which helps them mount a fantastic display every Christmas season that goes up on Thanksgiving and remains there until January 6. No one is sure what motivated them to do it, and the family is reticent about providing an answer, saying only that "Something special happened to the family on Christmas Eve in 1973." It must have been very special, since the insured display's value is about $4 million, and the electricity bill must be very large too. This is their way, they say, of recognizing the miracle and expressing gratitude to the Lord.

Thousands of people visit it every year. I first saw it some twenty years ago and have returned several times since, both to gaze and reflect upon it and to observe others taking it all in. Some people toss money over the fence, which is then donated to a local Catholic church. The house is a large two-story stucco affair, painted in bright pink with white trim, and on the right side a white porch is supported by Ionic pillars. The display consists of mannequins, statues, and other creations, some of which possess moving parts. These include actors Brigitte Bardot, Rita Hayworth, Audrey Hepburn, and Nicole Kidman, as well as various saints, the Virgin Mary, and Jesus Christ. There's a Santa Claus and his reindeer galloping along a roof, and a mysterious camel, with a glittering harness. Cherubs in various poses with silvery wings on gold-trimmed pedestals are everywhere, clinging to crystal chandeliers, and holding on to ropes with tassels. The garden area is covered with a red velvet-looking material, and a white baby-grand piano sits in the middle of it. A statue of a horse rearing up is stationed just behind a large golden harp. I could go on and on, but I believe the picture is clear and my suggestion is—it's definitely worth the trip to see the display during the Christmas season, particularly when it's lit up at night.

The homes here are fairly nice, with many semi-attached houses on the side streets. Perhaps the prettiest real estate is along Astor Avenue, especially as one goes east. One property, at number 1650, on the corner of Tiemann Avenue, would be more at home in a very upscale community, like Bronxville. It's quite opulent and really in a class by itself. A very large brick and stone Tudor with a slate roof, surrounded by a wrought-iron fence, it also has terrific landscaping in the form of sculpted bushes, and tall trees. The bricks have been fashioned in an interlocking checkerboard, with diagonals, and herringbone designs. There's a triple-arched stone entrance to the home. A huge stone chimney rises above the house, giving all of it a grand look.

Other luxurious homes on this block, like number 1662, are also worth taking in. I see a Tudor-style house at 1715, where bricks and stones are arranged almost haphazardly in unusual fashion. There are clinker bricks and stones embedded into the brick design. Another one, at 1739, is a brick Mediterranean home with a green-tiled roof,

French casement windows, and quoins wrapped completely around the front door. All in all, this is an area that feels like a world unto itself. It ends right near the Hutchinson River Parkway, and people driving by would have no idea of what they're missing—an oasis of peace and quiet, unknown to most New Yorkers.

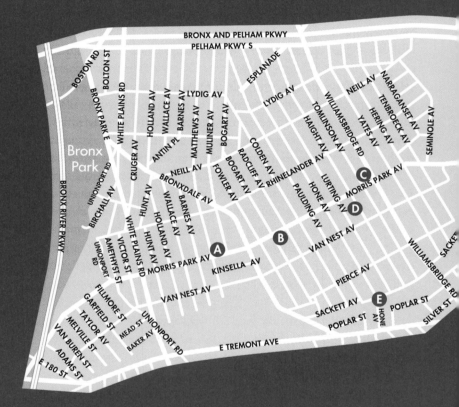

BRONX AND PELHAM PKWY
PELHAM PKWY S

Bronx Park

Bronx Park E
BOSTON RD
BOLTON ST
WHITE PLAINS RD
CRUGER AV
BIRCHALL AV
UNIONPORT RD
BRONX RIVER PKWY

HOLLAND AV
WALLACE AV
BARNES AV
LYDIG AV
MATTHEWS AV
MULINER AV
ANTIN PL
BOGART AV

ESPLANADE
LYDIG AV
COLDEN AV
RADCLIFF AV
BOGART AV
FOWLER AV

NEILL AV
BRONXDALE AV
NEILL AV
WALLACE AV
BARNES AV
HUNT AV
HOLLAND AV
WHITE PLAINS RD
HUNT AV
VICTOR ST
AMETHYST ST
MORRIS PARK AV

NEILL AV
NARRAGANSET AV
TENBROECK AV
WILLIAMSBRIDGE RD
HERING AV
YATES AV
TOMLINSON AV
HAIGHT AV
RHINELANDER AV
HONE AV
PAULDING AV
LURTING AV
MORRIS PARK AV
SEMINOLE AV

Ⓒ
Ⓓ
Ⓑ
VAN NEST AV

Ⓐ
KINSELLA AV
VAN NEST AV

FILLMORE ST
GARFIELD ST
TAYLOR AV
MELVILLE ST
VAN BUREN ST
ADAMS ST
E 180 ST
UNIONPORT RD
MEAD ST
BAKER AV

PIERCE AV
SACKETT AV
POPLAR ST
Ⓔ
HONE AV
POPLAR ST
SILVER ST
WILLIAMSBRIDGE RD
SACKET

E TREMONT AVE

Ⓐ Chocolate Place
Ⓑ Art Deco building at Bogart Ave.
     and Morris Park Ave.
Ⓒ John Dormi & Sons Funeral Parlor
Ⓓ "Nicky #1" mural
Ⓔ Sackett Ave. mural

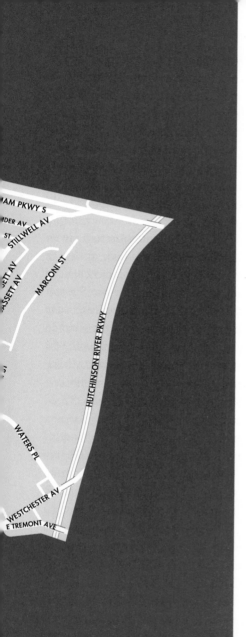

MORRIS PARK

MORRIS PARK OWES ITS NAME to John Albert Morris, who built the Morris Park Racecourse, which hosted the Belmont Stakes for fourteen years. He was born in 1836 into a family of great wealth. His father, Francis Morris, owned a 25,000-acre ranch in Texas, where he bred horses including Ruthless, who finished first in the 1867 Belmont and Travers Stakes. John Morris also bred horses in England. He was a majority owner of the Louisiana State Lottery Company and was nicknamed "the Lottery King" as a result. He also owned properties in various parts of the United States.

The boundaries of Morris Park are, generally, Pelham Parkway South on the north, the Hutchinson River Parkway on the east, E. Tremont and Blondell Avenues and Silver Street Avenue on the southwest, and the Bronx River Parkway on the west. It is today a predominantly Italian community, famed for its annual Columbus Day Parade. Long ago, it had been a vibrant Orthodox Jewish community, mostly on and near Pelham Parkway, but that is no longer the case. All that's left is the Young Israel synagogue, now located on Pelham Parkway, which serves a very small community. Demographically, the community is changing, as groups such as Hispanics, Albanians, African Americans, and South Asians continue to move in, attracted by its relative safety and good housing stock. Generally, the private homes in Morris Park tend to be nicer on the first block or two off Pelham Parkway South. Recently, more young people from Manhattan and Brooklyn have shown interest in moving here, attracted by lower prices than elsewhere, an easy commute, and the low crime rate. Perhaps one day it will gentrify. There's also ferry service to Manhattan twenty minutes away, from Clason Point. Finally, a Metro-North station will open here in the near future.

The main commercial thoroughfares are Morris Park and E. Tremont Avenues, White Plains Road, parts of Eastchester and Williamsbridge Roads, and the western portion of Lydig Avenue. The area is also home to numerous hospitals and medical centers, among them Jacobi, Albert Einstein, and Calvary, all of them east of the Indian Village section. Indian Village is a small upscale community with its own identity within Morris Park. The main recreational parks in the area are Bronx Park, along the community's western border, and Loreto Playground, on Morris Park Avenue between Haight and Tomlinson Avenues. The number 2 and 5 subway lines service the area.

Van Nest, a small triangular-shaped section which is today considered part of Morris Park, is bounded on the northeast by White Plains Road, on the south by E. Tremont Avenue and the Amtrak tracks, and on the west by the Bronx River Parkway.[44] The main shopping thoroughfares are Morris Park Avenue and White Plains Road. Named after Reyneier Van Nest, a saddle maker, it's a working-class area that has become more heavily Hispanic and African American, as well as home to Muslims from various countries. It's also considerably poorer than the rest of Morris Park and has a bit of a crime problem. For those interested in knowing what the old neighborhood looked like physically (Van Nest was founded twenty years before Morris Park), this is an ideal area to explore because it has so many older structures. Basically, with its narrow streets—Amethyst,

Fillmore, Garfield, Van Buren, Adams, and Taylor—it's what the Bronx used to look like many decades ago.

I begin my explorations in this throwback to the past, when so much of the Bronx was Italian, on the main drag of Morris Park Avenue, just east of where it meets up with White Plains Road. It's still very Italian, with many stores bearing the names of their Italian owners: Phil Napolitano's law office, Conti's Pastry Shop, and many more. There's the usual assortment of nail salons, supermarkets, including Pioneer (which has been around forever), barbershops, launderettes, realty and lawyers' offices, a car service place, repair shops of all kinds, and many delis, along with a couple of restaurants. But, in a sign of ethnic changes, hookah shops with Muslim proprietors, Hispanic bodegas, and an Albanian deli exist here too. In short, if you're looking for a community where big-box chain outfits haven't taken over, this is it. There are also a larger-than-usual number of churches—Assemblies of God on nearby Rhinelander Avenue, and on Morris Park Avenue, Our Lady of Lourdes, St. Francis Xavier, and a Seventh Day Adventist church.

Chocolate Place, at 839 Morris Park, with "Godiva" on the sign, catches my attention. It specializes in beautifully designed chocolates of all kinds, with the Godiva line as an alternative. The service is outstanding and super friendly. I speak with the woman behind the counter, who tells me: "We do deliveries, we make our own chocolates and have been doing it at various locations in the area for thiry-two years. People stay loyal and order by phone. Here are some truffle selections—tiramisu, coconut, whatever. We have almond clusters, you name it. We have done classes in the past, learning how to mold, how to fill, you know, how to put something together. New groups are coming in, but I believe if you're nice to people, they'll come in, and they do. I tell my people, 'Nobody needs to come here. If you're not nice they won't come back.'"

She's right about that, especially in a community with a small-town atmosphere. And it's all about her making eye contact and showing off photos of her grandchildren, recalling where she grew up (the South Bronx), anything that personalizes her to people.

At number 870, an unusual name for a store catches my eye—Odd Ball Industrial Solutions. Curious, I walk into the office where I meet Jose Rios, a youngish Puerto Rican man with a pleasant demeanor.

"What exactly does 'odd ball' mean?"

"We help people find stuff that they need, whether it's in Kansas, New York, or Germany. Often, they can't go out of their office or don't know how to find a part on the internet. I'll find a made-to-order type that people want."

"How'd you get into this business?"

"I used to work before in the power transmissions market—ball bearings, sprockets, all mechanical items. That was actually in Puerto Rico, and then I came to New York looking for the same type of work. Hey, you said you write books. Let me show you something." Jose takes me into a back room and shows me a collection of old books in some boxes, the kind often seen on the streets of Manhattan near Greenwich Village, where vendors sell these well-worn volumes for a dollar or two. "We're going to sell these books cheap to people."

"But you do realize there isn't much of an audience for these books, especially with people reading on Kindle and e-books."

Jose lowers his voice, almost conspiratorially and says: "This is my partner's idea. He's such a sweet person. His mother lived in Morris Park, she's Italian, and she passed away and she had all these books. He's gonna keep some of them, but he's selling the rest. And also, these old newspapers from years ago. Now that Mom's gone, he's cleaning up. You see these business cards? They're done in pink. It's because his mother had breast cancer. We actually wear pink shirts in a male industry. And you see," he continues, laughing, "in this industry, if we're not going to be known for the name, then we're going to be known for the color. Isn't that something!"

Basically, this is the plan of a man who wants his mom to live on in a way, through selling these books in whatever way he can, that

Art Deco building at Bogart and Morris Park Avenues

were so much a part of her life. He surely doesn't think he can make much money this way. But more important, whoever reads these books will be benefiting from things she cared about. The pink-colored business cards stem from the same motive. This is a common desire, one I constantly come across when people talk about their departed ones. For some it takes the form of memorial plaques; for others, charitable donations in peoples' names; but in all cases the motive is keeping alive the person's memory.

A couple of blocks farther east at the intersection of Bogart Avenue, I spot, on the north side of Morris Park Avenue what looks like a very old Art Deco building. Starting from the roof, it has an irregular-shaped design, with parapets at different heights. Below it, on the third and second floors are a number of really creative designs, rectangular, circular, diamond, and checkerboard, as well as Native American symbols, all set against a wall of different colored bricks in a pattern of wavy flattened arches. The entrance to the building has flattened-out pilasters on each side, with a whimsical sort of pediment immediately above it. I've seen more than a few six-story Art Deco structures with less to say for themselves. Special yet typical, in a way, of what is a preserved community with many Tudor-style brick homes on the side streets.

Four blocks later I see, on the right, a spectacularly painted three-story building. On the ground floor, it's Emilio's of Morris Park, a pizzeria, established in 1989. If you were driving by, you might not notice it, but walking past it it's impossible to miss. Their catchy motto is "We don't just make. . . . We create." It's at 1051 Morris Park Avenue, on the corner of Hone Avenue. It's painted in a wacky, modernistic style, with interlocking circles, diamond shapes, all in different very bright colors—orange, red, green, chartreuse, black, white, and gray. Interspersed throughout are these giant, luscious-looking red tomatoes, with drops of dew on them. Unlike most murals, this artwork is on two adjoining perpendicular walls, one overlooking Morris Park and the other, Hone. In addition, one rarely sees murals with multiple windows, on buildings inhabited by people. In a way, it reminds me of a Maurits Escher painting, an artist known for his expressionist drawings and lithographs. The creator of this mural was David Louf, an artist from the Netherlands, and it was commissioned by Richie DiNardo, the owner of both Emilio's and the building.

Whether or not this building is tasteful depends on whom you ask. DiNardo himself acknowledged that not everyone likes the mural, such as the "more mature type of audience that lives around here, like my mom. They don't like change." Typical of this attitude was comments by Joanne Guglielmo Murphy, who said: "Was their business doing so badly that they had to make a spectacle of themselves?" Joe Barile had a different take: "I really like it. Let's face it. The Bronx is a really dull place and Morris Park Avenue is regarded as number two to Arthur Avenue, so why not?" Kristina Myers Reed agreed, noting: "I love it. This is a great way to bring some color and art into our daily lives. Be radiant!"[45] So there you have it. If nothing else, it leads to active and pretty harmless debates.

Continuing east on Morris Park Avenue, just beyond Tomlinson Avenue, I enter the John Dormi & Sons Funeral Parlor at number 1121 in search of the Bronx Veterans Museum, founded by Joseph Garofalo, a local resident and World War II veteran. It displays his medals and war memorabilia as well as war memorabilia of other

Morris Park residents. Model airplanes hang from the ceiling. It's the first thing one sees as one enters the parlor. The room is carpeted, with easy chairs for visitors, and it has subdued lighting. Many of the medals and other items are inside glass cases and in glass frames along the walls. They mostly date back to World War II, the Korean War, and the Vietnam War. One prominent example is a Purple Heart for Sal Canizzaro for wounds received in Vietnam. Above him is a gray-and-red prisoner-of-war uniform from 1974, also from Vietnam, in Hoa Prison, the infamous "Hanoi Hilton" where many Americans were incarcerated. I also look at medals received in battles with Germany, along with helmets and military hats of every description. There's a can of Spam (a staple food for soldiers), a razor kit, a hand grenade. It's an incredible exhibit filling every corner of the room. I think about the juxtaposition of all this inside a funeral home where the dead are remembered and memorialized. How appropriate, I conclude. My reverie is interrupted by an older man with a shock of neatly combed wavy gray hair wearing a suit on this, the day after Christmas.

"Hi, I'm Chris."

"You're just the man I want to see. This is a really impressive display. Can you tell me about it?"

"Sure. This guy here, Joe Garofalo, decided he wanted a place for his medals and other items from when he served in World War II." Chris, whose full name is Crescenzo DiCostanzo Jr., is one of the funeral directors here. He has a great smile and a very welcoming manner, punctuating his comments occasionally by putting his arm around me.

"I was in 'Nam, and met Bob Hope there while he was doing one of his tours. What a great guy he was! I took him from the helipad when he flew into Saigon and brought him to the embassy. And his hair, back in '67, was as white as anything. I was like so shocked to be right next to him. But I just kept my composure. I knew I was there for a reason, to make sure he got to where he needed to go." Chris begins laughing, recalling what happened, exclaiming, and giving me a couple of playful jabs for emphasis. "Can you imagine, me, plain old me, standing right next to him as we rode up the elevator?"

"Anyway, Garofalo, who lived in Morris Park, wanted people to remember the history of our wars. He had this terrific collection, but nobody wanted it. The local library wasn't interested. SUNY Maritime has a museum, but where they wanted to put it was so out of the way that nobody would ever see it. And there was this place nearby in Westchester Square, but they wanted to put us in the basement. I said, 'Joe, nobody's gonna see it.' 'Well,' he says, 'maybe we could put it here.' I said, 'Why not?' And so we put his collection in this glass cabinet. And before you know it, people were coming in for funerals, and they would say, 'My dad was in World War II and could we bring in his picture?' I said, 'Yeah,' and we began a book with war photographs. And it just grew and grew. People even called from far away, East Harlem. . . . 'My dad was part of the Tuskegee Airmen unit.' But most of the stuff was brought in by people from the community. Then the local school, P. S. 108, started bringing the kids over to see it. We also have a film of what was created here."

"I don't understand why [places] like SUNY Maritime or the library weren't more interested in this concept."

"Well, it's ironic. Even the people in our industry said, 'What, is he crazy? That doesn't belong in a funeral home.' But let me tell you, through my forty years of experience. . . . People come to a funeral, and they're standing in the lobby [the museum's location] and what are they talking about? The last time they saw somebody, their retirement, their golf club, whatever, like a social event. When we put this in, it was a whole different thing. Little kids with their grandparents, they'd take them over and show them the pictures and medals. The time was spent much more respectfully. And people brought in books about the military, first-person stories about their units and what happened. And Angelo Pinto, he's like the curator, he brought in other things, like this model of a clipper ship from the eighteenth century. Angelo talks to the kids when they visit, not about the horrors of war, but about how this rifle works or where the soldiers went. The goal in my mind is for people to learn that many sacrifices had to be made for America to be what it is today." I bid Chris goodbye, thanking him for the interview.

In truth, this was an idea that came about by chance. When Joe Garofalo decided to donate his war memorabilia, he had no specific place in mind. Chris suggested several places, and they were both disheartened by the lack of interest and real commitment. Given the objective of showing respect for the American military and its critical role in the country's history, they seemed to see the responses as a lack of respect. Were they right? Possibly, though it may have been due to the lack of good spaces. Still, if it had been a real priority, a prominent location would have been found. Doubtlessly, those approached may have been uncomfortable saying they didn't want it, especially given the fact that the request was being made by a true war hero. Yet with each rejection, it appears, they became more determined to find a home for it.

Then came the almost offhand suggestion by Joe to situate it in the funeral parlor. Chris's response was immediate and spontaneous. No surprise, since he, a war veteran and booster of Morris Park had expressed enthusiasm for it from the start. The funeral parlor was indeed an odd choice, yet Chris found good reasons to support it retrospectively. He noted that his colleagues in the industry thought he was crazy. In his view, after putting it there, it seemed like an inspired choice because people were now discussing important issues relating to the exhibit instead of inappropriate conversations about matters unrelated to why they came to the funeral in the first place, namely to respect the departed. Thus, Chris and Joe had the last word, in effect. Having youngsters visit it was the icing on the cake. It was now an important educational experience for the young. In this way, an idea became a phenomenon of lasting importance. To wit, Chris says: "And it just grew and grew. People even called from far away." Apparently, he wasn't crazy. He was a man with a vision who made it happen.

Turning left on Haight Avenue, one block west, I pass a colorful mural just beyond Morris Park Avenue on my right at number 1727.

It's unusual in that it's not on an apartment or commercial building wall, but on a front wall on the private property of a home. It's across the street from Loreto Playground and appropriately so. Kids are playing basketball inside the playground and this mural, dedicated to the memory of "Nicky #1," has a basketball, a baseball, and a Yankees insignia on it, plus the letters SFX on the basketball, for the St. Francis Xavier school, which happens to be located on the same block. His full name was Nicholas Musto, and he died at the age of twenty-two (1975–1997). Interestingly, it was created much later, in 2014, by an artist named "James." I wonder what prompted that much more recent decision. Musto was killed when a car in which he was a passenger crashed into a tree on nearby Pelham Parkway after the driver fell asleep. A life brutally extinguished at an early age, I think. What might he have become? But, at the least, those who loved him remember him in this way. A gravestone is private, but this is public, very public. In this way, others are reminded that life can be fleeting and that remembering loved ones is so important.

Heading south to the end of the block, I turn right, and soon go left onto Hone Avenue until it dead ends after three blocks on Sackett Avenue. The street runs parallel to the Amtrak railroad tracks, and in front of it, off to the right, on a small cement wall is a three-panel color mural celebrating one hundred years of Morris Park's history, from 1913 to 2013. It was painted by Lovie Pignata, a Bronx artist who studied fine arts at Pratt Institute. While there is no explanation of the panels, it's clear enough for those familiar with the community's history.

The first panel, on the left, features a crowd of people, a man holding on to his hat, next to an automobile, and a flying contraption. Morris Park was the site of one of the first public air shows in the United States. In 1909, Glenn Curtiss, a renowned aviator and a founder of the American aircraft industry, presented a flying performance at the Morris Park Racecourse, and the panel depicts Lawrence J. Lesh guiding a glider. Curtiss is famous for having made the first long-distance flight in the United States. The center panel has a drawing of a distinguished-looking bearded man, John Albert Morris, who built the racecourse. The last panel, on the right, depicts the racecourse, which could accommodate up to 15,000 patrons. The figure in the foreground is that of Morgan Powell, who did prodigious research on the history of people of color in the Bronx and whom Lovie Pignata particularly admired. The turquoise and terracotta tile representations surrounding it are based on the original tiles of the old Morris Park train station, still viewable from the mural's location. They were designed by Cass Gilbert, the architect of the iconic Woolworth Building. This rich portrait is well worth seeing.

Sackett curves right a block later and here I see a one-story structure on which is painted a rough equivalent of the American flag, also along the Amtrak border, with a small door on which there's a sign reading "R&R Gun Club." This turns out to be a rifle range currently used by the New York City Police Department. Off to the right behind me, is Giordano's Wholesale Market. There are no other businesses here, which means that it's so good that people will make a special trip here. A man standing outside confirms this, saying: "It's been here for, maybe, thirty years, and they have everything you need, fresh cuts of meat, pasta, paper goods, and at great prices. People travel from all over to buy here. And they deliver also."

Angelo, a middle-aged man, grew up here. He says the community used to be all Italian but that it's changing, though he hastens to add that it's still a good place to live in, along with Throgs Neck. People inside the market are friendly. The young woman at the counter looks at my two-box purchase of farfalle and says in a joking tone: "That's it? That's all ya buyin?" I tell her I'll come back for more next time and she laughs.

Walking farther along Sackett I angle right onto Bronxdale, which is a mix of residences and businesses, many of which have Italian names on them, all attesting to the continued presence here of Italians. Here and there are some Yemeni-owned grocery stores. I go left at Matthews Avenue, drawn to it by curiosity about a small structure I see down the block. It's number 1839, and it's a very well preserved house with a wrought-iron fence, featuring pretty curlicues at the bottom and top of the fence. There's a small porch in front of the entrance, with an overhang supported by marble Doric columns. The home itself, with a prominent bay window, looks very old and was, in fact, built in 1905. The outer facing consists of raised, white-painted cement blocks that give it a stone-like look. There are corbels and cornices on the roof too.

Returning to Bronxdale, I hang a right and almost immediately come to number 1913, the address of F&J Pine Restaurant. While a couple can certainly have dinner there, it's a large place that tends to attract families and groups in general. The prices are reasonable, the fare is Southern Italian, the portions gigantic. It's a local favorite, but it has also attracted Yankee players and celebrities since opening in 1969. Very successful, it's the brainchild of Frankie and Johnny Bastone, two brothers who immigrated here from Calabria with a dream of opening an eatery that served the same hearty food they enjoyed as children back in Italy. What makes it worthwhile seeing is the atmosphere—noisy and decorated in Italian motifs, with photos of the rich and famous who have eaten here. Originally it was the Pine Saloon, and they kept the name Pine because they couldn't even afford a new sign when they first opened. Speaking of famous people, there are some very well known figures who, while they grew up in Morris Park, lived in totally different worlds—Regis Philbin, the TV personality; Kwame Ture (formerly Stokely Carmichael), the Black nationalist; and Jake La Motta, former boxing champion.

As I look around on a Sunday afternoon, it's very crowded with people of seemingly every nationality and race dining, many with young children. You don't always see such an ethnic mix in Italian restaurants in Italian communities. The interior has brick red walls with simulated old newspaper clippings and headlines painted on them. There are Yankees jerseys in frames hanging everywhere, red-and-white checkered tablecloths. I see a photo of Frank Sinatra with Phil Rizzuto. There's a long bar too, a gas fireplace, and a pressed-tin ceiling, all of which convey a feeling of warmth and welcome. It's a place to keep in mind if you want lots of good Italian food, at least according to the reviews I've read.

Turning around, I go half a block to Matthews, make a right this time and take it up one block to Neill Avenue, where I make another right and hoof it about a half mile up to Williamsbridge Road. Heading left, I walk up Williamsbridge, which is the western border of Indian Village, until I come to Pelham Parkway South, where I go right for one block, turning onto Yates Avenue. Indian Village is a subcommunity and part of Morris Park. It has some cachet and is a bit more upscale than the rest of Morris Park. A number of the homes on these blocks are nicer and more spacious, and most are in a brick Tudor style. The most magnificent such home is on Hering Avenue, one avenue east of Yates and parallel to it. There, at number 2064, I'm treated to a view of a drop-dead-gorgeous mini-mansion made of brick, stucco, and irregularly shaped colored stones, with a stunning scalloped slate roof. There's also a crenelated turret with a cone-shaped slate roof. The home is quite large, and clearly the dream residence of someone who took literally the idea that "A man's home is his castle."

Nevertheless, this area isn't entirely a Shangri-La. The farther south from Pelham Parkway you go, the more ordinary the homes are, looking indistinguishable from the rest of Morris Park. One drawback of this area is that the houses are quite close to Jacobi Hospital and other medical centers, not to mention the Hutchinson River Parkway. There's also the noise from the ambulance sirens wailing away night and day, although that's true of Morris Park in general. Part of the cachet is the name and the gently winding streets. Reportedly, people in Indian Village are more likely to have higher incomes and to send their children to private schools, like Fordham and Iona Prep for boys and Ursuline or Maria Regina for girls. This has a cumulative effect, as more people come to believe it's a more desirable and chic community, becoming a self-fulfilling prophecy. And so ends my journey through this fascinating community.

Ⓐ *Fantasia* (Aileen Ryan Fountain)

PARKCHESTER

PARKCHESTER WAS DEVELOPED by the Metropolitan Life Insurance Company as a planned community, and was the model for Manhattan's Stuyvesant Town. Technically, it's part of the Soundview community but is treated separately here because, like Co-op City, it's a distinct and unique place. Its boundaries are E. Tremont Avenue on the north, Castle Hill Avenue on the east, Westchester Avenue on the south, and White Plains Road on the west. Its name is a combination of two former Bronx neighborhoods once located nearby—Westchester Heights and Park Versailles, with most of the latter being on the actual grounds of present-day Parkchester. Founded in 1939, the community discriminated against minorities, as did other developments during that era. Today, it's integrated, with over 40,000 residents in its condominiums and rentals, and welcoming to all. There are 171 brick structures, ranging in height from eight to thirteen stories, and spread out over 129 acres. Condos sell at reasonable prices, depending on current market rates, with studios going for about $90K and two-bedrooms for $180K. Many have been renovated with new appliances, parqueted floors, and other amenities. Rentals are also available for approximately $1,500 a month for a one-bedroom apartment and $1,800 for a two-bedroom unit.

As a self-contained space, Parkchester has shopping within its boundaries, with chain stores like Marshalls, Macy's, Bolton's, Applebee's, Zaro's, Starbucks, and supermarkets, along with banks, a fitness center, mom-and-pop style stores selling jewelry and clothing, dry cleaners, pizza shops, delis, convenience stores, and restaurants, not to mention several parking garages and an urgent care center. While all this is inside Parkchester, many of the shoppers come from the surrounding communities and beyond. The main thoroughfare running through it is Metropolitan Avenue.

Parkchester has its own security force and is safe, day or night. Transportation is available within walking distance via the number 6 train and various bus lines, and plans are underway for a Parkchester stop on Metro-North. The train ride to midtown Manhattan takes about thirty-five minutes; the express bus takes an hour. Houses of worship, including historic St. Raymond's Church, are a short distance away. There are programs and activities, especially for seniors and youngsters, plus recreational facilities like basketball, baseball, and handball courts as well as playgrounds. The makeup of the groups residing here is that of a veritable United Nations, with a potpourri of ethnic and racial groups, making it appear that this is likely a tolerant place. Conversations with residents strongly support these impressions. In general, it's a working-class community, with firefighters, technicians, nurses, small-business owners, and many other occupations.

I begin walking Parkchester through one of its many entry points, Archer Road. The buildings look somewhat timeworn, with the color fading on many of the red bricks. Yet there are plenty of workers engaged in maintaining the property. There's no central air-conditioning and no large picture windows, and from the outside it looks basically like it did when it was first constructed—okay but nothing spectacular. Then again, many apartments are being upgraded. The prices are reasonable, transportation isn't a problem, there's excellent shopping within, and it's safe.

One attraction that was present from the beginning and endures is the artwork: 600 plaques, mostly above the doors, of animals and people and 500 terra-cotta statuettes of soldiers, mermaids, Native Americans, and the like. While some no longer exist, due in part to careless maintenance, the majority of these are still there and in reasonably good shape. They are often found on the corners of the buildings. The first one I see is of a sailor playing the guitar. Above several first-floor doors, I take note of wildlife plaques—two ducks, a deer lying down, seals, two more featuring monkeys—and a statuette

Fantasia (Aileen Ryan Fountain)

of a man singing and accompanying himself on a concertina. Another one is of a man with an umbrella. One could easily spend an entire day viewing them, as they are everywhere throughout the development. They were created by Raymond Granville Barger, Carl Schmitz, Theodore Barbarossa, and Joseph Kiselewski, an award-winning American sculptor best known for creating the Good Conduct Medal presented to soldiers who served in World War II, as well as other medals.

I turn left and head over to the main drag, Metropolitan Avenue, and here the buildings are in better condition. This is a major commercial thoroughfare. In one block, I come to the Oval, which contains the Aileen Ryan Fountain, called *Fantasia*. Surrounded by a grassy area with benches, this is the pièce de résistance of Parkchester.

The spouting bronze sculptures in the fountain are the work of Raymond Granville Barger, a highly regarded sculptor who specialized in bronze artworks. The fountain area is decorated according to the changing seasons. For example, during the winter there's a marvelous Christmas display, including an elaborate nativity scene, multiple Christmas trees, candy canes, nutcracker wooden soldiers, and more.

I meet an older Jewish man with a thick Russian accent. There are very few white people in general left in Parkchester, which he confirms, adding that the number of devout Muslims residing here makes him nervous because of what he feels are their anti-Jewish attitudes. He lives here because he's retired, and it's inexpensive. The Muslim population here is fairly large, though not dominant. In fact, the surrounding areas, namely Soundview and Castle Hill, also have significant numbers of Muslims from various lands, and many are traditional.

I enter Macy's, the second one to open after the main Macy's store in Manhattan's Herald Square on 34th Street. It's not as large as other Macy's branches, but it's quite substantial and has all the usual departments—clothing, housewares, shoes, jewelry, and so on. Next, I sit down in Starbucks, next to a Jamaican man named Tim, who's busily working on bracelets and other items made from copper which he mostly gives to friends. I ask him about the neighborhood.

"It's pretty nice and safe here. I've lived here since 2000."

"How does it compare to Co-op City?"

"Co-op City is okay, but it's farther up and too big and impersonal and doesn't have all the shops inside it. Transportation here is better. In general, this is a very friendly place. And the schools are decent. And we have a charter school."

"But where are all the kids? I mean, it's Christmas week and school's out."

Tim makes a motion with his fingers, mimicking working on an iPhone or something similar. "They're all playing on their tech toys and phones. Kids don't go out much anymore, it seems. They just play video games. You go to the park and you see them on the swings, clicking away. So, it's like, okay, I get it. That's the way it is. Nobody plays hide and seek or anything else that's outdoors." To be fair, it's winter and I see plenty of young people playing ball outdoors when the weather is warmer.

An older African American woman sitting at the table next to him and making a blue and white pom-pom for a hat, says: "I've lived here for twenty-three years, and it's a great place. And now we have a ferry going from Clason Point, not far away. It makes three stops in Manhattan, 90th Street, 34th Street, and Wall Street. It takes about forty-five minutes to get to Wall Street, and it's a beautiful ride. The apartments are nice, and I feel very safe here. There are some three-bedrooms, too, that go for about, 250K, I think."

Tim adds: "In the 1980s, they were going for twenty thousand, so a lot of people bought them up. Many of these apartments are owned by people who own maybe twelve of them that they rent out. To tell you the truth, I've lived all over New York City and what I like here is that it's a very comfortable vibe. It's a real community where I can spend all my time in it, and at the same time it's in a great city, where I can go to Manhattan or anywhere else whenever I feel like I want to do something else that's interesting."

And that pretty much sums up Parkchester.

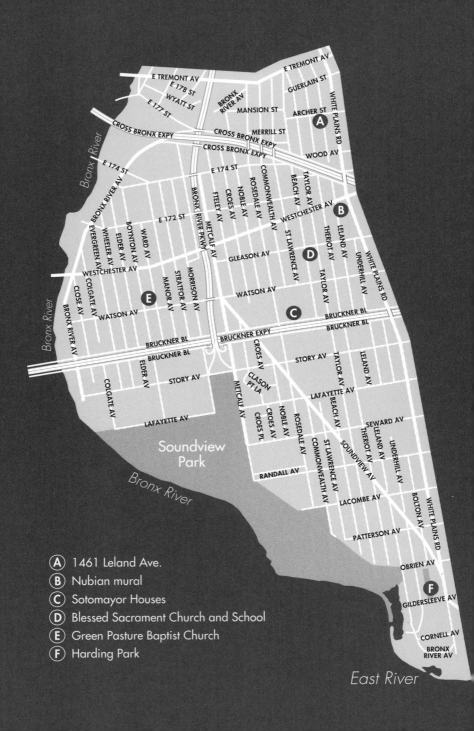

E TREMONT AV
E TREMONT AV
E 178 ST
WYATT ST
E 177 ST
GUERLAIN ST
ARCHER ST
BRONX RIVER AV
MANSION ST
WHITE PLAINS RD

CROSS BRONX EXPY
CROSS BRONX EXPY
CROSS BRONX EXPY
MERRILL ST
WOOD AV

Ⓐ

Bronx River

E 174 ST
E 174 ST
BRONX RIVER AV
E 172 ST
BRONX RIVER PKWY
FTELEY AV
CROS AV
NOBLE AV
ROSEDALE AV
COMMONWEALTH AV
BEACH AV
TAYLOR AV
WESTCHESTER AV
ST LAWRENCE AV
LELAND AV
THERIOT AV
TAYLOR AV
WHITE PLAINS RD
UNDERHILL AV

Ⓑ

Ⓓ

GLEASON AV
METCALF AV
WATSON AV

WARD AV
BOYNTON AV
ELDER AV
WHEELER AV
EVERGREEN AV
WESTCHESTER AV
COLGATE AV
CLOSE AV
WATSON AV
BRONX RIVER AV
STRATTON AV
MORRISON AV
MANOR AV
Bronx River

Ⓔ

Ⓒ

BRUCKNER BL
BRUCKNER BL
BRUCKNER BL
BRUCKNER EXPY

BRUCKNER BL
BRUCKNER BL
ELDER AV
STORY AV
COLGATE AV
CROES AV
CLASON PT LA
METCALF AV
CROES AV
CROES PL
STORY AV
TAYLOR AV
LELAND AV
LAFAYETTE AV
BEACH AV
NOBLE AV
ROSEDALE AV
ST LAWRENCE AV
COMMONWEALTH AV
SOUNDVIEW AV
SEWARD AV
THERIOT AV
LELAND AV
UNDERHILL AV
WHITE PLAINS RD
BOLTON AV

LAFAYETTE AV
RANDALL AV
LACOMBE AV
PATTERSON AV

Soundview
Park

Bronx River

OBRIEN AV

Ⓕ

GILDERSLEEVE AV

CORNELL AV
BRONX RIVER AV

East River

Ⓐ 1461 Leland Ave.
Ⓑ Nubian mural
Ⓒ Sotomayor Houses
Ⓓ Blessed Sacrament Church and School
Ⓔ Green Pasture Baptist Church
Ⓕ Harding Park

SOUNDVIEW

THE BOUNDARIES OF THIS RATHER LARGE COMMUNITY are E. Tremont Avenue on the north, White Plains Road and a small slice of Soundview Avenue on the east, the East River on the south, and the Bronx River on the west. Throughout the nineteenth and early twentieth centuries, the area was rural, with farms predominating. Its name is derived from the Long Island Sound, because early maps described the southern border, the East River, as being part of the Sound, which lay to the east. The major park here, Soundview Park, was largely marshland when the city purchased it, and while parts of it remain swampy today, it has other things to offer, as discussed below.

When the Lexington Avenue subway line, today the number 6 train, was extended along Westchester Avenue, builders developed the area, constructing small detached and attached homes and apartment houses, most of them three to five stories high. Incidentally, the IRT (Interborough Rapid Transit) lines did not initially have numbers, designating them as such only after 1948. Until the early 1960s, those settling here were predominantly Jewish, Italian, and to a lesser extent, Irish. The construction of the Bruckner Expressway, completed in 1972 at great cost, resulted in large-scale building of both middle-income high-rises and low-income public housing.

Today, Soundview has one of the largest number of NYCHA projects in the city. This, accompanied by a rising crime rate, has dampened the enthusiasm of working- and middle-income people of all races and ethnicities for living here. While this demographic still exists here, its numbers have gone down. The population today is a mix of African Americans, West Indians, Guyanese, Puerto Ricans, Dominicans, and South Asians. The main commercial streets are White Plains Road and Westchester, E. Tremont, and Soundview Avenues. The largest shopping center is where White Plains Road and the Bruckner Expressway meet.

My day begins with a stroll through what I would call northern Soundview, immediately south of Van Nest and north of the Cross Bronx Expressway. I walk up Wood Avenue and turn right onto Leland Avenue. Soon I pass what looks like it was once a synagogue at number 1461, and architectural signs identify it as such. There's a sign outside, referring to Christmas, declaring "Jesus is the reason for the season." The cornerstone tells the tale—organized 1929, erected 1950—and further research reveals that the name was Congregation Beth Abraham. Jews, Italians, and Irish predominated in this Bronx community from the 1930s through the 1960s.

Turning left on Archer Street, I walk one block to Theriot Avenue and make another left. Here are several co-op buildings, among the nicest in the area. The lobbies are in excellent condition, as are the exteriors, and I can see colorful and vibrant Christmas and Hanukah decorations. The community here is largely working class, with police officers, nurses, bus drivers, and business entrepreneurs. I speak with a Puerto Rican man on Commonwealth Avenue. Gabe is outside his two-story home, tinkering with his well-maintained eighteen-year-old white BMW. I ask him what it's like to live here.

"Actually, I'm a returnee, I guess. I was raised here and, as it happens, we were the first Puerto Rican family to become members of St. Anthony's Church. In fact, we were the first Puerto Ricans to move into the area. When I got older and married, I moved out to New Jersey, where I raised my kids. I bought this house cheap in the 1980s as an investment but never thought about moving back because the area was so bad then."

"Is the community safe now?"

"Yes, more or less. I've had my run-ins with some of the locals, but I'm a New Yorker and I know how to deal with that. In the winter it's crowded; in the summer it can get pretty lively. Now I live here. I'm semi-retired, I'd say, because I teach. Before that I was in the corporate world. It's my house, and the best way to protect it is to live in it. But it's much better now than it was twenty years ago."

While Gabe isn't exactly a gentrifier, he's one of a number of people who have returned to their roots later in life, and I've met others like him. The area draws him in because it was nice when he grew up, not nice in-between, and is now improving. That there's a large Puerto Rican presence here today probably makes it even more attractive. St. Anthony's Church, which still exists on Mansion Street near St. Lawrence Avenue, was established in 1908 as a personal Italian parish, but today it's mostly Hispanic. Most parishes are organized along geographical lines. Sometimes, however, they are assigned on a nonterritorial basis—in this instance, to serve a particular ethnic group that resides in a larger area. The school, also on Mansion and now closed, is a beautiful building, Italianate in design, with rich-brown terra-cotta trim, and a motto "Religion Patriotism Knowledge" carved above the entrance to the building. There's also a marble plaque from the old days memorializing those killed in World War II.

From here I return to White Plains Road via Mansion Street and Archer Street and head south to Westchester Avenue, where I make a right and turn left a block later onto Leland. Almost immediately I come face to face with a jaw-dropping large mural on a four-story building wall on my left. I've seen countless murals in my meanderings through the city but never quite like this one. It's very intricate, not amateurish in any way. The colors are bright blue, yellow, and peach. The main character is a giant fish-like creature in bright blue, with peach-colored eyes represented by big scary-looking blank spaces with no eyeballs and a downturned mouth. It has fins and a tail. On the side of its body are four rows of windows of various shapes, round, square, and oval. The windows have multiple panes and shapes as well, with elaborate designs. Beneath them are two rows of portholes, with open square covers. This combination fish/vessel seems to be in swirling peach colored water or perhaps clouds. There's a floodlight atop the object's head, shining, perhaps, into the night. Summing up, it needs to be viewed in person to be fully appreciated.

So many of the city's communities have sections dominated by one style—blocks of ranch homes, dull apartment buildings, or long rows of two-story brick homes—which are often quite monotonous. That's not the case in this part of the Bronx, Leland Avenue being a perfect example, where the streetscape has many varieties and sizes—colonials, capes, multistory brick structures, done in brick, stucco, aluminum siding, and shingle—not especially attractive, just basic. But they are different, and variety can hold the explorer's attention. One exception sits on the corner of Leland and Gleason Avenues, where a gracious colonial home rests on large property. Another is plain-looking except for a giant picture window, showing off some very impressive plants. Other blocks are completely made up of two-story semi-attached red-brick row houses that are well maintained and quite attractive.

I turn right onto Bruckner Boulevard, the service road of the Bruckner Expressway, and soon see the first of a series of modest brown-colored plastic signs, reading "Welcome to Justice Sonia Sotomayor Houses." This twenty-eight-building property is situated between the boulevard and Watson Avenue, running east-west from Leland Avenue to Soundview Avenue, with 1,500 apartments. Originally called Bronxdale, it was renamed in 2010 after the Supreme Court justice, who once lived there. Clearly, it's a matter of great pride to the residents, with its underlying message that despite one's humble origins, anyone can succeed in America. Residents in the houses are actually very proud that a Supreme Court justice's roots lie in this community. They also speak about how she graduated from Princeton and then from Yale Law School. She is the first Hispanic and Latina to be named to the court and has served with distinction since being appointed in 2009.

As I walk through, it's clear that it's still a low-income development, but not as problematic as are others in the city. There's litter on the ground, but it's a Sunday; the garbage cans are full and have not been emptied, so what can one do? In fact, CBS News aired a story the day before I visited about a pile of uncollected garbage on

Watson Avenue. It was all in bags but created a terrible stench that made it necessary for Bronx borough president Ruben Diaz Jr. to get involved. He said: "Somebody in City Hall just doesn't care. Have the New York City Housing Authority do its job." This isn't an unusual situation. There have literally been thousands of similar as well as more serious complaints about NYCHA in the past several years— rats biting children, employees involved in sex scandals, lack of heat for weeks or even months, mold and rotting ceilings, and the like. In this case, a NYCHA spokesman said that the trash compactors "had been broken." Residents asserted this was an ongoing problem, not as bad as that day, but something that needed to be addressed.[46]

Not surprisingly, simply naming a project after someone famous isn't like waving a magic wand. Much more needs to be done, and the name, while helpful because authorities fear negative publicity, can't by itself result in the massive resources required to really fix such a large system. There are benches, green grass, and playgrounds, which at least suggest possibilities for a better quality of life. Looking through the windows, I see signs that residents take pride in their apartments, however modest they may be. There are hanging plants, nice curtains, and neatly arranged furniture. There are no knots of young, hard-looking men hanging out, though this isn't the case in the summer. One thing is clear—many of the residents live in poverty. On the other hand, it's in a fairly safe area and is viewed as average among the NYCHA locations, neither terrible nor great.

Walking along Beach Avenue, I come across quite a few Hindu temples, serving Guyanese residents and others; and mosques, with adherents from Bangladesh, Guyana, and other countries. I also take note of a beautiful edifice housing the Church of the Blessed Sacrament at number 1170. It's made entirely of stone and has graceful arches and turrets. The interior is made of dark, tan-colored stones. There are niches in the walls depicting the life of Jesus. Most striking are the lovely stained-glass windows. Justice Sotomayor attended grammar school here, as did her brother Juan Luis Jr., who later became a physician—another success story. Coincidentally, her

Church of the Blessed Sacrament

abuelita (an affectionate term for grandma), with whom she was very close, lived on Kelly Street (as did she in her earliest years), where former secretary of state Colin Powell also resided as a child. Justice Sotomayor's deeply moving memoir, *My Beloved World,* presents a poignant and unforgettable portrait of the challenges, joys, and sorrows of living in the Bronxdale Houses and attending Blessed Sacrament, and of growing up in the Southeast Bronx in general.[47] Coincidentally, the Sotomayor family moved to Co-op City in 1970 because Bronxdale had deteriorated, with gangs moving in and taking control of the housing project. One of the main gangs operating there was the Black Spades, who were influential in the development and spread of hip-hop culture.

While this book doesn't focus on famous people who lived in the Bronx, some of those who grew up in Soundview deserve mention not only because of their renown but because of their diversity. They include the cartoonist and author Jules Feiffer, the actors Yaphet Kotto and Wesley Snipes, the serial murderer David Berkowitz ("Son of Sam"), the record producer and musician Phil Spector, and the all-female vocal group the Chiffons, of "He's So Fine" fame. I can't imagine what it would be like if they, plus Sotomayor and the rap groups from the Bronx River Houses, could all magically have a reunion in the same room.

At 1246 Beach Avenue, I see a home that's completely encased in bars. It was probably constructed during the much more dangerous 1980s. Other houses in the area also have many protective bars, but few completely cover a house. On the corner of Beach and Westchester Avenues, there's a restaurant called South of France. Curious, I ask the Hispanic manager about it and am informed that the previous owner twenty years ago was North African, from the "south of France."

Going left on Westchester Avenue, I enter John's Diner, at number 1786, which looks exactly like a regular diner except it's not on a separate detached property. The sign proclaims "We Serve Breakfast All Day." The red-and-gray vinyl-upholstered banquettes, the turquoise-painted walls from the 1950s, and the checkerboard designs throughout, plus the boomerangs drawn on the formica table surfaces, not to mention the counter stools for quick service, all scream "Diner!" There are large framed photos of Elvis, Marilyn Monroe, fifties-vintage automobiles, posters of films like *Rebel without a Cause* and *Casablanca*, plus, in a nod to the location, a photo of Dr. Martin Luther King Jr. together with Malcolm X. The menu is completely American—no Hispanic, African, or West Indian dishes for the locals, the way I've seen in other communities like this one—despite the fact that almost all of the customers are either Hispanic or Black. I speak with the owner, John Sarantis, a pleasant, voluble, middle-aged gentleman from Greece, who opened the diner twenty years ago:

"How come you built a diner here?"

"I came here as a teenager, worked as a dishwasher in a Manhattan restaurant and was promoted to busboy in two weeks. Then I was a pastry chef, and then one day I got the idea that I'm gonna make something from the past that many people forgot about, a diner. I like the old times. I grew up in the church, I never used bad words, I like old cars—I like the old times. And next door, in my pizzeria, we only have Yankees who have been around a long time. These tables here sell for a lot of money today, just the formica is $360 a tabletop. There's no diner like it in this part of the Bronx."

"Is this community safe?"

"I never have no trouble because I'm good with the people. That makes a big difference. I live in Flushing, and I have two kids. One is a teacher, and the other works on air conditioners. I'm a good and honest person, and that's why," he adds with a smile. "I'm not rich. I'm here twenty-three years. I open early in the morning, and I close at 10:00 p.m." This is a happy man, dedicated to what he does and proud of his ability to run a restaurant, one he built and designed with his own hands. And if the crowds that fill his eatery are any indication, he has a very strong following.

A bit farther down the street, I spy a cigar lounge, called Don Luis VIP Cigars. It's one of about five such enterprises in the Bronx, a place where people can engage openly in an activity now banned in almost every public space. I remember meeting former Mayor Giuliani in such a lounge in Manhattan when I was doing my first book on New York. Here the setting is much more modest, a couple of chairs crowded together in a small place, with several TVs along the walls. But like Giuliani's more elaborate establishment, it's filled with the aroma of cigars, expensive and cheap ones. Through the haze, I see a lone older woman among the men, all of them local, according to the manager.

Tiny, a man who is actually very large and quite gregarious, tells me about the competition, one of which is a Riverdale shop that I've written about in this volume. The swankiest place, Tiny tells me, in a class by itself, is the one on E. Tremont Avenue and Southern Boulevard. The owner's name is Ramon, and the place is called Maduro's. Tiny says that Ramon put a lot of effort into setting it up. He doesn't knock anyone, and seems to be happy with what he has, just like John. He has his people; the others have theirs.

Strolling along Noble, Croes, and Fteley Avenues, I notice that there are hundreds of similar-looking semi-attached red-brick homes here, almost all of them in excellent condition. The people are working class and enjoy living in a private house. I cross over to the west side of the Bronx River Parkway along Watson Avenue and notice that while the housing is the same, including the red-brick homes, the area is not as well-kept and, at times, even looks run-down; avenues like Morrison, Stratford, and Manor. Bronx River Houses, run by NYCHA, lie on E. 174th Street between Manor and Harrod Avenue, and they have an unusual form of cachet— hip-hop culture. A number of people who lived there were stars in the movement: Sean Perry, DJ Jazzy Jay, Eshawn Hall (DJ Mista Smoke), Afrika Bambaataa, and others. It all ended in the 1990s, when the police drove out the drug gangs that had taken over the housing project.

On Ward Avenue, at number 1115, I see what was once a synagogue, today the Green Pasture Baptist Church. The name Linas Hazedek is still carved on the cement wall in the front in large letters. The full name, Chevra Linas Hazedek of Harlem and the Bronx, indicates its Manhattan origins, and the building, very well-preserved, has been on the National Register of Historic Places since 2014. It's a beige and yellow stone structure in the Romanesque Revival style, with arches and stained-glass windows and entrances, and was built between 1924 and 1932.

Farther up Ward, there's an ad at Westchester Outlet Shoes, near Westchester Avenue, for what's called a "butt-lifter," with women wearing underwear drawn on a wall in what's a visual explanation of how well this item works. Slightly graphic, but it makes its point. Crossing Westchester, I pass more houses in below-average condition. As I head west, there are more apartment buildings, because as one comes closer to the south-central portion of the borough, population density increases. On Boynton, walking south, I glance at a curious memorial to a young man known as "Headache Nelson." Why he was a headache is unknown to me.

Upon reaching Bruckner Boulevard, I turn right and right again and walk up Elder Avenue, reaching a three-story brick building at E. 172nd Street, number 1521, where it intersects with Elder. It looks like it could once have been a Jewish school of sorts, again attesting to the strong Jewish presence here in the past, especially from the 1930s through the 1950s. The synagogue to which it is attached, which still has all the Jewish symbols—two menorahs on the front wall and a large Star of David on top—is at 1310 Elder and was established in 1939. Today, it's home to the Emanuel Pentecostal Faith Baptist Church. It was formerly Emanuel Synagogue and I wonder if the present church's name, "Emanuel," is a coincidence. I go left at 172nd and make another left onto Wheeler at the first corner, heading south.

At Wheeler Avenue, on the southwest corner, just beyond Westchester Avenue, Wheeler is also identified on the street sign as Amadou Diallo Place. Diallo was shot and killed in the hallway of his home on February 4, 1999, by four policemen looking for a rape suspect. Altogether forty-one shots were fired, nineteen of which hit Diallo. The officers were later acquitted after being charged with second-degree murder. The incident became a cause célèbre, as the police were widely seen as having used excessive force against an innocent and unarmed man. A mural of Diallo, who was twenty-three years old when he died, traces with painted footsteps his trek to the United States from Guinea, Africa, to New York City. It was completed in 2017, and his last words to his mother on that fateful day are reprinted: "Mom, I'm going to college." The mural was a necessary memorial because there's no sign of what happened at 1151Wheeler. Diallo's mother sold the home and moved away. The new owners, as is often the case, probably did not wish to have tour guides and people stopping and gaping at their home.

Heading east at the end of Wheeler along Bruckner, I return to White Plains Road and cross over the Bruckner Expressway into central Soundview. Here is the largest shopping center in the area. There's a strip mall just south of the intersection with various major outlets, and more emporiums along White Plains Road, stretching for several blocks. These include well-known places, like Kmart, Marshalls, Modell's, GameStop, Toy City, Sprint, Old Navy, the Children's Place, and dozens of other stores. I go right one block later onto Story Avenue. It's a depressing story with numerous NYCHA public housing projects, five of them along this avenue, and therefore a dominating presence. This is the 43rd Police Precinct, a high-crime area. I speak to a policeman, who is emphatic about the dangers of living here.

"There's robberies at the ATM. There's drugs, as you can see from the discarded needles all over the place. It's just horrible. The hallways in many of the buildings smell from weed. The only good part of the area is at the end of Soundview Avenue, where they have condos and a few gated developments, but even there you still have to go outside and shop and take kids to a park. I wouldn't want to live here. We try our best, but there are so many problems here."

"Do you think the ferry will improve matters?"

"Yes, it probably would, but it will take years."

He has a point, I think, as I pass streets littered with refuse, and inebriated people, some of them staggering in the street, on a Monday morning. The NYCHA complex looks bad, even by NYCHA standards. In the midst of this are several tall buildings, in good condition with pretty balconies, built decades ago in the early 1960s, when there was greater hope for the future of this area. It's well patrolled, and it's privately owned. One, the Brittany, is at 875 Morrison Avenue. Nearby, there's the Deauville, both part of what's called Lafayette Estates. Most of the people who live here tend to be retired and lower middle class—like postal workers, police officers, and medical technicians—and they are generally Hispanic or Black. In recent years, more younger people have been moving in. There are express buses to Manhattan, and of course there's now the ferry.

Turning right on Lafayette, I head over to Soundview Park, a 205-acre recreational center that boasts great walking trails, bike paths, fishing, terrific views of Manhattan and Long Island Sound, and sports fields galore. It even has a well-landscaped dog run. There's a wild look and feel to the place, enhanced by the marshland that makes up a good part of the park. An unusual attraction is a butterfly meditation garden and a daffodil project, where volunteers have planted over six thousand bulbs to connect visitors to the city's official flower. An annual music festival is held every year on the last Sunday in June. I speak with a parks employee who advises me to be careful when walking the park: "It's safest in the winter when no one's around. In the summer people can get rowdy. There's a lot of riff-raff in the area."

Outside I meet an older Puerto Rican woman who has lived in Lafayette Estates for over forty years. She says it's a nice place and that the area is safe, but not near White Plains Road where the James Monroe NYCHA Houses are. I tell her I'm taking a walk through the park, and she advises caution. I expect her to tell me about getting mugged, and to my surprise she says: "I was walking there yesterday and a big raccoon jumped out at me. I was really scared."

"Do you think I should move to your building?"

"You want to? Okay, but there are only a few white people living here. African people are moving in, but they're so afraid of dogs. I ask them why, and they say, 'Because in our country, the owners teach the dogs to bite the people.' And I say, 'Here we don't do that. Don't be scared.' We have younger people moving in now, but you have to have a job and good credit ratings, or they don't qualify you. A studio is about $900 and a one-bedroom, maybe $1,600." I find myself wondering why she doesn't feel the danger that the police spoke about. In part, as a longtime resident who lived through the crime-ridden 1990s and early 2000s, her expectations may be lower.

She also knows what areas to avoid, and she's not involved with criminals the way the cops are. Nevertheless, the crime rate in this area is, objectively speaking, quite high. As to the dogs, both the woman and the Africans she has met are probably overstating their situations a bit to make a point.

As I walk the streets in the southern portion of Soundview, beginning with Lacombe Avenue, along avenues like Leland, Beach, Taylor, St. Lawrence, and Underhill, I take notice of all the small, modest, and neatly kept homes, many of them single family, with small houses of worship mixed in. Ethnically, it's probably still Puerto Rican and other Hispanics, but South Asians are also becoming a presence. And I think to myself, the police may see this community as a horror show, but literally thousands of law-abiding citizens—one could call them homesteaders—live here, struggling to achieve "the Dream." And while they are aware that danger lurks outside, this is what they can afford, and they are determined to stay and overcome the odds and protect their loved ones from harm. They're not that different from the gentrifiers around the city who bravely move into communities that aren't completely safe yet either. In both instances, it's worthwhile to keep in mind Jane Jacobs's wise observation that it's the presence of "eyes," regular folks on the streets, that makes a community safer.

My trip through Soundview ends in Harding Park, or, as it's also known, "Little Puerto Rico." It's at the southernmost edge of the community, and the boundaries are O'Brien Avenue on the north, White Plains Road on the east, the East River on the south, and the Bronx River on the west. The area is about twenty acres in size, with about four hundred homes. It's best approached and entered along Leland Avenue, on the western edge where it passes O'Brien. Another marker could be a large statue of a Greek god on the right, possibly Hercules from its appearance, which a homeowner has placed very near the road. There are lions at his feet and he seems to be subduing them. About three yards down, there's another statue of a Greek maiden. Ramshackle homes, actually tarpaper shacks, were first put up here in the early 1920s, and the area was named Harding Park, after then president Warren Harding (1921–1923). The Higgs family, which had an amusement park in the vicinity, leased land to people and it became a summer resort. It all fell apart during the Depression. But after World War II, when housing was in great demand, about 250 people settled in the area, paying rent. In 1979, the city took over the properties after a failed effort by Robert Moses to demolish the homes and relocate the population elsewhere in the Bronx.

As I proceed, I see small pathways between the roads. Here several chickens and roosters are taking noisy notice of my arrival and strutting up and down. Many of the homes consist of small bungalows with screened-in porches, whose exteriors show signs of aging through the years. The streets are very quiet, with few people out and about, and the roads still flood even after a moderate rainfall. The only noise interrupting Harding Park's tranquility is that of planes on their way to and from LaGuardia Airport.

Writing in the *New York Times*, Lizette Alvarez described the movement into Harding Park by Puerto Ricans and other Hispanics bent on improving their lives as a "a matter of pride for a group of people tired of being blamed, historically, for degrading entire neighborhoods." It became predominantly Hispanic in the 1980s and '90s. One of the early homesteaders, who steadily improved his bungalow, was Pepe Mena, who recalled shouts of "Spic, get out" when he first arrived in 1964. Eventually, after a protracted legal battle, the city settled with those who took over unused land by selling the area to a homeowners' association founded in 1982, selling the property for $3,200 a plot.[48] Then mayor Ed Koch was helpful to these poor but resolute new homeowners when he exempted these homes from building code regulations.

But change is coming to Harding Park. The African American population has steadily grown through the years. New homes are sprouting everywhere, some of them quite large and elaborate, with new immigrants from both Hispanic and non-Hispanic lands. After all, the prices aren't as high as elsewhere, and one can have a million-dollar view of the Manhattan skyline, while those lacking one are but a five-minute walk from a public grassy area (actually part of Soundview Park), where they can see water for miles. On the Fourth of July, hundreds of people come here to picnic and celebrate, and in front and to the side of the skyscape, they can also see Rikers Island and Hunts Point. An active homeowners' association is quick to step in to protect the residents' interests. Townhouses have also been established on empty land bordering Harding Park. And now, there's a ferry to Manhattan five minutes away, on the other side of White Plains Road. Considering all this, this section could gentrify in the near future, bringing with it all the benefits and deficits associated with gentrification. For now, serious shopping and eateries are still far away, about two miles up near the Bruckner Expressway.

I turn right off of Leland onto Cornell Avenue, named after the first family, English, to settle here on what was land once occupied by the Siwanoy. I stride out over the grassy waterfront area, wending my way between thick underbrush and small boulders that have been here for centuries. So peaceful, I think, as I gaze upon the gentle waves lapping up against the uneven shoreline, with a sandy beach just off to my left. Two older men are fishing from the shore, a schooner glides by, and off in the distance I see Manhattan in all its splendor. It's an uncharacteristically warm Bronx day in January, with fifty-degree temperatures. And everything seems right with the world.

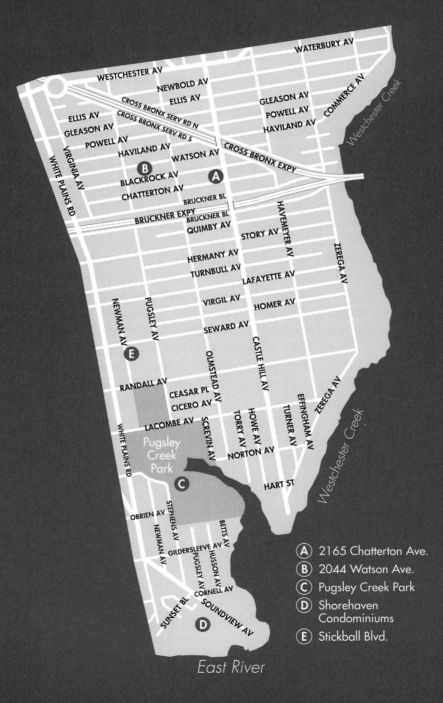

WATERBURY AV

WESTCHESTER AV

NEWBOLD AV

ELLIS AV

GLEASON AV

POWELL AV

HAVILAND AV

COMMERCE AV

Westchester Creek

CROSS BRONX SERV RD N

CROSS BRONX SERV RD S

ELLIS AV

GLEASON AV

POWELL AV

HAVILAND AV

WATSON AV

CROSS BRONX EXPY

VIRGINIA AV

WHITE PLAINS RD

Ⓑ

BLACKROCK AV

CHATTERTON AV

Ⓐ

BRUCKNER BL

BRUCKNER EXPY

BRUCKNER BL

QUIMBY AV

STORY AV

HAVEMEYER AV

HERMANY AV

TURNBULL AV

LAFAYETTE AV

ZEREGA AV

VIRGIL AV

HOMER AV

SEWARD AV

NEWMAN AV

PUGSLEY AV

Ⓔ

CASTLE HILL AV

RANDALL AV

CEASAR PL

CICERO AV

OLMSTEAD AV

EFFINGHAM AV

ZEREGA AV

LACOMBE AV

SCREVIN AV

HOWE AV

TORRY AV

NORTON AV

TURNER AV

WHITE PLAINS RD

Pugsley
Creek
Park

Ⓒ

HART ST

Westchester Creek

OBRIEN AV

STEPHENS AV

NEWMAN AV

BETTS AV

GILDERSLEEVE AV

PUGSLEY AV

HUSSON AV

CORNELL AV

SUNSET BL

SOUNDVIEW AV

Ⓓ

Ⓐ 2165 Chatterton Ave.

Ⓑ 2044 Watson Ave.

Ⓒ Pugsley Creek Park

Ⓓ Shorehaven
   Condominiums

Ⓔ Stickball Blvd.

East River

CASTLE HILL

THE BOUNDARIES OF CASTLE HILL, generally, are Westchester and Waterbury Avenues on the north, Westchester Creek and the East River on the east and south, and White Plains Road on the west. The name came from a hill, which reminded Captain Adriaen Block, a Dutch explorer and trader, of a castle. Block was also the first European to establish that Manhattan and Long Island were indeed islands. The earliest occupants of the land here were the Siwanoy. In earlier times, most of Castle Hill was also called Unionport. The area was undeveloped land until the 1920s, when there were only a few houses and small farms, as well as resorts in Clason Point. Over time, beginning in the 1940s, people moved here in greater numbers, especially when subway service began and low- to middle-income housing was built.

Ethnically, Castle Hill is home today to Muslim and Hindu South Asians and to Guyanese, Puerto Ricans, Dominicans, Jamaicans, Ecuadorians, and Colombians. There are issues with respect to safety and crime, but the condos near the water where Soundview Avenue ends, which have security, are quite safe and so is the northernmost section of the community around the Cross Bronx Expressway. In terms of transportation, the number 6 train stops at the Castle Hill Station on Westchester Avenue, and there are buses, plus the new ferry at Clason Point. The main commercial streets are Castle Hill and Westchester Avenues and White Plains Road.

I begin my trip on Westchester Avenue and White Plains Road, heading east. A good example of syncretism can be found here. Many stores advertise *halal* (sanctioned by Islamic law) meat, but this one says Musa's Halal Chinese Food. There's a drawing of a chicken on one side of the sign and a cow on the other side, meaning, by its absence, no pork. Two doors down is the Mexican El

Texano eatery, and there are other restaurants too. That the owners of these shops are located cheek-to-jowl with each other assures that they will have contact with and get to know one another, as will their clienteles. Sometimes the appeal is explicit, as in the sign I saw outside a Harlem pizza/chicken joint proclaiming "No Pork on My Fork." Yet there's more to a community's identity than food. These food stores identify an area as multiethnic, but the real contacts take place in the communities themselves—in the buildings, on the streets, in parks, community centers, schools, and sometimes houses of worship, all places where successive waves of immigrants have met and mingled for more than a century.

When Westchester swerves left in a few blocks I walk straight ahead down Waterbury and I soon arrive at Intermediate School 194, built in 2003 on Waterbury Avenue east of Castle Hill Avenue. Castle Hill has a large South Asian community, especially Bangladeshis and Guyanese, and smaller numbers of Pakistanis and Indians. There are pretty collages on both sides of the entrance. I speak with an administrator who informs me that the school is about 55 percent Asian and 45 percent Hispanic, most of them Puerto Rican and Dominican, and it also has some white and Black students, a good number of whom come from nearby Parkchester. It's a beautiful, spacious, and spotless institution. But most important, it's the perfect place for groups to learn about and appreciate each other.

Waterbury becomes industrial, with storage facilities, lumberyards, concrete factories, and the like. It's understandable, as several highways converge nearby. I come to Zerega Avenue, the entire length of which is industrial. I turn right onto it and right again, heading west on Newbold Avenue. Just off Zerega, at number 2365, on the right, is the home of Bronx Indoor Paddleball Courts, with paddleball, racquetball, and handball available. This kind of indoor facility isn't easy to find in these parts. The courts have been there for twenty-five years, and the online reviews on Google are great. In general, the area just off Zerega on either side is industrial, but west of Havemeyer to the Cross Bronx Expressway, it's residential. The houses are nicer than in Soundview, but they're small and crowded together. I also pass a Mormon church on Ellis Avenue, at number 2055, a block south of Newbold, just west of Olmstead Avenue.

Powell Avenue, two blocks south of Ellis, is one of the prettiest streets in the area, with number 2238, an updated beige-painted stucco home, the most elaborate one. It is Victorian in style, with Tudor elements, and Art Moderne glass blocks. At the intersection of Powell and Castle Hill Avenues on the left, I see a beautiful apartment building, made of dark-red brick, with Tudor lines near the top. I go through an arched entrance into an indoor courtyard, a rarity here. It's circular, with a fountain and greenery around it and there are Gothic entranceways. A block wide, it has another similar entrance on the next block, Haviland Avenue. I walk north on Castle Hill and then left on Ellis heading west to Pugsley. The Cross Bronx Expressway bisects this community at an angle and I'm now exploring the southern side, having completed my visit to the northern portion. At the corner of Pugsley, I jump into the Yoselin Deli to use the lavatory. To get there I must go through another small room where two regular customers are relaxing on a small couch and watching a boxing match. Many bodegas have such spaces and the people give me a friendly hello as I pass through.

Walking south on Pugsley I soon discover that this section is decidedly nicer than the one I've just left. The homes are larger and better maintained, and more than a few are detached, with garages to boot. In general, even the northern section of Castle Hill, between Westchester Avenue on the north and the Cross Bronx Expressway, is a more upscale area than nearby Soundview, with far less public housing. To my left, at 2016 Gleason Avenue, I can't help but notice an eye-catching day care center, called Kids World. The low brick wall around it is painted in alternating bright hues of blue, pink, yellow, green, red, and purple. Every single brick needed to be painted individually with care taken not to spill any paint on the next one. Imagine how much work and commitment to the center was required to make that happen.

At 2044 Watson Avenue, two blocks south of Gleason and not far from the corner of Olmstead Avenue, I come across an unusual home. It's set high off ground level, with steps that have a red stripe painted down the middle, leading to the entrance. Beneath the first-floor stucco wall are a number of ancient stones, clearly the original stone of the land on which it was built. A wishing well with a bucket stands here, next to welcome signs. The rocks have been painted in various colors. Off to the side are andirons for a fireplace, a poker, brush, and other items. "I LOVE NEW YORK" has been spelled out, using dozens of small stones. There's a shrine to the Virgin Mary and Jesus, stating: "You will not be able to love your children if you do not love your mother." Inside the driveway, toward the back is a statue of a life-sized soldier standing guard, if you will, over the house. At number 2136, I see five concrete globes atop five fence-posts. Each one has been colorfully painted in great detail. They look exactly like soccer balls, which was obviously the intention, and they're the right size. I've not seen that before anywhere in the city. Someone here is a real soccer enthusiast.

At Castle Hill Avenue, I turn right and then left a block later onto Blackrock Avenue, named after the Black Rock Farm that stood on land in the 1800s, which later became part of Soundview Park. Specifically, it was named after a large boulder made of gneiss, a coarse-grained rock that has light and dark bands across its surface. But for millions of people, what matters most is that Jennifer Lopez grew up on this block at number 2210 in a detached fairly large home, with metal grillwork in front. There's also a side yard with a white picket fence running along it. The block dead-ends at the Cross Bronx. Lopez actually had a 2002 hit song dedicated to where she lived, called, "Jenny from the Block." Here's a small sampling of the lyrics:

> Don't be fooled by the rocks that I got
> I'm still, I'm still Jenny from the block
> Used to have a little, now I have a lot (Southside Bronx!)

No matter where I go, I know where I came from (From the Bronx!)

Although the critics gave it a mixed reception, it was a rousing success financially. Some in the community were offended by it, asserting that Lopez never did much for the community she came from. Others praised her for writing a song (with others) that at least acknowledged her Bronx roots.

At 2165 Chatterton Avenue, on the corner of Castle Hill, stands a fine-looking brick apartment building, with a neat cloth canopy over the entrance. The bricks are intricately designed with all manner of diamond and square shapes in various shades of tan, dark brown, and pale yellow. The keystones above the windows are in the shape of scalloped seashells, and the bricks underneath all the windows are arrayed in a checkerboard design. Inside, there's a large coffered ceiling with floral arrangements painted onto it. The floor has a terrazzo design, and there are sculpted sconces along the walls. There's an old-fashioned elevator with a semicircular dial identifying the floors in Roman numerals.

The streets below the Bruckner Expressway—Hermany, Turnbull, Lafayette—consist of homes that pretty much resemble the homes discussed until now. One disadvantage of living here is that not far away is the notorious Castle Hill Houses, considered by many to be one of the worst NYCHA housing projects in the Bronx. It's roughly bounded by Seward and Cincinnatus Avenues on the north, Havemeyer Avenue on the east, Lacombe Avenue on the south, and Olmstead Avenue on the west. Constructed in 1960, the twelve- and twenty-story high-rise buildings have 5,500 mostly lower-income residents, with many single-parent homes and high unemployment, and are a problem in terms of keeping the area safe. I pass by the childhood home of former first baseman Ed Kranepool at 847 Castle Hill Avenue, near the corner of Hermany Avenue, and five blocks from Castle Hill Houses. It's a modest, two-story home with vinyl siding. There are simple metal awnings on the second-floor

The intricate design on 2165 Chatterton Avenue

windows. Kranepool's father was killed in battle during World War II the year Ed was born, and the family had very little money.

I walk the streets south of Lacombe, along Norton Avenue and the side streets branching off from it. Overall, it looks fairly nice, but many of the houses are plain-looking. Next, I head south on Castle Hill Avenue, which soon ends at the East River. Just before that, I turn right at Hart Street, a one-block affair. Here, I take a brief hike along the shore of Pugsley Creek. The waters are still, and the area is very quiet. It's a pleasant interlude. Crossing Castle Hill, I check out the YMCA, which offers gorgeous indoor and outdoor swimming pools, an excellent library, basketball courts, workout rooms, and many activities. Someone has painted a detailed map of the entire United States, with each state drawn and identified, on an outdoor concrete surface. All this can be had for a mere $100 a month for membership for a couple and five children. One of the most outstanding features is the terrific view. Sitting astride the shoreline of the East River, you can see a large expanse of water and great views of the Whitestone and Throgs Neck Bridges. How many YMCAs in the city can claim to have such an extraordinary vista?

From here, I hike back up Castle Hill Avenue, past the tract housing that lines the street to Lacombe and make a left, and then another left onto White Plains Road. In a few blocks, I turn left once again onto Gildersleeve Avenue. The homes here are a mix of pretty nice and average, with some of them quite old. These streets are very quiet and have the feel of a small village. I walk the streets off Gildersleeve—Newman, Stevens, and Husson—and see that my presence is duly noted by one or two residents. They're probably surprised to see anyone taking a walk. It's a racially mixed section that feels quite safe. At the end of Husson, I make a left onto Cornell Avenue, where I enter Clason Point Park.

This scenic park is landscaped and surrounded by water. It makes for an excellent walk. There are curved concrete paths and pretty benches, with old-fashioned streetlamps lighting the way. There are grassy areas where people can simply lie down, relax, and gaze upon the water and the boats passing by. There's a state-of-the-art playground, with the latest varieties of climbing equipment. In the summer, the park is crowded with people of all nationalities. I walk onto Soundview Avenue and head toward the ferry to Manhattan, which costs but $2.75 a trip, with free transfers available. It's a nice boat and the ride is thirty to forty-five minutes, depending on where you're going, with stops on E. 90th Street, E. 34th Street, and Wall Street. I meet Marvin Torffield, a tall, gray-haired man wearing a fisherman's cap and a black-and-white scarf, who is on his way to the ferry via a small scooter he owns.

"Do you live around here?" I ask him.

"Yes, in Soundview, on Lacombe, near Rosedale Avenue. I moved here about two years ago because they had a great deal on an apartment. I'm an artist and it gave me the light and room that I needed for my work."

"Did you grow up in New York City?"

"I was raised in East New York. I had lofts in Manhattan on 21st Street near Gramercy Park, 23rd Street, and then Greene Street in the seventies and eighties. Until I came here, I lived in Staten Island, in Saint George, near the ferry, for about twenty years. The condo people have waited thirty years for this ferry."

"Where did you study art?"

"At Pratt Institute, and then I did a masters at Yale. Today I'm seventy-five, but I still work on sculptures. I'm not retired. I started with xenon, a colorless odorless gas, doing light projection in fog." Torffield is, as they say, the real deal. His work has been discussed and reviewed in the *New York Times*, the *Boston Globe*, and elsewhere. He was awarded a Guggenheim fellowship and was also a research fellow at MIT and Harvard. His work has been analyzed by the prominent sculptor and artist Robert Morris and by Dore Ashton, a well-known critic and art historian. And why does this prominent individual live in Soundview, an out-of-the-way-part of the city? Because the rent is great and so is his studio, and he has "drop-dead views of the Manhattan skyline and the East River." Marvin doesn't seem to need the crowds or the Manhattan vibe and art scene. Plus, as he says, "This is an up-and-coming community." And if he wants to go to Manhattan, the ride is a mere thirty minutes.

I walk into Shorehaven Condominiums on Soundview Avenue. The name, Shorehaven Condominiums, gives it away to those few in the know. This was formerly the site of the Shorehaven Beach Club, located where Kane's Casino once stood. Jeffrey Wiesenfeld, who spent summers there as a child, described Shorehaven as a mostly Jewish club established in the 1940s and 1950s. But Bronx historian Lloyd Ultan says it was intended for middle-class people. Regardless, the owner, a Dr. Goodstein, arranged for buses to take people there from all over the Bronx. Everything has to have a "hook" to sell. The people were told that the surrounding waters were those of Long Island Sound, when, in fact, it was the much less attractive-sounding East River.

While it may not have been the Catskills, it had the same amenities: ping pong, shuffleboard, volleyball, tennis, and square dancing, as well as appropriate entertainment. The latter meant people like Buddy Hackett, Myron Cohen, and other Jewish comedians. Those who frequented the club still speak fondly of the end-of-summer highlight—the Miss Shorehaven contest. Those who were there back then are obviously no longer there today. But for those still alive to reminisce, the Bronx lives on in their minds as a place that was fun. In this sense, today's population carries on the tradition, even if the new places have different names and are enjoyed by different ethnic groups.

I end my trip with a visit to Stickball Boulevard. Yes, that's really the name of this street, formerly known as Newman Avenue. Stickball, played with a Spaldeen (a pink rubber ball made by the Spalding company but pronounced "Spaldeen" in New York City) and a broomstick that served as a bat was once played on streets everywhere in the city. I played it as a kid. The bases were the manhole covers in the street. A "three-sewer-man" was a demigod because he could hit the ball a distance of three sewers. An ESPN reporter describes the scene here:

Stickball Boulevard

It is a sunny Sunday afternoon on Stickball Boulevard in the Bronx, and the future of a sport steps up to the plate. Jayden Carrasquillo inches closer to the dry paint on the scorching blacktop and taps his stick once, twice, as his parents Russell and Jennifer, look on. . . . A hit here would mean far more than on a baseball diamond. Today is Jayden's first game with the Silver Bullets up in the bigs—the New York Emperors Stickball League.[49]

Sports need not die permanently. If people want to, they can be revived generations later. Today, shuffleboard, a game for older folks at resort hotels, has caught fire among the gentrified set. In Gowanus, Brooklyn, there are leagues with lots of teams, and the courts are thriving. And now we have stickball, declared all but dead decades ago, enjoying a revival among youngsters, not only in the Big Apple, but elsewhere in the country. Who can know where it will go?

THROGS NECK

PELHAM BAY

WESTCHESTER
SQUARE

CO-OP CITY

CITY ISLAND

MIDDLETOWN RD
ROEBLING AV
ZULETTE AV
WELLMAN AV
MAITLAND AV

GILLESPIE AV
CROSBY AV
DUDLEY AV
HARRINGTON AV
CODDINGTON AV
LA SALLE AV

JARVIS AV
MERRY AV
HOBART AV
HOLLYWOOD AV
KEARNEY AV
BRUCKNER EXPY

DWIGHT PL
ROBERTSON PL
KENNELWORTH PL
OHM AV
STADIUM AV
GRISWOLD AV

WATT AV
BAY SHORE AV

AMPERE AV
GRISWOLD AV

SPENCER DR
RANDOLPH PL
COUNTRY CLUB RD
VALHALLA
PARSIFAL PL
RAWLINS AV
STADIUM AV

CAMPBELL DR

Eastcheste
Bay

E TREMONT AV
EDWARDS AV
BALCOMB AV

PURITAN AV
WATERBURY AV
EDISON AV
BRADFORD
MAYFLOWER

WATERBURY AV
FAIRFAX AV
ELLSWORTH AV
THROGMORTON AV
FAIRMOUNT AV

LAYTON AV
BARKLEY AV
SHORE DR
DEAN AV
CLARENCE AV
WILCOX AV
VINCENT AV
THROGS NECK EXPY

Westchester Creek

Old St.
Raymonds
Cemetery

BRUCKNER BL
BRUCKNER BL
BRUCKNER EXPY

OTIS AV
LOGAN AV
EDISON AV
HOLLYWOOD AV
THROGS NECK EXPY

BARKLEY AV
SWINTON AV
HUNTINGTON AV
BRINSMADE AV
BALCOMB AV
CROSS BRONX EXPY

E TREMONT AV
LAFAYETTE AV
REVERE AV
QUINCY AV
CALHOUN AV
PHILIP AV

RANDALL AV

CLARENCE AV
SCHLEY AV

SCHLEY AV

E

BRUSH AV

St. Raymonds
New
Cemetery

CROSS BRONX EXPY
CROSS BRONX EXPY

LAMPORT
PL
SCHLEY AV

D

ADEE
DR

MILES AV
BLAIR AV
LO

BUTTRICK
AV

SCHLEY AV

DEWEY AV
BALCOMB AV
SAMPSON AV
SWINTON AV
BRINSMADE AV
HUNTINGTON AV

REVERE AV
CALHOUN AV
QUINCY AV
LAWTON AV

E TREMONT AV
HARDING AV

MILTON PL

THROGS NECK EXPY
THROGS NECK EXPY

THROGS NECK BL
KEARNEY AV
MEAGHER AV
PRENTI

PENN

Hutchinson River Pkwy
HUTCHINSON RIVER PKWY

SCHLEY
AV

MILES AV
GRAFF AV
BUTTRICK AV
DAVIS AV
ROBINSON AV
HOSMER AV
EMERSON AV

SCHURZ AV

MSGR
HALPIN PL

SUNSET TR

C

POPL
INDIAN

Westchester Creek

Ferry
Point
Park

HUTCHINSON RIVER PKWY

East River

G

F

THROGS NECK

*Long
Island
Sound*

THE GENERAL BOUNDARIES OF THROGS NECK are Middletown Road and Watt Avenue on the north, Long Island Sound on the east, the East River on the south, and Westchester Creek and the Hutchinson River Parkway on the west. The precise boundaries of the neighborhoods within Throgs Neck have long been, and continue to be, a matter of dispute. Many residents are fiercely territorial about the subject. But it doesn't matter that much in this ethnically homogeneous area. Furthermore, most of the homes in this largely middle-class community range from modest to nice, with few mansions or, as people like to say, "McMansions"; and the housing stock consists of colonials, splits, capes, and ranches, along with upscale condominiums, a good number of them on the water. There are attached, semi-attached, and detached homes. Furthermore, most people consider these sub-areas to also be a part of Throgs Neck. For these reasons it makes sense to group them all under the name of Throgs Neck, by far the largest single community. (While some sources spell it "Throggs," the more current spelling, "Throgs," will be employed.)

For the record, nonetheless, here are the names and very approximate locations. Looking north from where the bridge first crosses land, we have the State University of New York (SUNY) Maritime College, followed by the small enclaves of Silver Beach and Locust Point on the left, and Edgewater Park on the right. To the north of Silver Beach, there's Throgs Neck, Middletown, Schuylerville, Pelham Bay, and Co-op City; and to the left of Pelham Bay is Westchester Square. These last three neighborhoods are treated separately, as they are distinct in terms of their appearance and population makeups.

On the eastern side, generally speaking, of the Bruckner Expressway are the subcommunities that can sometimes straddle the Bruckner. These are, heading north after Edgewater Park, Eastchester Bay, Country Club, and Spencer Estates. To the first-time visitor, be they tourists or New Yorkers, these names will probably mean nothing. For those interested in learning more about the specific boundaries and distinctions, call Community Board Ten.

Throgs Neck was originally home to Native Americans, then claimed by the Dutch and settled by the British, who departed after the Continental Army was victorious in the American Revolutionary War. It was largely farmland through the nineteenth century. Near the end of that century, the area was a summer resort, attracting many Germans from Yorkville in Manhattan who were particularly fond of the German beer gardens that flourished here at the time. When public transportation became more available early in the twentieth century, large numbers of Italians flocked to the area. Today, it is a largely Catholic and white neighborhood consisting mostly of Italians, Irish, and Germans. There is a small Black and Hispanic population here too. It's a very safe community, and has lots of parkland available to the public for recreation. The main commercial thoroughfare here is Tremont Avenue, which runs through the entire neighborhood. There's also a shopping mall along the Hutchinson River Parkway west service road.

My walk through Throgs Neck begins at Pennyfield Avenue where it crosses Lawton Avenue on the west side of the Throgs Neck Bridge. A block later I go left onto Harding Avenue, pass the New York Tennis Club, which has nice courts, and then make a right just before a bridge toll entrance, onto Longstreet Avenue. In one minute, I turn left onto Chaffee Avenue, which swings right and soon becomes Locust Point Drive. This is the small community of Locust Point, a tiny part of Throgs Neck that lies along the bridge as it ascends. No driver will notice it because it's situated behind high walls that shield it from the constant din of vehicular traffic on the bridge.

Since Civil War symbols of the Confederacy are being torn down all over the country, it's interesting to note that Longstreet Avenue is named after James Longstreet, a leading general of the South and the main subordinate to General Robert E. Lee. Lee referred to him fondly as his "Old War Horse." So why is his name still up there? Could it be because this is a politically conservative neighborhood and the people are uninterested in this controversy? Absolutely not. After the war, Longstreet, a longtime friend of President Ulysses S. Grant, became a vocal opponent of the South's position, supporting Reconstruction to the point of leading an African American militia into battle against those opposing it. Historians say he was a talented battlefield commander. But no one is perfect. In a battle at Seven Pines in Henrico County, Virginia, he ordered his men to follow him down what turned out to be the wrong road, arriving late to the battlefield in a fight which turned out to be inconclusive.

Most of the homes here are detached. They're not fancy, but nice enough. Religious statues of Jesus and Mary are quite common here, reflecting the Catholic makeup of the neighborhood. It's also politically conservative, as attested to by the many American flags that typify such communities, some of which are quite large. I turn right into Hatting Place. At the end of the block I turn left onto a dirt path and come to the next parallel street, Glennon Place and turn left again. At number 3247, I see twin stone chimneys. One of them has an unusual triangular shaped crest, with a blue and gold cross on a black eagle's chest.

On the next block, Giegerich Place, I look at the well-tended gardens, the many stone figurines of rabbits, frogs, and birds, and the patriotic signs adorning many homes and am struck by the fact that, on the whole, people here care very much about how their homes look and decorate them very tastefully. Outstanding examples of this can be found at numbers 3221 and 3217. I turn left onto Longstreet and pass Tierney Place, soon after which Longstreet dead-ends at a property that faces out to the water. On my left, at the intersection, is what looks like a typical multifamily development. It's a beige-brick building, very tastefully done and yet, due to its size, somewhat extravagant in appearance. Four stories high, it's divided into three sections, with ten small balconies. The rear of the property faces out onto the water and there's a very large patio which fronts out to the water itself. I think to myself that those living in what looks like a condo building must be very fortunate to be on the water.

The other properties on the south side of Tierney face the water too, but they are all single-family semi-attached and detached dwellings. Here, on Longstreet Avenue, I come face to face with the bridge, the East River, and off to my left, Long Island Sound, with Nassau County visible but quite far away. I'm looking out over a waist-high picket fence, with an unlocked gate, belonging to the development. The vista is very inspiring, especially as I see sailing vessels of all kinds gliding by. There's something about these water-side communities that feels as though one is in touch with nature in a way that evokes the smallness of human beings when in the presence of large bodies of water and an open sky above.

My wife is my research associate and sometimes accompanies me on my trips. We decide to enter the apartment complex through an opening on the side. Now we're strolling through the property for a few minutes. There's no one around. It's a hot weekday, about 90 degrees at noon in late August, so we assume that people are probably at work. We think about sitting down on some comfortable-looking chairs but decide against it because we don't live there and, if truth be told, I want to continue walking. I wonder how people on these blocks feel about having near their home what seems to be the only apartment building in Locust Point. Do they think "There goes the neighborhood" or does it not matter to them? I look around, hoping to engage some people on this topic, but the street is deserted. Little do I know that I will soon learn more about this building in a different way, secondhand but pretty reliable, to wit, an analysis of the Mafia that appears by pure coincidence two days later in the *New York Times*.[50]

My wife and I read this article and are transfixed by it. Exhibit A is the Zottola family, which resides on Tierney Place, a street we walked on forty-eight hours ago. What a coincidence. Locust Point is a tiny sliver of a community in Throgs Neck. Who knew that such sinister figures made their homes here, but then again, why not? They have to live somewhere. Which house was it, we wondered. So, we surfed the net, looking for photos of the house, and we soon found it and received a shock. It turns out that what I described above is not an apartment complex, but a huge compound, consisting of three similar-looking private homes, all of which belong to the Zottola family, who, according to the police, are closely affiliated with the notorious Bonanno Mafia family, led for many years by Joseph Bonanno, an immigrant from Sicily who died in 2002 at the ripe old age of ninety-seven. I remember being entranced by Joseph Bonanno's nickname, "Joe Bananas." It seemed so evocative, the stuff that makes the serious and deadly seem oddly, if inappropriately, comical. After all, these people are killers.

About a month earlier, on July 11, 2018, Salvatore Zottola had been shot several times in a mob hit near his home on Tierney Place around 6:30 a.m. as he was leaving his house.[51] Gravely injured, he nevertheless survived. A month earlier, a similar attempt had been made on his father, Sylvester Zottola. When I speak with old-timers in these neighborhoods they often express appreciation for these families, saying they "knew how to take care of business and kept the neighborhood safe." Younger Italian Americans are less charitable in their assessments, seeing them as criminals who give Italians a bad name, though they're sometimes afraid to speak out. Both views were expressed here too in the aftermath of the shooting.

A seventy-eight-year old man named Joe Peloso said: "Almost every weekend he'd have the whole neighborhood over. It's like an open house over here. He's good to the neighborhood." On the other hand, a woman who didn't want to be named commented: "It's not a surprise. Look at what he does for a living. I can't say any more. It's not worth my life. It's not worth my daughter's life." Who had the last word? Perhaps a man who answered the phone at the Zottola home and warned the caller: "Don't f---king call me no more!" More permanent than this admonition is a sign outside one of their several homes on the block that proclaims:

OUR FOUNDATION IS BUILT FROM LOVE. OUR STRENGTH KEEPS US TOGETHER

A plaque on another Zottola home, underneath an engraved flower, evokes memories of *The Godfather*:

OUR WALLS ARE BUILT THICK. OUR LOVE FOR EACH IS THICKER

One thing is certain. The family does not take kindly to the publicity. Leaving Jacobi Hospital, where Salvatore was hospitalized, a family member said, according to the *Daily News*: "We want to thank everyone for their kind words, but you can go f--- yourselves."[52]

In a way, this event is stereotype-defying. Throgs Neck is supposed to be, along with Riverdale and Woodlawn-Jerome, a "safe" part of the Bronx, where violence doesn't happen, unlike Morrisania, Hunts Point, Melrose, and Tremont. Statistically, there is more violent crime in these communities by far. But, this case demonstrates graphically that no place is completely immune.

As for me, I asked myself what might have happened to me and my wife had one of the Zottolas walked out onto their patio and found us relaxing in their backyard? Would they, during this tense time in their lives, have believed my claim that I thought it was an apartment house? Surely they were on high alert after the two recent attempts on their lives. Ironically, if I hadn't read the story, I'd probably have written that it was an apartment house, an understandable and by no means terrible error, but nevertheless incorrect. In a grim postscript to the story, Sylvester Zottola was, in fact, killed by a Bloods gang member hired by the Mafia. Their fears were justified and borne out.

Researchers try to get it right, and for the most part they do, but not always. In this case it could have ended badly for us, since these are not the nicest of people, or they could have merely laughed it off as a mistake and nothing more. I've always felt it important to ask questions, but no one was around, and it really doesn't look like a private home. There are thousands of apartment houses in New York City, especially in Brooklyn and Queens, that look exactly like this structure. Still, this incident should serve as a reality check for researchers in general. On the other hand, the way it turned out made for a much more interesting story.

Leaving Locust Point via Tierney Place and then turning left on Chaffey, I retrace my steps to Pennyfield and make a left heading through an area that some call Schuylerville and others call Throgs Neck. It's a series of small and quiet dead-end streets that have nice homes of brick, aluminum siding, or shake shingle, situated right on Hammond Creek. There's a marina here by the same name, with many boats moored along the piers. Even though it's far away from Manhattan and sort of isolated, there's regular bus service here, as well as in Locust Point and everywhere else in the area, though subways are farther away. I turn left on Giegerich Place.

Here I meet Maria, a white woman, perhaps Italian or Irish, I would guess. These two groups and German Americans predominate in Throgs Neck. She's standing outside her pretty home.

"Hi," I say. "This is such a beautiful corner of the Bronx. What's on the other side of the marina?"

"That's Locust Point. Here it's Schuylerville."

"It's beautiful here."

"Oh, it's so nice here. And you should see the view from my deck on the second floor. People come here on my deck and they say: 'This looks like Cape May. It's gorgeous.' And then they say, 'This isn't the Bronx.' And I say: 'Yes, it *is*.' And we have a private beach club here too that a lot of people go to. Plus, you have Maritime College where they have a nice pool and exercise classes. We use it all the time there."

"And what's behind me on the other side of Pennyfield?"

"That's Silver Beach, a private community, and you have to go through a board to get in there, and three people who know you have to recommend you."

"And the schools are good here too, aren't they?"

"No. Not the public. We have two good schools here, but the rest I don't know. There's also Lehman High School down by Buhre Avenue and it's bad. You gotta send your kids to Catholic schools, which are very good, but you gotta pay $800 a month. But if you figure you go live in a suburb and pay twenty thousand a year in taxes versus $800 for four years and they're out, what's a better deal? It's obvious."

This interview is revealing in a number of ways. First, Maria loves it here. She's happy with the location, the view from her home, and the lifestyle. There's a private club, and there's also the facilities at Maritime College. When universities locate within a community, residents are likely to take advantage of what it has, and the school, which wants good relations with the community, is often happy to oblige. When she says the public schools aren't so good, she's basically referring to the high school, which is a bit far from her home.

She speaks about Catholic schools, taking it for granted that I understand why. This isn't surprising, since I'm white and it's a heavily Catholic neighborhood. She isn't at all guarded in her speech, letting it all hang out there. Thanking her for the advice, I continue on Pennyfield and soon come to the Bayview, offering breakfast, lunch, and dinner and advertising Italian cuisine.

There's no other restaurant nearby, so the Bayview has a captive clientele. On the other hand, if the food isn't good, people can drive to E. Tremont Avenue with its dozens of eateries in five minutes. The owners are local and have been in this business for many years. Their reviews are uniformly good. What you also get here is a place where you can meet local folks. A beautiful mural is painted on the window itself, with two palm trees and an Adirondack chair, thereby combining the tropics and upstate New York. This may seem unrealistic, but it's meant to be reminiscent of a place where one can relax as in their slogan, "Enjoy summer." Inside, there's another mural painted on the wall depicting perhaps twelve people fishing in the same spot. It must be a really good spot, but given the mountains in the background, it's nowhere near Throgs Neck. But who cares if it's far away? The artwork is excellent, and people like to think of enchanting vacation places. Certainly, the equally well-done ceiling, featuring birds flying overhead, is quite appropriate for Throgs Neck, or anywhere else where birds fly.

From here I continue south on Pennyfield to the SUNY Maritime College. It is affiliated with the United States Navy. Most of the students focus on maritime studies, learning about merchant vessels, cruise ships, and the like. There are also programs in engineering, business, and environmental studies, all of which can and do, in this instance, relate to maritime studies. A popular course of study involves obtaining a United States Coast Guard license. The college has master's and bachelor's programs, and students participate in internship programs relating to their chosen fields. It also has a Navy and Marine Reserve Officers Training Program. The institution is highly ranked academically in its areas of concentration and has a low faculty-student ratio of 16 to 1, insuring lots of personal attention. Fort Schuyler, a stone fortification dedicated in 1856, and built to protect New York from attack, is situated here, an integral part of the SUNY Maritime campus.

The college is its own world, in a sense. It sits on the coast and is isolated from any residential areas. The road around the school runs along the water. The buildings house administrative offices, classrooms, and dormitories. The president's home is a large colonial house with a great view of Long Island Sound. Walking toward Fort Schuyler, I suddenly hear bagpipe music from somewhere. Looking around I see a thin wiry man with a shaved head standing in a tufted grassy area along the coast, where water splashes over the craggy rocks. He's playing the bagpipes by himself. If I didn't know any better, I'd think I was somewhere on the Irish coast, especially because the sky is overcast. I introduce myself to Patrick and tell him how enraptured I am by his playing, inasmuch as bagpipes are my favorite instrument. Their music is at once uplifting, haunting, and spiritual.

"Why are you playing the bagpipes here?" I ask.

"I'm playing the pipes because I'm practicing. I'm a new student in the graduate program in transportation management and in the cadet program. I also graduated from West Point and played the pipes there for the academy's pipe band." Patrick tells me he served in the Army for ten years, which included a stint in Afghanistan, where he said the people were crazy but were excellent fighters. "They're not afraid of death like Westerners are."

He's pleased that I like his playing, but tells me: "There are people who don't like bagpipe playing. They say, 'Please, don't play that instrument. I can't take it.' They do have to be in tune. If they're not, it sounds really bad. The Scottish ones are the most popular, but you'll find them all over the world, in Africa, Sweden, France, the Middle East." As I prepare to leave, he plays "When the Caissons Go Rolling Along" and says "The people here don't like it when I play that because it's the Army song and this is the Navy." Patrick finishes up

Fort Schuyler

with "Amazing Grace," which sounds especially beautiful on this instrument. I consider myself lucky to have unexpectedly had this unusual experience. As I look at the trees, the fort, the cannons, the bridge, the water, and the rocks, it all feels very peaceful and special.

My last stop is the library and museum in Fort Schuyler itself. The interior of the library is made of brick and the same stone as the fort walls, but it's really fascinating to see such large stone blocks inside a library. Attached to the library is a museum specializing in all aspects of the maritime industry. Most notably it is filled with replicas made from wood, wire, and other materials, down to the last detail, of various ships, a number of which are quite famous. Some of them are at least ten feet long. It's a very large exhibit and also includes ship steering wheels, flatware from the Queen Elizabeth ocean liner, a special collection of life preservers, many large bells from various vessels, paintings, uniforms, maps, and much more. All in all, it's a remarkable exhibit. And yet it's almost totally unknown. A few school groups have come here in the last few years. But for the most part, the museum is virtually devoid of visitors, perhaps fifteen to twenty a week. I urge everyone to see it. It will definitely be enriching, as it was for me.

I walk back up Pennyfield and make a left into the private community of Silver Beach at Plaza Place. It's a private co-op development of about 450 homes. The residents own their homes but lease the property from owners' collectives. It's fenced in from the rest of Throgs Neck, and there's a guard booth with no guard in it when I pass through on a Monday in August. In fact, I've been here several times and have never met a guard, though reportedly there is one working here part-time. Instead there's a jacket on a wooden hanger, which faces the approach and looks, from afar, like a real person, sort of a scarecrow strategy. A bit to the left of the entrance and straight ahead there's Sunset Trail, and walking down I turn right and skirt a park-like area on the water with some benches spaced at intervals. The vista here is enormous in width and distance, as I can even see the faint outlines of Manhattan from here.

Turning around, I head in the opposite direction on a footpath called the Indian Trail, which soon leads to the top of a cliff and wends its way past some private houses. Offering a magnificent view from here, the trail also leads to a private beach, accessible except at high tide. I walk along some other avenues, and the houses are pretty but not fancy; some are simple bungalows. Clearly the recommendation process for gaining entry to Silver Beach, namely the recommendations from three residents, ensures a certain degree of homogeneity as opposed to diversity among the population. Also, rentals are not permitted here. Despite the feeling of privacy and getting away from it all, the Bronx 40 bus runs here along Pennyfield.

I return to Pennyfield, hang a left and then a right at Lawton Avenue. Crossing over to the other side of the expressway, I turn left and enter Edgewater Park community on my right at Miles Avenue. The streets here are divided into sections, running from A to E. They are identified as such instead of by the street names they now have. Like Silver Beach, this 675-home community is private, so if you don't look familiar to the residents you might well be told that it's a private community.

Entering the community is worth a shot, because it looks and feels very different from the city. The properties are small, twenty-five by forty feet, and they either have a small front yard or a small backyard. The streets are very narrow, allowing for only one car to pass at a time, and there are no sidewalks. Originally, the wealthy who lived on estates overlooking the bay leased the lots with bungalows for the summer to people in search of a getaway from the heat of the city. When tastes shifted and the wealthy began vacationing elsewhere, the lots were permanently leased through a co-op association, which owns the property but not the homes. Over the years, most of these homes, which began as bungalows, were expanded upward. The prices here are somewhat lower than those in Silver Beach, and the most expanded ones are on the water. I suggest going down a street on the left, after passing the parking lot and Ruane's

Deli on the right. Soon you'll come to the water, which has terrific views to the north over Eastchester Bay and to the east over Long Island Sound.

Founded in 1916, Edgewater Park conveys a real sense of community, and it even has a charitable association that gives financial help to those in need. Most of the homeowners are police and fire department employees or other city workers. Flags can be seen everywhere, including ones that say "Edgewater Park." An express bus provides transportation that can reach Manhattan in less than an hour. There are Halloween and Christmas festivities and an Easter egg hunt. The opening of the summer season is marked by a Memorial Day parade led by the local fife and drum band, the Edgewater Redcoats. There are social clubs, but mostly people just socialize by the beach and in each other's homes. Ethnically and economically, it's similar to Gerritsen Beach in Brooklyn, which is on the water and not far from Sheepshead Bay. These communities definitely add to the city's diversity, even though their members are not especially diverse as a group. I've explored Edgewater Park several times and saw no evidence of change here, but there's more to see in Throgs Neck, and as I return to the expressway service road, I make a right.

Almost immediately on my right, I enter Bicentennial Veterans Memorial Park to eat a quick lunch and enjoy the view of the bay and the sound. It's actually the exact same view as in Edgewater Park, only it's free, public, and quite tranquil. The park has a heavily used baseball field. I continue walking along the service road, make a right onto Philip Avenue, and arrive at a tavern called P. J. Brady's. It's more than a tavern because its nicely appointed restaurant has a full menu, in an area with almost no other eateries. Its real claim to fame, however, is that for a number of years it was the place of employment of Louie Palladino, one of the great pizza pie makers of all time in this city, and a man who views making pizza as an art. And indeed, that's what it is for him. I asked him to explain how he creates culinary magic from these pies, which he's been serving up in Throgs Neck for almost seventy-five years. In his own words:

"If it [the pie] starts out thin and then gets thicker, you've got an amateur making the pies. And there's also stretching the dough right, as well as the edges of the pie. Seasoning's important too. When I make a mushroom pie, I throw in garlic powder. On the other hand, if it's a sausage pie, then I use oregano. You gotta know what goes with what. I must've made over a million pies in my life and I put my heart in every one of them. . . . I'm a pie man, that's what I am. . . . I love what I do."

Louie began coming in less often as he got older and eventually retired in his early eighties. But according to a waitress who's been there for years, he passed on the recipe to the younger people who work there. "He loved training them, and he still comes in. Louie definitely had his following. He was a crazy old man, but I loved him," she tells me. In short, he's a community fixture and a real character. A copy of a *New York Times* piece about him is proudly hung on a wall inside for all to see, read, and remember.[53]

Before I leave I take a look at two framed displays on the wall of the bar that house a collection of shoulder patches in various colors. The names tell a story of what matters in this place and in the community. Among the groups represented here are: Missouri Patrol, US Border Patrol, Sheriff's Pride of Texas, Pleasantville Police, Botanical Gardens Security dated 1891, New York State Correctional Services, Co-op City Bicycle Patrol, Steuben County Sheriff's Department. Obviously, it's heavy on law enforcement agencies, and that's no surprise since so many of their members reside here. Someone might wonder why these patches were collected, but the reason is obvious. These agencies are united in a national fraternity of people with a culture and value system that's pretty similar everywhere in the country.

Heading north along Shore Drive, I see many nice homes, some of them quite elegant, along the water. If there's any area that's upscale, it's in the Country Club and Spencer Estates sections, which run northward roughly from Waterbury Avenue to Middletown Road and Watt Avenue, where Pelham Bay Park begins. Shore

Drive turns into Stadium Avenue after it crosses Baisley Avenue, and two blocks later I go right on Agar Place, where I see some amazing large homes, quite a few directly on the water. Take 3355, with a tiled roof, and the one across the street from it at 3380. The house of the ages in terms of size is being constructed here next to 3441. It will be 3421 Country Club Road, which is what Agar turns into. This small area is really worth seeing for the sheer beauty of the residences here.

The Villa Maria Academy is also here, at 3335 Country Club Road. It was founded in 1886 by the Sisters of the Congregation of Notre Dame, an order dating back to 1653. A private Catholic institution for grades K–8, it sits on a beautiful property along the water. Its main building is a Tudor-style brick and stucco structure with half-timbers, almost like a mansion. This is a serious school, whose thirty-five graduates in 2018 went off to some excellent high schools, earning over $1 million in scholarships. All, except one, Stuyvesant High School, were Catholic. Throgs Neck is heavily Catholic, with upwardly mobile but traditional families for whom such a school is perfect because it teaches not only academics but religion and Christian values.

Spencer Estates is immediately north of Country Club and is bordered on the north by Pelham Bay Park. It has some streets with highly unusual names, a collection such as I've never seen before in any community—Outlook, Library, Research, Ampere, Ohm, and Watt Avenues, not to mention Radio Drive. It sounds as if it was once a community filled with research scientists working in an advanced scientific institute with a campus, but I see no evidence of that. As is almost always the case, there's a reason. It's just a matter of doing the work required to find it.

Ohm Avenue ends at Pelham Bay Park, right where the Aileen B. Ryan Recreational Center is located. Until 1989, this was Rice Stadium, named after Isaac Leopold Rice. Rice had been president of the Electric Storage Battery Company. His widow, Julia, donated $1 million toward the stadium's construction. In honor of the family's generosity, some of the streets near the stadium were given "electrical" names in October 1922 by the New York City Board of Estimate. George Ohm was a famous German physicist who specialized in research about electricity. Rice also headed the Electric Boat Company, which built submarines for use by the United States and British navies during World War I. His involvement was critical because submarines used electricity while underwater.

Rice's wife, Julia, worked with him on these projects and was a talented musician, to boot. She also founded an important organization in 1907, called the Society for the Suppression of Unnecessary Noise. The main object of her ire was the loud noises made by the whistles and horns of ships, which her family experienced firsthand while living on Riverside Drive overlooking the Hudson River. This might sound like an idiosyncratic organization that "tilted against windmills," as they say, but it made at least one lasting contribution: its efforts were instrumental in establishing the quiet zones that are today the norm in school and hospital areas and elsewhere.[54]

There's also a very strange looking home at 3317 Ampere Avenue, made of painted brick and cement. There are very few windows on the side of the house. The picture window in the front on the first floor behind an open porch is painted on the glass itself with pink flowers and purple tulips, butterflies, and grass. On the upper level, I see a terrace area enclosed by a curving wall around each end. On the corners of the wall are two carved lions, and in the center are two bears, perhaps two feet in height. It almost looks as though these creatures are guarding the house, especially because the bears are standing stiffly at attention. On the bottom is a sculpture of a soldier in a robe with a spear. The first-floor yard features statues of nude women. I don't believe I've ever seen a house in this shape and form. Outside the home, on Ampere, are some parked vintage classic cars. The gleaming white Ford pickup truck, manufactured in 1952, is a real standout. Just beyond Ampere on Bayside Avenue, there's a great view of the water and a stupendous one of Pelham Bay Park.

I walk west on Ampere to Robertson Avenue, hang a right onto Jarvis, and cross over into the Middletown section on Middletown Road. I traverse Roebling, Zulette, and Wellman Avenues, as well as Crosby Avenue, which has several commercial blocks. This neighborhood between the Bruckner Expressway and the Hutchinson River Parkway (known affectionately as "the Hutch" by New Yorkers) is not as upscale as the Country Club area. It's more working class, with old tenements and small homes. But it's not a high-crime section. It's just a community where the people aren't rich or even, in many instances, middle class. Heading south I stroll through the streets. The area that abuts St. Raymond's Cemetery is pretty quiet, and the section below E. Tremont is most often referred to as Schuylerville.

The cemetery is quite interesting too. Jazz singer Billie Holiday is buried there, and so is a brother of St. Elizabeth Ann Seton. A convert, Seton was the first person born in the United States to be canonized a saint, and she also founded the Sisters of Charity. On the more sensationalist side "Typhoid Mary" (Mary Mallon), also found her final resting place here. Mallon, a cook, was the first-known asymptomatic carrier of typhoid fever in this country and was suspected of having infected fifty-one people with the disease. She lived in isolation for almost three decades before she died. Finally, Charles Lindbergh allegedly met with his child's kidnaper in the cemetery to pay a $50,000 ransom, all in vain, since the child was found dead a few months afterward.

South of the Bruckner Expressway, I walk up and down Revere, Calhoun, and Swinton Avenues. Like the section between Middletown Road and the Bruckner Expressway, the houses here are quite modest, whether detached, semi-attached, or attached, most with tiny front yards. The entire area is ethnically mixed, and these homes may be a step upward for those striving to do even better. A good number of the residents take pride in homeownership as they reminisce about their origins in South or West Bronx apartments or the countries they left. To my left are the Throgs Neck Houses, one of the earliest public housing projects, dating back to the 1950s. Despite evidence of mismanagement in 2018, it remains one of the safer public housing complexes in the city. It seems that a sex scandal involving the workers resulted in the entire forty-person staff being transferred to various sites throughout the city. The surrounding neighborhood is called Throgs Neck, just like the larger community.

Turning right, or west, from Swinton Street, onto Sampson Avenue, I soon come face-to-face with Ferry Point Park. The park is large, half the size of Central Park, at 413 acres, stretching from Balcom Avenue on the east to beyond the Hutchinson River Parkway on the west. Here I see basketball courts in excellent condition opposite a housing project that are in use on the hottest of days (peaking today at 98 degrees). There's a baseball field, also in good shape, where, I deduce from a quick look, hitting the ball into the weeping willow tree just beyond the outfield must be a home run. There are also picnic areas in various parts of the park. Just inside the entrance, I meet Elander Gadson, the park attendant in charge, a lovely gracious woman in her forties, and have a fascinating conversation with her. She's a Black, middle-aged mother of four who lives with her husband on the opposite side of the Bronx, on Willis Avenue in the southwestern community of Mott Haven. She travels here every day to do her job, one she's seriously committed to. I greet her and praise the way the grounds look.

"Thank you. This is what makes my day, when somebody notices."

"Well, I'm writing a book about the Bronx, so I pay attention to these things."

"I was wondering who you were when I saw you heading towards me."

The only problem, Elander tells me, "is we don't have the tools to do our job but we try. I'm what they call a SCPW [Seasonal City Park Worker]. I've been here four years, and I believe they like me and my work. I report here at 7:00 a.m. and open up the gates, and I leave here at 3:30 p.m. And when I'm not in season, I work with the mentally disabled in a community group home. Before I got this job, I was working in a juvenile detention center for troubled youngsters."

"What's the hardest part of your job here?"

"The people. It could be a bad day for them, a bad day for you, you don't know. But I'm respectful to them. If I see people smoking or drinking I tell them to stop, nicely but firmly. I raised four sons, all of them good kids and responsible people, so I know what to do." I think to myself that in addition to her street smarts and people skills, and experience with four boys, she's a large woman who doesn't look like a pushover, which has to help. In short, she's perfectly suited for this job.

"Are you from New York?"

"No. I was born in Eutawville, South Carolina, and came to New York when I was five. I went to public high school, but I went back for high school to Eutawville. My mom was a single mom raising two younger boys and she wanted to work. Plus, she worked late hours and didn't have anybody to keep an eye on me. So, I came back to South Carolina to my grandmom. My first job was as a hostess at a Days Inn in Santee, South Carolina. Then I came home to my mom who was living on 146th Street in the Bronx, because she needed me to help watch my younger brothers who were getting older."

"Would you say the area here is safe?"

"I'd say yes. I come home sometimes at night. I've never seen any 'activity' here. I don't go into the projects though, so I can't speak for them."

"Do you have children?"

"Yes, I have four sons, twenty-five, twenty-two, twelve, and nine. My oldest went to the High School for the Visual Arts. He went to college for a year. Now he works for a charter school. My second oldest was on a school basketball team and went to a tournament and was in the newspaper for his playing because they won at the Barclay in Brooklyn. He works for UPS. One of my kids is in a charter school, which I think are good. He's so smart, but they put a lot of pressure on them. On weekends my husband and I take the younger kids to New Roc City in New Rochelle or Riverbank Park on 145th Street in Manhattan where they can play, skate, run around, and enjoy themselves."

"How were, or are you, able to protect your kids from all the bad stuff—gangs, drugs, crime—that's going on in the streets?"

"You have to be active with them. Don't hide anything from them. Be honest and open with them. Let them know what could possibly happen to them if they go out. They tend to think everybody's a safe person to be around. You have to have boundaries. And [I tell them] if you have a problem, don't be afraid to tell your parents. At the same time, I let my nine-year-old go outside to teach him independence, because I can see him from the window if anything goes wrong. My husband's also involved. He's a supervisor at a women's shelter in the Bronx."

"What do you think of the rap music lyrics?"

"Not much. They're not good. But a child will hear things in the streets and you can't stop it. But if the lines of communication are open and there's love, they'll trust you and ask you: 'We heard this and that. Is it right?' And we tell them what's tolerable and what isn't."

"Did you go to college?"

"I did for half a year, but I got pregnant. My husband and I have known each other since I was ten years old and have been together since I was nineteen."

"What's your secret to such a long marriage?"

"Understanding and being tolerant of each other and knowing what's important in life. Of course, once I had a baby I had to drop out of college and work part time. But I keep dreaming that I'd like to go to college. It's just that when you have no money and responsibilities, it gets really hard to go to school. And you're older and it's maybe too late."

"Where did you get your values from?"

"I got it from the roots of my grandparents."

This story is remarkable for its unremarkable nature. We read so many stories about the needs of the millions of households raising children in poverty, particularly single moms. They deserve the best help that the government can give them. They are, shall we say, stuck in place. This case is somewhat different. Elander was raised in a poor Bronx neighborhood by her mom who sent her to a safer community in the South, where she had a grandmother who gave her love and a home. The high school she attended there was most likely a better environment than one in the Bronx would have been. She went to college for a short time but then became pregnant at an early age, which prevented her from continuing her education.

Elander and her husband raised a family together, and their values helped them direct their children and kept their family intact. Precisely what these values are would require a longer discussion, but the results speak for themselves. Yet even people in this situation need help. Perhaps with financial assistance she could have sent her children to college and advanced their careers, and even gone back to school herself. People like this, whom we might call the working poor, considering that Elander and her family still live in a South Bronx apartment, also merit help and should receive it even as they continue working. Their stability means that they might be able to accomplish a great deal with such assistance.

The eighteen-hole golf course known as Trump Links, designed by Jack Nicklaus, is on the western side of Ferry Point Park and cannot be accessed by walking due west through the park from this part. To get there I take Balcom north to Lafayette Avenue and then go left to the southbound Hutchinson Parkway where I again go left down to Schley Avenue. There I see the entrance to Ferry Point Park. On the right are many picnic tables. The path winds around leftward under the Whitestone Bridge in a circle to the golf course entrance. In characteristically outsize fashion, the words TRUMP LINKS are carved into the ground and are clearly visible from the air on the right side, one could say, as drivers descend from the Whitestone Bridge. I speak with a man who works in the pro shop.

"Have you found that people care about the fact that the golf course is named after Trump?"

"Not personally, but I'm sure people do care. But golf is golf. I think it matters much more to people that the golf great Jack Nicklaus designed the course. We're doing extremely well." This is corroborated by several other people. But, of course, we don't know about politically liberal golfers who opt not to come here. It's the highest-rated course in the city and third best in the state. It was certainly crowded when I visited on a Monday afternoon. It's a bit out of the way and probably not worth the trip unless you're into golf. Several golfers noted that the course is treeless, which can be a bit disorienting since most courses do have trees. It's also expensive for a public course. It strikes me that this isn't a political statement about Trump's ego or politics in general. Given the hostility to Trump by many New Yorkers, it's more an expression of the city's tolerance, for to date there have been no demonstrations demanding that it be shut down or that the name of Trump, offensive to many people, be taken down from a public space.

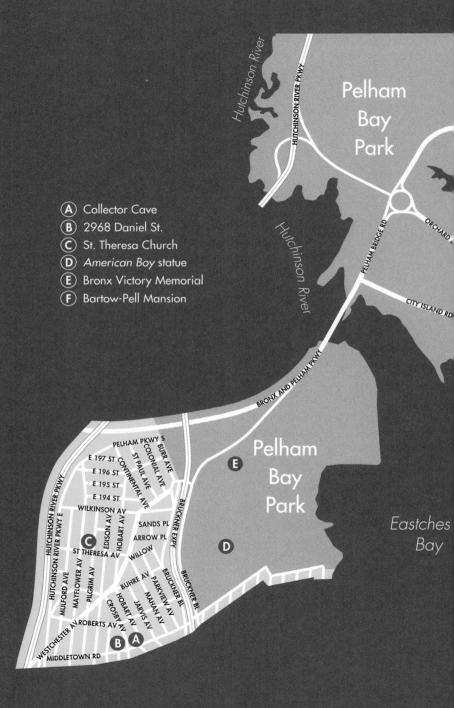

Hutchinson River

HUTCHINSON RIVER PKWY

Pelham
Bay
Park

Ⓐ Collector Cave
Ⓑ 2968 Daniel St.
Ⓒ St. Theresa Church
Ⓓ *American Boy* statue
Ⓔ Bronx Victory Memorial
Ⓕ Bartow-Pell Mansion

Hutchinson River

PELHAM BRIDGE RD

ORCHARD

CITY ISLAND RD

Hutchinson River

BRONX AND PELHAM PKWY

Pelham
Bay
Park

Eastches
Bay

Ⓔ

Ⓓ

PELHAM PKWY S

E 197 ST
E 196 ST
E 195 ST
E 194 ST

COLONIAL AVE
BURR AVE
ST PAUL AVE
CONTINENTAL AVE

WILKINSON AV

SANDS PL
EDISON AV
HOBART AV

ARROW PL

WILLOW

Ⓒ ST THERESA AV

HUTCHINSON RIVER PKWY E

BUHRE AV

MAYFLOWER AV
MULFORD AVE
PILGRIM AV

HOBART AV
CROSBY AV

PARKVIEW AV
MAHAN AV
JARVIS AV

BRUCKNER EXPY

BRUCKNER BL

BRUCKNER BL

Ⓑ Ⓐ

WESTCHESTER AV ROBERTS AV

MIDDLETOWN RD

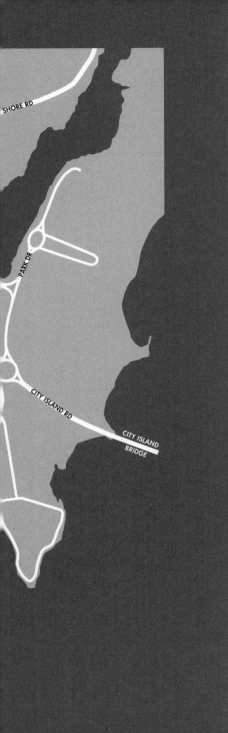

PELHAM BAY

THE BOUNDARIES OF PELHAM BAY ARE Pelham Parkway on the north, the Bruckner Expressway/Interstate 95 on the east, Middletown Road on the south, and the Hutchinson River Parkway on the west. The area was acquired from the Dutch by Thomas Pell in 1654. Pell, a physician who was born in England, attended Cambridge University before coming to America. The area was built up in the 1920s when mass transit arrived. Many brick apartment buildings, now showing their age, were constructed then, as well as modest private dwellings, both semi-attached and detached. The groups who settled here during the early twentieth century were largely Italian and Irish.

The main commercial thoroughfares here are Westchester, Crosby, and Buhre Avenues, plus Middletown Road. There are some small parks and playgrounds, but the crown jewel is Pelham Bay Park, the largest park in New York City. It's a quiet and safe community with one of the lowest crime rates in the Bronx. Its current ethnic makeup is largely Italians and Hispanics, most of them Puerto Rican, with a smaller Greek population as well. Public transportation to Manhattan is basically a long ride on the

IRT number 6 subway. This line was immortalized in the hit film, *The Taking of Pelham One Two Three*.

I come to Crosby Stop Pizza at 1731 Crosby Avenue. This modest establishment was voted "best pizza in the Bronx" by Fox Five News, and it says it's the home of exotic and round Sicilian pizzas. Many people from the Bronx have told me the pizza here, which is the traditional thick slices, is the best in the borough. It is certainly crowded, and the booths are very basic, nothing fancy. A bit farther south, at 1300 Crosby, there's Louie & Ernie's Pizza, which also has a strong following. On the corner at Westchester Avenue is George's Restaurant, a Greek-infused eatery, because there is a Greek population here too, though not as large as the Italian representation. I angle right onto Buhre Avenue. Here you can find Italian delis, Yemeni grocery shops, a sushi place, a Tex-Mex joint, a hookah smoke shop, which is also a mini-supermarket. But the hookah pipes and smaller glass pipes are the draws, hundreds of them on display, and inside there's a little bit of everything.

Making a right onto residential Mahan Avenue I stride through an area of smaller modest homes, detached and semi-attached, mostly brick and made of siding or shingle. I turn right at Middletown Road and come to Collector Cave, at 3021–23, a store that specializes in collectibles of action figures, CDs, and old comic books. In the windows I see figurines of superheroes and monsters from various movies, Spider-Man, Freddie Kruger, Joker, and others, selling on average for $45 to $75. I enter and speak with an employee in his late twenties.

"That's quite a collection you have here. Do you have anything outstanding to recommend?"

"I have the first comic book of Deadpool Comics in 1991 for $400. The first one ever. It's rated a 9.2; nothing ever gets a ten."

"What about all these games?"

"Here's the Infinity Gauntlet toy, part of the Marvel Legends Series. It's that big glove from the movie that killed the universe. It's 130 bucks."

Collector Cave

"Why is it such a big-selling item?"

"Well, everybody wants to rule the universe."

"What do you do with it? How does it work?"

"You put the glove on. It glows. You walk around your house. You rule your cat, your dogs."

"What's your customer base?"

"People like eighteen and up. I get old people like you too sometimes."

Curious and perhaps vain, I say: "How old do you think I am?"

"Oh, about sixty-five."

"That would be nice if true," I say, laughing. I'm not sure if he's goofing on me or serious.

"Well, you were around when this stuff started. You're surely retired now. What else are you doing? You read comics. You watch movies. You said you do. So, you could become a collector too. It would be better if you'd been a collector when you were young. Then your stuff would really be worth something. I also have parody books of Trump. If you're a Trump supporter you're not gonna be happy with those." I remember where I am. I've passed more than a few Republican headquarters in these parts.

"Do you have parody books on Hillary?"

"Sure, but not as many. It's more fun to make fun of the president. I'm not especially political. Whatever makes me money I'm interested in. This is a business, ya know."

This is an opportunity to relive your childhood if you're my age, but nostalgia isn't the main market here. They're dealing with younger people for whom this is either the present or the recent past. I feel this is like being in a time warp, only it's me, not them, that's in the time warp. I catch one or two names like Spider-Man, but most are unfamiliar. These stores sell fantasy, but the buyers take it seriously, and the employee, in a cynical tone, describes living in that world as walking around the house in your game attire and acting like a big boss, but over what—a cat or dog? Someone once said that in America, 95 percent of the population is bored 99 percent of the time. Escaping into another universe is a way of relieving boredom. And taking on an identity is a way of escaping who you are or aren't. It's the same as fans who wear hockey, baseball, or basketball uniforms with the names of their heroes emblazoned on their backs.

The fellow with whom I speak isn't really into it, though he's definitely in it as a seller. He creates a connection to the game by saying it's fun to ridicule the president, but it's really nothing more than fun; it's not real. He tries to encourage me to become a collector, noting that I'm not exactly busy these days, given my age, but acknowledges my limitations. I'm too old, not cool, and he says I should have begun collecting long ago. It's a rebuke of sorts, but he understands that I couldn't really appreciate that these items would be worth real money someday.

What we see is that this is a viable industry. There are stores like it in many communities, and they and their clientele are part of the city's landscape. As I leave, I note that across the street is a florist, with the equally fantasy-world name of Ava's Rain Florist, which sounds suspiciously like rainforest. Will that bring in any more customers? I don't know. Perhaps they have flowers or plants from the real rainforests. The Amazon Rainforest has over 40,000 varieties of plants, and one of its many flowers is the orchid, which Ava does sell. Alas, the shop is closed so I can't get closure on this, but it's not a critical issue for me. I also wonder whether a store around the corner on Crosby Avenue, at number 1633, named Lettuce Eat, which sells wraps, burgers, milkshakes, and salads, attracts anyone because of the name. At least it's subliminally creative.

At 2968 Daniel Street, a one-block affair that runs from Crosby to Plymouth Avenue, my attention is drawn to a narrow, attractive Dutch colonial home, whose steps and garden are literally chock-full of potted plants. I don't believe I've ever seen so many plants on such a small piece of property. The number of plants is probably around eighty. Because of their abundance, one can only walk up the eleven steps to the entrance in single file. These include hibiscus, coleus, wandering Jew, and cockscomb. It's worth a minor detour if you're walking by on Crosby, depending on the season, of course. Late summer is a good time to see the greenery at its best. And while you're at it, don't miss the pretty Victorian home at the top of the hill on the right, with its striking turret, wraparound porch, and extensive grounds.

From here I turn right, or north on Plymouth, left on Roberts Avenue, and right again on Edison Avenue. This is a quiet area, with quite a few nice homes. In a few minutes I arrive at St. Theresa Avenue, where St. Theresa Church is situated. It was here on a Sunday that I stumbled upon the annual Italian American Family Feast celebration along the avenue and in honor of St. Theresa, usually from Wednesday through Sunday in June, around the time that school ends, so as to attract more families. The feast is sponsored by the church of the same name, and there are at least two thousand people there. I join the procession and walk behind a statue of the Virgin Mary. It feels strangely peaceful even though I'm not Catholic, perhaps because of the somber music played over a loudspeaker and the slow gait of the marchers, whose gazes suggest peace and reverence. The avenue is lined with stands selling sausages, pizza, and other delectable foods, the aromas filling the open air. There are also games of chance, hit the dummy, and sink the basket. But, of course, even these stands stop selling and enticing as the religious procession passes by.

In front of the church are several religious functionaries, dressed in robes of various colors, one of whom, perhaps a priest, begins speaking. "I think you will agree with me," he says, "that St. Theresa was very anxious to do this procession. And I think she was nice to cool things off a little for us. There is much to give thanks for, which is what we're all about. The greatest gift, of course, is the gift of our faith." With these opening comments he humanizes her to the audience. He invites all to hear the choir after he finishes. He prays for the assembled, and acclaims Theresa as the greatest saint of modern times and asks for a moment of silence. A shower of rose petals—red, white, and yellow—drops, seemingly from the sky, but actually tossed from the roof of the church. Everyone oohs and aahs appreciatively, perhaps imagining it as a miracle.

As I survey the scene I'm reminded once again of the centrality of religion in the lives of millions of New Yorkers. There are many other feasts, with multitudes winding their way through the Catholic areas of New York City, drawing thousands of devotees, but largely unreported by the mainstream media. These celebrations bind the community together, providing opportunities for religious expression and venues for social life. There are so many people in the city for whom religion is just a bunch of baloney, and then so many for whom it is everything. This is not an area likely to be gentrified. It's too far from Manhattan, and only the number 6 line, a local train, comes here. If it does gentrify, then the traditions that are a hallmark of the community will be affected and perhaps erode over a period of time.[55]

Regrettably, space does not allow for an-depth discussion of Pelham Bay Park, a 2,772-acre park—about three times the size of Central Park, which covers about 843 acres. Still, it deserves to be mentioned here since, because of its remote location, it's not well known at all to most New Yorkers even though it's the last stop on the number 6 train. I enter the south end of Pelham Bay Park off Watt Avenue. Just beyond the parking lot is the Aileen B. Ryan Recreational Complex. It has tennis courts, soccer fields, and even an outdoor gym with stationary bikes, shoulder rotators, chest presses, and something called a "captain's chair" to improve one's abs. It's almost like a small outdoor fitness center. The centerpiece is an outstanding running and walking track that encircles the soccer field. The alternating colors are blue and beige, and the ground is made of a synthetic substance that feels very comfortable. Overlooking the field is a statue of a young man with a finely chiseled body wearing just a pair of shorts. A sculpture created by Louis St. Lannes, it's named *American Boy*. It's in the style of ancient Greek and Roman statues and was meant to encourage young people to engage in healthful recreation.

I walk north along some very appealing and wide concrete walkways offering pleasant shade from large trees and barbeque areas for picnickers. Eventually I come to the Bronx Victory Memorial. Erected in 1927, it's a truly inspiring war memorial dedicated in memory of Bronx soldiers who sacrificed their lives in the "Great War," or World War I. The Corinthian column is about 120 feet in height, topped by a large superb bronze statue painted in bright gold of a winged woman, connoting victory in battle. It is easily visible even from a distance of a quarter mile. There are bas reliefs on each side of the pedestal of soldiers marching off to war, as well as large urns and carvings of animals, birds, floral designs, and a clipper ship. It's also a popular location for wedding photographs.

The park has many walking trails, extensive woodlands, two golf courses, a wildlife sanctuary, and, of course, Orchard Beach, which is worth seeing if you've never been there. It's the prototype of a working-class beach paradise and has terrific views. For precise locations of park attractions, simply download a map from the internet. There's also the outstanding Greek Revival-style Bartow-Pell

Mansion, built between 1836 and 1842. Mayor Fiorello LaGuardia lived in it for a summer while Orchard Beach was under construction. All of these can be found on the park map and are well worth exploring. In the spirit of this book's theme, I strongly recommend visiting the relatively unknown mansion's gardens, which are exquisitely designed and very well cared for. Unlike the New York Botanical Garden, located in the Bronx, it is never crowded. Few people visit, and most have never heard of it, which is a shame. Of course, there's far less to see, but it's the way it's preserved that stands out. I had given an evening talk there years ago, but it was dark and I didn't see the outdoor area.

I meet Guy Johnson, the gardener in residence and ask him what there is to see here. He's a handsome, aristocratic-looking man in his fifties, fit and trim, and friendly in a sort of quiet way and is possessed of a soft gentle voice similar to that of Mr. Rogers, that exudes kindness and caring. "We have water lilies, Angelonia, tulips, boxwoods, and statues of peacocks. There are different herbs growing here too in a separate little garden—garlic, thyme, Japanese basil, horseradish, fennel, rosemary, sage, parsley. There are trails around the gardens, but I would recommend walking them in the fall, when you can see the foliage. There's also a children's garden with different kinds of vegetables."

In a way, the garden strikes me as a miniature version of the gardens I saw at Versailles a number of years ago. Mostly it's the stone steps that lead down to the ornamental pool, the stone walls, and the wrought-iron fences. There's a winged cupid holding a fish as water is spouting from its mouth. Goldfish are swimming in the water. I decided to speak further with Guy and ask him what he did before coming here.

"I worked in the New York Botanical Garden."

"What's the difference between working there and here, besides the size?"

"A lot less visitors, much quieter."

"Did you like making the switch?"

"Yes. Here where the park ends and the mansion begins is a gray area. I come here in the winter and use a brush cutter to keep it clear from the mansion. If I don't do it, everything will become thick and overgrown." It's an interesting response, demonstrating how a reward of this work is making certain everything is delineated and orderly, even if the contribution isn't recognized. It's the joy of the work itself.

"Like my wife, who's also a teacher, I taught kindergarten for ten years after leaving the Gardens," Guy continues. "But it was similar work because I went to schools all over New York, the Bronx and Manhattan, teaching little kids about gardens and gardening. I did this part-time at first, but now I'm here full-time. As I walk here in the morning I feel my blood pressure go down because it's so peaceful. My predecessor was more of a vegetable gardener, but my background is in ornamental gardening. And I look forward to coming here every day. In fact, it's appealing to my basic personality. I spend a lot of time, in fact, going to places in the city like small museums, where most people don't go. There are no lines; it's peaceful, nice, and pleasant. It's similar to this place, where there are, on average, only about twenty visitors a day."

Guy is a New Yorker, raised in Manhattan and still living there in Inwood. He interacts little with people on a regular basis, and he clearly enjoys solitude. While appearing diffident, he's very approachable if you make the effort and says that while he took a cut in salary there are more important reasons for taking a job. He's the opposite of the brash, garrulous, somewhat rough-talking New Yorker. He sounds like many people who come here from small towns and find Gotham a bit overwhelming. But there are thousands of people like him living in this city, many of them from here, thus proving that there's no one-size-fits-all person in this city. In a way, Guy is from the city, but he's not really in the city, at least most of the time.

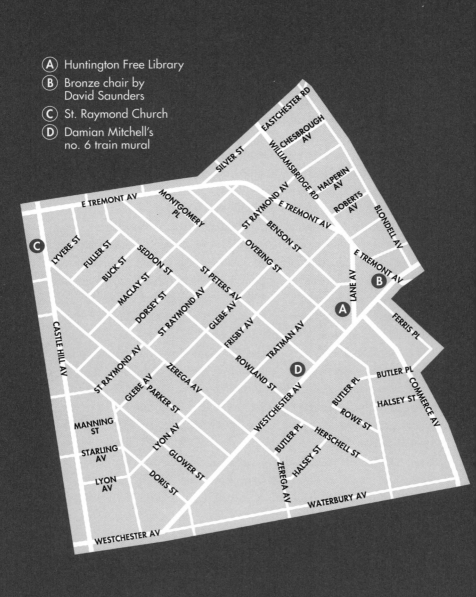

- (A) Huntington Free Library
- (B) Bronze chair by David Saunders
- (C) St. Raymond Church
- (D) Damian Mitchell's no. 6 train mural

WESTCHESTER SQUARE

WESTCHESTER SQUARE'S BOUNDARIES ARE, roughly, E. Tremont Avenue and Silver Street on the north; Blondell Avenue, Ferris Place, and Commerce Avenue on the east; Waterbury Avenue on the south; and Castle Hill Avenue on the west. This area was founded in 1654 by the English, who had purchased the land from local Native American groups. The Dutch also had claims to the land and wrested control back from the English, with the British regaining full ownership after signing a treaty with the Native Americans in 1692.

In the modern period, the town of Westchester became part of New York City in 1895 along with other parts of the Bronx. With the advent of mass transportation, many people, the majority of them Catholic, moved here. Irish and, to a lesser but still substantial extent, Italian immigrants were already here in the nineteenth century. Today, the area is mixed with a polyglot representation. Many South Asians, in particular Bangladeshis, have made this community their home, along with Hispanics, African Americans, and a small, mostly older Italian and Irish population. The commercial streets are Westchester, E. Tremont and Castle Hill Avenues, and Williamsbridge Road. In addition, Blondell Avenue and the streets branching off it, as well as Waterbury Avenue to some degree, are populated by light industry enterprises. It's a pretty safe, largely working-class community, with a smaller middle class as well.

I begin my walk in this small community on E. Tremont Avenue and in a few blocks, veer left onto Silver Street. Both are commercial streets without much of interest. I walk a few more blocks and turn right onto Blondell Avenue. This is sort of an industrial area and I notice a familiar pattern. A section like this will have small factories, wholesale warehouses, and light manufacturing, with a sprinkling of private homes—lonely outposts where people live, but with very few residential neighbors. Turning right onto Halperin Avenue I wonder who Halperin was. Normally the city's Transportation Committee handles street name requests, with input from Bronx officials, especially the local community. It's only one block long. Much to my surprise, the deservedly renowned expert on the subject, John McNamara, author of an entire book on the origin of Bronx street names, writes: "No one knows who Halperin is or was." All that is known, according to him, is that the street was opened and named on March 17, 1936.[56]

Is it worth having a street named after you if no one besides you and whoever you told knows that this is the case? It depends on the individual. Researching the matter through various source materials, I came up with several possibilities, based on when they lived and what they did. Victor Halperin (1895–1983), a film director most famous for his film *White Zombie,* starring Bela Lugosi, the first feature-length zombie film, released in 1932. A sequel, *Revolt of the Zombies*, came out in 1936, the year Halperin Street was named. A Victor Halperin lived at 842 Kelly Street in the 1930s, but there's no indication it was the same person. There's also Maurice Halperin (1906–1995), an American writer, professor, and diplomat; and Sol Halperin (1902–1977), a special-effects artist. It could also have been a person of no particular renown who had the connections with City Hall to make it happen. The answer to this can probably be found with more digging through old city records. But when writing a book of this sort, one must decide how much time to put into a mystery in terms of how important it is to what one is doing. Since McNamara, who was only writing about street names, couldn't come up with an answer, and he knew almost every other street's origin, it would probably involve more effort than it's worth.

I speak to a man named Edwin, who owns a pretty Dutch colonial house on Halperin across the street from an old apartment building and has lived in it for years. He has no idea of why it's called that. The man is a Fedex employee working out of Manhattan.

"What do you like about the community?" I ask.

"It's really quiet. When I first moved here there were old Italian guys who would sit outside on chairs and tell you what things used to be like. I'm Puerto Rican and was raised in the Bronx. I lived on Jerome Avenue and 167th Street, then on 163rd Street, then on Walton Avenue. And I went to Taft High School. I'm a Bronx person and many of my friends are from here."

"Is there a nightlife in Westchester Square?"

"Well that would have to be on East Tremont but I don't really know."

"Who was Halperin?"

"You know, I don't know. I've lived here for twenty-one years, but I've never thought about it. Now you've made me curious. I'll have to ask around." This doesn't surprise me. If I were living on a street with an unusual name, I'd be asking about it right away. But not everyone's like that. His attitude is that it doesn't affect his life, he has a family and a job, and knowing the answer would not materially influence or change his life. This tolerance of a narrowly circumscribed existence is reflected in his lack of knowledge about his surroundings. He knows there's a nightlife somewhere, but he's not certain exactly where. Similarly, when I ask him about the area on the other side of Williamsbridge Road, a few blocks away, he says: "I believe it's changed a lot in terms of who lives there. It's more Indian, Hindu. I see a lot of cabs parked there, so they're not rich. There used to be a lot of drugs there twenty years ago. But I really don't know much about the area. There's a library there where my kids take out books. I feel it's like a secret area."

"Secret in what way?"

"No one talks about the area. No newspaper articles about it. It's not upscale."

We're suddenly interrupted by a shabbily dressed perhaps inebriated homeless, African American man. Being New Yorkers, we talk to him and tell him to take care of himself. He tells us: "I'm no Vietnam vet but I'm a Bronx vet. Ha ha." Edwin's small dog begins barking at the man, and he steps back cautiously despite Edwin's assurances that he's friendly. Suddenly he says to me: "I believe we've met before in Queens. You were with your wife. Be good and may the Lord protect you." As I look at him, I suddenly remember that he is the same man who worked for a tax return company wearing a Statue of Liberty costume to attract customers. I'm not surprised that he turns up here twenty miles away because he had told me then that he lived in the Bronx, traveling several hours every day to his job. As to his appearance on this day and his slurred speech, he had said at the time that this temporary job "keeps me out of trouble." The chances of my ever meeting this man again were very remote. I guess that's what they mean by "It's a small world," even in the Big Apple.

Bidding Edwin good day, I continue walking down Blondell to Westchester. Edwin turns out to be only partially correct. The area in question isn't very Indian nor Hindu, but predominantly Bangladeshi and quite Muslim. Such an error isn't so unusual because people from other parts of the world often look like an amorphous mass to those who have only superficial contact with them, and that's certainly true of Edwin. This is how many people make their way in the city. They live side by side but know very little about those not in their group and don't go out of their way to find out. They have their circle of friends and family and that's enough for them.

I turn right off Blondell onto Westchester Avenue. Westchester, E. Tremont, and Lane Avenues all come together at what is the commercial hub of the community. Here at 9 Westchester Square is the location of the Huntington Free Library. Built in 1891, it has a beautiful Gothic-style wood-paneled interior that includes a reading room and an excellent collection of books and other materials about the Bronx. It's also where one finds Owen Dolan Park, which underwent a major renovation in 2011. Dolan was an educator and lifelong resident. He had died in 1925, right after giving a speech dedicating a granite memorial in the park honoring soldiers who had perished in World War I.

Huntington Free Library

Another major feature of the park is a large bronze chair, erected in 1987, the work of Australian sculptor David Saunders. An award-winning design, it features stars and stripes and a laurel wreath. Images of wild boars are engraved into the boulder upon which the chair rests. Underneath the seat is a dictionary opened to a page containing delicate drawings of birds commonly found in America. The intent is to symbolize human objectivity, as opposed to the wild boars, meant to represent human emotions. The chair is taken from various nineteenth-century monuments to respected individuals who are shown seated amidst indicators of wisdom and learning. All this comes from the explanation provided by Saunders to the Parks Department about the meaning of his work. Saunders explained that the unoccupied chair makes it possible for any viewer to imagine themselves seated in the chair. It's the first time I've seen a sculpted chair inside a park. I wonder if people ever dare to sit in it. I wouldn't be at all surprised. The park can also lay claim to status of some sort. The granite for the boulder was taken from the same quarry used for the pedestal of the Statue of Liberty.

I cross the park and begin walking southwest on Tratman Avenue, a street teeming with children playing in front of old dark-brick apartment buildings that suggest faded glory. I see wires hanging from ceilings, where, I understand, there once were chandeliers. The first two buildings I see have large interior courtyards with gardens, not well maintained but pretty, nonetheless. Conversations with people reveal that the area is predominantly Muslim and largely Bangladeshi. I see many green cabs parked on the streets, and this is a line of work where Bangladeshis and Pakistanis are dominant. It's a working-class immigrant population and quite a few of those I encounter speak little English. Why are these people here? Because rents are cheap, and the immigrants prefer to be with their own. A Bangladeshi man who cleans buildings at night tells me in accented English: "All get along here. But we are poor."

I cross the street and meet another man, of Italian descent. He's not at all pleased with the residents: "I help out the super sometimes.

I live about a mile away but I'm here a lot. These people are like roaches. They don't care how they live. Mohammed goes home for a visit to his country, and he comes back with other people in his family, and suddenly there are twenty people living in the apartment. I know because I have the keys, and I have to clean these dirty people's apartments. They got bedbug-infested cots all over the place, and they sleep in shifts. One comes home. The other gets out of the bed, goes to work, and the guy who just came in sleeps in it until eight hours later, when someone else replaces him. They're friendly but nothing beyond hello. They only hang out with each other. I tell you, I don't trust none of 'em. They're not like us. If ICE would come over here, they would have a field day." He's standing in the courtyard, looking at residents with evident distaste even as he nods hello to some of them.

"But couldn't you try to become friendly with them? I mean, you're in their apartments a lot."

"Yeah, but you gotta understand. It's not like the old days." He whispers into my ear conspiratorially: "*We're a minority.* We used to be the majority, our way of life was important. You were clean, you respected people, you went to church. Now, it's all gone. Nuttin' but the memories. These people got garbage everywhere. They must be coming from a Third World country. It feels like it's Iraq." He laments the extinction of his way of life. He continues: "I never, never turn my back on them. You can't trust them. It's not so much because they're dirty, but because they're making a dirty bomb in those apartments. And then, one day, I could lose my life. My head could fall off. They're mostly Muslims, and we know they want our way of life to disappear. I will say this. There's no danger here when it comes to crimes. They don't do no muggings. But I feel isolated here. I got no friends here, nobody to talk to."

It's this feeling of not belonging that disturbs him so much that even though he says they commit no crimes, it doesn't matter. In a sense, this rant is self-explanatory, the story of ethnic succession laid bare, with the hostility open for all to see, that is, if he'll open up to them, which he won't. Soon he will be gone, and in a matter of years, the newcomers at whom this commentary is directed will acclimate to life. After all, once upon a time, the same stereotypes and invective greeted the Italians, Jews, and Irish who came here. In the larger sense, when he describes their living conditions—how they sleep in shifts, living in very crowded conditions, the bedbugs—he's unwittingly testifying to the hardships they must endure to live here and how hard they are willing to work to build a new life for themselves and their families. His only positive statement about them is that there's no crime here: "They don't do no muggings." Most revealingly, it's followed by a comment that reveals the underlying basis for his hostility to the newcomers: "I feel isolated here. I got no friends here, nobody to talk to." If nothing else, this account has deepened my understanding of what many of the Bangladeshis whom I meet in taxicabs, or as students at City College, that diverse institution of the city where I teach, go through on a daily and nightly basis.

I continue on Tratman to Zerega Avenue, make a right and then a left onto Lyon Avenue, crisscrossing back and forth, trying to get a feel for the neighborhood as a whole. Some blocks have nicer homes than others, and one can see Bangladeshis and other people of South Asian origin whose homes are detached. Generally, their English is better, and the clothes they wear seem of better quality. Queries about the apartment buildings substantiate my opinion that the more recent immigrants and those with far fewer resources tend to reside there. I return eventually to E. Tremont Avenue and am intrigued by a store at number 2465, called There Should Always Be Cake. It's a Dominican pastry shop that specializes in elaborate cakes with different themes. It's a recurring experience, as the Bronx, Queens, and Upper Manhattan have many of these types of bakeries, mostly run by Dominicans. They're small, nicely done inside, and the people have a welcoming attitude to the customers.

At the intersection of Castle Hill Avenue and E. Tremont, I arrive at a very large church, called St. Raymond. The architecture is traditional in the Byzantine Revival style, with twin towers, and quite imposing. It was the first Catholic church in the Bronx, dedicated in 1845. It grew rapidly as more Catholics moved to the borough and, attracting two thousand worshippers a week, became so crowded that a new building was constructed in 1897, which stills stands today at this site. It's a very active church with a school and many activities.

I head east on Tremont for a few blocks and turn right onto St. Peter's Avenue. Here I pass some charming homes on my way to Westchester Avenue, where I see on my right a delightful mural of two elevated 6 trains arriving at a station simultaneously and heading in opposite directions, next to a Transport Workers' Union counseling center. It's an ideal and surely not coincidental placement, since the 6 runs overhead on Westchester. I cross the street to get a better look at it. It's a very well-crafted rendering, known as a trompe l'oeil: an optical illusion creating the appearance of a three-dimensional drawing. Limiting it to shades of blue, black, and white and a green-colored backdrop around the "6" gives it a very realistic appearance. Using my imagination, it's almost as if the oncoming train is about to continue onto the sidewalk in front of it. The gritty subway look is adhered to via what appears to be white vertical streaks running down the gray-and-black wall on the side, built to support an apartment building above it. The 2016 work by the artist Damian Mitchell was supported by the Public Arts Project. It's a great scenic way to end my trip through these streets.

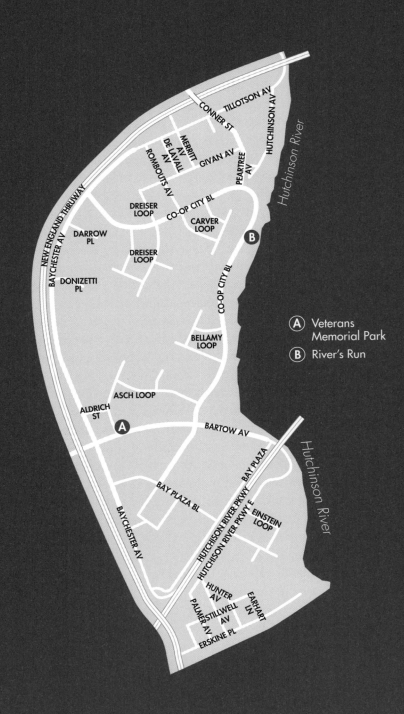

CONNER ST

TILLOTSON AV

HUTCHINSON AV

MERRITT AV

DE LAVALL AV

ROMBOUTS AV

GIVAN AV

PEARTREE AV

Hutchinson River

DREISER LOOP

CO-OP CITY BL

CARVER LOOP

DARROW PL

DREISER LOOP

NEW ENGLAND THRUWAY

BAYCHESTER AV

DONIZETTI PL

CO-OP CITY BL

(B) River's Run

(A) Veterans Memorial Park

(B) River's Run

BELLAMY LOOP

ASCH LOOP

ALDRICH ST

(A)

BARTOW AV

BAY PLAZA

BAY PLAZA BL

HUTCHISON RIVER PKWY

HUTCHISON RIVER PKWY E

BAY PLAZA

EINSTEIN LOOP

Hutchinson River

BAYCHESTER AV

HUNTER AV

EARHART LN

STILLWELL AV

PALMER AV

ERSKINE PL

CO-OP CITY

CO-OP CITY (SHORT FOR COOPERATIVE CITY) is a predominantly lower- to middle-class community made up entirely of a 320-acre cooperative building complex. It has over 15,000 apartments, thirty-five high-rise structures ranging in height from twenty-four to thirty-three floors, plus 236 townhouses, and about 35,000 residents. When it opened in 1968, it was the largest co-op housing development in the country. There are five sections, set apart by the fact that their streets all begin with the same letters, from A to E. Four of the sections are on one side of the Hutchinson River Parkway, with the fifth close by but on the other side of the highway. While many people recognize the name of the complex immediately, there are lesser-known aspects of it, both historically and currently. And while it is one large commonly owned development, it's a community like any other in terms of how people identify with it. There's even a thirteen-screen movie theater in the Bay Plaza shopping center. It has organizations, shopping areas, activities, streets, transportation, schools, and all the aspects that exist in other Bronx communities, which justifies its separate inclusion in this book.

Generally speaking, the boundaries of Co-op City are Co-op City Boulevard on the north and east, Bartow Avenue on the south, and Baychester and Tillotson Avenues on the west. The boundaries of the irregularly shaped separate section nearby are the Hutchinson River Parkway on the north, Hutchinson River and Erskine Place on the east and south, and the New England Thruway on the west. Co-op City is considered to be a separate area, but it is also part of the Baychester community. The Mall at Bay Plaza shopping center is immediately south of Bartow Avenue and is seen by many Co-op City residents as "theirs" because of its proximity. However, since it's open to all customers and is situated right where Interstate 95 and the Hutchinson intersect, it's really part of the northeastern Bronx as a whole.

Co-op City was preceded by Freedomland U.S.A., whose founders built their amusement park on what was once a municipal landfill, basically swampland. It lasted from 1960 to 1964, and though short-lived, was well known to most New York residents. It was based on US history with eight different themes and shaped like a map of the United States, with visitors entering at "Little Old New York." It was a really fun place, as I remember from my youth, with lots of rides. I recall lining up to dedicate a song to a humorless administrator in my school. The show was broadcast by a major New York radio station, and the host mispronounced the administrator's name in a comical way. As a result, I got into trouble at the school, but my classmates loved it! While Freedomland was larger at the time in area than Disneyland, it ultimately failed. There were financial issues, and unlike Disneyland, the park was unable to remain open for all seasons in the outdoors. After all, New York does not enjoy the same weather conditions as California. It was also hard to get to. Both Co-op City and the Bay Plaza mall are today located on what was once Freedomland.[57]

Co-op City, known today as Riverbay at Co-op City, was the brainchild of Abraham Kazan, who established the United Housing Foundation. The Amalgamated Clothing Workers of America was also an active participant in the project. It was under the auspices of the New York State Mitchell-Lama Housing Program, otherwise known as the Limited Profit Housing Law, and was aimed at attracting moderate-income families and promoting racial and ethnic diversity. Naturally, over a period of time, conditions deteriorated, but in the past twenty years more than $240 million has been spent on renovations.

Today, perhaps 60 percent of the residents are African American, West Indian, or African, and an additional 30 percent are Hispanic, with the remainder either non-Hispanic white or Asian. At one time Co-op City was predominantly Jewish, Italian, and Irish, and today these groups still have some older residents who are comfortable here. Riverbay has a reputation for tolerance, and most people seem to like the diversity. The main commercial street is Bartow Avenue, and the Mall at Bay Plaza is quite large, featuring JCPenney and Macy's as anchors, with P.C. Richard, Stop & Shop, Staples, Bob's Discount Furniture, Marshalls, and many other stores located in or next to it. There's also the Bartow Mall, which has smaller shops and restaurants. The development has its own police force and is considered very safe.

In an attempt to better appreciate what this place is really like, I spent some time walking through the various sections observing and chatting with residents. Visually, the apartment buildings are in very good shape, as are the townhouses. The grass is cut, and there are different varieties of trees. Of course, these meadows and trees are completely surrounded by tall structures, so no one is under the illusion that they're living in the country, but it's quiet and there are benches to sit on and concrete paths to stroll on. Due to the landscaping, it actually feels like a more open space than one would expect. There are playgrounds, baseball fields, and basketball, hand-ball, and tennis courts, which all appear to be in excellent condition.

A sample trip I took began with walking down Baychester Avenue to Aldrich Street, where I turned right and then right again, onto Asch Loop. Within two minutes I was passing by a park dedicated to the memory of armed forces veterans. It was dignified but not particularly elaborate, the most distinguishing aspect being a flagpole that was at least six stories high. The other streets are the same in terms of how the buildings look, something true of all the sections. Thus, if individual style is what you're looking for, you won't find it here. I turn around and head north on Asch Loop, making a right and then a left, walking up and down Adler Place. Venturing off the road, I come to some attached townhouses and note that they have quite a few varieties of plants in the small gardens in front of them. I speak with Maria, a resident.

"Are these nice gardens the responsibility of the residents or management?"

"Well, the co-op takes care of them, generally, but I have a bigger garden as you can see, and the management is fine with that as long as I maintain it. We have coleus, azaleas, hostas, and other plants."

"Is it safe here?"

"Very. I've been here many years and not even a broken window, not even a flower picked from my garden. That's why there are no bars on the windows. Most of the people living in the apartments have been here thirty or forty years. I moved to this townhouse nineteen years ago. I have a one-bedroom, and upstairs there's a three-bedroom. An apartment became available and there were six people vying for it. A bus gets you into Manhattan in less than an hour, or you can take a bus to the 5 train. We have Pelham Bay Park, Orchard Beach, City Island, a movie theater, restaurants. There are many elderly people, still some Jews from the old days, with two synagogues. Everybody from the Concourse moved here," she says, laughing. She's Hispanic and many of her friends are Jewish. The people are clearly happy here.

Another woman says: "My daughter comes to pick me up for the day to take me to her house in Long Island. She thinks she's doing me a favor, but I have plenty of friends here and good restaurants. And everybody meets at the beauty parlor. She loves me and I love her, but she's not a good cook. We all get along here. We have Nigerians and especially Ghanaians. And we also have Muslim women from the Middle East."

I return to Asch Loop, turn left, or east, and in a few minutes arrive at Co-op City Boulevard. Here I turn left and cross the street to the east side of the boulevard where I walk along the perimeter of the community. I pass several Little League baseball fields and then come to a magnificent community garden called River's Run, at number 675 if you're trying to get a precise location, cared for by the residents of Co-op City. It has gardens behind white picket fences. Suddenly I spot a groundhog that has just stolen a tomato and is devouring it. It looks up, and seeing me staring, it darts away. I also discover a first-rate screened-in gazebo. Well, I think to myself,

River's Run Community Garden

here one can enjoy nature even on a warm summer night without getting bitten up, the best of all worlds. Next to it are some of the largest sunflowers I've ever seen, perhaps eight feet tall or more, and the flowers themselves have a nearly two-foot diameter.

In conclusion, this looks like a sterile place when driving by, but once you enter and speak to the people, this perception quickly changes. The people here have friends, activities, nice living spaces, amenities, clubs, and a sense of community. In the end it's the people that make a community vibrant, and when the place is well taken care of, with transportation, eateries, schools, and the like, that's good enough for them. And so, what looks like anomie is actually bonhomie. One of the most attractive aspects is that people will pay much less than the market rate. A one-bedroom apartment will go for maybe $14,000 and a three-bedroom goes for about $30,000, with the monthly carrying costs ranging from about $700 to $1,400. Eligibility for these great rates depends on income. One must make enough to afford these costs, but not too much. Judging from my conversations with people here, there's very little jealousy or hankering for more. They believe living here's a good deal and that's more than enough.

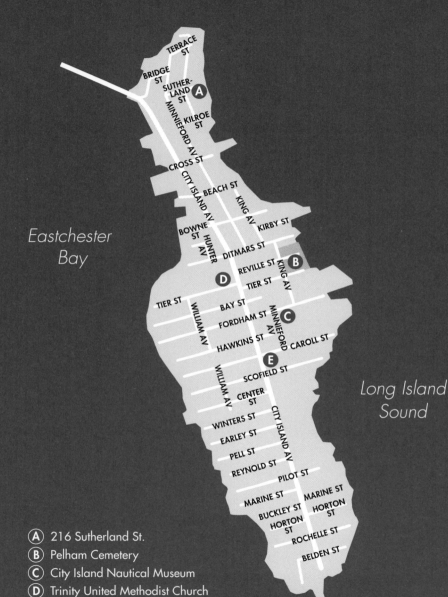

Eastchester
Bay

Long Island
Sound

TERRACE ST
BRIDGE ST
SUTHER-LAND ST
(A)
KILROE ST
MINNIEFORD AV
CROSS ST
CITY ISLAND AV
BEACH ST
KING AV
KIRBY ST
BOWNE ST
HUNTER AV
DITMARS ST
REVILLE ST
(D)
(B)
KING AV
TIER ST
TIER ST
WILLIAM AV
BAY ST
(C)
FORDHAM ST
MINNIEFORD AV
HAWKINS ST
CAROLL ST
WILLIAM AV
SCOFIELD ST
(E)
CENTER ST
WINTERS ST
CITY ISLAND AV
EARLEY ST
PELL ST
REYNOLD ST
PILOT ST
MARINE ST
MARINE ST
BUCKLEY ST
HORTON ST
HORTON ST
ROCHELLE ST
BELDEN ST

(A) 216 Sutherland St.
(B) Pelham Cemetery
(C) City Island Nautical Museum
(D) Trinity United Methodist Church
(E) Caroll St. mural

CITY ISLAND

THIS IS A SMALL ISLAND, about 1.5 miles long, surrounded by waters, with no street boundaries. Instead the boundaries are defined by its general location. On the north is Pelham Bay Park, on the northeast is the privately owned High Island, on the east and south is Long Island Sound, and on the west is Eastchester Bay. Originally inhabited by the Lenape and then the British, it changed hands after the American Revolution. The main industries here, besides fishing, were shipbuilding and sail making. In the twentieth century, it became a resort community for the wealthy and those who were not. Today, it attracts many tourists who frequent the numerous restaurants, perhaps thirty in all, and antique shops along and just off City Island Avenue. There are three yacht clubs and one kayak club here too. Visitors also charter boats for fishing trips and cruises, and go scuba diving.[58]

The population, numbering about 4,500 residents, is mostly white, but there are also communities of Hispanics and Blacks residing here. Deer, monk parakeets, and turkeys are present on the island as well. Residents also have the advantage of being right next to Pelham Bay Park. City Island has been used as a setting for several well-known films, including *Butterfield 8* and *Long Day's Journey into Night*. With a population of about 4,500 residents, it is a very safe and quiet community. Finally, despite being on the water, it was spared the wrath of Hurricane Sandy.

My walk begins after the bridge on City Island Avenue, the main and only commercial thoroughfare in this island community. Immediately I see all the trappings of what could be a New England coastal town, perhaps in Massachusetts or Rhode Island. There are bait and tackle shops, marinas with many small boats, and restaurants specializing in seafood. There's also a Catholic church—St. Mary Star of the Sea. Other categories of eateries such as sushi, Italian food, American fare, and Chinese places have a presence here as well. There are combinations too, like a Japanese-Hispanic restaurant called Ohana, offering "Japarican" food, an eight-course "fusion" chicken dinner that includes Japanese onion soup and traditional Puerto Rican beans and rice.[59] After all, not everyone coming here wants to eat seafood all the time. Nonetheless, there is an emphasis on this cuisine.

While overwhelmingly Christian, there is a small red-brick Jewish house of worship too—Temple Beth El. I turn left onto Bowne Street, my interest aroused by some of the gracious homes on the block. It dead-ends in three blocks at the water's edge. Sitting on it are a group of modern-style condominium homes. These have become increasingly popular in recent years, affording people the chance to have a gorgeous waterfront home at a reasonable cost. Turning around I go right, or north, onto King Avenue, a tree-lined street. Here, most of the homes are detached, many of them sporting nautical symbols like anchors and replicas of lighthouses. There are Victorians, brick homes, others with aluminum siding, and even one or two with stucco. I make a left onto Beach Street and, in one block, turn right onto Minnieford Avenue. I spot several bed-and-breakfast places here as well.

At 640 Minnieford, my attention is drawn to a home where the owner simply can't wait for autumn to begin. There's a large block-lettered sign bearing the friendly greeting of HELLO FALL though it's still early September, presenting a display with multicolored ears of corn and Halloween appurtenances like pumpkins. Along the side of the home, on a white picket fence is a painting depicting a blue sky and birds in flight. Its somewhat frayed condition suggests it has been here for quite a while. Despite having bed headboards and empty garbage cans partially obscuring it, when taken together, it suggests a warm, welcoming home.

I make a right on Cross Street and then a left onto King Avenue. In a few yards, I see a really beautiful home on the water. It's a large stucco structure with a green-tiled roof and tan marble pillars, with red-brick trim around the windows. Shortly thereafter, I see a Victorian home with a fencepost made entirely of ancient-looking cobblestones. Attached to it on either side of the fence are large cylindrical pillars. Both the fenceposts and the pillars are topped with lovely pieces of jagged fieldstone, and there are flowers inside the jagged stones atop the pillars. This is followed by a very large Victorian edifice with an enormous wrap-around porch and painted gray-blue. I cannot identify the house number. Very distinguished statues of eagles, their wings spread wide, look out from each side of the fence around the home. Nice windows with grids around the panes add to the home's attractiveness. The property is quite large too, and has a spectacular view of Long Island Sound. There are also modest small bungalows mixed in here as well. At Sutherland Street I swing right and after a short distance of maybe two hundred yards, I see on my right a huge structure on the water at number 216 that appears to be a white painted home, which, with its tower and crenellations around the walls, is reminiscent of a castle. Perhaps it's someone's fantasy home.

This is but one example of what a residential section here looks like. I walk the island's length, angling off on the side streets, and in general it's pretty similar on either side of City Island Avenue. If this is what interests you, just spend two days and walk every block. It's not wide either, perhaps about five city blocks in all. King and Minnieford, east of City Island Avenue, and William Avenue, on the other side, are not contiguous; they stop at dead ends and pick up a block or two later. There are also narrow one-block lanes that, nonetheless, have homes on them. On the west side, Hawkins and Earley Streets, the latter where one of my City College colleagues, Betty Yorburg, used to live, are especially pretty.

At King Avenue farther south, I pass by the old Pelham Cemetery. It affords a great view because it stretches all the way to the shore, where one can see sailboats and other vessels gliding over the water. Not many cemeteries have this kind of a scenic backdrop. The

Pelham Cemetery

graves go back to the 1800s, and many of Pelham's prominent and not-so-prominent families are buried here. I see a young woman walking into the cemetery alone carrying three balloons that read "Happy Birthday." She approaches a gravestone and places them there. All I can think of is how incredibly sad this must be for her. I assume she lost a child and is commemorating its birthday. I decide not to approach her, feeling it would be too intrusive.

Fordham Street is where one will find the Nautical Museum at number 190. The street, off City Island Avenue, is named after Rachel Fordham, who was a schoolteacher in the first schools that sprang up in City Island in the 1830s. Photographs from the museum's collection line the walls, depicting maps, boats of every type, and bridges. There are books about the island's history and the people who built up and lived on City Island. Arrowheads from Native Americans and tools employed by sailmakers and ship-builders are an integral part of the museum's collection. There are many items reflecting the island's history, such as an old icebox from pre-refrigerator days and a century-old typewriter.

I use the restroom in the City Island Diner at 304 City Island Avenue and am not surprised to discover that the wallpaper is covered with anchors and other emblems of sea life. Across the street, one block north, is Papa John's Deli, no relationship to the pizza chain. City Island is generally thought of as an expensive place in which to live, with high-priced restaurants. But there are also inexpensive eats available at places like Papa John's, where a robust cheddar cheese or smoked turkey sandwich can be had for a mere $4.50.

I ask a customer, a middle-aged woman, what it's like to live here and she says: "If you don't mind living in a community where not a lot happens except local gossip, it's fine. And people here are very friendly, as they would be in any small town. But there are no movie theaters, major department stores, or anything like that. The good part is it's pretty, safe, and quiet, except on the weekends in the warmer months when the tourists come, mostly for the restaurants. I love it here, but then again, I'm a 'clamdigger.' That's what they call the folks who were born here."

I buy some snacks and obtain a sense of what small-town life can mean here when I go searching for a place to sit down. There being no park nearby, I enter the launderette next door and ask the proprietors if I can sit in their backyard. "Sure," they say, and I sit down in a swinging easy chair speaking with the Hispanic family that runs it. And by the way, if you're interested in enjoying a brief, perhaps five-minute hymnal concert played over the loudspeakers at 331 City Island Avenue, home of the Trinity United Methodist Church, you can hear it on a daily basis outside the church or nearby at 12:00 noon, 3:00 p.m., and 6:00 p.m.

I continue on my way to the southern end of the avenue, where there are some more restaurants, unsurprising since it has a terrific panoramic view of Queens and Long Island off in the distance. In general, the venues for fine dining prevail on both the northern and southern ends of the island, with the middle having more of the stores providing the necessities of life—grocery stores, beauty and barber shops, shoemakers, nail salons, and the like.

Returning up City Island Avenue toward the bridge, I spy at Caroll Street, a mural memorializing 9/11. They're all over the city, but this one's a bit different. Uncle Sam, hat off, dressed in full regalia, head bowed in mourning, has an expression of great sorrow on his face. A nude woman, with her hair flying in all directions and her red, white, and blue wings spread out, is gazing over the Manhattan skyline. There's an oversized Statue of Liberty looming over the skyline behind it, holding up its torch. Beneath an American flag are an ambulance, a fire truck, and a police car, with angels standing by weeping. Alas, the mural is peeling. It was probably painted many years ago, but still, the obligation to never forget involves preserving the art in its memory as much as possible. It may be time for a makeover, however.

ACKNOWLEDGMENTS

After my husband, William Helmreich passed away, I found an incomplete list of people whom he intended to acknowledge for their contributions toward the successful completion of this project. I know that, had he lived, there would have been many more, including all the people at Princeton University Press who brought the book to fruition, even in his absence, such as: Meagan Levinson and Erik Beranek (editorial), Mark Bellis (production editorial), Amanda Weiss (text design), Chris Ferrante (cover design), Erin Suydam (production), Maria Whelan and Kathryn Stevens (publicity), Molan Goldstein (copyeditor), Chris Holewski (photographer), and Mario Torres (driver).

The following are the individuals he listed, in alphabetical order: Nicole Barton, Joe Cicciu, Mary Coughlan (McGoo's Bar), George Crinnion (CCNY security), Nate Goldman, Sam Goodman (reader), Jeannie Hoag (Fordham University), Helen Ishofsky (reader), Rob Katz, Sydelle Knepper (reader), Ben Lunzer, Josh Martin, Alison McKay (executive director, Bartow House), Janet Munch (Lehman College Library archivist–Navy WAVES), Jack Nass, Lovie Pignata (muralist/artist), Chris Pignone (reader and helper), Constance Rosenbloom, Rene Rotolo (VP for campus planning and facilities, Lehman College), Fred Shaw, Rana Smith (Woodlawn Heights Library), Harold Stern (reader), Laura Tosi (librarian, Bronx County Historical Society), Lloyd Ultan (interview), Al Weinstein, Jeff Wiesenfeld, and Sharon Wolfe (reader).

To all of you listed above, and to anyone who should have been listed but was not, I thank you in Bill's name, as I know he would have wanted.

Helaine Helmreich

APPENDIX

1. Be alert at all times.
2. Dress innocuously and not very well—no loud colors.
3. Never stare at anyone, but if you should make eye contact, and the person isn't looking at you in a hostile manner, smile and say "Hi." It's a counterintuitive, disarming approach that has served me well, though gauging this can sometimes be tricky.
4. Avoid groups of people congregating on the street, especially teenagers, but do not cross the street if you feel they've already seen you approaching. You don't want to look nervous or fearful. This is obviously not easy to determine with certainty.
5. Walking at night, on weekends, and in the summer is riskier than at other times.
6. Do not walk with more than one person since you don't want to attract attention.
7. Avoid areas where it's difficult to exit, such as neighborhoods without nearby transportation.
8. Avoid deserted areas.
9. Don't carry a lot of cash, but have some. Having nothing on you may increase the likelihood of physical attack from a disappointed assailant. Never fight back unless all else is lost.
10. Be careful about giving money to panhandlers. Generosity can lead to trouble, especially if others take notice.
11. Always be respectful. If someone is walking toward you be ready to give way, as you are not on your home turf.
12. Never try to project an image of toughness. It won't work and, in fact, people may judge you as either insecure or challenging them if you try it.

These are not hard-and-fast rules. Circumstances may dictate a different response or approach. Each situation is, by definition, unique, and you need to be flexible and adapt. Having and using common sense is an essential quality.

Women, as a rule, should exercise more caution and should not walk in these areas alone. Walking with a man is less likely to attract attention. Walking with a man and a dog is even better. It suggests that you are local, or at least visiting someone local. Older people, provided they are physically fit and can walk at a reasonable pace and without using a cane, are actually at less risk than those who are younger. A younger person who looks like an outsider—such as of a different race or ethnicity—may be seen as a challenge to a resident of similar age. People who look like they could be a cop or worker in the area—for example, a teacher, social worker, delivery person, or store employee—are at less risk.

On a personal note, I walked over ten thousand miles of city streets in the last eleven years, at all times of the day and night, and was never attacked. Why? I grew up in a rough area of the city and was familiar with life there. I hung out on the streets and developed the usual sixth sense about danger. Even more important, perhaps, I was just plain lucky. One incident brought this home to me. I once walked into a public housing project at midday. As I passed a teenager who glanced at me, I said, "How ya doin'?" His face was expressionless as he said something into a walkie-talkie. I looked around and saw seven heads go up about fifteen yards away across a small grass oval. Without any hesitation, I said, "Have a nice day," and walked out, neither quickly nor slowly, toward the street, never looking back. I had, I suspected, interrupted a drug deal or other illegal activity. My goal was to indicate that I wasn't a threat to what they were doing. In this case, being seen as a cop might have made things worse.

Nothing happened to me. Again, I was fortunate.

NOTES

1. Roberts 2019; Ultan and Olson 2015; Rosenblum 2009; Ultan and Unger 2000; McNamara 1989. Readers can also benefit by looking at the "Bronx" entry in *The Encyclopedia of New York City* (Jackson 2010).
2. Allyn 1958.
3. Kaufman 1993.
4. Helmreich 2013: 231–95.
5. Fernandez 2006.
6. McNamara 1984: 40.
7. For more on Mott Haven, see Ultan and Olson 2015: 153–67.
8. Berger 2012.
9. Rosenblum 2009: 66.
10. White and Wilensky 2000: 559.
11. Roberts 2013.
12. Fordham University's Walsh Library has an archival collection about African Americans and West Indians who moved into Hunts Point.
13. Ultan and Unger 2000: 246–47.
14. Roberts 2019.
15. Stern, Fishman, and Tilove 2006: 1212–17.
16. Interview with Lloyd Ultan, August 6, 2018.
17. Fordham University's Walsh Library has an archival collection of documents about African Americans and West Indians who moved into Morrisania.
18. Rosenblum 2009.
19. Berman 1982; Caro 1974.
20. Helmreich 2013: 214–15.
21. Hughes 2018.
22. McNamara 1984: 550.
23. For an excellent history of this parish and its role in Highbridge see Kevin T. O'Reilly's account on the church's website.
24. Allyn 1958; Kaufman 1993; Freuchen 2013: 63–64.
25. Billings 1997.
26. Although I discovered this mural on my own as a result of walking the community block by block, I later came across an article that has more to say about it, in particular regarding its creators. See Gonzalez 2015.

27. Goodstein 2010.
28. McNamara 1989: 111.
29. Ultan and Unger 2000: 255–56.
30. Rosenblum 2009: 149–51; Duffy 2002.
31. Munch 1993.
32. McNamara 1989: 132.
33. McNamara 1989: 140–41.
34. McNamara 1989: 145.
35. McNamara 1989: 154.
36. McNamara 1989: 14.
37. Woodlawn Taxpayers Association 1970.
38. McNamara 1989: 226; Browner and Hamill, 2006.
39. McNamara 1984: 33.
40. Tracy 2018; Wirsing 2018.
41. Ultan and Unger 2000.
42. Thomas and Thomas, 1928: 572.
43. Deutsch, Armaghan, and Fisher 2012.
44. While at one time the eastern border extended to Bronxdale Avenue, Van Nest is widely considered by those living there to only extend to White Plains Road, according to Albert D'Angelo, the current head of Community Board 11, where these neighborhoods are situated. Lasky 2018.
45. Guiliano 2017.
46. CBS News 2018.
47. Sotomayor 2013: 3–87.
48. Alvarez 1996.
49. Gold 2017. http://www.espn.com/espn/feature/story/_/id/20670727/welcome-stickball-boulevard.
50. Watkins 2018.
51. McShane, Tracey, and Ruscoe 2018.
52. Shrier 2018; Celona, Moore, Sheehan, and Musumeci 2018.
53. Feuer 2002. The quotes are a combination of Feuer's interview and mine, stitched together to make it more seamless.
54. McNamara 1984: 189–90; Smith 2013.
55. This procession happened while I was working on *The New York Nobody Knows*, but is described here again because it's important and an annual event. Those interested in observing or participating in it should contact the church in whatever year they plan to attend to find out the dates of the event.

56. McNamara 1984: 124.
57. McNamara 1989: 179, 197–98.
58. Boyer-Dry and Falkowitz 2019.
59. Such a term actually exists and has been written about. Generally, it refers to someone whose ancestry is half Japanese and half Puerto Rican. Cohen 2002.

BIBLIOGRAPHY

Allyn, Donald. 1958. "A Short Historical Sketch of the Highbridge Neighborhood." Unpublished paper. Highbridge Public Library, Bronx, NY.

Alvarez, Lizette. 1996. "Hispanic Settlers Transform Harding Park in Bronx." *New York Times*, December 31.

Baver, Sherrie, Angelo Falcon, and Gabriel Haslip-Viera (eds). 2017. *Latinos in New York: Communities in Transition.* 2nd ed. Notre Dame, IN: Notre Dame Press.

Bellafante, Ginia. 2019. "At Last, a Bookstore Comes to the Bronx." *New York Times,* April 28.

Berger, Joseph. 2012. "No Longer Burning, the South Bronx Gentrifies." *New York Times*, March 25.

———. 2007. *The World in a City: Traveling the Globe through the Neighborhoods of the New, New York.* New York: Ballantine Books.

Berman, Marshall. 1982. *All That Is Solid Melts into Air: The Experience of Modernity.* New York: Simon and Schuster.

Billings, Molly. 1997. *The Influenza Pandemic of 1918.* https://virus.stanford.edu/uda/.

Boyer-Dry, Margo, and Max Falkowitz. 2019. "Visiting a New England Seaside Village in the Bronx." *New York Times*, August 1.

Bridges, William. 1974. *Gathering of Animals: An Unconventional History of the New York Zoological Society.* New York: Harper and Row.

Browner, Frances, and Patricia Hamill. 2006. *While Mem'ries Bring Us Back Again: A Collection of Memoirs.* Yonkers, NY: Aisling Irish Community Center.

Caro, Robert. 1974. *The Power Broker: Robert Moses and the Fall of New York.* New York: Alfred A. Knopf.

CBS News. 2018. "Huge Garbage Pile at NYCHA Building Creates Awful Stench." December 30. https://www.cbsnews.com/newyork/news/massive-pile-of-garbage-nycha-sonia-sotomayor-houses-bronx/?intcid=CNM-00-10abd1h.

Celona, Larry, Tina Moore, Kevin Sheehan, and Natalie Musumeci. 2018. "Son of Bonanno Crime Family Associate Shot Near His Bronx Home." *New York Post,* July 11.

Chen, Stefanos. 2018. "The Bronx Is Great, Thonx." *New York Times,* September 14.

Cohen, A. M. 2002. "The Japa-Rican Dream." *Japan Times*, February 6.

Deutsch, Kevin, Sarah Armaghan, and Janon Fisher. 2012. "Firefighter, Three Geriatric Gangsters Accused of Running Gambling Ring for Genovese Crime Family." *New York Daily News*, March 2.

Duffy, Peter. 2002. "The Boy Who Saw the Virgin." *New York Times*, December 22.

Fernandez, Manny. 2006. "As Maps and Memories Fade, So Do Some Bronx Boundary Lines." *New York Times*, September 16.

Feuer, Alan. 2002. "Secrets of the Dean of the Pie Men: Hints from 59 Years in Pizza: Crust Is Thin, and No Avocados." *New York Times*, April 2.

Freuchen, Peter. (1935) 2013. *Arctic Adventure: My Life in the Frozen North*. Reprint, Brattleboro, VT: Echo Point Books and Media.

Gold, Jonathan. 2017. "Welcome to Stickball Boulevard." ESPN. September 11. http://www.espn.com/espn/feature/story/_/id/20670727/welcome-stickball-boulevard.

Gonzalez, David. 2015. "On a Wall in the West Bronx, a Gentrification Battle Rages." *New York Times*, November 29.

Gonzalez, Evelyn. 2004. *The Bronx*. New York: Columbia University Press.

Goodstein, Laurie. 2010. "For Catholics, Interest in Exorcism Is Revived." *New York Times*, November 13.

Guiliano, Bob. 2017. "Reactions Mixed over Mural at Emilio's Pizzeria." *Bronx Times*, November 4.

Hall, Ben M. 1961. *The Best Remaining Seats: The Story of the Golden Age of the Movie Palace*. New York: Bramhall House.

Helmreich, William B. 2013. *The New York Nobody Knows: Walking 6,000 Miles in the City*. Princeton, NJ: Princeton University Press.

Hermalyn, Gary, and Robert Kornfeld.1989. *Landmarks of the Bronx*. New York: Bronx County Historical Society.

Hu, Winnie. 2015. "Bronx Koreans Cope as Their Population Shrinks." *New York Times*, April 1.

Hughes, C. J. 2018. "Flora, Fauna and the Random Roar of Lions." *New York Times*, June 17.

Jackson, Kenneth T. 2010. *The Encyclopedia of New York City*. New Haven, CT: Yale University Press.

Jacobs, Jane. 1961. *The Death and Life of Great American Cities*. New York: Vintage Books.

Jonnes, Jill, 2002. *South Bronx Rising: The Rise, Fall, and Resurrection of an American City*. New York: Fordham University Press.

Kaufman, Michael T. 1993. "About New York: A Museum's Eskimo Skeletons and Its Own." *New York Times*. August 8.

Lasky, Julie. 2018. "Morris Park, Bronx: Where Congeniality Flourishes." *New York Times*, August 29.

Mahler, Jonathan. 2005. *Ladies and Gentlemen, the Bronx Is Burning: 1977, Baseball, Politics, and the Battle for the Soul of a City*. New York: Farrar, Straus and Giroux.

Mark, Jonathan. 2018. "Yiddish Hoedown in an Old Folk Shule." *Jewish Week*, June 1.

McNamara, John. (1978) 1984. *History in Asphalt: The Origin of Bronx Street and Place Names*. Rev. ed. Harrison, NY: Harbor Hill Books. Reprint, New York: Bronx County Historical Society.

———. 1989. *McNamara's Old Bronx*. Bronx, NY: Bronx County Historical Society.

McShane, Larry, Thomas Tracey, and Emily Ruscoe. 2018. "Attempted Mafia Rubout Eyed in Bronx Shooting of Man Whose Father Was Targeted Just Weeks Ago." *New York Daily News*, July 11.

Mueller, Benjamin, and Al Baker. 2016. "An Enduring Heroin Market Shapes an Enforcer's Rise and Fall." *New York Times*, June 27.

Munch, Janet Butler. 1993. "Making Waves in the Bronx: The Story of the U.S. Naval Training School (WR) at Hunter College." *Bronx County Historical Journal* 30, 1 (Spring): 1–15.

Newman, Andy. 2015. "A Hotel in the Bronx Gets High Marks from Guests, if They Can Get There." *New York Times*, June 1.

O'Reilly, Kevin T. n.d. *The Story of Sacred Heart and Highbridge*. Website of Sacred Heart Church, https://bronxaltar.org.

Roberts, Sam. 2013. "Fewer People Are Abandoning the Bronx, Census Data Show." *New York Times*, March 14.

———. 2019. "Five New York Buildings that Changed American History." *New York Times*, November 1.

Rodriguez, Clara. 1991. *Puerto Ricans: Born in the U.S.A.* Boulder, CO: Westview Press.

Rojas, Rick. 2017. "Doctor's Killing at Bronx Hospital Called a 'Monumental Loss.'" *New York Times*, July 2.

Rosenblum, Constance. 2009. *Boulevard of Dreams: Heady Times, Heartbreak, and Hope along the Grand Concourse in the Bronx*. New York: New York University Press.

Rothman, Joshua. 2013. "A Walker in the City." *New Yorker*. September 18.

Samtur, Stephen M., and Martin A. Jackson. 2003. *The Bronx: Then and Now*. Scarsdale, NY: Back in the Bronx Publishing.

Shrier, Adam. "Reputed Bronx Mobster Survives Botched Hit by Masked Gunmen." *New York Daily News*. July 13.

Smith, Peter Andrey. 2013. "The Society for the Suppression of Unnecessary Noise." *New Yorker*, January 11.

Sotomayor, Sonia. 2013. *My Beloved World*. New York: Alfred A. Knopf.

Stern, Robert A. M., David Fishman, and Jacob Tilove. 2006. *New York 2000: Architecture and Urbanism between the Bicentennial and the Millenium*. New York: Monacelli Press.

Thomas, William Isaac, and Dorothy Swaine Thomas. 1928. *The Child in America: Behavior Problems and Programs*. New York: Alfred A. Knopf.

Tracy, Thomas. 2018. "Woman Shot in the Head outside Bronx Nightclub Dies." *New York Daily News*, August 28.

Ultan, Lloyd. 1979. *The Beautiful Bronx, 1920–1950*. New Rochelle, NY: Arlington House.

Ultan, Lloyd, and Shelley Olson. 2015. *The Bronx: The Ultimate Guide to New York City's Beautiful Borough*. New Brunswick, NJ: Rutgers University Press.

Ultan, Lloyd, and Barbara Unger. 2000. *Bronx Accent: A Literary and Pictorial History of the Borough*. New Brunswick, NJ: Rutgers University Press.

Watkins, Ali. 2018. "Echoes of Gunshots and 'Goodfellas' on a Quiet Bronx Street." *New York Times*, August 26.

White, Norval, and Elliot Wilensky. 2000. *The American Institute of Architects Guide to New York City*. New York: Crown Publishers.

Wirsing, Robert. 2018. "Police Investigate, 4 Shot, 2 Stabbed in Allerton." *Bronx Times*, August 25.

Woodlawn Taxpayers Association. 1970. *Welcome to Woodlawn Heights 75th Anniversary Year*. Bronx, NY: Woodlawn Taxpayers Association.

INDEX

Note: Page numbers in italic type indicate illustrations.

Art Deco style, xx, 29, 30, 35, 74, 113, 116, 120, 126, 129, 287–88, 303
Arthur, Chester, 148
Arthur Avenue Retail Market, *146*, 149, *150*
Art Moderne style, 126, 129, 287, 337
Aruba, 243
Ashton, Dore, 342
Asians, 192, 253, 278
Assemblies of God Christian Church, *54*, 56
Assemblies of God churches (Morris Park), 301
Augustinian Fathers, 136
Ava's Rain Florist, 375
Avitabile Deli, 229–30

bagpipes, 356
bakeries, 59, 219, 230, 276–79, 388
Bambaataa, Afrika, 327
Bancroft, Ann, 223
Bandidos, 207
Bangladeshis, xxii, 138, 169, 174, 323, 336, 381, 384, 386–88
Bank of the United States, 69
Barbarossa, Theodore, 315
Barbosa, Rafael, xii, 12–13
Bardot, Brigitte, 296
Barger, Raymond Granville, 315–16
Barile, Joe, 304
Barretto Point Park, *54*, 56, 64–65
Barrymore, Ethel, 8
Barrymore, Lionel, 218
bars and taverns, xii, xxv, 12–13, 222, 229–31, 360–61. *See also* beer gardens; music and nightlife
Bartow-Pell Mansion, 234, *370*, 377–79
Basilio, Carmen, 292
Bastone, Frankie and Johnny, 310
Battaglia's Market, *284*, 294–95
Baychester. *See* Eastchester and Baychester
Bayview restaurant, 355
Beame, Abraham, 73
Beautiful Mind, A (film), 164
Beaux-Arts style, 20, 74, 113, 199
Beckford, William, 218

Bedford Park, 169–79; crime and safety, 170; ethnic groups, 169–70, 172, 174–76; famous people, 171, 173; history, xxii–xxiii, 169; housing, 169; map, *168*; parks, 170; religious life, 170–75; schools, 169–70, 174, 176–77
Bedford Park Congregational Church, *168*, 170
Bedford Park Presbyterian Church, 174–75
Bedford Park Seventh Day Adventist Church, 170
beer gardens, 15, 348
Bellevue Hospital, xi
Bell Tower Park, 205
Belmont, 42, 147–53; crime and safety, 148, 151–52; ethnic groups, xxi, 147–49; famous people, 148; food and drink, 148–49, 151, 152; gentrification, 149, 152–53; history, 147–48; housing, 149; map, *146–47*; music and nightlife, 151; parks, 152; reputation, 147; tourism, 149, 151
Belmont Stakes, 169, 192, 299
Benzaquen, Yair, 219–20
Berkowitz, David ("Son of Sam"), 325
Berlin, Irving, 237
Berman, Marshall, 108
Bernadette, Saint, 172, 288
Bertine, Edward, 6
Bertine Historic District, 2, 5–6, *5*
Bette's Rose Garden, *26*, 38
Bhutanese, xvii, 120, 126
Bicentennial Veterans Memorial Park, *346*, 360
Bissel, Israel, 248
Bissel Gardens, *238*, 248, *249*
Black Panthers, 49
Black Power, 87
Black Rock Farm, 338
Black Spades, xv, 324
Blessed Mary Convent, 290–91
Blessed Sacrament Church and School, *318*
Blige, Mary J., 199
Block, Adriaen, 335
blockbusting, 4, 162

Hunts Point Market, 56
Hunts Point Produce Market, 63
Hurricane Sandy, 397
Hutchinson River, xx, 257
Hutchinson River Parkway, 297, 299, 311, 347, 348, 364, 371, 391

Iglesia Vida, 170
immigrants, xvii, 50, 102, 120, 230–31, 233, 235–36, 239, 336, 386–88
Indians, 336, 383
industry, xxv–xxvi, xxxiii, 10, 29, 55–56, 62–64, 66, 257, 336, 381–82, 397
Institute for Special Education, 290
Intermediate School 194, 336
Inuit, xvi, 118–20
Inwood, 222
Inwood Hill Park, 212, 223
Iona Prep School, 311
Ippolito, Justin, 151
Irish, 3, 15, 28, 49, 69, 77, 87, 112, 117, 125, 156, 169, 170, 181–83, 187, 191, 193, 204, 218, 222, 227, 229–31, 233, 235, 239, 252, 272, 275, 319–20, 348, 354, 371, 381, 388, 392
Irish food, 182, 235–36
Irish Republican Army, 3
IRT subway, 55, 57, 77, 127, 240, 275, 319, 372
Islam. *See* Muslims
Italian American Family Feast, 375–76
Italianate style, 173, 291, 321
Italian food, 47, 91, 148–49, 152, 229–30, 276–79, 294–95, 304, 310–11, 355, 372
Italia 90 Club, 280
Italian Revival style, 6
Italians, xxi, 3, 15, 28, 42–43, 49, 69, 77, 87, 91, 112, 117, 147–49, 151, 152–53, 156, 169–73, 181, 196, 227, 229, 239, 252, 263, 271, 272, 275, 278–80, 286, 290, 292–94, 299, 301, 309, 319–21, 348, 351–52, 354, 371–72, 375–76, 381, 386–88, 392

Jackson, Kenneth, The Encyclopedia of New York City, xxxii, xxxv

Jackson, Washington and Rosetta, 81
Jacobi Hospital, 311, 352
Jacobs, Jane, 145, 331
Jamaicans, 239, 266–67, 278, 335
James Monroe Houses, 330
Japarican, 398, 409n59
Jerome, Mark, 166
Jerome Park Racetrack, 169, 192
Jerome Park Reservoir, 169, *190*, 192, 232
Jesus, 20, 93, 138, 172, 245, 290, 296, 320, 323, 338, 349
Jewish, 15
Jews, xv, 3, 24, 28, 39–44, 49, 56, 69, 77, 87, 88, 91–92, 99–100, 112, 117, 125, 148–49, 152, 156, 169, 181, 183–84, 188–89, 192, 200, 204, 211–12, 214, 216, 218, 252, 263, 272, 275, 283, 286, 295, 299–300, 316, 319–20, 327–28, 343, 388, 392, 394, 398
J. M. Kaplan Fund, 65
John Dormi & Sons Funeral Parlor, *298*, 304–7
John Paul II, Pope, 212
John's Diner, 325–26
Johnson, Guy, 378–79
Jolson, Al, 156
Jordan, Michael, 71
Jose Caraballo Art Gallery, 164
Joseph Rodman Drake Park, 56
Joyce Kilmer Park, 29, 51
J. P. Morgan, 65
Judith K. Weiss School, 228
Junior High School 98, *68*, 74, *74*
Justice Sonia Sotomayor Houses. *See* Sotomayor Houses

Kane's Casino, 343
Kazan, Abraham, 392
Kennedy, John F., 183, 199
Kidman, Nicole, 296
Kids World, 337
Kilmer, Alfred Joyce, 51
King, Martin Luther, Jr., 325
King Bee mural, *262*, 267–68
Kingsbridge, 191–201; crime and safety, 192, 198; ethnic groups, xxii, 191–93, 200; famous people, 199; food and

ALSO BY
WILLIAM B. HELMREICH

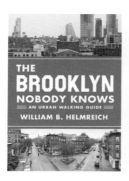 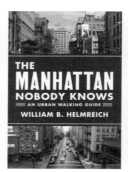 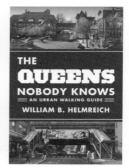

 PRINCETON UNIVERSITY PRESS

AVAILABLE WHEREVER BOOKS ARE SOLD
FOR MORE INFORMATION VISIT PRESS.PRINCETON.EDU